Handbook of Corporate University Development

Handbook of Corporate University Development

Managing Strategic Learning Initiatives in
Public and Private Domains

Edited by
ROB PATON, GEOFF PETERS, JOHN STOREY
and SCOTT TAYLOR

GOWER

Published by
Gower Publishing Limited
Gower House
Croft Road
Aldershot
Hants GU11 3HR
England

Gower Publishing Company
Suite 420
101 Cherry Street
Burlington VT 05401–4405
USA

British Library Cataloguing in Publication Data
Handbook of corporate university development: managing
    strategic learning initiatives in public and private
    domains
    1. Employer-supported education 2. Employees - Training of
    3. Organizational learning
    I. Paton, Rob
    658.3'124

    ISBN 0 566 08583 6

Library of Congress Cataloging-in-Publication Data
Handbook of corporate university development: managing strategic learning initiatives in public and private domains / by Rob Paton ... [et al.]. – 1st ed.
        p. cm.
    Includes index.
    ISBN: 0-566-08583-6
    1. Employer-supported education. 2. Employees–training of. 3. Organizational learning. I. Paton, Rob.

    HF5549.5.T7H293 2005
    658.3'1243--dc22

                                                                                2004026214

Typeset in 9 point Stone Serif by IML Typographers, Birkenhead, Merseyside and printed in Great Britain by MPG Books Ltd, Bodmin

Contents

Preface

We use the term 'corporate university' (CU) to encompass a range of initiatives that carry cognate titles such as academy or institute. As a working guide we include all initiatives, whatever the term in use as a label, which:

- are wholly owned by a parent work organization;
- have as their primary focus the provision of learning opportunities for employees of the parent organisation (even though it may also offer learning to suppliers and customers);
- utilize symbols and language from the educational sector.

These criteria thus exclude institutions such as the Arthur D. Little School of Management, which although originating as a corporate university in our terms, metamorphosed into an institution, which now places it in the conventional mainstream educational sector. Our focus in this volume is upon those strategic learning initiatives whose prime objective is the use of learning as a vehicle of corporate strategy targeted on a particular corporate or industrial constituency, whether located in the 'public' or 'private' sector.

The first set of challenges facing any such initiative concerns how a CU is positioned within the company or field. Questions being asked here include who the managerial 'owner' of the initiative might be, how funding is managed, how continuing strategic alignment is sought and achieved, and how the new initiative relates to other powerful groupings in corporate 'space'. These issues are the focus of Part I.

A second set of challenges is more internal to CUs. They concern how CU directors and project managers acquire and deploy resources, how they deal with suppliers, and how they report and measure CU performance. Part II contains seven chapters exploring different aspects of these issues.

The third set of challenges arise at the professional level and concern the nature and methods of workplace training and learning at a time of considerable change. Here, in Part III, seven chapters address the processes and technologies needed to provide and support different forms of learning, how to blend different media, and ways to assess the learning that has taken place.

The fourth and final part assesses the future prospects and possibilities for CUs.

The collection encompasses a variety of voices and perspectives – as it should, in dealing with a disparate phenomenon, and one which frequently constitutes a meeting ground for very different business and professional expertise. The criteria in selecting pieces – beyond a basic coverage of the main topics – has been a concern to provide those with responsibility for strategy and for learning, at senior levels in business and government, with an overview of the range of practice, the key choices and the important debates. We have not tried to replicate more prescriptive offerings from consultants. We do not presume to know whether a strategic learning initiative should be a corporate priority in your context, let alone what form it should take. It is not, in other words, a recipe book. Rather, to continue the culinary metaphor, it is meant to inform those who are contemplating or already involved in a new approach to catering, and who may have to recruit and manage the chef.

We are grateful to many people who have helped us bring this collection together. Kitty (Lady) Chisholm had a bee in her bonnet and clearly has a lot to answer for. The Open University provided financial support for our wider and continuing research in this area. Senior practitioners in extremely demanding roles took time out to write and rewrite their contributions. Jackie Connell provided her usual cheerful, careful and dedicated support. Gower take the credit for spotting this particular publication opportunity. We hope they are all content with the result.

Rob Paton, Geoff Peters, John Storey and Scott Taylor
2005.

Notes on Contributors

Jonathan Andrews is the Managing Partner for Accenture Human Performance for Europe, the Middle East, Africa and India. Accenture Learning focuses on implementing innovative learning solutions that help transform the performance of Accenture's clients' workforces. He has extensive experience within the Learning and Human Performance domain having managed significant workforce transformation programmes in several industry sectors including Financial Services, Government, Pharmaceutical and High Tech.

Jonathan Andrews is a graduate in Psychology with an additional qualification in Applied Psychology. He joined Accenture in 1989 and was promoted to Partner in 2001. He is married and lives with his wife and three children in the UK.

Peter Bentley (Peter_Bentley@btinternet.com) is a member of the Chartered Management Institute and has worked in several parts of the world with people from many different cultures. Before joining Shell his career had been in procurement management, which he continued to develop, influencing group policy and strategies, before moving into learning and development at the Shell Learning Centre in The Netherlands in 1996. Peter was involved in creating the virtual Shell Open University and influencing new ways of distance learning. He was the architect of the Shell Group learning strategy and more recently has been working with two Middle East Oil Ministries advising on learning and development strategies.

Beate Bungartz is Director of Corporate Human Resources Development, Cegelec Group, Brussels/ Paris who is also in charge of the Cegelec Group University. After completing her studies in business management and several positions in personnel development, she focused her professional activities and part-time PhD at the Open University on organization development, organizational learning and top management development. Beate did further training in systemic consulting and coaching and spent some years as a managing consultant where she also headed a corporate university initiative. In 2000, she was entrusted with Deutsche Telekom's top management development.

Peter Clist (peter.clist@allianz.de) is Head of Succession Planning and Top Management Communication at Allianz AG Head Office in Munich. He is currently on an extended assignment from the UK subsidiary of Allianz. He studied modern languages (French and Spanish) and has three post-graduate diplomas: education, management studies, human resource management. He has worked in France and Germany, as well as his native UK. He started his working life as a teacher of Modern Languages before switching to a career in Human Resources. After a period with a manufacturer of electrical power cables, he joined Cornhill Insurance, holding a number of different positions. In October 2000, he was seconded to Cornhill's parent in Munich, with a brief to set up and develop the international part of Allianz's Management Institute (AMI). As AMI grew, he concentrated on the group of programs focusing on strategy development and communication. In January 2004, he also acquired responsibility for succession planning, covering the whole group. Married, with three children, he now speaks passable German as well as fluent French and good Spanish.

Daniel Dirks is a Senior Vice President at Fireman's Fund Insurance Co., a member of the Allianz Group, based in Novato, California. Currently on a two-year overseas assignment, he has been managing a comprehensive change management program for the claims operations and is now in charge of Product Innovation at Fireman's Fund. Prior to his current assignment, he was Head of Global Management Development Activities within Allianz AG, with a focus on top management and high potentials. In that capacity, he was also the director of the group's corporate university, the Allianz Management Institute. After a formal qualification in banking, Daniel studied Business Administration and Economics at the Private University of Witten-Herdecke (Germany), were he also received his PhD in International Management. From 1994–1998 he was a Senior Researcher at the German Institute for Japanese Studies in Tokyo, Head of the Economic Department and co-director of that Institute. Daniel has published numerous articles and books on Japanese management practices as well as, more recently, on aspects of training and (executive) development.

Jim Flood (jimflood@btinternet.com) is a freelance consultant and specialist in developing successful learning, especially within online environments. He was formerly Director of Learning at COROUS and a Sub Dean in the Faculty of Technology at The Open University.

Bob Fryer was Chief Executive of NHSU from February 2002. Before joining NHSU Bob was Assistant Vice Chancellor at the University of Southampton and Director of New College, a post he occupied from 1998. Between 1999 and 2000 he was on secondment to Ufi Ltd as an Executive Director, and before that was Principal of the Northern College for Residential Adult Education for 15 years. Bob is a member of the English Learning and Skills Council and a Director of Investors in People UK Ltd. He was Chair of the National Advisory Group for Continuing Education and Lifelong Learning, a member of the 'Moser' Committee on Adult Basic Skills and of the Policy Action Team on Skills for Neighbourhood Renewal. Bob was awarded a CBE for services to Community Education in the 1999 New Year Honours.

David Jackson has worked in education since 1971, between 1987 and 2000 as headteacher of Sharnbrook Upper School and Community College – a community comprehensive of 1550 students. In November 2000 David became the National College for School Leadership's first Director of Research. The success of the Networked Learning Communities programme led, in April 2002, to the founding of NCSL's Networked Learning Group, based at the University of Cranfield, specifically to focus on this programme. There are 130 NLCs (incorporating over 1500 schools) across the country. David is currently Director of the Networked Learning Group. David obtained an MA more than 20 years ago and is currently completing his EdD. He has taught on educational Master courses at the Universities of Cambridge and Nottingham and tutored on the Cambridge International MPhil programme. He has undertaken educational research and evaluation projects and has published articles on a range of topics – including school improvement, school-based enquiry, leadership, student voice, knowledge management and networked learning communities. He was previously involved in supporting and leading school improvement projects both in the UK and abroad. David is married with three children and lives in Bedford.

Thomas Kraack is a lead partner for Accenture's global learning services business, *Accenture Learning*. In that role, he is responsible for leading the firm's initiative in learning transformational outsourcing (LTO). Tom is an industry leader in the learning and human resources outsourcing marketplace, responsible for developing and leading several market-defining engagements. He is based in Accenture's Minneapolis Office.

Tom holds a PhD in Industrial and Organizational Psychology from the University of Minnesota. His BA and MA in Educational Psychology are from Ball State University. He has over 20 years of experience in developing human resources strategy and systems linked to market and business strategy. His expertise lies in human resource strategy development, organization change, business process outsourcing, executive development and leadership, and organizational systems and process. He is also a national resource in the financial services industry practice, where he has over 15 years of experience in line, staff and consultant roles. His client list includes Bank of America, Morgan Stanley Dean Witter, Lockheed Martin, Lucent Technologies, Agilent, Blue Cross Blue Shield, Allianz , 3M, Nortel Networks, Hewlett Packard, Imation, Best Buy, Sharp Electronics, NCR, Best Buy, and several Wall Street and regional investment banks.

Kieran Levis (kieran@cortonaconsulting.com) heads Cortona Consulting, which develops marketing and business strategies in new media and technology markets. Cortona's clients include the BBC, BT, HP, Intel, Oracle and several start-up companies. His consulting focus is helping clients to understand complex, rapidly changing competitive environments. Kieran has worked in new media since 1979, as both a consultant and an executive, and has started and taken to profitability businesses in online information and satellite television. He has led several large-scale studies analysing business issues in immature and rapidly changing markets, shaped by technology – e-commerce, e-business, collaborative working, Internet video and e-learning. He is the author of *The Business of (e)Learning* (2002), based on a year-long study of corporate and university e-learning markets in Europe and North America. He is currently working on a book about disruptive competition and new markets.

Paul McCoy (paul@capsconsulting.co.uk), MSc CEng, is particularly interested in the areas of organizational development, change and performance improvement. His early engineering-related career focused on introducing technological change as a means of enhancing performance. Subsequent management positions in operations, strategy and planning saw Paul successfully introducing new processes and ways of working, and taking on broader business-related change. His role as Head of Organizational Learning within the BAE SYSTEMS Virtual University saw Paul addressing the barriers to effective sharing and learning of know-how across large corporations. This involved the introduction of cultural-related change programmes, along with the introduction of leading-edge online learning and best practice resources. Now acting as an independent consultant, Paul works with both private and public sector organizations to deliver optimized capabilities and performance.

Raymond Madden is Executive Director of Education Training and Development at the Institute of Chartered Accountants and formerly Head of Learning for ABN AMRO Group N.V. In addition, Raymond is part of a team of internal coaches who provide feedback to the bank's top executive group. From 1998–2001 Raymond was Associate Dean for Executive Development at City University Business School, London. His clients included BT, Bank of

China, Prudential, Texaco, Erste Bank and Coutts. Prior to this he was Director of Research Support at London Business School from 1990–1998. Raymond has over fifteen years' experience in management development.

Robin Mason is Professor of Educational Technology at the Open University. Robin is a specialist in the design and practice of online teaching and learning. Her research interests centre on learning objects, the e-learning potential of broadband and the processes and technologies of student-centred learning. Her most recent book is entitled *The Connecticon: Learning for the Connected Generation* and concerns the ways in which the Internet has changed the nature and content of learning. In 2003 she was nominated Australian Scholar of the Year and toured the major universities of the country lecturing on the current state of e-learning. Her website is http://iet. open.ac.uk/pp/r.d.mason

Peter Matthews worked in water services from 1965 to 1999 and in particular for Anglian Water from 1974 onwards; he experienced all the major changes in those services culminating in privatization in 1989. He is a chemist by background, but he filled a number of wider technical and management roles, leaving when he was Deputy MD Anglian Water International. He was appointed Director of Innovation in 1994 (in fact the first such post in the UK) and identified radical changes to the way in which knowledge, or indeed wisdom, is managed as being a key to success in the overall transformation process of the company. He founded and led the University of Water until he left in 1999. Since then he has run his own consultancy and sits on the boards of a number of organizations including Anglia Polytechnic University and the Environment Agency of England and Wales. He has always seen the value of learning in his personal and corporate life and has been active in environmental professional bodies; recently he has been a leader in a project to create a confederation of such bodies and created the Society for the Environment which has just obtained a Royal Charter and can award the Chartered Environmentalist qualification.

Jeanne Meister (jeanne.c.meister@accenture.com) is a globally recognized expert in the design and management of corporate universities. She is currently Vice President, Market Development for Accenture Learning, and is responsible for working with clients in the design and management of corporate universities, identifying emerging enterprise education opportunities, and communicating the complete range of Accenture Learning's offerings to the enterprise learning marketplace. Over the past decade, Jeanne has consulted well over 100 enterprises on launching and managing a corporate university. Jeanne is the author of *Corporate Quality Universities*, as well as *Corporate Universities: Lessons in Building a World-Class Work Force*. Jeanne has written extensively for such publications as *Harvard Business Review Japan, Financial Times, Chronicle of Higher Education, Journal of Business Strategy, TRAINING, T&D magazine* and *Chief Learning Officer*. Jeanne currently writes a monthly column on enterprise learning trends for *Chief Learning Officer* Magazine.

David Morris. Born in Cincinnati, Ohio, raised in a village in India by missionary parents, graduate of a boarding school in the Nilgiri hills, with undergraduate and postgraduate studies in America, David Morris earned a MA in History and a PhD in Educational Administration, becoming a university instructor, development officer and Dean. Following a trip to China in 1978, he became a consultant for American companies setting up shop in Asia. After CEO-ing his own company, he returned to roots in south India and became

Executive Director of the Hospital & Educational Foundation. Following acquisition of an OUBS MBA, he is a pioneer in social entrepreneurism and on the board of numerous NGOs.

Jean-Claude Nataf is ST University and Corporate Training Director, STMicroelectronics. Jean-Claude is an Engineering Electronics graduate from the Institut Administration des Entreprises in Paris. He has over 23 years' experience in the high technology and semiconductor industries. In 1994, he took on the challenge to start up ST University. Under his direction, ST University evolved from a start-up organization into a leading-edge corporate university, receiving two excellence awards from Corporate University Xchange and the Eurotraining Quality label. Jean-Claude is an active member of several worldwide benchmarking associations in the educational field such as ASTD, Corporate University Xchange and *EFMD*. He is a board member of the DEFI Club. Jean-Claude is a regular speaker in conferences organized around strategy, human resources, knowledge sharing, learning and cultural topics based on his international and multicultural experience.

Rob Paton (r.c.paton@open.ac.uk) is Professor of Social Enterprise at the Open University where he pioneered the use of Supported Open Learning for management development. He initiated the OUBS work on corporate universities and has been active in the UK's Learning and Teaching Support Network, assisting staff in other business schools respond to the structural changes affecting higher education. However, his main research interests concern the leadership and organization of social enterprises: *Managing and Measuring Social Enterprises* was published by Sage in 2003, and he is currently working with nine public and non-profit chief executives on 'the inside story' of their working lives. He is head of the Centre for Public Leadership and Social Enterprise in the Open University Business School.

Geoff Peters (g.peters@open.ac.uk) is Professor of Systems Strategy at the Open University and Chairman of UKERNA Ltd, the company that manages JANET, the UK's academic and research network. His main research interests are failure in complex human systems and changes in higher education systems including corporate universities. He has been the Open University's acting Vice Chancellor, Pro Vice Chancellor and a Dean as well as President of US Open University and the Board appointed to restructure and wind down UK e-Universities Worldwide Ltd. He has also edited and authored books on information systems, system failures, systems behaviour, and the works of Sir Geoffrey Vickers.

John Rogers (john.rogers@barclays.co.uk) is Head of Leadership Programmes, Barclays University Business School. He is responsible for the development of programmes for Barclays senior leaders covering leadership, business strategy and value-based management. John has held a number of senior management positions in the Barclays Group learning and development function over the last 10 years, including Head of Resourcing and Learning for the Group's 30 000 retail staff. He has specialized in the leading and shaping of business change in learning across Barclays. Prior to joining the business school team, John was responsible for directing the implementation of Barclays' award-winning corporate university – Barclays University ...be you (bu). This was created through a £15 million change management programme that delivered a step change in the perception of learning, confirmed through employee research. The achievement has been recognized externally through the awards for Innovators in Learning (Businesslab awards 2002) and excellence in marketing and branding (Corporate University X-change awards 2002).

Crystal Schaffer (crystal.schaffer@capgemini.com) is Director of Knowledge & Development, Les Fontaines Business Learning Forum, Capgemini. Her expertise lies in networked learning, human asset research, innovative program design, employee and corporate coaching and communications, consumer marketing and business writing. Her proudest accomplishment is having created and managed the International Workforce Management Study – a massive research effort spanning 13 countries to uncover the attitudes and issues of the industrialized workforce – and integrating these findings and further research into the development of learning methodologies for Les Fontaines' award-winning curriculum. Crystal has researched and published numerous articles on the impact of people in the workplace. She is also the founder and editor-in-chief of the business community e-zine, *Focus*.

Peter J Scott (Peter.Scott@open.ac.uk) is the Head of the Centre for New Media in the Knowledge Media Institute of the Open University in the UK. He has a BA and PhD in Psychology. He is a founder board member of the company WebSymposia Ltd, an internet multimedia webcasting company. Before joining the Open University in 1995, Peter lectured in Psychology and Cognitive Science at the University of Sheffield for ten years and has an undegraduate textbook in each of these subjects. He has managed over 15 major grants, and has over 40 research publications.

Michelle Selinger is executive adviser for education at Cisco Systems, based in the UK but working across Europe, the Middle East and Africa. Her work involves research and dissemination of effective solutions for e-learning in all aspects of education and training. She works at the interface of academia and industry, drawing on successful experiences from both sectors to help organizations develop their e-learning strategies and competences. She has an academic background in ICT and education and has worked at the UK Open University and the University of Warwick. Michelle is a member of the Advisory Group for the European Commission's e-Europe 2005 Action Plan.

Gordon Shenton (shenton@efmd.be) is currently working part time for the Brussels-based efmd (European Foundation for Management Development) on secondment from EM LYON as Associate Director of EQUIS, the efmd's quality improvement and accreditation scheme for business schools and university faculties of business and management. He holds an MA from Oxford University and a PhD from Harvard University, where he taught as an Assistant Professor of French from 1968 to 1975. From 1976 to 1980 he was Head of Studies at ISGC (Institut Supérieur de Gestion Commerciale) at Saint-Etienne in France. In 1980 he joined EM LYON, a French Business School, where he was Head of the Language Department from 1980 to 1987 and Academic Dean from 1987 to 1997. In 1997 he became the first Director of EQUIS when it was launched by the efmd. For the past three years, he has also been Project Director for the efmd's new Corporate Learning and Improvement Process (CLIP).

Steven Smith (steven.smith@capgemini.com) is Director of Capgemini University, Capgemini. Capgemini is Europe's largest consulting, technology and outsourcing firm. Its unique approach focuses on building collaboration with clients and partners to deliver the best solutions to meet each customer's specific need. Steven's background is in economics, marketing and strategy – all of which he integrates into his approach to learning. His focus is delivering learning solutions which bring measurable results to individuals, teams and the Capgemini organization. His approach facilitates the creation of professional communities which contribute to the continual updating of Capgemini's knowledge and methodology bases. As Director and CLO of Capgemini's university, he has implemented his model within the group's different disciplines and it has delivered more than 500 million euros in business results and contributed to Capgemini's university being a benchmark for numerous European and American corporate universities.

John Storey (j.storey@open.ac.uk) is Professor of Management at the Open University Business School and a consultant to a number of leading corporations and public sector organizations. His latest book *Managers of Innovation: Insights into Making Innovation Happen* (co-author Graeme Salaman) is published by Blackwell (2004). This research monograph reports a three-year research project in 21 international organizations. He has also edited *The Management of Innovation* (2004) a two-volume collection published by Edward Elgar. John Storey is a non-executive director on two management boards.

Lee Taylor was Head of Curriculum at NHSU, having been involved with it since its inception in 2001. Lee's previous experience is within distance and open learning, primarily at the Open University where she has held a series of posts including Director: OU-NHS Partnerships, Director: Administration, Open University Business School and Director, Organizational Development. She is a non-executive director and vice chair with Milton Keynes Primary Care Trust. Her research interests are in organizational development, equal opportunities and space planning.

Scott Taylor is a lecturer in organizational behaviour in the International Management and Organization group at Birmingham Business School, University of Birmingham, where he teaches human resource management and organizational behaviour to undergraduate students. Previously he worked as a research fellow at Manchester Metropolitan and Open Universities, investigating the management of people in small companies and corporate universities. He has also published recently on the Investors in People training initiative and the workplace spirituality movement.

Stacia Vigne (stacia.vigne@st.com) is ST University Communication Manager, STMicroelectronics. American-born Stacia started her career as an editor and has held various writing, editing and translating positions. After moving to France to complete her studies, she joined the Corporate University of STMicroelectronics to manage communication and e-learning programs. Stacia holds a BS degree in mathematical sciences and an MA in French Literature. Stacia is responsible for defining and implementing the ST University communication strategy. She also develops and teaches programs, including communication for managers, writing skills and creativity tools. Stacia has written a number of self-training guides on communication topics, such as presentation and writing skills.

Richard D West (richard.west@baesystems.com), BEng (Hons) MIEE MRaS, has worked in a variety of senior roles with British Aerospace, Matra BAE and BAE SYSTEMS. He has significant experience in defining key business processes supported through the use of technology and currently leads the companies' approach to e-learning and knowledge-based learning. The strategy and products developed have been recognized as best practice – BAE SYSTEMS received the International Corporate University Exchange/*Financial Times* Award for its innovative utilization of technology in creating a continuous learning environment for all employees.

Perry Williams (perry.williams@LMD.co.uk) is Research Adviser at Learning Materials Design (LMD). Formerly a lecturer at the University of Cambridge, in 1994 he joined LMD as an author and producer of educational and training materials, working with many professional and government bodies, charities and companies to develop course materials – both printed and online – to their specific requirements. Since 2003, he has also been conducting research with the Open University's Institute of Educational Technology into the use of 'learning objects' in e-learning, as experienced by learners themselves. His aim is to help those involved in producing e-learning to do it better.

Positioning the Corporate University

1 *Introduction*

Chapter 1 opens this part and the book by explaining the origins, the nature and the variety of corporate universities (CU). One purpose is to delineate the topic more clearly by developing and illustrating our definition of CUs as strategic learning initiatives. Another is to provide (briefly) a historical sketch. By setting this new wave of corporate academies in an economic and an educational context, it is easier to see both the continuity and the changes in corporate learning. But the main purpose is to illustrate the variety of strategic issues for which a CU may be created as (part of) a response, and to review the formative choices that face those sponsoring or initiating a CU. This means the chapter is necessarily wide-ranging and generalized – in contrast the remaining chapters in this part provide a range of illustrations for what the struggle to position the CU can mean in the untidy complexities of strategic management.

Many of the chapters in this collection – rightly – present CUs as an exciting arena of management action. Yet at the same time CUs are also vulnerable to all manner of challenges. As important new initiatives they often initially attract passion and enthusiasm as visionaries and corporate change agents mobilize tremendous energy and raise expectations. These aspects are evident in many of the chapters and case studies portrayed in this volume. And yet, as the chapters also reveal, it is not unusual for CUs to lead a precarious existence.

Hence, following Chapter 1 this part explores the high-level political work that has to be accomplished – and sustained – in order for these strategic learning initiatives to succeed and to last. These four chapters help to clarify and demonstrate the kinds of organizational issues and obstacles that frequently have to be confronted. CU initiatives do not always succeed; indeed they could be characterized as continually struggling for their very existence. However, despite the countervailing forces of alternative priorities, budget cuts, new brooms, changing priorities, apathy and neglect, many CUs do succeed – perhaps even after initial failure and subsequent second phase relaunch.

Chapter 2 (by Storey and Bungartz) describes and analyses an important case in Europe, which in many ways is prototypical in the range of issues that it surfaces. The case is revealing because the initiative that it describes was large-scale, it had an international reach, the level of investment was substantial, and its infrastructure and objectives reflect those found in many other CUs. The main reason it is included here, however, is because it clearly reveals the kinds of intra-organizational struggles that champions of corporate universities so often face. This large German corporation explicitly modelled its form around the kinds of principles found in Jeanne Meister's influential 1998 CU guidebook; however the case described here reveals the obstacles faced in reality when the 'best practice' guidelines were followed.

Chapter 3 (by Fryer and Taylor) continues these themes in its exploration of the progress made by the putative 'largest corporate university in Europe'. This account of a major learning initiative with aspirations to become a fully fledged university for the British National Health Service (NHS) demonstrates the issues faced when attempting to operate on a massive scale. Once again this account of the interplay and tension between vision and aspiration on the one hand and difficulties and obstacles on the other helps to ground our understanding. The chapter also helps position the nature of CUs by surfacing the range of issues that pioneers of these sorts of learning initiatives encounter, revealing how key actors responded to the issues and obstacles. This chapter has gained an increased relevance since it was written in mid 2004. At much the same time a thorough review of all the 'arms-length bodies' that supported the NHS was being conducted. As a result, it was decided by the Department of Health that a new NHS Insitute for Learning, Skills and Innovation, should be formed to replace the NHS University, and two related bodies, the NHS Modernisation Agency and the NHS Leadership Centre, as well as supporting the creation of a new Innovation Centre. Such changes in the wider environmental context of the whole organization that a CU seeks to support, and the rethinking of how strategy can best be supported, are common.

Chapter 4 (by Selinger) explores the case of a company that has attempted to exploit the potential of e-learning not only to train its own workforce, but to extend that training to partners and customers – and even into the community at large. It also links into the corporate social responsibility agenda in developing countries, providing the corporation's perspective to contrast with Chapter 11 (by Morris). The scale of the vision of this initiative is expansive.

This part of the volume ends on a salutary note. Chapter 5 (by Matthews) recounts the story of the rise and fall of a major corporate university initiative. The tale of Anglian Water's 'University of Water' is important because this particular initiative was planned and developed in a systematic and substantial manner. It was a serious initiative accompanied by substantial investment, consistently held up within the industry and by the British government as an example of best practice. The Anglian Water champions, ostensibly at least, did many of the 'right things' as conventionally understood – and yet the initiative failed nonetheless. The chapter helps to underline the scale of the potential difficulties in initiating and maintaining a corporate university. It, along with other chapters in this part, and indeed in the volume as a whole, demonstrates clearly that corporate universities are often unstable and need to be continually refreshed and even redrawn periodically. The motto is not, as Homer Simpson would say, 'Don't try' but rather learn from previous failures and successes.

1 Corporate Universities as Strategic Learning Initiatives

Rob Paton, Geoff Peters, John Storey and Scott Taylor

Introduction

No two CUs are alike – indeed, they sometimes differ enormously. For those new to the field, or even just moving between organizations, the extent of this variety can be unsettling. So what should you expect from a corporate university? Does it make sense to talk of 'best practice'? Why is it that for every CU that swears by a particular approach, there is another that does the opposite? And if your board decided, in the end, *not* to label their new approach to corporate learning a University – does that mean this book is no longer relevant? Alternatively, if the 'U' word is not essential, then just what are we talking about?

This chapter has two aims. The first is to delineate the focus of the book and to resolve such 'ground-clearing' questions. In doing so we show what CU initiatives do and do not have in common; what is new and significant about them – as well as their continuity with earlier generations of company training colleges; and why they have emerged at this time. Our argument centres around and develops the concept of strategic learning initiatives.

The second aim is to map the variety of forms such strategic learning initiatives commonly take. This is done by considering the main options – concerning *function, form* and *funding* – open to those who initiate or sponsor them. Thereafter, we offer a simple typology of the main forms, and suggest what may be a trend underlying the apparent profusion of different approaches. In this way, the chapter provides a backdrop to the various positioning strategies discussed and illustrated by the other chapters in this section.

We start by setting the CU phenomenon in its wider context.

The scale and significance of corporate learning

Market intelligence companies such as IDC or Datamonitor estimate that almost 30 billion pounds is spent in the UK alone each year on training. Figures from surveys in the USA yield similar expenditure per worker. Unfortunately, beyond such indications of widespread activity, more detailed and reliable information about training and development investment by employers is unavailable: it is not a cost that employers monitor closely (Keep et al., 2002), definitions of training and learning vary from company to company, and informal training is often excluded from such calculations. So we know that structured learning in and for the workplace is a now pervasive feature of contemporary employment, at all levels of organizations and all around the world. But we know far less about how that learning is arranged and the relative frequency and success of different approaches to enabling (and guiding, providing, monitoring and resourcing) that learning.

Nevertheless, over the last 15 years the number and visibility of corporate universities has grown sharply, initially in the USA and subsequently in other areas of the globe. Over this period the number of conferences, consultancies and publications devoted to corporate learning practices and issues has increased steadily. By no means all corporate learning takes place within or through CUs, and a number of large prestigious companies have invested heavily in corporate-level initiatives that are specifically not branded as CUs. Others utilize the CU label while pursuing training and development through separate training departments at business unit level. Inevitably, managerial practice, consulting and academic work are all to some extent creating and following fashion in this area, but to ignore or dismiss the CU phenomenon as 'only a fad' seems overly cynical and misguided – too much has been happening, and for too long.

It is not just that 'a lot seems to be going on'. CUs have emerged at the same time as four major developments have been taking place in industry, education and society:

- the emergence of the knowledge economy and learning organization as key managerial discourses;
- the frequency and rapidity of corporate restructuring, leading managers to focus on common corporate principles and practices in order to maintain some corporate glue;
- the pervasiveness and potency of communication technologies and their application to training and development;
- the increasing diversity of educational systems, moving away from curriculum-centred to work role centred, from campus-based to distributed learning, from pre-vocational to timely continuing development, from a single, standard progression route to a multiplicity of pathways.

The CU phenomenon is situated at the confluence of these four powerful currents in the contemporary economy.

The origins and spread of the corporate university phenomenon

As with many apparently novel managerial initiatives, the roots of the contemporary CU movement can be traced through the course of industrial society. Eurich (1985) reports the concerns of managers in the earliest US industrial organizations about the state educational system, and how it was not providing the 'right kind of person' to work for their rapidly expanding corporations, either in terms of skills or attitudes. Corporate colleges were set up to fill this gap, in the mid-nineteenth century USA. The spread of such activity was moderated by reforms to state education to achieve a better fit with the new conditions of work and the subsequent arrival of business schools and commerce departments in universities and colleges in the early twentieth century.

However, by the mid-twentieth century, managers in large corporations (such as Disney, McDonald's, and Motorola) began once more to find that employees recruited out of the state education system lacked the attributes they required, and set up provision within organizations to enable more specific training and development (see Wiggenhorn, 1990).

These new institutions moved from the shadows in the early 1980s as they began to acquire degree-granting powers, and a definition of the hybrid corporate educational institutions emerged:

> [A corporate college is] an institution offering postsecondary degrees which was initially established by an entity, profit or non-profit, whose primary mission was something other than granting collegiate degrees.
>
> *(Hawthorne et al., 1983: 2)*

Hawthorne and her colleagues were able to identify 14 of these colleges and argued that they would become significant competition for established educational institutions. (Indeed, they argued that academics were in part to blame for this competition because of their reluctance to acknowledge the legitimacy of corporate education until then.) More recently, the dean of a former corporate training facility that now trades independently as a private business school, has argued that a significant number of business schools will soon disappear, and that the role of the 'management professor' would change (Moore, 1997). Such developments would be driven by changing rules in a more competitive marketplace, and in particular by the expansion of degree-awarding CUs. Currently, however, CU initiatives that seek degree-awarding powers and to become competitors with 'traditional' business schools are in the minority, particularly in Europe. An alternative scenario sees managers within CU initiatives working closely with academic partners to jointly determine course content and methods of delivery, closely tailored to the corporate definitions of relevance, while continuing to draw heavily on the research of leading business schools and at the same time cherry-picking faculty members as course contributors and staff (Paton and Taylor, 2002). Far from being competitors, the relationship may be more symbiotic and collaborative.

This cursory sketch of the historical and institutional context is enough to suggest that corporate education and training has co-evolved with public and private education, both stimulating and responding to developments. At a time when higher education is currently undergoing very rapid change around the world, such co-evolution seems likely to continue. It would be a serious mistake, however, to locate CU initiatives within the conventional (further/higher) educational domain. One aspect of CU activity that is clear, in the UK and Europe at least, is that the various academic labels used by companies – institute, college, academy, university – are generally more symbolic than literal (which does not mean the label is unimportant). One can point to interesting similarities between CUs and various other types of university (Paton and Taylor, 2002), but profound differences are also obvious. This means that in some respects the notion of a 'corporate university' is bound to be misleading.

What's new and different about corporate universities?

Hence, rather than argue about whether or not they satisfy the requirements of a particular essentialist definition, it is more useful to examine the rationales for these initiatives and the activities they encompass. To this end, we suggest that what the CU tag refers to, and what this handbook addresses, is a new generation of *strategic learning initiatives*. Three features make them different.

1 **They are corporate-level initiatives in large, highly complex and differentiated settings**

As can be seen from the chapters in this book, organizationally CUs tend to be located in or near to corporate headquarters, have a board-level sponsor, and are often distinct from the Human Resources (HR) function within business units. Decision-making is evident at a higher level of the organization in the management of these initiatives than is common in managing training and development. They aim to deliver on a specific *corporate* contribution, to provide 'corporate value added', as one CU manager put it. This means avoiding the replication of what is done well at a local level, such as specialized skills training, while seeking to promote corporate consistency in relation to common terminologies and approaches, transnational working and communication, or instilling of common corporate values. The scope of such content varies between organizations (and within them over time), but CUs tend to be given high priority and significant resourcing.

2 **The pursuit of continuing strategic alignment**

A fundamental driver for CUs appears to be gaining control of training and development activities more effectively in relation to strategic priorities. Such priorities vary; some are concerned with post-merger integration, others with building customer loyalty, cross-cultural working, high-flier retention and development, making training more cost-effective and timely, or developing leadership. Clearly, strategic business priorities are continually changing, and as a result CUs frequently have to be repositioned and programmes have to be redeveloped. Traditional universities are among our oldest and most stable institutions; but everything about CUs is provisional.

3 **They attempt to raise standards, expectations and impact as regards training and development**

This aspect of CUs reflects the strategic priority afforded to learning. It may be seen in attempts to identify and engage the highest-quality providers almost regardless of location, the development of frameworks intended to increase consistency of provision, reinforcement of key messages and competences between levels and across diverse business and cultural settings, innovative programme designs including much greater attention to pedagogy, the use of information communications technologies (ICTs) through e-learning and blended learning, by fostering distributed alumni communities, and rationalizing the sourcing of learning services from external providers. This is not to suggest that everything CUs do is new and that all previous corporate training was non-strategic, unsophisticated, non-innovative, and so on. Nevertheless, what emerges from the chapters in this handbook is the explicit aspiration of CU managers operating at very senior levels and from within the corporate centre, to more closely manage standards of provision and ensure alignment with organizational strategy.

A public and private phenomenon

The factors that have led to the emergence of CUs in the private sector have in several respects been mirrored in the public sector too. The governance and management processes may be different, but many of the imperatives are seen to be similar: keeping pace in a knowledge-based society, the frequent reform and restructuring of institutions, the commitment to an e-society and the increased concern for demonstrable quality improvement in education. Furthermore, privatization, other outsourcing initiatives and public private partnerships have blurred the distinctions between these sectors.

There is in any case a long history in parts of the public sector of dedicated and sometimes high-level training provision in the form of 'staff colleges' – noticeably in the military and allied services and the civil service. Over the past 30 years in the UK there have been a number of attempts to create new public educational providers such as The Open University, and Ufi/*learndirect,* but these have been institutions open to the public at large. In this handbook we have included examples of two more recent cases that fit easily into the strategic learning initiatives space. The National College of School Leadership sees its clientele as half of all the teachers in state schools, and the (NHS) University aimed to address an even wider audience of not just health and care staff, but carers and patients too.

New modes of knowledge creation and knowledge sharing

It is also necessary to attend to what is new and significant about the learning *processes* fostered by these initiatives. A description of learning in the workplace from around a century ago would look something like this:

- knowledge capture and creation through some form of research or enquiry focusing on those who have the relevant practical 'know-how';
- codification of that knowledge in terms of abstract principles, techniques and frameworks;
- communication of de-contextualized knowledge to those who plan and deliver education and training;
- delivery of the general principles to practitioners-as-trainees to be applied in working contexts;
- contextual adaptation and application of the general principles by the practitioners to their particular situations.

This is represented in Figure 1.1. It is immediately obvious that the communication chain is long and prone to varying degrees of failure, and that if and when practitioners facing similar challenges in comparable contexts can communicate directly, they may devise solutions to their practical problems a lot more quickly. This is precisely what has happened in a wide range of settings and in different ways since the beginnings of industrial work. Skilled and knowledgeable practitioners, drawing on the experience and tacit knowledge of colleagues, create new knowledge in the course of tackling novel and complex challenges in the field, and in so doing become sources of advice for colleagues.

Equally, it is clear that such collaborative learning processes are not new. What *is* new is the extent to which their importance as part of a highly competitive knowledge economy is being recognized, encouraged and facilitated. This is happening in a range of different ways, as many of the chapters that follow illustrate. Just as new CUs often co-exist with training departments at the business unit level, so new modes of learning extend and complement the more traditional modes of training and learning. It is not necessarily 'all change', with the new supplanting and replacing the old. Rather, the new strategic learning initiatives encompass, integrate and go beyond the more familiar and established structures and processes of corporate learning.

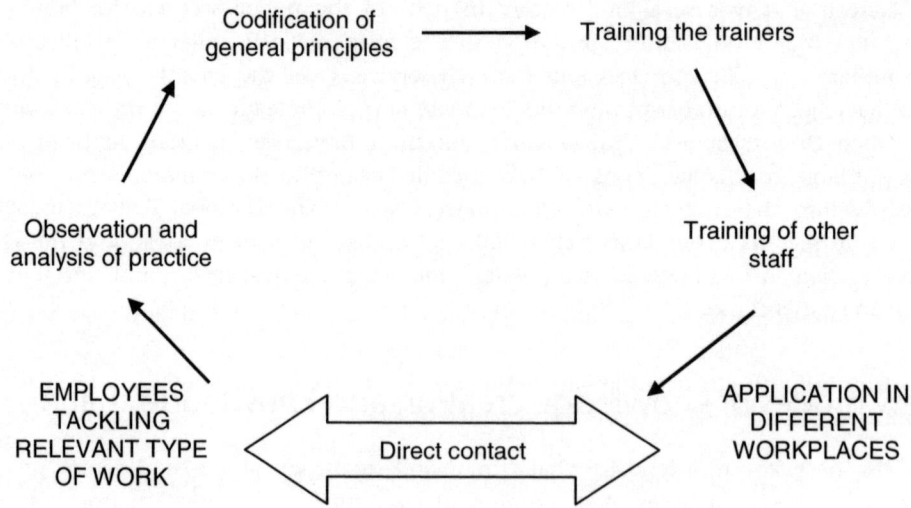

Figure 1.1   Training versus knowledge sharing approaches to learning

Types of corporate university

If we accept that CUs are usefully viewed as strategic learning initiatives, it is important to explore the space that such new entities and groupings occupy. CUs have to take some structural form no matter how limited this might be, and hence to understand them necessitates examining managerial practice and language. We try here to make sense of the profusion of different forms by offering an overview of their key dimensions and the formative choices that generate that variety. In doing so the discussion will chart more clearly the boundaries and interfaces of the CU phenomenon as we have defined it. The diversity of CU activity arises in large part from the different sorts of strategic challenges for which a substantial, corporate-level learning initiative may provide an appropriate response. Thus, for example, where the preservation, dissemination and reproduction of a company's distinctive expertise is seen as vital for future success, we can expect to find certain sorts of initiatives, with strong links to knowledge management activities and processes. Alternatively, where labour market shortages of appropriately trained labour threaten to constrain or undermine business development, externally focused initiatives, involving partnerships and with corporate citizenship dimensions, can be expected. Or, as another instance, where the strategic issue is a longer-term concern with ensuring the development and availability of sufficient numbers of high-performing leaders, the CU will take a different form again (Paton et al., 2004).

Part of our intention, then, is to make the observed diversity of CUs intelligible in relation to the strategic issues they are designed to address. We approach this by considering the key choices facing managers in organizations that are either setting up a CU or trying to renew the relevance and effectiveness of an existing CU. Notwithstanding the manifest variety, we think it is also possible to distinguish some broad types of CU and an underlying trend towards arrangements that provide and support different forms of networked learning.

Formative decisions

When corporate or industry leaders are minded to create – or re-create – a CU, the first decision tends to relate to the shape and structure of what is envisaged: both the characteristics they seek and those they expressly wish to avoid. In doing so they take formative decisions in three areas. These concern:

- the **function** of the initiative – including its central role and contribution to the parent institution;
- its organizational **form** – including strategic choices over how 'real' and how 'virtual' it may be, or how much to 'make' and how much to 'buy';
- its **funding and governance** – including choices that concern how it can be effectively embedded in the wider systems it is designed to serve.

These choices are of course interrelated, but nevertheless they provide a convenient framework for starting to explore the variety of CU practice.

FUNCTION

The corporate or strategic challenges to which the CU is a response shape its central purposes. These purposes are likely to be expressed in three key areas:

- **The scope of the initiative**: Does it have a 'tight' remit, for example focused around leadership, or is it intended to encompass a much wider range of learning? Examples of the former are the Boeing Leadership Centre (and its Institute for Aerospace Leadership), while initiatives like the BAE SYSTEMS Virtual University (Chapter 19) and ST University (Chapter 7) have a much wider remit including technological learning.
- **The range of learners**: Reflecting the scope of the initiative the possibilities here range from an expressly elite body of learners through to a more or less 'mass' or 'open' approach. The NHS University (NHSU) – in Chapter 3 – with its early emphasis on providing elements of a common induction programme for *all* staff, exemplifies the latter approach. A related choice concerns whether to invite the involvement of supply-chain partners in the learning provided as a way furthering common practices and approaches. This is an approach that has been taken by ABN Amro; CU staff there routinely deal with requests from clients of the bank for training and development in areas such as global financial markets and loan products. This is intended in part to strengthen relationships between the bank and its clients, and in part to enable the CU to become an independent profit centre. It has the additional role of providing a feedback mechanism to the bank on its products. Finally, some initiatives focus on improving the supply of labour – they train *potential* employees (see Chapters 4 and 11).
- **The nature of the contribution**: Some CUs are programme-focused – that is, their role is centred on directly addressing particular learning needs. Often, however, the central contribution relates more to providing some form of learning infrastructure. This may be technological, such as 'putting in the plumbing' for e-learning, or it may be in terms of generating a company-wide competence framework in order to provide a consistent terminology and shared reference points for staff development programmes across an industrially and geographically diverse group of business. Finally, such a contribution may

involve managing the sourcing of learning services from providers perhaps appraising, negotiating with and accrediting selected consultants and universities.

FORM

Clarifying the nature of the CU's central contribution is closely tied in with decisions about the form it should take. Many CUs are more or less 'virtual'. Learning@Intel, for example, is said not to appear on any organizational chart and is said not to have any single point of hierarchical accountability. However, most of the 50 or more entities that comprise Learning@Intel are much more tangible and familiar organizational units firmly located in corporate space. These include services and programmes reporting to corporate HR, notably Intel University Operations, which provides company-wide booking and housekeeping services, and the College of Employee Core Practices. But most are major geographical or business unit training operations based in sites or on a separate campus. In this context, Intel's virtual university concentrates on coordination through ad hoc working groups of those directly involved; sharing processes, tools and methods for learning, and essential standardization to ensure consistency with manufacturing specifications.

By contrast, other CUs take a more familiar organizational form as a distinct entity with a bricks-and-mortar site reporting either to the board directly, or to corporate HR. A related choice concerns the extent to which a company will rely on external providers to supply or support corporate learning activities or, alternatively, cultivate and draw on its own expertise in the form either of its own full-time learning specialists, or through regular contributions by senior executives and professional experts.

FUNDING AND GOVERNANCE

CUs are commonly funded through some combination of central corporate support and payments earned from business units. Typically, central funding is targeted on infrastructure development, or as pump-priming to expedite the creation and testing of new programmes. Thereafter, however, many CUs are expected to earn their living within a managed internal market. The situation is more complex with industry-wide or collaborative initiatives that may involve several partners or that are funded in whole or in part through a corporate affairs budget (see Chapter 4). In CUs, as elsewhere, financial dependencies always concentrate managerial minds and they are central to ensuring the accountability of the initiative and to embedding within the wider organization.

That said, the oversight arrangements for CUs often embrace other contingencies and stakeholders. Some companies have experimented with making a CU role – for example, as Dean of a Faculty – an aspect of the role of senior executives or directors. The purpose here is not just to ensure an alignment between CU supply and business needs, but to make a statement to all managers and professionals about the importance of activities aimed at cultivating talent and knowledge. Arrangements for advisory councils involving both internal sponsors and external partners and experts are also common. Such formal arrangements for multi-level governance are more common and elaborate in the public domain, but CU initiatives also have to negotiate space within a jungle of professional and regulatory bodies, staff and employers groupings, and existing training providers – all of whom may be both obstacles and resources, depending on the issues in question (see Chapter 3 on the NHSU).

Diversity – and convergence?

The downside of outlining – as we have done – the range of important choices is that it results in a profusion of possibilities. It is then hard to discern underlying trends and to grasp the broad contours of what may be happening in corporate training and education. For this a higher-level map is needed. To this end, we suggest that it is useful to think of contemporary CUs as varying on two dimensions. The first concerns the nature of the learning; this axis ranges from a narrow training focus (imparting information, developing specific vocational skills), through broader forms of education and professional development (including a socialization into organizational values and practices), and finally on to those that encompass forms of research as well as higher-level teaching and learning. In knowledge terms, the dimension ranges from the transfer of explicit well-codified information, through to knowledge sharing and creation.

The second dimension concerns the spatial organization of the CU, specifically whether it is focused on a specific facility that people attend (the campus model), or whether it is primarily distributed. Thus it may be either 'virtual' (such as BAE SYSTEMS VU) or employing a mix of media, including print, and providing support locally, perhaps through a network of learning centres.

Combining these two dimensions highlights four different types of CU; Figure 1.2 illustrates these and indicates what kind of 'output' we can expect from each.

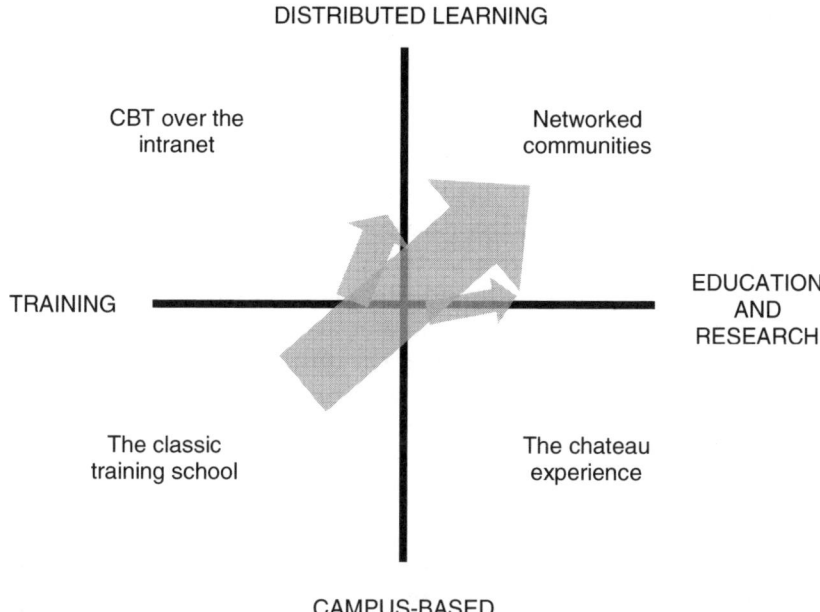

Figure 1.2   A typology of corporate universities

The most familiar type represented here is the classic company training school or college, based on the nineteenth century model of corporate education and socialization. This type continues to form a large part of the CU landscape, upgraded in various ways to raise the status and profile of training both inside and outside the organization – McDonald's Hamburger U can be seen as an exemplar of this type of CU. They are heavily focused on delivering the skills needed for consistency, quality and efficiency in core operations. Such initiatives are often represented as compensating for the shortcomings of secondary educational systems, as at one of the original CUs, Motorola U.

A second type of CU – encapsulated as 'computer-based training (CBT) on the intranet' – is much more recent, but has been the focus for very considerable investment in particular industries and contexts and provides the basis for much popular press coverage of CU initiatives. The reason is obvious: whenever large numbers of staff have to be regularly retrained (to use new software tools, for example, or to comply with new legislation), or updated (for example, on the features and terms of the latest products they sell), the costs of providing such training on a face-to-face basis have been considerable. By switching to electronically delivered training, companies may save on staff travel and accommodation costs, particularly when they are internationally distributed. Managers have also found it easier to provide the training consistently in a timely manner, with less disruption to work schedules (not least because delivery of training in this way enables it to take place outside work time and the working environment). Debate continues over the scope for this method of delivery in the longer term, particularly whether and how far it can be used for 'softer' topics less amenable to right and wrong answers, or how far it can develop beyond its pedagogic origins in programmed learning. Nevertheless, that there are important contexts in which it can be highly cost-effective is no longer in question. The Shell Open University (see Chapter 16) provides an example of reducing training spend in a highly distributed organization that needs to pass on information quickly; a second is Unipart, where (it is said) you can learn in the morning and apply it in the afternoon through using dedicated desktop computers, linked to the Unipart U, provided on every shop-floor.

The third type of CU – designated the 'chateau' or 'country house' experience – was also a familiar feature of the corporate landscape before the term CU became common. Management, leadership and executive development has traditionally taken place in well-appointed rural locations away from corporate headquarters, but in recent years such expensive initiatives have had a renaissance. They are now seen as one way of addressing a major corporate challenge – how to promote cohesion across highly differentiated international businesses, especially those that have grown through acquisition and merger. The importance and difficulty of building a common understanding and effective management teams out of diverse national and corporate cultures cannot be over-stated. The reinvention of the management college as the incubator of a shared corporate culture, through intense face-to-face development activities and the creation of cross-organizational networks, may be a result of the increased frequency of multinational mergers. Being semi-detached from the pace and pressure of mainstream corporate life, such facilities may also provide a social space where the normal codes are to a degree relaxed, and assumptions can be questioned. To this extent they may also have a role as corporate 'think tanks' where senior figures or rising stars can take time out to analyze, debate and think through emerging challenges, in relation both to internal issues faced by the organization and also in relation to wider concerns over, for example, the natural environment or the location of production. High-profile examples of this sort of CU are the Rüschlikon facility in Switzerland owned by Swiss Re (see http://www.ruschlikon.com) and Boeing's Leadership Development Centre in the USA.

Finally, there are the CUs that exist and operate as networked communities. They embrace a wide range of learning (technical and professional as well as business management) that is supported in diverse ways (combining e-learning with face-to-face elements, mentoring, action learning, placements, and so on). Their form and focus change frequently in response to emerging professional needs or shifting perceptions of strategic priorities, particularly as it appears that restructuring has become a normal rather than an exceptional occurrence in corporate life. The Capgemini University has several of these features, having played different roles at different points in the 12 years of its existence. While the campus near Paris remains the hub of the corporate university, CU staff are distributed around the world. Increasing use is made of e-learning and blended learning, and professional updating in a very fast-moving industry is provided through an online magazine. Great emphasis is also given to fostering communities and networks among the different sorts of professionals that work in the company. The UK's National College for School Leadership (see Chapter 18) is another case in point: it has a well-appointed central facility, but great effort is given to facilitating and supporting continuous distributed learning.

As the arrow on Figure 1.1 suggests, if there is an underlying trend in the development of CUs, it is towards the last of these types: a CU that may possess a central facility but need not remain forever identified with or limited to it.

Conclusions

In this introduction we set out to provide a roadmap through the various territories that CU managers inhabit. In particular, we have pointed towards a number of formative decisions concerning the function, the form and the funding of CUs through which a CU is located, shaped and oriented. It is important to stress, however, that these will rarely be one-off decisions; they will be revisited – typically every five to seven years, if not more frequently – causing the CU to evolve either by providing a new strategic focus or by adding additional functions. In addition, some of the choices concerning the form of the initiative – for example, how much to do in-house, and how much to buy in; whether or not it is important to have a branded campus or centre – may swing back and forward (because there is no stable 'best' solution).

As is to be expected from such a broad review drawing on examples of practice across the entire CU field, there can be few conclusions. Rather, this chapter is intended to illustrate the very range and variety of initiatives currently flying the CU flag in its diverse symbolic, organizational and managerial aspects. However, this is not to suggest that anything goes and everything works. Our review is also intended to emphasize that the strategic choices available to managers exploring this territory have very real material effects, in terms of cost to the host organization, the long-term success of the initiative, and the effectiveness or utility of it. Ultimately, as Chapter 5 outlines through telling the story of a 'disappeared' CU, if these criteria are not met then these strategic learning initiatives will fail.

References

Eurich, N. (1985) *Corporate Classrooms: The Learning Business*. Princeton, NJ: The Carnegie Foundation for the Advancement of Teaching.

Hawthorne, E., Libby, P. and Nash, N. (1983) 'The emergence of corporate colleges', *Journal of Continuing Higher Education*, Fall: 2–9.

Keep, E., Mayhew, K. and Corney, M. (2002) 'Review of the evidence on the rate of return to employers of investment in training and employer training measures', ESRC Centre on Skills, Knowledge and Organisational Performance Research Paper No.34, Warwick Business School.

Moore, T. (1997) 'The corporate university: Transforming management education', *Accounting Horizons*, 11(1): 77–85.

Paton, R. and Taylor, S. (2002) 'Corporate universities: Between higher education and the workplace', in: G. Williams (ed.) *Enterprise in Universities: Evidence and Evaluation*. Buckingham: Open University Press.

Paton, R., Taylor, S. and Storey, J. (2004) 'Corporate universities and leadership development' in, J. Storey (ed.) *Leadership in Organisations: Current Issues and Key Trends*. London: Routledge.

Wiggenhorn, W. (1990) 'Motorola U: When training becomes an education', *Harvard Business Review*, July–August: 71–83.

2 Using a Corporate University Initiative to Drive Strategic Change

John Storey and Beate Bungartz

Introduction

This chapter explores the experiences of one major corporation as it sought to bring about substantial change in strategy, structure, culture and working practices and also sought simultaneously to build an integrated international organization. Although the corporate university (CU) initiative was not the only device used in order to meet these objectives, it did constitute an important and significant part of the management of change programme and the case reveals the problems and possibilities associated with using CUs in such a strategic way. Additionally, because the initiative also generated a number of other major issues of the kind that typically occur in many other CU ventures, the chapter will also help to illustrate the kind of tensions that often surround CUs in large organizational contexts. The political struggles involved in the attempts to establish and gain approval and funding for the CU were considerable and they reflect tensions that we have observed in many other companies. Even today, as is the case with many other corporate universities, the institution in this case remains vulnerable. On the other hand, despite the difficulties encountered, the case also points to a number of ways in which worthwhile gains have been achieved.

This case is also of some special interest because it tells the story of a large multinational corporation headquartered in Germany. The corporation has a legacy based on a sound tradition of education, training and development. What provokes special interest is the fact that the head of the CU in this case explicitly sought to learn from, and import, the American model(s) of the CU. Indeed, there was an explicit intent and attempt to draw on the work of Jeanne Meister (Meister, 1998) as part of a strategic intent to shift from the tradition of the German training pattern to a more commercial mode.

This declared purpose provides an opportunity to compare idealized prescription with the messy reality of practice. Meister's (1998) book, *Corporate Universities: Lessons in Building a World-Class Workforce*, portrays abundant examples of apparent success in numerous organizations such as GE, National Semiconductor, Tennessee Valley Authority, Bank of Montreal, Chase Manhattan Bank and so on. Each seems to have secured top management commitment from chief executives and others providing visible support; they appear to have a 'guiding coalition of board members' (p. 68) who proffer a compelling corporate vision. These visions are 'inspiring, memorable, credible and concise' (p. 69) and so on.

While these accounts of 'best practice' can be instructive and thought provoking, what they do not reveal are the many obstacles invariably faced in practice and the difficulties in maintaining any progress made. And yet we know from a range of cases that managers who seek to introduce CU initiatives face many obstacles. The account one receives of corporate practice is highly dependent on how organizational research is conducted. When spokespersons are invited to tell the story of success they of course readily rehearse the script familiar to them. The complexities of opposition, of uncertainty, of partially understood messages, of contradictions with other corporate activity, and the myriad other ways in which reality confounds the digest of events tend to be glossed over.

In this chapter we focus on one large European corporation that illustrates the difficulties as well as the successes. The case is instructive because it is an organization rich in resources, with a long proud history of training and development, and, at the time of this study, it had a small number of senior managers with a clear and serious intent to introduce the CU concept. At the same time there were a number of other senior managers who remained unconvinced of the idea and their support or acquiescence was, at best, highly conditional. The unfolding dynamic between these different positions forms the central theme of this chapter.

The case in the context of the debates in the literature

As CUs have increased in number over the past few years, much analysis has naturally been about making sense of and interpreting the meaning and significance of the phenomenon. Thus, for example, one distinct approach has been to compare and contrast CUs with traditional universities (Blass, 2001; Antonacopoulou, 2002). And one aspect of this has been to address the question of whether CUs are a threat to, or opportunity for, conventional universities (Meister, 1997). In this chapter we do not concern ourselves with this part of the debate. For our purposes here, the extent to which CUs should be rated as 'real universities' or whether they dilute the label or present a growing threat is not the issue. Rather, we want to examine what senior managers are *doing* with these organizational forms; how they have been shaped, rationalized and received. In other words, to a large extent to assess them in their own terms. We do not seek to assess the implications for the world of education at large; rather we want to assess CUs as organizational phenomena.

Our own approach to the concept of the CU is to regard it as a cluster of ideas and a set of institutional and technological possibilities that can be mixed and re-mixed in various combinations. So, for us, the interesting question is not 'What is a CU?' but rather how the cluster of ideas and the mix of possibilities are used in particular settings. Further, we are also interested in the extent to which, and the ways in which, the configurations and possibilities are constrained and with what consequences.

This chapter reports on a case study research in the German headquarters of a corporation that, for purposes of anonymity, we label 'Utility Co.'. Our research methods in this case included the collection of relevant documentary evidence and in-depth interviewing of key informants. The documentary sources were comprised of policy papers prepared for the Board of Directors, background analyses of the nature of the education, training and development provision and the analyses of what needed to be improved, and other documents including organization charts, training needs analyses, curriculum content and so on. The interviews were conducted with key players at various levels and from a number of functions and product divisions. We interviewed the head of the CU – a senior director who reported directly to a main board director. We also interviewed board-level members of the main product divisions of the corporation, the head of e-learning and various other managers who represented both the supply and the demand side of the equation. Our sample included idea champions, senior managers who had acted as 'faculty' of the university, third-party customers (senior divisional managers whose budgets paid for the CU) and consumers of the universities courses. The interviews were conducted at the company headquarters in 2003. Each interview was between one and a half and two hours in duration and all interviews were tape-recorded and transcribed.

Background to the case

Utility Co. is a major corporation headquartered in Germany. It was formerly a public sector utility company. In this former state it held a monopolistic market position, had an almost entirely German orientation and was characterized by rigid employment policies and practices. Its employees were, in formal terms, civil servants and were protected by the laws and regulations governing such state employees. But since it was 'privatized' (its shares were made available on the stock market) in 1995 it has grown into an equity-based company with international reach and with aspirations to be entrepreneurial in character.

The corporation employs around 200 000 people, of whom some 25 per cent are located outside Germany. There are four main divisions and a multiple set of businesses. The CU's mission is to offer a service to all these businesses and to achieve some common capabilities and some common values across them. Commitment to training was an integral part of its public service ethos and legal duty. Many categories of staff were (and to a lesser extent still are) contractually entitled to a certain minimum number of staff training days per year. Nearly half the total workforce of the parent company are still civil servants and as such are protected by public laws. Following agreement with the works council and the labour union, it is mandatory for the company to provide career development (and even promotion rights) to this category of employees. Thus, co-determination and the wider pattern of corporatist policies in Germany have a direct impact on the organization of training and development provision in this case.

Vocational training and development had traditionally been firmly established within the company and it has a legacy of a generously staffed training and education function. Indeed, the corporation even had its own technical universities, although these were by no means perceived as carrying the attributes associated with the contemporary idea of a CU. This legacy proved to be a significant factor within the narrative of this case because, when the idea of launching a CU was first mooted in the late 1990s, the initial draft proposal was actually built around the existing technical universities.

One of the initial objectives was to focus on the managers – the key constituency that lay outside the formally 'protected' group within the co-determination legislation. So the CU was, in part, designed for the management group – a cadre neglected by the mandatory training provision.

The corporate university

In this section of the chapter we first describe and analyse the origins and rationale of the new CU. We then explain its functions and its range of products and service. Third, we examine its location and sponsorship within the organization and assess its strengths and vulnerabilities. Fourth, we consider the take-up of its products and the way it is perceived and received by its clients.

ORIGINS AND RATIONALE

The story of the *competing rationales* and competing conceptualizations of what a CU is for, and should be, as illustrated by this case, has a resonance in many other companies. The playing out of these tensions is, however, unusually stark in this case. Different stakeholders were found to have different objectives.

The nature of the initiative that unfolded was influenced by the company's historical legacy. As one senior manager observed:

It is important to understand its history as a state-owned company. When the company was launched to go public in the mid-1990s it left behind many of the public sector development practices. The abrupt ending of these development practices left a gap. In particular there was a serious neglect of young professionals and of management development. In fact, when I joined in the late 1990s, the company really had no management development at all.

In 1997, the main board Human Resources (HR) Director established a task force to examine the options for establishing a CU. According to a range of informants we have interviewed and according to documentation, there were four main reasons for this move. The first was a general feeling that other leading companies were establishing CUs and so this organization should possibly follow this trend. A second reason was that the inherited legacy of an elaborate education and training infrastructure was perceived as expensive and outdated. It was judged that much of that could be reduced or dispensed with and the money invested in a more targeted way elsewhere. The third reason was that the management cadre had been neglected from a development viewpoint and that the needs of this target group needed to be addressed at a time when a more entrepreneurial and commercial outlook was required. There was also the view that new capabilities were required under the new, competitive, privatized regime. Different attitudes and competences had to be nurtured in order to address the new market conditions facing the company. Finally, as an array of international businesses had been acquired, there was a view that the group required some common leadership and management development activities in order to provide some 'corporate glue' for the corporation as a whole.

Not all of these reasons were clearly stated at the time. Some were made explicit, others remained rather implicit. Some senior managers focused on one or more of these reasons, while other managers focused on a different mix.

The corporate glue argument was expressed by one board-level director as follows:

We are in the process of transferring business responsibility to the different pillars of the group. Our objective is to strengthen the different pillars in order to bring processes and decision making nearer to the very specific needs of those businesses. But as we begin to succeed in this what then holds the corporate bits together? One of these umbrellas in my view is to achieve a common understanding of the nature of 'leadership'. This gives us the opportunity to design common development processes for skills and competences at this senior level.

This informant went on to say that without an academy or CU, some other initiative would need to be put in place in order to help with the task of binding the corporate whole together.

There is a dilemma here, however, because other managers – especially those in the divisions – tended to be suspicious of new infrastructure at the corporate level. They preferred to take the proclamations of the priority of *devolved* management at face value. Thus there was resistance to more corporate training and development and a tendency to seek to be self-sufficient in the divisions and businesses.

To a considerable extent these arguments were accepted or at least heard at the centre and so means were sought to allow complementary provision and to limit the role of the centre:

> At the moment there is extensive duplication. We are struggling to find an acceptable design for personal development across the divisions. For example, with regard to policy towards high potentials, how do we devise a common competency model while also allowing for the special needs of the different pillars? My view is that we need some common model. Whether that extends to all functions and levels is more doubtful. To do that would imply adopting a centralized model. But that would inhibit responding to our new flexible, varied and dynamic environment. So in my view we need to at least have this at the top level in order to allow for a unified form of leadership. But it would be best not to try to replicate this at the technical and operational levels. Siemens, for example, introduced a sophisticated skill-based model. Thousands of skills had to be described. It turned out to be far too detailed. There was too much precision and it was too inflexible and not at all adapted to local special needs.

Some (but by no means all) directors of the company argued that the introduction of the CU at Utility Co. could be interpreted as 'an emergency measure'.

The first emergency to be tackled was the building of new management capacity and capability. As one of them claimed: 'The advanced management and general management programmes are focusing on this aspect, the tactic here is to see what can we do quickly with famous partners such as Harvard and Stanford in order to get managers up to speed.' To some extent these modules are tailored to the needs of the company. Nonetheless it was reported to us that it was 'tough' to convince top directors of the company that this management training was needed.

Another 'emergency' was the perceived need to increase the 'international mind-set'. It was noted, for example, that there was still a discussion in the company about what would be the appropriate company language. There was some consideration to the idea that possibly German should not be that language. Language aside there was also a concern that the ways of understanding markets was still too weighted towards a German set of assumptions and that these needed challenging and testing. As has been the case elsewhere, there was also some priority concern given to the concept of leadership and the promotion of appropriate leadership behaviours throughout the group. In addition, there was a concern that expertise was too narrowly focused within separate pillars and that the group lacked managers with the capability to operate in a cross-functional and cross-business manner. It was expected that the CU would crucially tackle this new requirement.

THE CHRONOLOGY OF ACTUAL DEVELOPMENTS

The initial proposal came in the form of a document presented to the HR Director by a working party that he had established. This team offered a blueprint that showed how the technical universities, which, notably, the corporation already owned, could be forged together as the basis for a revamped educational package. The plan also emphasized the potential for higher academic standing and accreditation by establishing a privately-owned university of applied sciences with an adjunct Master of Business Administration (MBA) programme. Despite intensive work by the task force over a period of 12 months the plan was rejected by the HR Director. As a result, a number of the architects of the plan resigned from the company and considerable ill-feeling was provoked.

As the current head of the CU observed:

> The first draft plan for a CU was not accepted by [the main board HR Director]. The proposers misunderstood the word 'university'. They wanted to build on the existing university of applied sciences and make it like a real academic university. But [the main board Director] wanted a corporate academy – a very different concept. Their idea was to improve the standing of the applied science university in the academic world getting them on ranking scales, with more academic standing, based on scientific research. But they neglected the internal needs and especially they neglected the needs of our executives.

The HR Director pursued another route. Two of the legacy universities were disposed of – through closure of their specialist facilities and through transfer of the more generic facilities to the state educational authorities. As the current head of the CU pointed out, the initial attempted design by the working party produced a plan that was based on the 'wrong' assumptions:

> The word 'university' led them down a particular path. They devised plans for an elite school which would have high academic credentials. Their idea was to have chairs in finance and economics and so on. But in fact what top management at Utility Co. really wanted was more like a commercial management college. Indeed the CEO, wanted something 'more American'.

Other associated desired attributes were described as being that it should be more virtual rather than physical, that it should only have small numbers of staff, and that rather than an in-house faculty the staff should be 'in-house organizers who hire and manage external experts'.

A new head of the initiative was appointed from outside the company. This newcomer was given the very general brief to construct a new proposal for a CU. He was then allowed a free hand to get on with this task. It is a matter of some interest that the new head, although located in Germany, which of course has its own distinct and proud vocational educational system, began by researching the nature of corporate universities in the USA. The models, as promulgated by Jeanne Meister and the Corporate Universities Exchange in the USA, proved to be influential. Indeed, the previous proposal was discarded completely and an American-influenced model took its place.

As this new head of the academy explained:

> At this point I came in and began to gather information. I had researched the framework of Mrs Meister and others. My remit was very open, I had lots of free space. I was especially

attracted by the Motorola model. The priority was – how do we get senior executives to work with us in an academy? It would have been difficult to integrate a vast system of pre-existing training provision into the new institution, it was too unwieldy. It was too big and too much of the wrong thing. So, to try to integrate all this would have been a liability. Also, if we had done so, another disadvantage would have been that other senior executives may also have looked at our new thing as part of the old thing!

This quotation is very revealing on a number of counts. The academy had to be seen as something 'new'. It had to be credible with the top team and be supported by them. For these things to happen, the academy had not to be encumbered by the pre-existing training and development provision and it had to be small and focused. There was a fresh start, working from a blank piece of paper.

One of the first steps was to abandon the term 'university' – a term that was perceived to send the wrong signals in this particular context. Instead, the term 'academy' was selected. This has the dual merits of (a) focusing attention on a select group of top managers (it was to this extent intentionally selective and elitist); and (b) directing attention to company capability development needs rather than wider educational provision. In such a context, as has been the case in a number of other settings, the term 'university' proved to be a hindrance.

FUNCTIONS AND ACTIVITIES

The Utility Co. Academy is a virtual institute with no own buildings or campus or faculties. The 34 staff of the academy – all of them located in Germany – are distributed among four sub-units: management development, college affairs, e-learning and knowledge management. These sub-units loosely express the ambitions of the academy.

The main target groups for the academy are senior executives, high potentials, young academic people, and, for certain specific learning initiatives, the whole company. Concerning management development, the academy is viewed as the appropriate supplier, particularly for training offerings and events in the field of general management, leadership, corporate governance, integration and internationalization.

A needs analysis of top management has been conducted and, as a result, a number of new courses have been devised in close cooperation with external business schools. The most important products of its management development unit are a General Management Programme, and an Advanced Management Programme.

The General Management Programme comprises two three-day modules that focus on enhancing the ability of senior executives to make measurable business impact in a context of rapid industry evolution. Guided by faculty from London Business School and Columbia Business School, the participants work to establish process standards for the areas of prime concern to the General Manager. The Utility Co. Toolkit created from this programme will drive the creation of a common general management culture in the functional practices and throughout the company. The tailor-made training is predominantly based on case studies. These cover issues such as general management, borderless action, business innovation and the management of people.

On the other hand, the target group of the Advanced Management Programme is Utility Co.'s top executives. The programme focuses on organizational growth driven by internal entrepreneurship. It uses faculty from Harvard Business School and Stanford

University. It includes not only analysis of organizational structure and growth, but also the deeper cultural issues that can prevent or foster an entrepreneurial spirit from taking hold in the organization. The two three-day modules emphasize subjects in the fields of corporate strategy, managing change and entrepreneurial leadership. Both programmes can be changed to suit the needs of the business. For example, at the time of writing, there is a strong focus on 'handling headcount reductions' in a newly emerging general management programme.

The integration of new hired executives is promoted by specific integration seminars and live current issues are taken up and discussed in monthly business forums.

The Utility Co. Academy also provides a career development programme. This programme is targeted at the individual promotion needs of identified potential candidates for top executive positions. The executives who are identified as top potentials in the annual executive-level meetings undergo a formal management appraisal. This appraisal is based on Utility Co.'s newly developed management competency framework, which seeks to identify individual strengths and development needs as a first step in the design of a personal development plan and targeted promotion.

But this formal design was not fully endorsed by our informants within the divisions. For example, one objection was that:

> There is a conflict between 'placement-focused' and 'development-focused' objectives for the programmes. The programmes often seem to have mixed functions. In my view, the academy should not be concerned with placement process, it should be about development.

The e-learning arm has a dedicated intranet presence. The company has recently purchased a Harvard CD-ROM, which acts as a taster and a pathway into the e-learning zones. The CD-ROM contains brief and palatable introductions to some 34 key management topics. Each of these topics can be studied on the CD-ROM in approximately 20–30 minutes. Each topic then has demarcated pathways into further resources such as further reading and also directions into further courses (if supplied by Harvard, these courses are then charged for, whereas the CD-ROM modules are 'free' at point of consumption). Beyond this particular initiative, the e-learning unit within the academy is responsible for the development and evaluation of a corporate learning strategy and for the coordination of virtual learning platforms.

An early experiment in e-learning was expensive and elaborate. A whole range of modules requiring two hours of study each was commissioned. This turned out to be rather a waste of money. Website usage was monitored and it was found that despite the huge investment made by the company in developing this elaborate package, the average stay in a module was less than five minutes. Less than 5 per cent of the employee population completed courses once started. Five per cent of 200 000 (10 000 people) could be made to appear rather good. But when compared to the costs and the provision, that was still expensive. As the manager in charge of the new e-learning initiative pointed out: 'We will not make the mistake again of having a library of courses and then hope someone will use them. Rather, we want to pay for actual specific usage'.

Another problem for the academy in general in relation to e-learning is that its aspirations for a common architecture across the divisions is not implemented in practice. Each division opposes the uniform approach; they try to be self sufficient in as many regards as possible. This causes tension with the academy. The divisions are powerful, they make a profit contribution and they enjoy, as a consequence, a certain freedom.

Overall, the products within the suite have been separately designed for different purposes and for specific target audiences. So far, there has not been an integrated, cumulative progression of product offerings by the academy.

The third arm of the Utility Co. Academy is its work on 'knowledge management'. This sub-unit seeks to capture, store and make available knowledge through use of a device known as 'Cockpit'. In essence, this is an electronic collection of readings that strives to display the range of knowledge in Utility Co. It contains, for example, a collection of articles and a series of links. In some respects it operates like an electronic encyclopaedia. At the time of our research, however, this knowledge management unit was being moved outside of the academy and was being located instead within the in-house consulting unit. The main reason for this shift appeared to be to meet a headcount audit need, rather than serving any pedagogic rationale. This in itself might not be a particularly significant development, but some key players interpreted it as indicative of a wider issue – the lack of a thought-through strategy for the academy. For example, a senior manager argued:

If you take the development of the structure of the academy, it shows that there is no real strategy. One year ago we integrated the knowledge management department into the academy. Now, it is being transferred to the in-house consulting unit. For both the academy and the consulting unit, there is some question mark over who will pay for them and whether they will survive over the long term.

Sometimes CUs are created in order to help rationalize pre-existing training and development departments. In the case of Utility Co., there was a clear attempt to achieve more standardization of training provision for managers and for e-learning in particular. Before the rationalization, even single divisions were found to have multiple and non-standard learning products and methods.

The academy is also used as a gateway to prestigious courses at Harvard and Stanford. Apart from the prestige, the networking permitted by participation in such courses is highly valued. But, of course, it can be reasonably argued that you do not need to establish a CU in order to send managers to Harvard or Stanford. For a brief time the academy also housed a team known as 'Top Executive Services'. This offered individual coaching to top managers. Another service within the embrace of the academy relates to 'teambuilding' for certain teams that are facing difficulties. However, the extent of this work is relatively obscure because, as was pointed out to us, 'no one is broadcasting these activities and interventions as there are certain sensitivities surrounding them; departments and units do not wish it to be known that they are dysfunctional and need help'.

There was also another reason for the low profile enjoyed by these activities. This related to the ongoing turf war between the Utility Co. Academy and the top managers in the HR function. The latter remained responsible for executive appointments, terms and conditions, individual competency development, open enrolment programmes at leading universities and so on. Meanwhile, the academy had responsibility for fostering networking among top executives and for their development as a collective. There was, of course, a very fuzzy boundary between these twin sets of responsibilities and, given the power struggle between the two parties, neither was willing to properly share information.

ORGANIZATIONAL VULNERABILITY

Even the initial investigation and planning stage which preceded the launch of the academy revealed the tenuous nature of the venture. As the head of the academy himself observed:

I had to gain the acceptance of various players in the company. It was a major challenge and it took me a whole year even to get basic agreement. During the process of negotiating acceptance I learned a lot about culture and power in this organization. The idea had to be 'sold'. I had to discover the potential bases and the different degrees of acceptance. I was surprised to discover that no one really even started out with the notion that management development was necessary. That assumption could not be replied on. Top management often argued, 'we have a lot of other things to do and we need to earn money, and then maybe later ...'.

Although it was found that few senior managers saw management development as a priority there was nonetheless a wide acceptance that something should be done about the newly emerging international character of the group:

There was a recognition that a common culture would not simply emerge naturally. We needed time and places and events to help build common values and culture.

Another plank on which the initiative could be built was the view that training provision needed rationalizing:

Everyone said we have problems with our training and that we needed a new coordinated architecture for our company's development. There was a perceived need to improve coordination of all the activities. Everyone seemed to agree with that – at least in principle. We had an over-elaborate training department and there was an opportunity to reduce this.

The divisional heads were suspicious about the costs of the academy as a central resource. The customer perspective is provided by one of the divisional heads:

The academy should not regard itself as a given function. It needs to prove itself. It needs to act as a market player. We have to deliver at least same quality as other potential providers. The benefit comes from synergies. It needs to be state-of-the-art in what we as individual business units cannot provide, also insight into what is going on externally, the extra perspective needed. A big risk for an academy is to be too internal focused. The academy has to offer something above and beyond what we could source ourselves.

Nor could it be assumed that HR would be natural champions and defenders of the academy. It was reported that there was ongoing effort to ensure that HR colleagues continued to support the idea. It was suggested that some HR specialists did not do so because they lacked knowledge and commitment in this area. Their expertise lay mainly within the traditional operating procedures – for example, dealing with terms and conditions, co-determination, labour law and other labour relations issues. It was suggested that they may be afraid of dealing with issues with which they were not familiar.

Discussion

This case illustrates the political tensions surrounding the introduction of this CU. It helps to surface the many disagreements about the aims, objectives, purposes and nature of CUs which, in varying degrees, are present also in many other cases.

The case also illustrates some of the differences between an American understanding of the CU phenomenon and a European perspective. The former is more normative in character. In so far as it is descriptive, it seems to be description that is offered in illustrative support of the normative account. In contrast, the European perspective is more alert to the pluralistic nature of organizations and to their political character.

Above all, the case reveals that CUs are not simply 'established', but rather that the process of introducing such initiatives is much more akin to a tentative, experimental, transitional process. Hence, culture change is not precisely 'managed' though the launch of a CU – even when this is one of its prime objectives. Rather the reality is more contentious and multiple agendas come into play.

The impact of the CU in this German corporation to date has been limited. In the face of competing expectations, the approach adopted by its champions has been pragmatic. In turn, the take-up and use by clients has so far been experimental and tentative. In the main, though, we did find that the General Management Programme and the Advanced Management Programme had been well received by the academy's customers.

Many difficulties remain, however. First, there are budget issues. Consequently, this has meant, for example, that the target of getting all the top 100 managers in the corporation through the Advanced Management Programme has not been met. In part, this is because of constraints – both the General Management Programme and the Advanced Management Programme have been subject to postponement and cancellation. Second, the academy is rather lacking in a coherent and compelling series of next steps. While those who actually attended the General and Advanced Management Programmes enjoyed them, there has now to be some follow-on activities. Third, and most crucially, the academy as an institution remains vulnerable to cuts and even to closure.

At the present time, its champions describe the academy as 'on the first rung of the ladder'. Its main function is to act as a department responsible for organizing courses and programmes targeted at certain key management populations. These key management groups are regarded as strategically important in various ways: either because they can help unite a now internationally dispersed corporation and/or because they are critical to redefining the nature and strategy of the 'new Utility Co.'

Part of this latter role is to instil a more commercial, entrepreneurial and innovative edge to a bureaucracy that is perceived as owing rather too much of its character to its public sector origins. The CU in this case is regarded by its champions as the catalyst for forging and diffusing a new set of core values. Its mission is to bring about culture change as well as capability change. The vision of its champions is also that the CU will be a key device to bind and hold together the multiple businesses, the multiple functions and the multiple international arms of the corporation.

These are objectives that we found echoed in many other settings where corporate universities had been launched. In practice, such ambitions are usually soon confronted with everyday realities, such as chief executives of businesses who have other priorities. And so it proved to be in this German case. Accordingly, CU champions are forced to spend much of their time trying to win the practical support (not just the rhetorical support) of powerful figures in the businesses. Resources of time, and money, have to be won. These are often only allocated conditionally and for limited time periods. In response, CU staff have to try to demonstrate the value of their activities. Some are tempted to hype up their contribution, others are more cautious – as one of them said in this case, 'I don't want to sell air balloons'.

But herein lies the dilemma. CUs are usually a central service function. They are, in the view of subsidiary divisions and businesses, a central 'overhead'. As such, they need to continually justify themselves. Unless they sell and project their contribution, they may be ignored. The academy team in this case were aware they had to create some sense of 'excitement'. On the other hand, if CU champions oversell the contribution, they risk being judged as failing if the measured contribution does not match the inflated claims. Hence, the pragmatic approach is often found – as it was in this case. Here, as elsewhere, CU senior staff seek to win the support of their top management colleagues by incremental progress. For example, this may be through involving them in quality courses both as participants and as speakers. The process is akin to gaining converts to a cause. In so far as this succeeds, this in itself may be judged as part of the culture change that is sought.

References

Antonacopoulou, E. (2002) 'Corporate universities: The domestication of management education', in C. Wankel and R. DeFillippi (eds), *Rethinking Management Education for the 21st Century*. Greenwich, CT: Information Age Publishing.

Blass, E. (2001) 'What's in a name? A comparative study of the traditional public university and the corporate university', *Human Resource Development International*, 4(2): 153–172.

Meister, J.C. (1997) 'Corporate universities: An opportunity or threat to higher education?', Paper presented at the Designing a Virtual University Conference, 12–14 March, Cambridge, MA.

Meister, J.C. (1998) *Corporate Universities: Lessons in Building a World-Class Workforce*. New York: McGraw-Hill.

3 Innovating at Scale: The NHSU[1]

Lee Taylor and Bob Fryer

Introduction

The NHSU, which was initiated following the UK General Election in 2001, aspires to be the university for the National Health Service (NHS), eventually becoming the largest 'corporate university' (CU) in Europe and, potentially, one of the largest in the world. Its radical vision promises a blueprint for innovation in work-based, lifelong learning that opens up participation in education and training to two million staff at all levels, as well as patients, service users and carers. This vision, and the overriding purpose of NHSU, is to contribute to radical change and improvement in health and social care through the transformation of learning. Bringing this large-scale vision to reality is already underway: there are learners on the first programmes, significant partnership working is taking place and NHSU is tackling the challenge of designing a robust, large-scale, distributed and largely work-based organization.

NHSU is part of the modernizing agenda for the NHS in England (Department of Health, 2000), which aims to put the patient at the centre of radically improved service delivery, providing greater choice and accountability. Health and associated social care depend fundamentally on the skills of a huge and extremely diverse workforce – employed by a plethora of public, private and voluntary sector bodies. NHSU aims to underpin and help to implement the ten-year NHS Plan and act as a catalyst for workforce skills' improvement. The NHS currently spends over £3 billion on education and training. NHSU aims to secure a better understanding of the development needs of over 1.3 million NHS staff and a further 1.5 million in associated health and social care. By working in partnership with the service itself, a wide range of education and training institutions, and by making extensive use of e-learning and a 'virtual campus', it intends to provide good-quality, timely learning opportunities, especially for those currently without a professional qualification. So, NHSU will help transform learning opportunities and achievement at all levels and significantly increase and diversify staff involvement in learning. It is aimed at securing a radical shift in workplace cultures across the sector, in order to embed learning in all workplaces for all staff in the service.

This chapter describes the context and history to date for this initiative, and discusses some of the key issues and challenges being faced by this new kind of educational organization.

Background information on the UK's NHS – its scale, its place in national life, the challenges it is facing – is provided in the box below for those unfamiliar with this unique British institution.

THE NATIONAL HEALTH SERVICE AND WORKFORCE DEVELOPMENT

In the UK, the NHS plays a remarkable and unique role in social and community life. Founded in 1948, post World War Two, the NHS provides high-quality primary and acute healthcare free to all citizens at the point of delivery. It is a prized and highly cherished part of the national culture as well as being a vital service for everyone; public opinion polls consistently demonstrate that more people value the NHS than any other British institution. However, this pre-eminent position also means there is a constant spotlight on the quality, effectiveness and timeliness of provision. Errors, delays and examples of poor provision are given hostile publicity in the British press and media, while thousands and thousands of successful and highly professional health encounters every day go largely unsung.

Of course, the effective provision and improvement of health and social care to the nation is a serious business, especially for the patients, service users and staff involved, and it makes great demands upon the public purse. The costs of the service to public expenditure already amount to more than £60 billion annually and are planned to rise by 7.4 per cent per annum until the total budget of the NHS is just over £100 billion annually, making the NHS one of the 30 or so largest economies in the world. Hence, healthcare is one of the core issues for public policy and public service reform in the UK – especially so as longevity increases, lifestyles change, expectations rise and social conditions and social relations in the community shift and change (See Wanless, 2002).

Advances in potential healthcare provision – in terms of new methods of handling illness and promoting good health, including the development, trial and application of new drugs, new equipment and innovative therapies – have meant that both life expectancy and patient expectations are rising. There is a consistent drive towards focusing on the patient, and providing services as much as possible in the community (primary care), blurring divisions between health and social care. Public access to healthcare knowledge, through the media and Internet is also increasing rapidly, accompanied by rises in public demand for high quality, more choice and diverse care. The wider social context of increasing affluence, changing lifestyles, a growing emphasis on choice and 'consumer' rights and inequalities that are hard to shift all contribute to a challenging backdrop.

In common with most developed and developing countries, UK health and social care already face a chronic shortage of the right mix of staff skills and competences. Both services face great challenges in securing the recruitment and retention of appropriately qualified staff. Moreover, the sheer time and scale of resources required to train healthcare professionals to the required high standards show clearly that continuing only with the same pattern of roles and staff development is increasingly unsustainable. Critical views of the NHS have insisted that, hitherto, it has paid far too little attention to the skills and undeveloped talents of large sections of its staff and that this situation should not be allowed to persist. This has led to a recent concentration of attention on workforce development to ensure that there is better recruitment, increased retention, a focus on improving motivation and morale, an emphasis on new ways of working and a commitment to continuous learning for everyone in the service (See Department of Health, 2001a).

Developing the ambition: Moving from concept to delivery

In October 2001 the Department of Health publication *Everyone: Introducing the NHS University* (Department of Health, 2001b) outlined the radical vision of an organization for everyone in the NHS, and associated social care, that both explicitly focused on those traditionally excluded from further and higher education and actively involved patients and carers in the new institution's development.

NHSU's first Chief Executive, Professor Bob Fryer, who was appointed in early 2002, assembled a Design and Implementation Team (DIT) to scope and plan the NHSU's initial vision and development. The 30, mainly part-time, secondees to the DIT came from a wide range of backgrounds in health, social care and education. These included especially colleagues from The Open University and Ufi/learndirect, the two existing national-scale distributed learning organizations in the UK, both of which were already successfully operating high-volume e-learning.

The DIT also included colleagues from staff-representative organizations, professional bodies and the trade unions. One of which, UNISON, Britain's largest trade union, had already pioneered a radical and hugely successful 'Return to Learn' programme for manual workers and routine administrative staff in this area (See Kennedy, 1995; Munro, Rainbird and Holly, 1997). The Department of Health and Department for Education and Skills (DfES) provided staff versed in relevant national policy and initiatives, especially the emergent reforms in education for young people, in higher education and the development of a national skills' strategy (DfES, 2002, 2003a, 2003b).

A development plan for consultation

Consultation on NHSU's first development plan, *Learning for Everyone*, published in November 2002 (NHSU, 2002), showed wide support for its eight guiding principles:

- **access** – available to everyone in healthcare (and associated social care);
- **relevance** – designed to improve healthcare outcomes;
- **choice** – delivered in innovative ways that suit individual learners;
- **support** – world class systems to help learners;
- **equity** – tackling barriers to fair opportunity and creating opportunities for inclusive learning;
- **multidisciplinary and multi-professional working** – towards common learning for shared and team-based practice;
- **partnership** – working with others and recognizing the good work already being done;
- **quality** – excellence in all aspects of provision.

The six month development plan consultation included a 'road show' of consultative stakeholder events involving an estimated three hundred separate organizations and more than 20 000 individuals. It yielded significant and enthusiastic support for the whole concept of the NHSU and its guiding principles, plenty of offers of collaboration at all levels and a healthy demand that NHSU should clarify its core functions. Respondents argued that NHSU should achieve focus and bring greater coherence, consistency and clarity to the complex patchwork of existing courses and qualifications. They urged NHSU to secure some 'early wins', to establish its credibility with the service, make partnerships work in practice, avoid unnecessary duplication of provision and move from rhetoric to reality as soon as possible. Some existing universities were concerned that NHSU should clarify the potential for confusion and contradiction between acting as both a direct provider of learning programmes and services and acting as a commissioner of them from others (MORI/NHSU, 2003).

Setting priorities: Initial learning programmes and services

After the consultation, NHSU needed to prioritize its planned activity and manage expectations. With no systematic and robust evidence on learning needs and service priorities, NHSU was obliged to piece together early requirements through discussions with key national officials and by reference to Department of Health policy documents and initiatives. We also benefited from a close reading of a large number of papers and reports, especially those linked to the implementation of the ten-year NHS Plan and the various strategies being developed and advocated for securing workforce development and achieving lifelong learning (Department of Health, 2001a).

On this basis, the development of a series of initial programmes and services is underway. A good example is the core initial development of a service-wide common induction programme entitled 'Working in the NHS' and prepared jointly with a leading, private sector e-learning provider, as well as with patients and service users. Perhaps surprisingly, there was no common programme of this nature already available in health and social care, although many organizations operate their own induction schemes. The NHSU's programme, which demonstrates many core NHSU tenets and principles, is delivered in close working partnership with the service and is aimed at all new entrants (estimated at a total of 140 000 per annum) whatever their level and previous qualifications. It covers the NHS's aims and values, the structure of the NHS, the individual's role, and, significantly, prepares for the learner's journey within the NHS. The programme is based on interactive and self-navigated e-learning, delivered through a 'blended' approach, supported by local learning advisers and hosted by the NHSU's virtual campus. The programme can be deployed flexibly and customized locally by the NHS and NHSU Learning Advisers, who themselves are offered training as NHSU tutors. The programme was extensively and developmentally tested within a few partner NHS trusts as well as with patients and users, and is being launched in each of the NHSU's nine regions in a variety of trust settings, prior to evaluation, further revision and full-scale rollout.

A second, learning services, example is the establishment of NHSU's dedicated national Information and Advice service concerned with learning opportunities in health and social care. Developed in collaboration with Ufi/learndirect for the first three years, it is based on Ufi/learndirect's existing database of over 240 000 programmes available in health and social care and uses a regionally based group of specialist advice staff in NHSU.

A third and defining instance of NHSU's approach is its determination to work alongside, and be an active part of, local health and social care communities, reflecting the planned shift of the balance of power in healthcare, in particular from national to local levels. Each of the nine NHSU regions is in the process of establishing close collaborative working relationships within local healthcare economies to secure the affiliation to NHSU of Local Learning Resource Centres that will serve as a network for local NHSU-supported learning and act as hubs of workplace learning activities. This approach is just part of the process of ensuring that NHSU is 'owned' by the sector and identifies closely with its aims, priorities and values.

Although the concept of the NHSU dates back to before the last UK General Election in 2001, it has only been actively in development since spring 2002. By early 2004, the initial largely part-time and seconded development team has been superseded by a full-time permanent group of more than 300 staff, split between a small headquarters and the nine regions. A draft strategic plan, *Forward to Delivery,* describing NHSU's intentions for the next five years and identifying key performance indicators, has been approved by the Minister of State for Health, and published (NHSU, 2003). NHSU was formally launched in December 2003.

Some tough issues for NHSU

Achieving the ambitious remit and vision of NHSU is challenging, and requires a carefully structured approach. Both the development and strategic plans recognize that there are tough issues to tackle, both in the short and medium term. Many of these take the form of continuing tensions, dilemmas or contradictions and will often need to be constantly managed and navigated rather than resolved 'once-and-for-all'. In exploring some of these tensions, it is possible to discern elements of the emergent distinctiveness of NHSU.

Establishing learner needs and matching them to curriculum provision

A first challenge is that NHSU should properly seek to meet the express needs and priorities for learning of the organizations and individuals that make up the vast sectors of health and social care. But there are serious difficulties here and the prospect of continuing tensions. First, there is currently no robust and reliable knowledge base of current and future learning needs, nor is there even a common and agreed methodology for discerning and collecting the data. Second, even when they are clearly articulated, the learning needs of both health and social care organizations on the one hand and those of individual members of staff on the other may be incompatible. Third, it is a gross over-simplification to assume that there is a fully common 'corporate' voice across this vast, albeit national, service. Fourth, senior managers will understandably press for immediate short-term requirements to be met, possibly at the expense of longer-term change and development. Indeed, in the NHS as elsewhere in business, most senior managers find it very difficult to 'imagine the future', especially given the here-and-now demands they face and the targets that they are required to meet.

There is already a complex set of provisions available and the NHSU has been approached with all sorts of proposals ranging from major suites of accredited learning to short programmes, and with different expectations of the NHSU role in their development and delivery. The NHSU is committed to discovering and understanding what learner needs really are, and how these can best be addressed by a national organization. Moreover, NHSU intends to adopt the role of 'broker' and commissioner of provision from existing educational institutions, acting as a market maker, at least as much as being a provider in its own right or acting as joint provider with others. Indeed, in seeking to emphasize this point, we in NHSU often say that our intention is to be a provider of 'last' rather than of 'first' resort.

NHSU will also co-badge and re-version existing and new learning services and products, through the development of its own quality criteria. It can co-develop or co-invest, for example, alongside other educational providers or with national organizations such as the National Patient Safety Agency. This potential range of roles requires careful consideration primarily of quality issues, intellectual property and contractual arrangements, and subsequent branding. So, partnership is at the heart of our curriculum development and delivery.

There has been widespread critique of the ability of the current providers to understand and then respond flexibly and rapidly to NHS needs, despite understanding 'customer' needs being part of the approval cycle for new provision in many colleges or universities. How can the NHSU do better? A Learning Needs Observatory has been established to undertake robust primary and secondary research of individual and organizational needs in partnership with a university centre of international excellence in this field. This work will be undertaken in partnership and joint ownership with the relevant national skill sector councils, Skills for Health and TOPSS, and in collaboration with Strategic Health Authorities and their workforce development activity.

The five target areas for analysing learning needs are:

- the implementation of the National Service Frameworks (which prioritize key areas for modernizing service improvement, for example, in mental health and cancer care);
- changing roles within the workforce;
- management and leadership;
- innovation and improvement of care;
- widening participation in health and social care training.

In the period before this research can inform curriculum development prioritization, a pragmatic set of criteria are being used to identify and phase programme proposals. The 20 plus programmes in development for rollout in the initial three years of delivery are clustered in the following areas:

- improving the patient experience (for example, a programme on customer care for multi-disciplinary teams);
- changing roles (for example, a programme to develop an Advanced Practitioner in Anaesthetics);
- aiming higher (for staff without professional qualifications – for example, foundation degrees);
- working with major (NHS) policy initiatives (for example, Disability Equality, supporting the rollout of the Agenda for Change pay initiative);
- statutory and mandatory skills (for example, Health and Safety).

One of the toughest challenges for NHSU is to ensure that the trajectory from learning need to delivery is as seamless and swift as possible. To this end, NHSU is putting in place systems to ensure that the 'corporate' approval gateways are in place to agree on learning needs prioritization in parallel with the academic gateways. In this way NHSU aims to secure both speed and quality.

Programme development models

In order to quickly address the needs of the huge workforce, patients and carers, and establish a balance of development activity, NHSU is currently evaluating a number of models for programme development. NHSU is also establishing a national Programme Development Unit, to set the broad framework and core academic 'architecture' of programmes and services provided or supported by NHSU in terms of modular organization, credit rating and accreditation, learning strategy and so on. This unit will also embrace a Rapid Response Team, with specialists and a small core of permanent staff, to meet calls from the service for the urgent provision of appropriate learning. The unit will work closely with three nascent schools – Interprofessional Care, Leadership and Management, and Knowledge, Information and Personal Development – which will house 'lead' experts, and bring in specialists to provide cutting edge knowledge, and be responsible for quality assurance.

NHSU may jointly develop programmes in association with educational partners, who may bring specific value and expertise to the table. An early example of this is the master's level programme in 'First Contact' in primary care, developed in collaboration with Sheffield Hallam University (SHU), which draws on SHU's extensive expertise in this area, and uses SHU quality frameworks for validation. NHSU has recently agreed plans to work in partnership with a principal academic partner – the University of Warwick – and nine regional higher education consortia.

But NHSU will also sometimes act as a commissioner or direct provider of courseware. For example, a private sector partner won the tender to work alongside NHSU staff and representatives of the service and service users to develop the induction programme, *Working for the NHS*. The programme is capable of being accredited through the NHSU's consortium providers in due course.

Academic organization

In developing NHSU's academic organization, we want not only to strive for the highest intellectual standards and quality, but also simultaneously to avoid the charges too often levelled at existing providers of a lack of responsiveness, inflexibility of provision, slowness of delivery and even academic 'superiority'. To assume that it will be easy to manage these tensions and dilemmas in understanding learning needs and developing an appropriate and highly regarded curriculum would be both naive and arrogant.

Our plan is to establish three major academic 'schools' in our main fields of operation to be the intellectual drivers of the curriculum. We will also create an innovative NHSU Institute, to coordinate key cross-cutting themes centred on work-based learning and practice, and set up a number of core research and development centres. The centres will focus on specialist concerns such as patient expertise, multi-professional learning, the pedagogies of work-based learning and e-learning, and public and patient involvement. We intend to involve patients, users and carers, as well as service providers, in the design and delivery of the learning programmes and services supported or provided by NHSU.

Making a reality of widening participation

Higher education in the UK has traditionally had a relatively poor record in reaching out systematically and extensively to those individuals and social groups typically under-represented in higher education, or largely excluded from higher levels of academic attainment. The current statistics make uncomfortable reading. We know that less than 40 per cent of all adults have had recent or current experience or are likely to be involved in adult learning (of any kind), while McGivney (2001) notes the obstinate persistence of social class as a major factor in relative rates of participation. Class also 'interacts with gender, ethnicity, age and disability in maintaining the overall elitism of the [higher education] sector and the continuing under-representation of lower income and working-class people' (McGivney, 2001, p. 20).

Nor are the data much better for involvement in learning at, through or for work. Those most likely to be offered or to take up such learning opportunities are concentrated among the already well qualified and those who occupy senior and professional posts in organizations, and over a third of British workers claim never to have been offered any chance to engage in learning at, through or for work.

Some respondents to our consultation (MORI/NHSU, 2003) raised two tensions in our aspirations to both open up 'learning for everyone' and attain full university status for NHSU. First, some who lack confidence as learners might be deterred by the very title of a 'university' that is, by definition, not for 'the likes of them'. Second, the pursuit of university status might militate against the introduction of desirable learning opportunities that are academically less demanding.

NHSU can best respond to these fears by not retreating from its desire to raise the levels of aspiration and engagement of people too often excluded from higher education. We accept that NHSU must ensure that its commitment to a genuine widening of participation is firmly underpinned by the establishment of well-supported learning pathways and by a range of relevant and inviting programmes and services. But we also need to tackle the cultural, material, organizational and psychological barriers that have so long stood in the way. Here the active support of health and social care managers for learning and for learners will be vital, as will the support of unions' learning representatives, in encouraging and facilitating access to learning and in securing the time, resources and staff cover required to make it possible.

One major contribution will be through targeting our NHSU Junior Scholarship scheme for 14–19-year-olds precisely at traditionally under-represented communities. Second, we will boost participation by making a significant contribution to literacy and numeracy through NHSU's Skills for Life and Health programme. Third, we will develop generic and specific modules for new health and social care foundation degrees that form part of a linked pathway of achievement for all staff currently without this level of qualification, in their first five years of joining the NHSU.

A key to supporting the much vaunted 'skills escalator' in health and social care will also be the establishment of a common credit 'currency' that is recognized, can be counted towards new qualifications and can be genuinely portable. This will enable individuals and whole cadres of staff to move through the gateways in terms of the knowledge and skills framework and into existing or, especially, new roles and responsibilities. This is a particularly tough challenge, as a common qualifications' framework, recognized across the country, has been sought after for many years. But, we are already working with a consortium of major further and higher education accrediting agencies to provide an accrediting framework for all those who wish to benefit.

We know too that many tentative learners can be put off by formal assessment. Thus, the proposal is that all NHSU programmes should be capable of attracting credit, but that wherever possible the choice of electing for formal assessment should be one exercised by learners themselves, on the basis of sound professional advice and guidance.

Stakeholders and interest groups

Healthcare and education are notably crowded with complex stakeholder arenas presenting a huge challenge to any new entrant to the field. There are already many powerful interest groups working in the field and many educational institutions depend heavily upon NHS contracts for income, having invested substantially in staff, buildings, equipment, programmes, know-how and relationships in order to deliver learning to current and future clinical and professionally qualified staff. So although working with stakeholders is a core value and favoured way of working for NHSU, the very scale and diversity of this challenge and the extent of diplomacy required to carry through successful consultation in these fields should not be underestimated.

Some idea of the size of the task, the range of interests to be considered and the inevitable sensitivity about learning and development can be gleaned from a brief summary of the main bodies most actively involved. They include almost 1000 healthcare organizations nationwide and tens of thousands of workplaces providing social care, in both the public and private sectors. They embrace thousands of representatives of staff, patients and the general public and a wide range of voluntary, special interest and community-based groups. Education and training for health and social care is already supplied by over 100 higher education institutions, nearly 300 further education colleges and several hundred private providers. Furthermore, education, training and professional qualifications are all overseen and supervised by dozens of powerful and high-prestige national bodies concerned with the regulation and continuing professional development of health and social care staff, many of them backed by statutory provision and the influential warrant of various royal charters. Partly in recognition of some of these sensitivities, an early agreement was made between the Department of Health and Universities UK that NHSU should not compete with existing undergraduate clinical provision and that initial ('pre-registration') clinical education would remain outside the NHSU remit.

Aspiring to university title

The NHSU seeks to become a full university with the same authority and responsibilities as others in the UK and to combine that with the very best features and behaviours of an excellent 'CU'.

Universities have existed in Europe for more than 800 years, and they pre-date all but a handful of institutions such as the Roman Catholic Church and the Manx Parliament. They have changed and evolved over the centuries, but new methods and ideas have often faced opposition. For example, when in the late nineteenth century Cardinal Newman gave his oft-cited Dublin lectures on the 'Idea of a University', he remained sceptical about the role of books in a university education.

The 1997 Dearing report into UK higher education concluded that there were four aims that captured the essence of higher education:

- to increase knowledge and understanding for their own sake and to foster their application to the benefit of the economy and society;
- to inspire and enable individuals to develop their capabilities to the highest potential levels throughout life, so that they grow intellectually, are well equipped for work, can contribute effectively to society and achieve personal fulfilment;

- to serve the needs of an adaptable, sustainable, knowledge-based economy at local, regional and national levels;
- to play a major role in shaping a democratic, civilised, inclusive society.

These objectives encapsulate much of what the fledgling NHSU aims to achieve. NHSU strongly believes that its value to the organizations and individuals that constitute health and social care will be greater and substantially enhanced if this new university adheres to the cannons of intellectual autonomy and academic freedom. We believe that a commitment to a genuinely critical intellectual perspective and the cultivation of a reflective approach to the development and application of knowledge, among both NHSU's staff and in its various communities of learners, are vital for our effectiveness (see Barnett, 1997). Independence of thought and reflection will be necessary to research the current and future needs of the service, and to develop the future subject matter and pedagogy to ensure those needs are effectively addressed. We believe that such approaches are not only valid in their own right, but they will also underpin our distinctive contribution to radical service improvement and change in health and social care.

Being a UK university is tightly controlled by law. The Privy Council awards the title to institutions on the basis of advice that, among other things, they meet stringent tests of quality of staff, provision and processes. Institutions seeking university title also need to demonstrate an appropriate range and level of learning programmes, that they have a given proportion of students following higher education courses and that they manifest wholly independent governance.

NHSU will seek fully to meet all of the appropriate and relevant criteria for attaining full university title, including independent governance. At present, NHSU programmes requiring accreditation are being handled by a consortium that straddles the further education and higher education boundaries, which provides NHSU with the opportunity to focus on core quality issues in an 'apprenticeship' model. However, we also firmly believe that none of this need necessarily be in contradiction to our continued commitment to the core aims, values and purposes of the NHS, nor should it require us to abandon our special, and very close, relationship with the service. It is our view that a clear demonstration of our independence and of the quality, standard and range of our planned provision are quite compatible with continuing an effective, focused and very special relationship with our chosen 'host' sector in health and social care.

We do not underestimate the skills, deftness of touch and fortitude that will be necessary to manage the continuing tensions inherent in our aspirations. Not least of these will be our desire to secure learning provision across the conventional divides of schooling, further and higher education and to provide, as far as practicable, seamless pathways for learners between these different levels of learning. We know we will come under constant pressure simply to meet urgent and immediate needs and will be criticized by some people in the service and government when we take a longer-term and often critical perspective. But none of these pressures are different *in kind* from those in many other fields of higher education, although admittedly NHSU may face them to *a greater degree* and on *a wider scale*. This is precisely what NHSU, through the leadership of its governing body and senior staff, will have constantly to manage and to navigate: there are no absolutes here.

Moreover, NHSU will need to ensure that it can also meet the more technical aspects of compliance with required norms and standards in respect of the volumes, proportions and range of learners required at higher education levels. We already intend actively to engage in, and cooperate with partners' centres of continuing education and the increased research capacity in the service. Where quality and standards are concerned, NHSU aspires to be counted among the very best, and to learn from and build on best practice. In this, we recognize the enormous challenges we face of upholding and improving standards in the delivery of work-based learning through a distributed network and by means of blended e-learning.

We recognize, but do not accept, the view of some commentators that, no 'CU' would ever be able to demonstrate and guarantee the full intellectual independence, academic freedom and self-governing community that they see as the minimal and non-negotiable defining features of 'genuine' or 'traditional' universities.

The current higher education sector in the UK already 'embraces a diverse range of institutions each of which is something of a palimpsest of successive social and educational ideals' (Collini, 2003). We see NHSU as one more contribution to the evolution of the concept of a University and the practice of being one.

NHSU as a corporate university

It can be seen that the aims and purposes of NHSU share several of the common attributes of CUs and much can be learned from the experience and best practice of those at the leading edge of corporate learning. In common with them, NHSU is intended to provide an explicit focus on work-based learning and development, in order to support the re-orientation of the business through championing investment in the skills, qualities and self-esteem of staff and expressing the core aims, values and priorities of its 'host' body.

NHSU also shares with some CUs and with much excellent traditional adult and community provision, a desire to recognize and to get learners themselves to acknowledge and value the many elements of informal learning, tacit knowledge, practical skills and everyday problem-solving that are already everyday features of their lives. Most of this learning is simply taken for granted and, usually, it remains largely non-accredited. All too often more formal and organized programmes of study overlook or discount these valuable aspects of learning. Yet they are well-tried means of boosting individuals' confidence and self-esteem that, at the same time, also enhance people's capacity to engage in the community as active citizens as well as underpinning many of their work-related competences (See Foley, 1999).

NHSU will also make extensive use of e-learning and expresses a bold intention to help transform workplace cultures, weaving learning into all aspects of work. In all of this, it places great emphasis on the contribution of management development and leadership to systematic service improvement. And it seeks to help re-focus attention on service users and the public and to involve them closely in reforming the design, control and delivery of services.

There are, however, several significant differences with most CUs. The new 'University for the National Health Service' that was proposed in the Labour Party General Election manifesto in 2001 would be the first completely new public university in the UK to be created entirely from scratch for over 30 years, since the foundation of the innovative and highly successful Open University. NHSU aspires to become an independent university in its own right, rather than simply acting as a straightforward creature of the NHS. NHSU also differs sharply from most in the sheer scale and broad spread of its planned operations across a wide range of educational and occupational levels embracing a plethora of jobs and professions. Its ambition to include patients, users and volunteers in the design, delivery and take-up of learning programmes and services is also somewhat distinctive.

Conclusion

NHSU has been established as an innovative, service-oriented and large-scale provider of work-based learning services and programmes, with a clear aspiration to become an entirely new kind of university and, eventually, to achieve full university title and status. It represents a whole new approach to corporate and individual learning and development in a vast and diverse health and social care sector already populated with many powerful stakeholders, interest groups and educational providers. NHSU needs to find effective and mutually respectful and trusting ways of working in partnership with many of these existing bodies at the same time as proclaiming and maintaining its distinctiveness.

Within the health and social care sector itself, although academic and intellectual attainment at the highest levels is already at world class standards, there is a compelling need to break down traditional educational and practice boundaries in a quest for genuine teamwork and multi-professional service delivery. Where staff have largely been excluded from systematic learning and achievement through work, it will be essential for NHSU to create pathways of support, opportunity and attainment that upskill the workforce. It should aim to enhance personal development, improve life chances and self-esteem and breathe life into the exciting idea of a 'skills escalator'.

As lifestyles, treatment pathways, social conditions and expectations change, new ways of involving and engaging patients, service users, carers and the public at large also need to be devised, including in the design, delivery and uptake of learning. This and the other transformations that NHSU will contribute to should all be set in the clear context of NHSU's overriding purpose, to help secure radical and palpable improvements in patients' experience and in the delivery of healthcare.

In focusing on all of this, it is clear that NHSU, with its chosen partners and centres of research and development excellence, will need to devise new sources of information and evidence on learning needs. It will be obliged to develop new methods of delivering high-quality distributed and work-based learning, based on its virtual campus. Finally, it will have to establish new and valid metrics for assessing the impact of learning on health and social care improvement in order to demonstrate its own value for public money invested and its value added to the nation's health.

Note

1.   This chapter describes the key issues and challenges faced by NHSU up until mid-2004, and prior to the major changes proposed in the November 2004 Department of Health Arms' length review (see page 4).

References and further reading

Barnett, R. (1997) *Higher Education: A Critical Business*. Buckingham: SRHE/Open University.

Burbules, N.C. and Torres, C.A. (eds) (2000) *Globalization and Education: Critical Perspectives*. London: Routledge.

Collini, S. (2003) 'HiEdBiz', *London Review of Books*, 6 November 2003.

Department of Health (2000) *The NHS Plan: A Plan for Investment, A Plan for Reform*. London: Department of Health.

Department of Health (2001a) *Working Together: Learning Together*. London: Department of Health.

Department of Health (2001b) *Everyone: Introducing the NHS University*. London: Department of Health.

DfES (2002) *Success for All*. London: DfES.

DfES (2003a) *The Future of Higher Education*. London: DfES.

DfES (2003b) *Twenty-first Century Skills: Realising our Potential*. London: DfES.

Field, J. (2000) *Lifelong Learning and the New Educational Order*. Stoke on Trent: Trentham.

Finegold, D. and Soskice, D. (1988) 'The failure of training in Britain: analysis and prescription'. *Oxford Review of Economic Policy*, 4(3).

Foley, G. (1999) *Learning in Social Action: A Contribution to Understanding Informal Learning*. Leicester: NIACE.

Giroux, H.A. and Myrsiades, K. (eds) (2001) *Beyond the Corporate University: Culture and Pedagogy in the New Millennium*. Oxford: Rowman and Littlefield.

Hayes, D. (2003) 'The case for corporate universities'. Available from <http://www.spiked-online.com/Articles>.

Hayes, D. and Wynyard, R. (eds) (2002) *The McDonaldization of Higher Education*. London: Bergin and Garvey.

Kennedy, H. (1995) *Return to Learn: UNISON's Fresh Approach to Trade Union Education*. London: UNISON.

McGivney, V. (2001) *Fixing or Changing the Pattern? Reflections on Widening Adult Participation in Learning*. Leicester: NIACE.

MORI/NHSU (2003) *Hearing What You Say: Summary of Consultation and Research for NHSU's Development Plan*. London: MORI/NHSU.

Munro, A., Rainbird, H. and Holly, L. (1997) *Partners in Workplace Learning: A Report on the UNISON/Employer Learning and Development Programme*. London: UNISON.

NHSU (2002) *Learning for Everyone: A Development Plan for the NHSU*. London: Department of Health.

NHSU (2003) *Forward to Delivery: NHSU Draft Strategic Plan, 2003–2008*. London: Department of Health.

Ritzer, G. (1996) *The McDonaldization of Society*. London: Pine Forge.

Sargant, N. and Aldridge, F. (2002) *Adult Learning and Social Division: A Persistent Pattern*. Leicester: NIACE.

Wanless, D. (2002) *Securing our Future Health: Taking a Long-term View*. London: Department of Health.

Williams, J.J. (2001) 'Franchising the university', in H.A. Giroux and K. Myrsiades (eds) *Beyond the Corporate University: Culture and Pedagogy in the New Millennium*. Oxford: Rowman and Littlefield.

4 Addressing Key Skill Shortages in the International Information Technology Industry

Michelle Selinger

Introduction

This chapter explores the benefits that accrue when a company exploits the full potential of e-learning solutions not only to train its own workforce, but also its partners and customers – and then takes those solutions into the community to address the needs of the business environment. Its primary focus is the Cisco Networking Academy Program. By early 2005, this substantial, certificated programme had been taught in 163 countries in 10 000 academies involving 452 000 students, and 22 000 instructors, and producing 300 000 graduates – making it, in all likelihood, the largest global e-learning programme to date. Important challenges in developing this programme are explained, and the case is then used to consider how those same technologies can advance the corporate social responsibility agenda in developing countries.

The chapter starts by describing the context in which the initiative arose. Cisco (see box below) is unusual in many respects. One of these is the way Cisco has pioneered in its management processes new applications of the generic networking technology it develops and manufactures. E-learning is one such application, and how this gave rise to the idea of the Cisco Networking Academy Program is outlined. The form of the programme and its worldwide delivery is then described. Next, the key challenges associated with *cultural adaptation, accreditation*, and *public–private partnerships* (PPPs) are discussed. Finally, the chapter looks ahead to the scope for further initiatives that can combine business and social returns.

CISCO AND IP NETWORKING

Electronic networks have become an essential part of business, education, government and home communications, and it is generally recognized that Cisco Internet Protocol-based (IP) networking solutions are the foundation of these networks. The Cisco Systems hardware, software, and service offerings help create Internet solutions that allow individuals, companies and countries to increase productivity, improve customer satisfaction and strengthen competitive advantage. These networks affect our everyday lives in multiple spheres such that 'at Cisco, our vision is to change the way people work, live, play and learn' (Cisco 2004a).

Cisco was founded in 1984 by a small group of computer scientists then working at Stanford University in the USA. Since the company's inception, Cisco engineers have been leaders in the development of IP-based networking technologies. This tradition of IP innovation continues with industry-leading products in the core areas of routeing and switching, as well as advanced technologies in areas such as home networking, optical storage networking, IP telephony, network security and wireless Local Area Networks (LANs). It now operates worldwide.

In addition to hardware and software products, Cisco provides a broad range of service offerings to its clients, including award-winning technical support and advanced services. Cisco sells its products and services directly through its own sales force and indirectly through a network of channel partners to large enterprises, small and medium-sized businesses, service providers and consumers.

In addition, Cisco has long been recognized as a pioneer in using the Internet for its own business practices and for offering consulting services to help other organizations around the world through its Internet Business Solutions Group. In the 2003 fiscal year, Cisco saved US$2.1 billion by relying on the Internet to provide customer support, offer employee services, sell products, provide training, and manage finances and manufacturing processes. Each year, the company introduces new applications, enhances existing applications, and increases adoption of these applications across the organization, which results in an incremental return on investment year-after-year.

E-learning at Cisco

Cisco makes extensive use of its own technologies to train and develop its workforce. Together with a number of learning partners, Cisco has evolved an e-learning strategy that in the financial year 2002–03 saved US$140 million in training costs. The wide range of training is available tailored to individual needs and job function. Using an online tool, 'My Development', account managers and systems engineers take a pre-assessment of their training needs and plan a programme of development that is personalized and tailored to their current product knowledge and to their job function requirements.

Courses are offered at three levels: entry, intermediate and advanced, and there is often a choice between modes of delivery from instructor-led training to virtual classroom and web-based teaching modules. Additionally, employees can select from a vast searchable database library of video-on-demand materials. Subject matter experts record presentations and employees can gain a quick update on products and services by searching for the relevant content as and when needed. Informal learning is facilitated through an internal messaging system, CiscoCast (a push messaging system that comes across the users screen and contains vital information and messages from senior executives), email, project spaces and bulletin boards. Entry to all e-learning is via a portal and each line of business has its own portal that is accessible through the main portal home page.

Since its introduction in 1998, there has been an increased uptake of e-learning options and the amount of training has increased, as have the satisfaction scores of employees. For example, 100 systems engineers taking an instructor-led version of the Network Certification Programs for Network Associates and Network Developers were compared with 100 employees who learnt through an e-learning programme. In the instructor led version, 77 per cent passed first time compared to 88 per cent in the e-learning group. Trainee satisfaction was also higher with e-learning. Another example is a survey of sales account managers. On a scale of 1 to 5 the following scores were assigned to these statements:

- Can directly apply to my job – 4.21.
- Courses match my job responsibilities – 4.30.
- Time spent was a good Cisco investment – 4.0.

Additionally, 87.5 per cent said that they would take another online course and that confidence in their own knowledge increased from 3.28 to 4.27 on the same 1–5 scale.

However, as with most large organizations, not all learning and development at Cisco is through e-learning. There are still face-to-face courses, particularly for leadership development, and some of the more heavily subscribed courses may be offered in more than one mode. Employees can select the learning mode according to their learning preferences or by choosing the mode that fits best with their work and travel commitments.

E-learning is now offered to partners and customers through the Cisco Learning Connection (CLC), a learning environment that provides anytime access to training on Cisco product and technology information. The course content is based on the training given to Cisco's own workforce, adapted for different client groups. By adopting technologies that permit reusability there are significant cost benefits. The CLC site also includes a range of learning options including video-on-demand offerings for information directly from Cisco experts, web-based training for in-depth interactive instruction, short flash and audio net bits for quick information, and online assessments for checking knowledge.

The Cisco Networking Academy Program – providing skills for the Information Age

Perhaps the most innovative aspect of Cisco's activities in this area relates to addressing skills shortages in the industry more broadly. That is, in addition to its internal training and training for partners and customers, Cisco offers e-learning to educational institutions and non-government organizations (NGOs) through its corporate philanthropy programme. This started in 1997 in response to demands from schools in the USA wanting to install networks but lacking the skilled staff to do so. Cisco identified a number of willing students who were keen to learn and started what quickly became the Cisco Networking Academy Program. This is an instructor-led course of 280 hours incorporating hands-on labs with e-learning materials starting from the fundamentals of internetworking, teaching students how to install, maintain and troubleshoot computer networks. Successful course completion provides students with the necessary skills and knowledge to take the industry-recognized certification, Cisco Certified Networking Associate (CCNA).

Shortly after this pilot, the Academy Program was rolled out globally as increasing demand for skills was highlighted in the late 1990s. A study commissioned by Cisco predicted that by 2002 there would be a networking skills shortage of up to 600 000 people in Europe alone (Milroy, 2001). Clearly, this was before the dot com bubble burst, but a later study supported the core finding that, despite the downturn, a skills shortage would still exist as more and more non-information technology (IT) companies demanded networking administrators to support their newly acquired infrastructure (Kolding, 2002). Senior managers at Cisco decided that 'traditional' education was not providing the skills, nor was there any short-term likelihood of it doing so. So, Cisco educational programmes are attempting to plug a gap, together with other companies such as Microsoft and Oracle. We believe this heralds a new departure for education – industry collaborations in the design and sponsoring of courses. Its global dissemination and appropriation has been remarkable. Over half the students are now from outside the USA. Decisions about what training to deploy and how to position it is subject to intensive review, with applications and courses piloted prior to wider rollout, and with evaluation and feedback a regular part of the review process.

The Academy Program is delivered through PPPs between Cisco, governments, educational institutions and NGOs. It was originally conceived to be taught in high schools to students aged 16 and over, but it is now taught to students from the age of 16 to 60 and includes a range of IT courses, some funded by other companies such as Hewlett-Packard (HP) and Panduit. In all courses offered through the Academy Program, the underlying teaching and learning model is based on a constructivist view of learning. Hands-on labs are included and given considerable emphasis, as they are seen as the pivotal element of the Academy Program. To support this, web-based materials have been written to help students make sense of the labs and provide a theoretical perspective. These resources make extensive use of flash animation, graphics and, more recently, video extracts, e-simulations and remote labs. The CCNA is based on four 70-hour semesters of study, each with a series of chapters and associated online and practical assessments at the end of each chapter and semester. The online assessment system was originally based on multiple choice questions, but now more procedural assessment tasks have been introduced using 'drag and drop' technologies and e-simulations. There is extensive instructor training supported by a global online community for the sharing of information and teaching ideas.

As part of an internal Cisco review process in 2002, the author undertook an evaluation of the Cisco Networking Academy Program in Europe, the Middle East and Africa (known as the EMEA region). The brief was to research the impact of the programme on students, teachers and educational institutions, and to draw lessons to be taken into account in designing future versions of the course. By the time of this review, the Academy Program had grown significantly from its small-scale origins: it was then taught in 95 countries in the EMEA region with nearly 20 000 students having already completed the programme in 3000 academies. For the evaluation, visits were made to 57 academies in 11 countries that included all areas of Europe, the Middle East and South Africa. Interviews were carried out with around 100 instructors and 300 students and classes were observed. Data was also gathered from other countries and other academies within the visited countries through a web-based questionnaire (see Selinger, 2002, 2004a, 2004b). Drawing on this data, the following sections address the central challenges that the programme has had to address, challenges that increasingly arise and are debated in other contexts as well.

Cultural relevance

It has been argued that cultural relevance is not necessary in a technical subject such as networking with strong US origins. Nevertheless, the way materials are presented and the language and standards used can present challenges in some countries where the cultural and pedagogical norms are different (Selinger, 2004a, 2004b). Previous research on cultural adaptation in global education has tended to focus on collaboration forum discourse in distance learning programmes, and either to ignore or marginalize the pedagogical style and approach of e-learning texts (which were seen as culturally unproblematic). Notable exceptions are Dunn and Marinetti's work (2002) and Bates' research (1999). The much referenced work of both Hofstede (1997) and Trompenaars and Hampden-Turner (1997) are also relevant in this context, as some of the dimensions they note are important to consider in the design of electronic learning environments that involve discussion and online teaching.

So, based on its own and other's researches, Cisco's approach is marked by the recognition that e-learning materials need to be reviewed for cultural relevance and then customized to accommodate the practices of the country. E-learning tools are ideal here, as they often make use of reusable learning objects that enable cultural adaptation, and it is relatively economic to customize resources for different teaching approaches to the same content. However, when an e-learning programme is taught in a blended learning environment with locally based teachers to support students, then the course materials can remain entirely unchanged to save costs. Adaptation then has to be made by the teachers, who will give students advice about what to read, or interpret and adapt the course to match prevailing pedagogy. However, *local support for the teachers themselves then becomes crucial.*

One example of this adaptation by local instructors was seen in the case of the Cisco Networking Academy Program in the Swedish institutions that were visited. A typical US model of teaching is to recap on previous concepts relevant to the content students are about to study; inform them about what they are about to study; give them the content; and review it at the end. However, in Sweden, students are given far more responsibility for their own learning than those in the USA and it is their job to ensure that they have the necessary knowledge and understanding to study new content. Teachers expect students to go back to previous parts of the course and review them alone if they find they are having trouble with new content. This means that Swedish instructors often tell their students to miss out the recap material.

Within Cisco, we believe that the Cisco Networking Academy Program has been successful because local instructors are trained to teach local students, but have the material of an e-learning program developed to a very high standard albeit with some inherent cultural biases. The instructors are trained locally in regional academies by people who have some experience of teaching the Cisco programme to students in the same country and in a similar environment (Selinger, 2004a). Additionally, because the programme has an extensive hands-on component, students are engaged in practical activity that links closely to the e-learning materials they have read and the animations they have observed on screen. This helps students in their understanding of the written materials. Instructors also support students' reading of the text by giving whole class presentations on key concepts and topics, advising on what to read and what to omit, and indicating where local networking or electrical standards may vary from the USA.

Recognition and accreditation

In many of the countries visited, discussion arose about the role of vendor programmes in schools, colleges and universities. Like Cisco, Microsoft and Oracle (among others) also offer IT courses in various guises. In some countries, it is difficult for such courses to be integrated into national curriculum frameworks, and the vendor qualification assessments are often seen as training awards rather than of educational value. In the case of the Cisco Networking Academy Program, much of the course focuses on the basics of networking, meaning that a considerable amount of content is vendor neutral. Where a country's or region's education authorities have been made aware of the overlap between Cisco's course and standard introductory networking courses, we might emphasize the benefits of obtaining up-to-date and relevant input direct from the related industry, and then allow educational establishments to integrate the program into their own course structures. In universities, the Academy Program might replace introductory modules on networking and add a strong practical component to what could be a highly theoretical course, while in schools and colleges it might be offered as a stand-alone course run after hours. In such situations, acceptance into national qualification frameworks of the course assessment in addition to acceptance of the educational value of the course materials has led to even greater potential for integration. Many universities report that they are keen for their students to be awarded a vendor qualification, while students delight in the opportunity to do some hand-on labs rather than studying theory all the time (as is often the norm for the majority of universities visited across the region).

Curriculum integration however varies widely from country to country and between different types of institution. We are often told that the Cisco 'label' on the curriculum is the key reason why the Academy Program has not been accepted; governments are concerned about potential fallout from showing preferential treatment to one company over another:

We have rules from the Ministry of Education ... It is not very easy to integrate a curriculum like the Cisco Curriculum. We have the subjects like Networking, IP Addressing and so on, so we can only try to integrate the Cisco Curriculum into the normal lessons in this way. (German instructor)

In Germany, another reason given for not integrating the Academy Program was its popularity! One school said they would not have enough teachers to teach the course if they offered is as part of their usual course of study as it would be so popular. In Hungary, the national curriculum for IT includes aspects of networking and incorporates some of the Academy Program curriculum. Schools, however, most often have to adhere to the national framework; in such cases, the Academy Program can only be offered as an elective with the danger of overloading students. Nonetheless, many students remain keen to gain the CCNA and are hence prepared to make the sacrifice, citing increased employment potential as the reason for doing so.

In the EMEA region, the Cisco Area Academy Managers work with country ministries and their curriculum and assessment authorities to find ways in which the Academy Program can be embedded into the curriculum. This has met with considerable success. In the City of Stockholm, the education authority funds the Academy Program in schools so that it can be a bona fide curriculum offering. It committed to integrating the curriculum in all its upper secondary schools, deploying it in some 50 to 60 local academies. More recently, the UK Qualification and Curriculum Authority (QCA) has accepted the Cisco and Microsoft joint program into the national assessment framework, while Cisco employees have worked closely with examination boards to offer accreditation that maps directly on to the CCNA curriculum. This means that funding can potentially be drawn down from the Learning and Skills Councils, allowing the course to be offered free of charge in 14+ institutions as well as being a course offering that would earn credits towards national vocational qualifications (see OCR, 2003).

Public–private partnership in education – the role of industry

In a consultation exercise by IPPR in the UK in 2002, a number of considerations around the role of PPPs in education were discussed that are relevant to this issue. These included:

- How should digital learning be funded?
- What roles are there for public broadcasters and commercial organizations in providing educational material?
- What are the consequences of making educational delivery dependent on large media corporations?
- Who owns national curricula?
- How can processes of procurement and tendering be improved?

This consultation process did achieve some consensus. It was agreed that there should be some element of risk sharing between partners (whether this be simply financial risk or reputational). There were questions raised about whether organizations involved should have shared objectives, or whether partnerships were an effective way of managing divergent interests, as well as whether there was a specific length of time over which partnerships could be sustained (IPPR, 2002). At the European eLearning Summit held in Brussels in 2001, Ferry de Rijke (Chairman of European SchoolNet) argued that the financial responsibility for basic education should remain with the public sector, adding, 'what businesses can do is to help fund elements of the innovation process'. Perhaps this is what vendor programs in education are for? The private sector is constantly seeking well-qualified individuals and recognizes the role of education for economic growth, so by supporting that process through provision of vocationally oriented educational programs with up-to-date and relevant curriculum resources through their corporate philanthropy programs, companies can ensure a steady stream of employable individuals.

In a recent article by Porter and Kramer (2002) on the benefits of corporate social responsibility (CSR), the Cisco Networking Academy Program is cited as one that fulfils the criteria to make it a successful endeavour. Porter and Kramer argue that, of the factors that make CSR programs successful, the Cisco Networking Academy Program displays the following:

- convergence of interests;
- free-riding; and
- signalling other funders.

Porter and Kramer argue that philanthropy based on pure social benefit is unsustainable; CSR efforts need also to have some economic benefits to the donor company, a state that they term 'convergence of interests' (see Figure 4.1). In the case of the Cisco Networking Academy this convergence of interest is demonstrated by the social benefits of the job opportunities that the programme can provide to many young people (this in turn provides relevance and hence incentive to study, and in some cases it has encouraged school students to pursue IT courses in higher education). The economic benefits to Cisco are the creation of a larger pool of well-qualified network administrators and technicians who can address the skills shortages that exist in the networking market (Kolding, 2002; Milroy, 2001), thus encouraging firms to install or improve their network infrastructure in the knowledge that network technicians

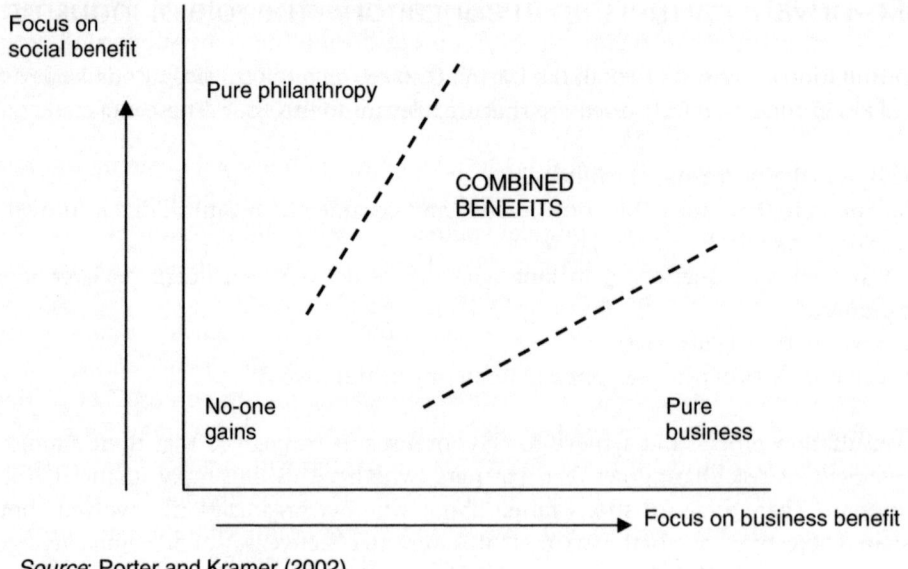

Source: Porter and Kramer (2002)

Figure 4.1   Combining business and social benefits

are available to hire at reasonable rates. This availability of a pool of labour not only benefits Cisco, but all those companies and public sector institutions who are seeking to recruit new employees to install and manage their networks. This is the essence of what Porter and Kramer mean by 'free riding'. In terms of 'signalling other funders', Cisco has partnered with IT course sponsors like Panduit and HP who see the benefits that have accrued from Cisco's own investment in education.

Looking ahead: Future education investments

Cisco's CSR programme is driven by a simple vision: 'We want to do our part in building stronger, more productive global communities. We believe that healthy, self-sustaining communities arise when every individual has the means to live, the opportunity to learn, and the chance to share those gifts with others' (Cisco, 2004b). The focal issues are basic human needs, access to education, responsible citizenship and technology and innovation in non-profit organisations.

The goals that Cisco (2004b) has set out to achieve these focal issues are:

- Overcome the cycle of poverty and dependence through strategic partnerships that help to provide food, shelter, and other essential prerequisites to self-sufficiency.
- Create educational opportunity and foster classroom innovation, thereby giving underserved students the chance to thrive, focusing in particular on young women and girls in least-developed nations.
- Promote a culture of volunteerism and social responsibility through programs and strategic grants that emphasize each citizen's role in serving and sustaining healthy communities.

- Transform the way non-profit work is accomplished and supported; by sharing best-of-breed strategy and technology with not-for-profit organizations, by supporting projects that find innovative ways to make an impact through technology, and by cultivating new avenues of philanthropic support to maximize the not-for-profit sector's reach and impact.

While Cisco as a company is always ready to respond to immediate community needs, particularly in times of crisis, senior managers believe that short-term community interventions must give way to lasting transformation if a cycle of self-sufficiency is truly to take hold, which is the rationale behind the last of these goals. Funds are allocated by the Cisco Foundation, or by Cisco depending on the nature of the grant.

As part of this ongoing CSR activity, a web platform for the Academy Program that drives curriculum assembly, delivery and assessment was developed by the Cisco Learning Institute, a not-for-profit organisation set up by the Cisco Foundation for this purpose. The platform, called Virtuoso, has been revised and developed over the last five years and is now available to organizations worldwide. It has enabled Cisco to partner with organizations to meet its philanthropic objectives. For example, in December 2003 Cisco announced collaboration with the World Health Organisation (WHO) to extend health education to the world. Virtuoso has been used to take the WHO's paper-based materials and turn them into a 400-hour interactive multimedia e-learning package for developed and developing countries around the globe. Pilots currently exist in Egypt and Jordan (Cisco, 2003). Another venture in this area is Cisco's support for the Jordan Education Initiative (World Economic Forum, 2004); particularly in the development of a mathematics e-curriculum with a strong focus on teacher support and development to improve students' application of mathematics by encouraging a strong collaborative and problem-based learning environment.

Referring back to Porter and Kramer's (2002) model, it could be argued that these two programmes do not have such strong economic objectives in comparison with the Academy Program, where direct links can be clearly seen to the company's core business, and therefore are not as likely to be supported. In such cases, the funding helps achieve the CSR vision and goals. Commitment to the Academy Program is ongoing with staff working for Cisco based in offices around the globe, while the other education initiatives focus on achieving pure philanthropic vision and the donations target cases where there are significant levels of support for capacity building in the partner organizations.

Cisco's CEO John Chambers believes strongly that the Internet and education are the two great equalisers in life. To this end Cisco's own workforce are well educated using the latest e-learning techniques and the tools that Cisco's technologies support. As a result, Cisco has become a showcase for the use of its technology, not only to improve the quality of the workforce and the competitiveness of the company, but also the application of those technologies to bring career opportunities to young people through the design and delivery of an education program that is relevant to the market needs. It has then gone further to use these technologies yet again to collaborate with less developed countries to improve the standard of health and education. CSR programmes can be both cost and socially effective if they build on current strengths and use the tools and artefacts already in use for the common good.

References

Bates, T. (1999) 'Cultural and ethical issues in international distance education', paper presented at the Engaging Partnerships Collaboration and Partnership in Distance Education UBC/CREAD conference, September 21–23, Vancouver, Canada.

Cisco (2003) 'The health academy', News@Cisco. Available from <http://newsroom.cisco.com/dlls/prod_121203.html>.

Cisco (2004a) 'Fact sheet', News @Cisco. Available from <http://newsroom.cisco.com/dlls/corpfact.html>.

Cisco (2004b) 'Corporate Philanthropy'. Available from <http://www.cisco.com/en/US/about/ac48/about_cisco_corporate_philanthropy.html>.

Dunn, P. and Marinetti, A. (2002) 'Cultural adaptation: Necessity for global e-learning', *LiNE Zine*. Available from <http://www.linezine.com>.

Hofstede, G. (1997) *Culture and Organizations* (revised edition). Maidenhead: McGraw Hill.

IPPR (2002) *Building Better Partnerships: Final Report of the Commission on Public Private Partnerships*. London: The Institute for Public Policy Research.

Kolding, M. (2002) *Networking Skills Shortage in Western Europe*. London: IDC.

Milroy, A. (2001) *Networking Skills Shortage in EMEA*. London: IDC.

OCR (2003) 'Vocationally-related qualifications news and updates.' *News and Updates*, 13 August. Available from <http://www.ocr.org.uk/OCR/WebSite/docroot/newsupdates/newslist/detail.jsp?anchorid=nav1&site=OCR&oid=12714&category=Vocationally-Related+Qualifications&server=PRODUKTION>.

Porter, M. J. and Kramer, M.E. (2002) 'The competitive advantage of corporate philanthropy', *Harvard Business Review*, R0212D. Available from <http://www.netacad.it/upload/pdf/HBRarticleCN.pdf>.

Selinger, M. (2002) 'An evaluation of the Cisco Networking Academy Program in Europe, the Middle East and Africa'. Cisco Systems. Available from <http://www.cisco.com/edu/emea/questionnaire>.

Selinger, M. (2004a) 'The role of local instructors in making global elearning programmes culturally and pedagogically relevant', in A. Brown and N. Davis (eds), *World Yearbook 2004: Digital Technologies, Communities and Education*. London: Kogan Page.

Selinger, M. (2004b) 'The cultural and pedagogical implications of a global elearning programme', *Cambridge Journal of Education*, 34(2): 223–239.

Trompenaars, A. and Hampden-Turner, C. (1997) *Riding the Waves of Culture: Understanding Diversity in Global Business* (2nd edition). Maidenhead: McGraw Hill.

World Economic Forum (2004) 'Jordan Education Initiative'. Available from <http://www.weforum.org/site/homepublic.nsf/Content/Jordan+Education+Initiative>.

5 The Rise and Fall of a Major Corporate University: The Case of Aqua Universitas

Peter Matthews

Introduction

This chapter describes the attempted transformation of a water utility through the means of a corporate university (CU) initiative. The CU provided the platform for the delivery of organizational development. In 1974 large regional water authorities were established based on river catchments. Hundreds of small operations were amalgamated into regional management with a new philosophy that transcended that of municipalities. Regional knowledge bases had to be established in order to migrate best practice. However, these authorities were still constrained by non-commercial rules and were purely UK operations. In 1989, however, the 'big bang' occurred; the privatization of public services as a means of increasing customer service, investment and efficiency. Utilities had to change from being public authorities to global companies (although in some cases they remained as UK companies). That change still continues as some UK water utilities themselves are absorbed by other commercial groups.

The role of one corporate university – one of the most significant in this sector – is described in this chapter. It recounts the story of what was then known as Anglian Water, the company that has grown into the present AWG. This initiative was one of the most fully developed in the industry. The story of its rise and demise is of some considerable interest as it carries a number of important learning points for those currently seeking to design initiatives of a similar kind. The chapter also seeks to explain why the CU has not survived within AWG in any recognizable form.

The origin of AWG lies in the creation of the Anglian Water Authority, which served some five million people in eastern England. In 1989, water utility functions were privatised, forming the core company of Anglian Water plc (the environmental water functions were incorporated into the National Rivers Authority, which was later incorporated into the Environment Agency). The non-core parts of Anglian Water grew both in commercial terms and in geographical terms; companies were acquired or established in the Americas, Europe, Scandinavia, Asia and Australasia. By the late 1990s customers overseas exceeded those in the UK. The core company in the UK operates according to the terms of a licence and settlements for charges, investments and services determined every five years by a state regulator.

The change drivers

After 1989, Anglian Water had to do a number of things at once:

- respond to a new commercial environment with shareholders;
- increase the levels of service, with a focus on customers;
- improve its cost efficiencies, knowing that water charges would have to rise to finance a massive capital investment programme;
- grow the business, particularly in overseas markets.

In other words, the company had to change, grow and improve simultaneously; in essence, however, such specific needs were expressions of the same fundamental need to become smarter. Within the company, it was felt that one means of achieving this was to focus on the notion that happy, committed, learned employees are more flexible and more productive than unhappy, uncommitted, ignorant employees. Learning and development were thus at the crux of change. Senior executives gained insights into the nature of CUs through attendance at Harvard Business School programmes, engendering the feeling that something radically different was necessary in terms of change management. A programme of organizational innovation in its broadest sense was conceived, beginning with a strategic review in 1993–94 focusing on a business process reengineering programme, implemented through total quality management; the company adopted the principles of the European Foundation for Quality Management (EFQM) and became a 'registered' learning organization in late 1994.

The early exposure of the leadership to 'executive stretch' programmes had been an important catalyst in the process. This resulted in an interesting learning loop, as the programme produced the idea of a CU – subsequently named Aqua Universitas, known within the company as the University of Water. The first manifestation of this was to produce a version of executive stretch for all employees, called the Transformation Journey.

Vision of the University of Water

While predecessor executives at Anglian Water were committed to training for craft and professional employees, little was available for front-line operational employees. Perhaps the first contribution of the CU was to broaden the notion of training to learning – examining processes to gain understanding of why, as well as how, work activities were completed in personal, team, group and social contexts. This evolution in thinking found its expression in the Aqua Universitas. As it was understood at the time, the principal objectives of a CU were to:

- create learning environments which actively promote learning;
- promote knowledge creation;
- allow learning to be linked into business needs, development and plans;
- allow measurement of learning processes and results;
- enable external partners, particularly universities, to collaborate;
- create a company-wide learning organization, while creating a local learning environment that reflects local needs and, more crucially, that individuals can relate to;

- permit a diversity of learning environments that will allow different cultural requirements to be built into group needs;
- allow the intellectual advantage of the concepts behind the university to be exploited;
- promote employability rather than employment.

A distinction was made between learning and cultural activities and the business activities, often characterized by the terms 'soft' and 'hard' issues respectively.

This CU was therefore not specifically targeted at management, but rather at all employees as part of a much wider programme of change.

A paradox of the CU was the balance of freedom to develop from experience through empowerment, versus the need to be structured in 'the way we do things here', to ensure consistency. This dilemma was also demonstrated in day-to-day operations. After extensive deliberation, Anglian Water launched the concept of a federal learning organization that was of a sufficiently unique and pervasive nature to give substance to Aqua Universitas. The University of Water was intended as a means of assisting the group to locate the best people, the best teams and the best organization to provide the best service – through wisdom, creation and exploitation. From the beginning, it was recognized that the university had to exist primarily in the hearts and minds of employees, but that there was also a need to have some tangible assets to satisfy the need to 'touch and feel' the university, even if this was personal experience rather than bricks and mortar. A sense of ownership by all employees was crucial.

I explained earlier that the concept of the CU arose out of an executive stretch programme. The first vehicle for bringing the CU to life was the provision of a modified stretch programme for all employees, which became known as the Transformation Journey. Groups of people travelled through the journey and some groups helped to provide greater substance to the practical structures of the university. This process was innovative enough to be described in a Harvard Business School case study.

The structure and operation of the Aqua Corporate University

The main focus initially was on providing the university with its own syntax within the part of the business known as Anglian Water Services, but people from other parts of the group were involved. It was intended that, with sufficient experience, the practices would be extended throughout the whole group, around the world. In essence, we began with a federal structure. A Learning Council advised the executive team on the Anglian Water brand of learning, comprised of learners from the university with a range of different activities and interests. The objectives included meeting the overall aspirations of the group through using a learning culture to develop business activities. These embraced the minimum acceptable achievement and rate of progress for all learning activities within the group, providing a central focus for audit feedback and high-level business synergies through learning. It sought to provide some understanding of the paradox in the balance of freedom to develop from experience through empowerment, versus the need to be structured.

Each of the companies within the group was responsible for developing a local learning organization or community. In the case of Anglian Water Services, the learning organization was sub-divided down into the business unit processes. Each business unit had a *learning champion*. This permitted unique needs to be satisfied; it encouraged experimentation; it encouraged local ownership and promoted teamwork. The results of each experiment had to be migrated to other business units in shared best practices. Formal mechanisms were also necessary to strengthen cross-process and organizational learning.

In 1994 the company established a series of networks to exchange knowledge and share best practice across the group, such as executive management networks and technology networks. Individuals were free to join and even establish new ones. Networks could be temporary or permanent and address issues of general or specific interest, but generally membership reflected the responsibilities and needs of an employment portfolio. Several of these were set up as 'catalysed networks', in which the organization set up an initial team by invitation around a key topic with a facilitator, and then left it to evolve as it wished.

By 1999 the company was well into the process of establishing company colleges as knowledge networks. In 1996 three colleges were started, based on the topics of creativity, open learning and international learning. These had the dual purpose of promoting organizational learning as well as allowing the participation of individuals to enrich their personal portfolio of knowledge. They provided a focal point for cross-company activities. So, for example, people from throughout the world working for Anglian Water could participate in the technology networks, as the purpose of the College of International Learning was to facilitate the University of Water's participation in the worldwide web of learning. It was to act as a focal point for an international scholarship programme and ensure that operational visitors were dealt with on a structured rather than an ad hoc basis.

By the summer of 1997 a number of key steps has also been taken to address the issue of what knowledge was needed in the business. A knowledge base 'layer' was identified at the bottom of the organization, which embraced the tacit knowledge associated with organizational culture and procedures, as well as explicit knowledge in the form of documents, filing systems and computerized databases. In terms of a corporate university this lower level may be seen as an 'archive', but one that is under continual change to be continually renewed. The second layer is the 'business system' (production and customer services in Anglian Water), where normal routine operation is carried out. The top layer relates to an area where multiple self-organizing teams create knowledge. These teams all shared in the joint creation of knowledge.

The knowledge base layer containing a number of core knowledge areas may therefore be perceived as giving a new insight into the way in which core competencies may be developed and as representing the knowledge assets of a company. Within a water utility we defined levels of knowledge in this way:

Fundamental (archive)	Social (business system)	Applied
Biology	Fiscal/economics	Ecology
Physics	Socio-politics	Construction engineering
Chemistry	Psychology	Education
	Sociology	
	Information technology (IT)	

These knowledge assets may be combined in knowledge application systems; the extent and depth of the combinations depend on what is needed by the business. For example, if an activity that was formerly in-house is outsourced, the extent of knowledge of the outsourced system will be diminished; it will have to be supplemented by an ability to manage the outsourced contract. An example of the knowledge application systems in a water utility might be fluid distribution systems (physics and construction engineering), environmental management (ecology, fiscal/economics and socio-politics) and capital management (IT, construction engineering, economics). Clearly this approach opened up a debate as to what core knowledge areas were essential for running the business. By 1999 the core knowledge areas identified became four faculties: – Engineering and Technology, Humanities and Social Sciences, Environment and Planning and Business Development and Management. The colleges were primarily mechanisms to take forward the key capabilities grouped within the faculties. Thus, the university began to take on a more structured form:

Faculties (with deans)	Key capabilities/college focus
1. **Engineering and Technology**	Pipeline management
	Operating treatment works
	Project management
	Waste/water treatment (treatment technology)
2. **Humanities and Social Science**	Customer service
	Change management
	Anglian brand
3. **Business Development and Management**	Negotiating and managing contracts
	Product offering and development
	Asset management
4. **Environment and Planning**	Water resource management
	Water quality
	Economic regulation

Most progress was made with the more 'tangible' colleges such as treatment technology, project management and water quality – not surprising when one remembers Anglian Water's origins and business needs. Each faculty had responsibility to ensure that it promoted creativity and used the facilities of the open learning network, with a lead team to ensure that the overall direction of the faculty was properly coordinated and supported, headed by main board directors.

The practical work in developing the university and supporting the faculties and colleges was provided by a small permanent team. It was inspiring to see these people work, particularly as two of them were recruited through the Transformation Journey process from the operational frontline. They worked on a Mastery of Best Practice, which embraced a number of our learning initiatives and recognized the egalitarian vision of 'fit for purpose learning', as well as exploring accreditation with a number of traditional universities. The level of demand that being involved in the university made on these individuals caused concerns about the balance of time spent on these activities, as opposed to their 'day jobs'. Efforts were then made to quantify how much resource the company could afford for learning and change, assessed as part of the annual business planning process.

Transformation Journey

The company launched its Transformation Journey in 1995 as an action learning programme rooted in the 'extraordinary', aimed at all employees. This approach was rather special as it was an executive learning programme that was extended to every level in the organization. Conceived as a means of changing the cultural and intellectual mind sets of everyone in the organization so that they could cope with the new faster and more flexible business needs of the developing group, it was central to the development of the university.

The Transformation Journey was, however, much more than just a change programme. It was about taking a whole organization through a process of renewal from the old way of doing things to the new. Success lay in its ability to galvanize an entire workforce to create a new future, not just for themselves, but for the organization as a whole, to release the unexplored capabilities of the people to sustain major growth without added cost, and to add to the intellectual capital of the company.

It was a voluntary process – therefore dependent upon capturing the imagination of those destined to 'travel'. Would-be 'travellers' formed groups of 6–12 and registered their interest; having 'bought a ticket' they began the journey destined to span two years. A model was used to describe this journey. Every traveller was invited to participate in three distinct opportunities:

- *A Traveller's Brief*: A two day 'think tank' using concepts designed to stretch thinking and create a new level in working relationships.
- *An Expedition*: A six- to nine-month undertaking designed and executed by the travellers themselves.
- *A Journey Review*: A one-day self-appraisal of achievements, both task and learning.

The pattern repeated itself three times over the two years. The first phase addressed personal learning development, the second team development, and the third organizational development. At each phase in the journey, travellers were asked to explore different aspects of development – from self through team to organization. At each point humanistic aspects were reconciled with economics. All the time travellers were exposed to those paradoxes that shape our choices in a business world.

The journey was a relatively unstructured ('untidy') mechanism because it sought to raise issues, the exploration of which was determined entirely by each group. Travellers themselves developed their own route map and began to shape their, and hence 'our', collective destiny. It became a dynamic undertaking full of rich and colourful stories about the exploits of the 'travelled', touching operational staff alongside directors, any combination, any level, any interests. The Transformation Journey was formally launched in January 1995, with five pilot groups already having started in November 1994. By 1999 almost 2 500 travellers had been or were involved on the Transformation Journey. It was felt that there were few rules; in addition, the company was grappling simultaneously with the development of a new 'balanced scorecard' of performance assessment, using the concept of intellectual capital and 'accurate anecdotes' that could be used to exemplify the benefits of transformation, as well as providing powerful metaphors to measure progress.

The costs of such journeys were wrapped up in the hidden costs of time and effort as much as the more obvious. The outputs were similarly encompassed not just in the achievement of self-determined objectives on the way to realizing the organization's vision, but in the unintended, unexpected new lessons learnt through experimentation. There was a marked improvement in the positive perception of the business on the part of travellers in comparison to non-travellers. This improvement continued but in 1999 there was still a need to find some way of measuring the benefits to the business. Thus, to develop the concept still further the company expanded the horizons of the model. For the travellers to experience new cultures, new thinking, new relationships, they needed to traverse the metaphorical world. Travelling was about connecting; the outward journey was to see new things, the inward journey was to see with new eyes. For the Transformation Journey to broaden the horizons of Anglian Water, the travellers must be able to connect with others in different places (seeing new things) and then to realize the value of those connections by revisiting the workplace afresh (seeing with new eyes). To be truly effective, wherever the business went, the journey had to go and, conversely, wherever the journey went, the business must go. Hence, any extension of the journey was really an extension of Anglian Water.

A significant result of the Transformation Journey was to induce more confidence. Individuals on the journey made observations about a prevalent fear culture; people were frightened to try new things or even speak up with new ideas because they did not want to make fools of themselves or see their ideas stolen by more politically adept colleagues. Peer group pressure and the 'Scrooge effect' with knowledge conspired to create barriers. The journey sought to remove these barriers, to cut away the blame culture without a loss of responsibility for actions taken.

However, the future of the journey was reassessed in 1999. Did we need to regenerate the pattern? What should we do about new recruits? How could graduates of the process continue transforming within the University of Water? How could the company ensure that it delivered benefits on intellectual capital? What were these benefits? It was clear that the process was less successful in the third stage when the teams were asked to engage in a business-orientated project. Having inspired people to look into themselves and their surrounding environments it was somewhat of a dampener to then ask them to look at the business benefits of mobile phone use, for example. Furthermore such business-based projects were usually the prerogative of work-based teams in business units and so there has been overlap and confusion.

The answer could have lain in the successes of the environmental and social projects. If the company aspired to be a good occupant of the environment and a good neighbour, it may well have been that these were the areas in which personal team and organization expression could grow. Another possibility was that the Transformation Journey might become an extension of existing induction programmes, including cultural aspects such as detailed examination of the vision and values of the company, empowerment initiatives, and total quality management. The Transformational Journey teams would then be cross-process, cross-disciplinary, and multi-level, bonded only by the common date of starting in the company.

Competencies, performance mangement and personal development plans

It is crucial to recognize also that structure was given to the way in which an individual related to these new and exciting opportunities in the University of Water. Primary competencies common to all employees were defined: teamwork, flexibility, initiative, getting on with others, and customer service. These were defined at three levels: foundation, management/supervisory and executive. Within the university, we also thought of these levels in terms of apprentice, journeyman and master, in the tradition of the learning guilds and within the concept of taking a journey of development. Each job role also used five secondary competencies from: empowering, motivating and developing others, communications skills, cross-cultural awareness, judgement, objective setting, knowing the business, strategic perspective, commercial orientation, innovation, self confidence and decisiveness. Again three levels of performance were defined.

Each year an individual had objectives and standards set together with appropriate measures and targets for business plan requirements, competency development requirements and personal development. There was a joint performance appraisal every six months. The personal development requirements were fed into personal development plans, which reflected the personal and company aspirations for an individual and took into account all of the learning opportunities provided through informal and formal training and through other opportunities such as secondment job application.

Examples will now be given of three separate and different processes, all of which drew on the same basic structural concepts and developed them in their own ways; each made distinctive contributions to the University of Water.

Innovation

The Innovation directorate was founded in 1994. It had a remit to develop technology innovation and stimulate organizational innovation and was the first directorate with such a wide remit in any company in the UK. Inevitably these were connected in many instances; from this group came both a structured 'knowledge creation' management process and leadership of the University of Water. Through practical observation of the way in which traditional research and development was conducted, it was clear that in many instances the process within commercial companies had been rather introverted, often self-serving and not linked in. The process of innovation was defined as a process of harnessing creativity within individuals and teams; the main difference between the Innovation directorate and traditional research and development was the notion of being extrovert and outward looking. In this sense it is probably more appropriate to think of innovation as being research and marketing rather than research and development.

Anglian Water distilled a vision for the development of its technology, not just for operations in eastern England, but to be shared commercially with other operations throughout the global group. This also provided a window on how the company thought in general. The technologists within the innovation process had a responsibility for inculcating innovativeness and creativity within the remainder of the organization and for participating in the marketing of new technologies. Their responsibilities extended to making sure that the processes were launched successfully and were supported properly once they were successful in the market place. The needs of the market place were a major driver in determining the nature of technology innovation in the spirit of the University of Water. A strengthening network had been established between the innovation technologists and colleagues responsible for technical marketing elsewhere in the group. This proved to be very successful in terms of determining the direction of both research and marketing.

By virtue of Anglian Water being an organization with strong technology needs, partnerships were established with leading universities such as Imperial College (London),

Cranfield, Cambridge, Trondheim and New South Wales. Staff of Anglian Water lectured occasionally, operational projects and site visits were provided for Master's courses, research assistants and PhDs were sponsored. The benefit to Anglian Water, apart from an extension to its knowledge assets and resources, was access to some excellent research. Individuals in the Innovation directorate were thus being developed themselves by the learning processes available to all employees, and by taking leading roles in giving the University of Water life.

Production

In the Production business unit, which was responsible at that time for all water resources, supply and wastewater treatment activities, a need was identified that, to meet the challenges of the next millennium, much higher skilled and competent individuals should be working in the front line. A review was carried out to visualize the type of workforce needed for after the year 2000, as well as the sort of work that would be done to enable the company to compete on a world stage.

With this in mind, total quality business improvement teams (BITs) looked at the work done at the time and how this might change. They identified many areas of current activity that, frankly, could have been carried out far more effectively and at lower cost by the type of contractor found in the 'Yellow Pages' telephone directory – for example, building maintenance, site amenity work and other areas of activity readily available in the market-place. At the other extreme, there was work which, although very 'high tech' in content, was done so rarely that to maintain an internal workforce with that capability was simply not cost-effective.

At the same time, other BITs were looking at what type of worker would be needed to respond to work challenges in the next millennium. The need to move from historic operations (primarily mechanical and electrical) to a far more process-related team idea, and for everyone to be much more comfortable and knowledgeable in process operations and techniques, was anticipated. Initially it was found that while 'maintenance' people were well qualified as electricians or fitters, they had no feeling or understanding of the processes that they were maintaining. On the other hand, industrial operators either had process skill and knowledge but no appreciation of the impact of mechanical and electrical work, or had no knowledge of the impact of their operations work on the underlying processes.

A further significant deficiency noted throughout the organization was the key competencies vital for success in a team environment. These include teamworking, communications (getting on with others), initiative, flexibility and, of course, a strong customer focus. The output from these BITs became the 'blue print' for the Production unit's Workforce 2000 initiative. One director commented at the time that although the basic concepts were simple, the translation on the ground would require one of the biggest business change operations ever contemplated in the company. Over 7 000 days of training were required simply to provide basic process qualifications to an accredited standard. Notwithstanding, these learning process and organizational changes were made successfully in 1997. This process revealed that some of the long-term employees from the old days of wastewater management had reading and writing difficulties that were tackled in a sympathetic way, ensuring that even if individuals could not pass the written and oral tests they left the company with increased life skills. The change was not without pain and distress, but there was no industrial action. Finally, during 1998 new recruits entered the company to fill vacancies created by the change, recruited via assessment centres. Despite the upheaval caused, most in the Production unit understood the importance of the combination of technology and teamwork in producing competitive advantage. Like other business units, Production applied the concepts based on personal development plans derived from the gaps identified in the development of the process outlined above.

Customer services

The Customer Services directorate was one of the largest processes in the company, with some 1500 employees whose skills ranged from dealing with customer enquiries, through to repairing leaks on the distribution system. This span of activities created great diversity of learning and educational needs. During the 1990s a strategy was developed to enable employees to deliver their maximum potential, through the ethos of total quality management and empowerment with the workforce progressively developing a portfolio of skills and competencies. By careful market research and service quality analysis, Customer Services created a picture of customer expectations, mapped these expectations against the business and identified weaknesses and opportunities for improvement. Using BITs consisting of representatives from the appropriate departments, solutions to the shortcomings were developed. Benchmarking best practice throughout the utility and commercial world further enabled baseline performance to be defined.

Inevitably the situation was dynamic, changing constantly as external forces came to bear. In the late 1990s the water industry in the UK experienced the climatic extremes of drought and a freezing winter. Handling difficult situations successfully with these varying pressures was testimony to effective learning.

During this early stage, there was also a period of active recruitment for new kinds of employee. Once selected the employee had a personal development plan customized to meet their individual needs and from this a training plan was created. Skills and training packages were prepared to match the competencies that are required for a job profile. Each profile consisted of development stages:

- Entry qualification
- Formal qualification required for the post
- Development opportunity to broaden experience
- Target skills/competencies.

The development stage was set against the National Vocational Qualification (NVQ) levels. This NVQ was unique at the time and was used as a learning tool as well as a team development aid.

Learning was not, however, restricted to those directly employed by the company. Strategic partnerships were developed with key suppliers and service providers, with relationships built around a mutual desire to grow the respective businesses. Such relationships could only prosper if they were founded on the process of learning. Anglian Water was a developing 'Learning Business'. Customer Services was using this platform to meet the growing expectations of its customers to ensure that it became their preferred supplier.

Some insights

Water utilities are still well placed to act as laboratories for creativity, innovation and knowledge creation. These cultural features remain essential to the success of an agile, smart organization. Anglian Water's progress, which had success and failure as learning experience, demonstrated what could be achieved with positive leadership. The Anglian Water Learning Management System recognized the importance of self-managing teams and groups. It encouraged mind opening as well as skill endowment. The long-term prospects of an individual and a company must be found together. Being learned, committed and happy is a better long term bet than ignorance, unhappiness and no commitment. Staff who feel valued will stay longer – we need to remember Maslow's hierarchy. The CU was a flag around which we sought to proudly gather. It needs to be founded on good communication of knowledge and best practice; vocational development should apply to all employees and should not be restricted to particular skill areas.

The University of Water, the unique Anglian Water learning organization, was right in making the changes that it did in the 1990s. It sought to be the culture and process by which the learning organization was brought into reality. The main strength was the federal concept which allowed a variety of learning initiatives to co-exist within a common vision, with a variety of needs represented. The university was linked to the operating company of Anglian Water through each individual, existing both in a tangible and physical form (the learning assets provided by the company) and in a virtual form (the intellectual, behavioural and cultural attitudes of each individual). This underpinned the unique character of the initiative, because it was made up of the aspirations and the wholehearted contribution of the employees. The employees were the learning organization. There was an essential quality of learning through teaching and teaching through learning. Employees became versatile and learned to cope with unknown circumstances.

There were, of course, many tensions and balances. For example, those involved in the university struggled with:

- delivering now versus future conceptual promise;
- stimulation of interest and expectation versus managing expectation and avoiding disappointment;
- abstract conceptual framework versus commonplace working language and practice;
- focused versus spontaneous and hence 'chaotic' change;
- mixing established and new employees' overload versus invisibility;
- structure versus flexibility and innovative freedom;
- coping with the 'day job' and learning at the same time;
- employee retention versus encouraging 'new blood';
- commercial versus social issues;
- measurement;
- conventional training versus the added value of a CU.

Of these issues, measurement was perhaps the thorniest. In the simplest terms the company knew that it had to be better at what it did, to change, grow and improve at the same time. In essence such specific needs were basically expressions of the same fundamental needs to become smarter. The answer to this conundrum was almost a self-evident truth: knowledgeable, committed happy people are more successful than ignorant, uncommitted, miserable people. Many within and beyond the company asked how this could be measured – and hence how could change be planned? The topic of measurement of learning is one that is of major fascination and debate. In response to this, I would ask what the measurements are that justify an athlete training for races. It is self-evident that untrained, lazy, unambitious people are not likely to be Olympic champions. The measurement of success is observed best in the outputs – speed and place. Commitment to learning takes an act of faith and commitment 'at the top' in just the same way as parents commit acts of faith when supporting children in their chosen field.

Another aspect of this tension is the boundaries between order and disorder. Order is that demand from within the business for rigour, objective setting, business plans and so on, whereas disorder is the much more chaotic opportunistic process of the entrepreneur or innovator. If these processes can co-exist, a debate can be constructed around the more productive combination. The chaotic phase may be much more organic, ad hoc, with much greater, even an explosion of, energy and activity. In the case of Anglian Water with its commitment to the order required by public service we had to always have consolidation dominant for a greater time than entrepreneurial disorder. Customers will want the reassurance of long-term stability in operational contracts. Perhaps it would have helped to think of the organization having the stability of explicit or recorded tacit information, expressed as best practice and quality assurance manuals, alongside the energy of tacit experimentation. Tacit learning and knowledge could thus be viewed as a living envelope that changes shape and size with time.

The concepts contained within the notion of the university provided the driving coherence for developing a Learning Business by which the day-to-day organization, technology applications, and employee activities were kept in balance so that customers, domestic or commercial, were kept in balance. Anglian Water was aspiring to be a Learning Business with its focus on people and value added profits rather than just a Learning Organization linked in an undefined way to profitability. The university provided integrated learning rather than fragmented learning for all. It allowed the company to develop as a distinct entity drawing on the strengths of transient individuals. The individuals and organization got progressively smarter.

Postscript: What happened after 1999?

In late 1998 the company decided to engage in what was described as a 'Giant Leap'. As a consequence, the senior managers who had been most involved with the launch of the University of Water, including myself, left as part of a restructuring in 1999. Not long after, the group acquired a large contractor with interests in facilities management. At the same time, the regulatory settlement for charges and services for Anglian Water Services imposed a very demanding regime for the period 2000–05, as it did for all water companies in the UK market. Anglian Water then embarked on a series of reorganizations and financial restructuring to deliver the regulatory settlement and to integrate the contractor with the aim of focusing the newly formed AWG group on facilities management and ring-fencing the old core. New people with different, sometimes non-utilities backgrounds, were appointed into senior positions. The group is still dealing with the challenges presented by these changes.

Simply put, after these changes of personnel, there was no-one left at senior level to champion the University of Water. Management focus after 1999 concentrated on an increasing list of immediate business problems and commitment to the university faded. Obviously, the provision of training in a conventional sense continued, but management of the training centre was outsourced. The added commitment of a CU was seen as a luxury and an expensive overhead. It had been difficult to prove the cost benefit of the original change project, so presumably it was even more difficult to prove ongoing benefits or to prove its value in integrating newly acquired subsidiaries with very different cultural backgrounds. The added value of a CU approach appears not to have been perceived as being consistent with the business demands.

It is very difficult to prove absolutely that the University of Water aided the change in Anglian Water in the 1990s. However, it is true that it flourished at a time when change and greater efficiency were needed – and the leaders of the company were committed to the approach. The university succeeded at the same time as the company succeeded. The new leaders inherited the benefits of the first change programme. But they did not have faith in the university to meet the new challenges.

This lesson is not unique; there are plenty of other, similar examples. Without belief and commitment from the highest level of the organization, a CU will not succeed, or even exist. There are a number of overheads that are traditionally cut when the going gets tough in business – research, marketing, training, learning programmes. Perhaps a CU is perceived to be at the luxury end of these vulnerable intellectual assets and overheads and hence will be one of the first to go. One lesson that might be drawn from this story is that standard business models of success have a use within CU management, so that a CU is not perceived to be a matter of personal leadership, to be dropped by successors. CUs have, therefore, to transcend the personalities that found them.

II
Organizing and Managing a Corporate University

II *Introduction*

This part of the *Handbook of Corporate University Development* examines how corporate university (CU) directors and project managers acquire and deploy resources, how they deal with suppliers, and how they report and measure CU performance. It covers a range of crucial managerial issues and problems including experimentation, piloting, control, relationships with stakeholders, measurement and evaluation, partnering and accreditation.

The contributors have selected valuable and distinctive insights into the thinking and experiences of the wide range of people involved in CU initiatives: directors, project managers, suppliers and faculty. People charged with the responsibility of managing and working with CUs have to handle often difficult interfaces with senior directors and with heads of operational department, as well as with the direct 'customers' or 'students'. Skilful diplomatic practice, political sensibility, well-conceived curriculum and pedagogical design are all prerequisites of the accomplished CU operator.

The first account (Chapter 6 by Storey, Taylor and Rogers) examines the case of one of the largest commercial banks in the UK, Barclays. The focus of this chapter is on the early stages of life of a CU. It highlights the need to develop and communicate a business case that convinces senior executives at group and subsidiary level to invest. In particular, it reveals one of the distinguishing features of many CUs, namely the development of these new institutions through experimentation and evolution. It underscores the place and importance of the underlying values and philosophy that gave a steer to those involved in the launch of this major initiative.

The second subject in this part of the book is centralization – and its counterpart, decentralization. Chapter 7 (by Nataf and Vigne) provides a thorough treatment of CU activity that is often noted in passing in prescriptive texts, namely, whether the initiative can enable the development of a corporate culture. This is an especially pressing managerial issue in organizations like ST that trade around the globe. As the chapter makes clear, a degree of centralization in training is unavoidable when the decision to cultivate and maintain homogeneous values has been taken.

The third topic is the relationship between business schools or universities and CUs. The account that explores this topic (Chapter 8 by Madden) is particularly interesting as it is written by a CU manager who has spent a number of years working in the university sector in the UK – a poacher turned gamekeeper, or perhaps vice-versa! Such a move is relatively common in the USA, according to the scattered anecdotal evidence available, but less so in Europe and particularly the UK. The chapter is especially valuable as it sheds light on what we see as a central dynamic of CU management; the attempt to redefine the relationship between content providers (particularly academics and their host business schools) and their corporate clients. The chapter also provides ample evidence of the difference that concentrating training and development activities within one structure can bring in terms of negotiating power.

Chapter 9 (by Williams) focuses on an area that provided much of the impetus for the popularity of CUs as a concept in the 1990s, e-learning. As the author makes clear, this is the sharp end of CU management; after managerial micro-politics, structural decisions, and negotiation with content providers, something tangible has to be offered by the CU to employees. As the author outlines, the key issue here is the balance of cost, quality and time, underpinned by people and processes. This method of delivery is neither cheap nor easy.

One of the issues raised by Williams is the topic of measurement and evaluation; this is tackled in more detail in Chapter 10 (by Paton). He provides an outline of the reporting mechanisms that can be adopted within CUs and the measurement processes that underpin them. This chapter notes the popularity of models of measurement such as that of Kirkpatrick, but also emphasizes that calculating return on investment on training is something that is unlikely ever to be reliable (in numerical terms). In the end, CU directors are under an obligation to engage with measurement and evaluation in some form, but it is important to shape the agenda towards a multi-faceted approach.

Chapter 11 (by Morris) expands the focus of attention and shifts perspective away from inside CU initiatives: it describes and explores a partnership between a CU and a number of local educational providers in a developing country. This chapter illustrates the potential extension of the mission of CUs and once again emphasizes the importance and complexity of intra- and inter-organizational relationships in the management of CUs. It provides a useful counterpoint to accounts that emphasize the benevolent role of CUs as educational providers. Finally, in Chapter 12 Shenton, Clist and Dirks examine an initiative that has recently emerged from the European Foundation for Management Education (efmd). In collaboration with CU managers, efmd has developed a framework for accrediting initiatives in the style of ISO certification for manufacturing processes or the British Investors in People accreditation framework for training activities. This chapter is both retrospective in that it tells the story of how the accreditation framework developed and Allianz Management Institute's experiences of it, and prospective in that it indicates an approach that CUs may increasingly turn towards – formal quality control and differentiation.

As a whole, the chapters in this second part of the book demonstrate that the organization and management of CUs is at the very least a difficult task. There are varied and sometime conflicting demands upon CU directors and managers, with multiple stakeholders able to request that the CU deliver or be something very specific. Managers in this area require extensive knowledge across a wide spectrum – for example, knowledge of learning needs, knowledge of organizational politics, knowledge of suppliers and delivery modes, knowledge about measurement and evaluation, knowledge about the gamut of stakeholders, and knowledge of educational quality control. Taken together, the chapters in this part offer some vital clues as to how to approach this range of challenges.

6 Evolution and Experimentation: The Barclays University Case

Scott Taylor, John Rogers and John Storey

Introduction

This chapter helps to surface one of the distinguishing features of many corporate universities (CUs) – the development and growth of new institutions through experimentation and evolution. Barclays University is rightly well known for its scale and ambition. But the architecture of this initiative was not designed at the outset. Rather, the distinguishing feature of this case is that the platform was a well-honed 'philosophy' and set of beliefs and values. In contrast, the structural features and programme content were not at all well developed and indeed even today are still in a process of evolution. This case reveals therefore some important lessons about the building of a CU and the way in which the range of stakeholders were involved and played a part.

Barclays University uses the acronym 'bu' (be you) as part of its logo and identity. There is an unusually strong emphasis on learning per se. For example, in its internal documentation to staff it poses the question and the challenge: 'Imagine how much better you'd feel about your job, or yourself, if you sharpened your skills or simply took the time to discover something new? Barclays University (bu) is all about taking control of your life, and it provides a huge number of opportunities to help you and your team discover who they can be'. The introductory brochure even accepts the open nature of its invitation with the prominent question: 'Love the idea but can't decide what to learn?' It reassures staff that browsing the bu website will open up a host of new opportunities. These statements set the general flavour of what this particular case is about. They indicate the aspiration and hint at some of the potential problems.

Origins

The initial impetus for setting up a CU within Barclays came from a newly appointed CEO, Matt Barrett. Barrett came from the Bank of Montreal in Canada, which runs its own Institute for Learning near Toronto, and he suggested a CU project as one of the first initiatives of his stewardship of Barclays. Those responsible for operationalizing Barrett's vision attribute the realization of the initiative in part to the CEO's own personal history, noting that he left school relatively early, worked his way up through his first company, and read the books recommended for Master of Business Administration (MBA) students without attending the courses or taking a degree. During his first few weeks, Barrett toured the country visiting many of the outlying branch operations of the company, getting to speak to between 10 and 15 per cent of the organizational population; one of the key aspirational subjects he spoke about was setting up a CU. In this respect, he began to make the project central to his own personal credibility with lower level employees. The company, according to those working within the CU, has traditionally been generous in terms of training budgets for business units and individuals. Despite this, some senior management perceived that the extent of *learning* and its impact were open to question. For example, one manager observed:

> The value that individuals perceive of [the CU], and also I suppose crucially the people who are paying for it, is that training is not doing what it's supposed to do. It's been very supply led as a philosophy, very production led, so we concentrate on trying to produce perfect courses. We're trying to fill gaps and not really concentrating on what learning is occurring or what the business line really wants out of all of this – which of course is actually improved performance. If you look at the sales directors in this world, and I've talked to them a few times, they're confused by the whole training thing because it's not their world, and what they see is lots of activity without much benefit. The Barclays University thing is in a different space altogether.

MAKING A LEFT-BRAIN CASE

The idea was then passed on to a newly appointed CU director working with a small team of project managers and administrators. This group works from a central head office location; the project managers spend most of their time moving around the company's training locations across the country. One member of this team outlined two more business-oriented issues that the team faced at the outset:

> We could see quite pragmatically that at a commodity level, banking was pretty similar – you needed to do something else to be able to create the differentiation, and some of these differentiators would come from other areas, so I think that this was being driven by a recognition that you had to do something different. You had to attract people, you had to kind of get them going, to be able to start to create some kind of quantum leap in the business at some future date. All that's fine as a kind of conceptual stuff, but of course you've got to pay for it.

Thus, the team then had to make a 'left-brain business case' for the CU, to go with the enthusiasm provided by the new CEO, and provide the funding for the investment and structure that employees now expected. The case was put together within months, and very simply: managers within the 26 individual business units that form the group were asked to calculate total training spend (including outgoings such as travel and accommodation, or building costs), and then to provide figures to estimate both the size and cost of staffing the training-related support functions of the business unit. The director of the fledgling CU then proposed to the board that the budgets and structures of training and HR within the business units could be reorganized entirely, and a new approach taken that would be more employee led and a lot cheaper. As one project manager explained:

> When we started out down this road the context of this is, we got the money to do what we're doing because of the restructure of the wider training function in Barclays. The big

picture for Barclays University was about this being a separate model. We had the Barclays University [here], and we had the learning development thing over here which was being restructured – we created a shell organization with its own branding. Part of the original deal was that you create the shell of Barclays University and at some stage you bring the existing training function into that.

One central, front-end team working on training and development, located within the CU, is the first stop for line managers and heads of business units in Barclays when a training need has been identified. Where considered appropriate, work was outsourced. If the CU could save Barclays money both on training supply and on the cost of the Human Resources (HR) function in business units, the CU director argued, then part of the saving could be set aside to support the core team that manage and deliver the saving, as well as providing capital for initial setup costs.

RESHAPING CONTROL OF TRAINING BUDGETS

This in effect means that the CU costs the company relatively little; it is set up and funded with a percentage of the savings from the two budgets of training and HR. Savings such as these do not come easily – for example, headcount in the HR functions in the business units has been reduced by 40 per cent in one year, which the bu Director admits hasn't always been easy, and there has been some resistance from business unit managers. In part, this may be a result of control over training budgets coming out of the business units and into the CU:

It's a quite important financial structural thing that's happened. Each of the businesses that make up Barclays were running their own training budgets and they've had to offer up those training budgets to the central organization, and we create value contracts. So there's a sales manager, for example, within the bu that agrees a value contract with, for example, Barclaycard as to how much training will be done for that particular business. That's obviously an internal contract, but that sets certain financial parameters round it. (CU project manager)

However, support from the top of the organization, and the strong business case framed in terms of shareholder value, provide arguments so strong that to argue against the bu would be difficult, financially and politically. Such an approach also protects the CU from short-term change:

Each of the business units had to sign up to the idea of the university, and in a proportion to the amount of training budget they let go. They had to hypothecate a certain amount of money to go into the university funding. That we've now got, and it's completely protected – that investment in Barclays University is sacrosanct. (CU project manager)

Senior project managers at the bu also recognize the responsibility they have towards business unit managers and remaining HR/training managers, as a result of the funding structure; one bu project manager described himself as an 'investment manager', managing the funds of the business units and providing a return for the shareholders on training investment.

The bu Director made clear, however, that such an approach was only possible because Barclays had not until that time gone through the cost-cutting exercises that other high street banks completed in the early 1990s. Essentially, at Barclays there was a lot of waste to get rid of, and a cushion of legacy costs to work with in making a business case for the bu. One project manager explained:

> At the time the restructuring proposals were being put together, Barclays was employing one member of HR staff for every 30 staff, and the best in class externally was something like one to a hundred, at least. A large part of the HR over-manning was in the training area – we had about one third of the HR staff employed in training in one way or another, whether that was designing, delivering, administering, or running their own training functions. We had 26 training functions in the UK – we had 26 different training organizations, companies, if you like, within the Barclays group.

This potential resource was clearly not available to other bank groups in the same way. The bu Director, who had himself worked in another large UK high street bank, pointed out that there were limitations on the scope and funding of other corporate universities because the potential to leverage new savings from cutbacks in HR and training had already been missed. That other company went through significant restructuring in the early 1990s, including cost reduction within HR and training; the CU there is perceived more as a means of further reducing training spend than anything else.

OPERATIONS – BUILDINGS, WEBSITE, BRAND

Operationally, the CU is currently organized around a number of 'metro centres' in cities around the country (for example, Birmingham, Bristol, Manchester, Luton, Newcastle), a publicly accessible website, and a strong branding focus. The metro centres are found above existing branches, making use of buildings that the group already owns and maintains. A central reception area leads into quiet spaces for study, a library area, a social 'forum' where drinks and food are served, and a number of rooms of varying size; computer terminals enable students to access materials online from the centre, and a whiteboard carries comments from previous users. The website (http://www.barclays-university.com) offers employees news, information, booking services, self-assessment tools, career advice, and summaries of the six 'Barclays behaviours' that underpin training for self development:

- **Drive performance:** Constantly challenge yourself and inspire others to meet ambitious goals, which deliver exceptional performance.
- **Build pride and passion:** Be passionate about Barclays because you are Barclays – take responsibility for making us a great company.
- **Delight customers:** Always strive to see the world through the eyes of your customers.
- **Grow talent and capability:** Be as consumed with the development and success of your colleagues as you are with your own.
- **Execute at speed:** Focus your energy on excellent execution.
- **Protect and enhance our reputation:** Respect the standards that are our licence to do business and find intelligent ways to apply them.

Currently a new website is being developed that focuses entirely on developing leaders (http://www.taketheleadbu.com). The course content and structure provided through this website replaces the 12 different courses previously available across the group; bu project managers hope to rationalize training supply in this way, and simultaneously to provide a higher quality of provision. In addition, significant investment in bricks and mortar complement this; the metro centres are seen as central to convincing employees that the bu really does exist. One project manager spoke of the need employees express to 'come and touch' the bu in the metro centres, and of the way in which such a space demonstrates the financial commitment of the company.

The central project team working within the bu currently numbers around a dozen full-time senior managerial staff, while each outlying metro centre employs around a dozen more full-time staff. In addition, in a further significant development the bu has spawned an extension in the form of a 'Business School'. The initial launch of the bu had been geared towards the needs of skills development in applied areas. What had been missed, in consequence, were the development needs of senior managers. The Business School, which currently sits on the periphery of the bu, is designed with these management development needs very much to the fore. This is a further example of the experimental and evolutionary nature of the growth of the CU idea within Barclays. The Business School contains four faculties and the Faculty Executive Committee is chaired by the CEO. A small number of external academic advisers are also retained, and information technology (IT) support is sourced within the organization.

The bu brand within the Barclays Group is a strong one. While the bu is firmly located within the Barclays Group, it remains a discrete entity within the organization, with a brand that is gathering value to itself. Longer term, plans are being made to 'stretch the brand' beyond the company and its employees, in two key ways. First, a division has been identified between the 'mass market' for training, and a 'niche market' for more individualized development. Unusually, Barclays is seeking to bring these together within the bu. To this end, a Director of Talent and Organizational Development has been appointed to set up a business school, which will be composed of four faculties. The basic bu brand will continue to provide the mass market training such as induction, and the business school will be devoted to high-level management development, organizational learning, retention of high flyers, and defining and achieving organizational competencies. Second, senior managers within the bu see a strong future for brand stretching beyond the company, of both the core corporate brand and the associated CU brand. Franchising has been considered, and opportunities for associating the bu brand with other training events and suppliers are plentiful. The bu infrastructure is seen as a good delivery channel that can go beyond supplying learning to employees, beyond even the supply chain, and into supplying learning for customers and the wider community. Small business owners, in particular, may be targeted if the bu brand can become recognized beyond the company.

Staff at the bu see themselves as providing a structure for employees to use according to their individual needs and desires. They acknowledge that the company is responsible for providing necessary regulatory training, and will require all new employees to undergo basic induction and legally required training. Beyond these, however, Barclays is responsible only for the *provision of possibilities* for self development, with the aim that a more voluntarist approach to the provision of training will result in employees that do take up the offer being more committed 'heart and soul', as one manager explained:

In the back quarter of 2000 we had a large consultation exercise – the largest consultation ever undertaken in Barclays with its staff, around what the CU was about. We ran a whole load of focus groups to ask people, 'what is it that you want from a CU, what does it mean to you?' And they told us some things like, we'd like to have control of our own learning, we'd like to do stuff which isn't necessarily bank related, we'd like e-channels, we want to be able to do some stuff in our own time. [We were] encouraged by the very positive response and the deep seated urge to learn, which in a sense had been knocked out of them by the normal corporate structures – 'you go on this course and you *must* go on this course', all this school type behaviour. At the heart of it there was a lot of desire on the part of the individuals to learn, so armed with that and the money to do it, we embarked on this marketing campaign. Our approach was to target those people who were going to touch us.

It's your responsibility to do what's best for you. We're trying, through what we're doing, to set a psychological contract with the individuals who will use the university, which is a massive step change from the kind of menu-driven training business which tends to do things, or should do things, as efficiently as possible to meet the fundamental needs of the organization – the university is something else. What we've tried to do is put it into the context of saying 'you're an adult, you have some responsibilities for yourself in terms of your career and indeed the life you lead outside the company, in the community, maybe as a parent or whatever', and so what we've done is raised awareness of the reality of those things. The model we're trying to put in place for the university is one that says 'you are learning all the time, it's just that you need to recognize when that's happening'. The way we put a training programme together will help to facilitate that. We've plugged into that as our first step to encourage individuals to see for themselves – normally speaking what people often say is well, '[learning] is not part of my job', or 'it's your responsibility to give me training and therefore if it's not available I'm not learning and therefore it's your fault'. It's a parent-child kind of philosophy going on and therefore what we're trying to do is raise awareness of something else, something different. The challenge is to try and push that as far as we can so that a large percentage of our target group, as large a percentage as possible, of the target group have heard it, and get it, and do something about it – but by no means will everyone get it.

bu in operation: The sub-case of Barclaycard

So far we have referred mainly to the operation of the bu as it operates within high street banking. The metro centres were built in order to meet the need of branch and regional staff. But in addition the reach and impact of the bu concept can be illustrated by attending to the special case of the Barclaycard business. This credit card business is headquartered in a large modern and purpose-built state-of-the-art building in Northampton, a town in the English Midlands. Barclaycard is regarded as comparatively innovative and creative and, some say, 'quite entrepreneurial compared with the rest of the bank'. This business has taken the bu concept and applied it to significant effect. But the Barclaycard story is interesting also because it again reveals the nature of continued experimentation and incremental build in the bu concept.

Barclaycard began in 1966 as a division of the Barclays Group, and was a founder member of the international VISA credit card system in the mid-1970s. At the time it was the UK's first credit card; Barclaycard currently has more than eight million customers, issuing around one in five credit cards in the UK. It was also the first card services provider on the Internet, a service that more than 800 000 customers regularly use.

The bu within Barclaycard has strong physical presence. This is achieved through the location of a bu local hub in a very prominent position in the 'High Street' of the ultra-modern new building. From here the bu is able to advertise its wares to passing employees through street advertising boards and posters akin to a local travel agency or newsagent. Typical enticing offerings include 'taster sessions' offered every lunchtime for talks and courses in popular subjects such as financial planning. Courses are also promoted in team meetings. Moreover, each member of staff was given £150 to spend on whatever they wanted in the first year of bu operation. People embarked upon learning of a general life skills kind, including how to do beauty treatments, singing lessons, languages, snowboarding and bricklaying. Some people, not surprisingly, were cautious and wanted to know what the catch was.[1] Team leaders perceived the initiative as 'clever' on the part of the company as it indicates that the company is interested in, or values, employees as people beyond the job role, and develops a store of goodwill that managers can draw on subsequently. In 1993 there were, in total, 3300 separate footfalls (physical visits and not including web access) to the bu area in the head office building.

bu was set up specifically as a separate entity from existing learning provision in order to be able to brand it 'cleanly' – so that it wouldn't be associated with any 'previous cloudy clutter' in anyone's mind. We interviewed a range of stakeholders within Barclaycard in order to ascertain their expectations and evaluations of bu. These respondents included line managers, team leaders and staff who had been users of the bu.

The reports of the line managers again revealed the evolutionary and experimental nature of the bu experiment. For example, one line manager of a significant number of staff pointed out how she had tentatively explored the phenomenon:

> I had done my staff's personal development plans with them and helped them develop their learning plans and then I thought, 'Oh I had better do something for myself'. And it suddenly occurred to me that unless I got myself involved with the bu and got to understand how it works, otherwise I simply wouldn't get any development at all. So, I went down to the bu space and had a little nose around. I then booked myself in to see one of the bu people and spent an hour being talked though possibilities given my aims and objectives.

This tentative approach is revealing. The line manager had virtually no idea what was on offer from the bu. She had certainly been made well aware of its existence and presence through a variety of media, but its actual content and potential remained a mystery. Its discovery and uncovering required some active 'nosing around'. Such a stage can, however, present a critical moment of truth for the would-be customer. In this particular instance the judgement was that, despite the staff time proffered by the bu, the diagnostic experience was rather too general and not sufficiently pitched at the right level. Despite this experience, however, this line manager has continued to support the bu as a sponsor of her staff.

She was in fact sufficiently impressed at one level to be prompted to ensure that all the remainder of her staff who had not so far visited the bu should be encouraged to do so and to talk with a member of the bu learning support team.

> I set each of them an objective: to have a personal assessment by a bu person before the end of May. Out of that came their own detailed development plans. Everyone in the organization is in fact supposed to have a personal development plan, whether you actively link that up with the bu is up to you. That part is optional.

This same line manager eventually decided that the bu was useful for her staff but could not substitute for her longstanding ambition to do a short residential course at Ashridge or Cranfield. In the end she won approval for an executive course at Cranfield. When she was asked if the bu had in fact had a similar course would she have been happy to take that she gave a revealing and honest response:

> It's a good point. Even if the bu had exactly the same course as the one I am attending at Cranfield then probably yes I would go on it. But in my heart of hearts I would still be thinking, 'Would I have been better to go to Cranfield?'

In effect, she was evidently pleased that the bu did not have a similar (let alone exactly the same) course and thus force her to make such a choice.

In the development and survival of CUs it is evident that the evaluation by line managers is critical. In this instance the bu had been appraised and the judgement was mixed. The nature and approach was found suitable for staff development purposes. To this extent it had been deemed a success. On the other hand, it was judged as having, to date, produced a portfolio of provision that was by no means sufficient to be a substitute for external management development. In the current stage of evolution of the bu this state of affairs was not deemed too much of a problem. However, with the introduction of the Business School, this dilemma might in future present some further challenges and some need for greater clarification of remit, intent and aspiration.

From other line managers it was also evident that the tentative, experimental approach had a downside. Managers were generally not aware of the full range of offerings by the bu. There was, they reported, no equivalent of the traditional glossy course brochure that has now gone out of fashion in so many companies. But as a consequence, while there was wide awareness of the existence of the CU, there was at the same time little understanding of what it could, or could not, offer. As one manager observed, 'I get far more brochures from external trainers than I do from internal sources. In fact I am not aware of ever having received an internal training brochure. Maybe one has passed me by.'

If we now turn to perspectives from a number of team leaders, we find that there was, in general, considerable optimism that the organization was gradually creating the appropriate kinds of provision. As one observed:

> You have to get people involved in learning in easy steps, because there is a perception – which is quite an interesting challenge for me – that even coming here [the bu space] to learn this is a big step. It's just one small step, because once they've opened the door the opportunity is clearly there. So part of what I have to do is sell the idea. [But] once they come through the door, there's usually no turning back, but I've got to get them into the door. I am feeding [them] information. If you want more – you've got the taste – come down and get more. The same way you go to a point like McDonald's for food when you're hungry. (bu team leader)

The Barclaycard bu team tends to use learning opportunities that are 'personal' rather than professional in order to get people involved in the venture. The thinking is that people will then progress into professional development.

Another emergent feature is that there are multiple routes that may lead to locating relevant training. But sometimes none of them work. There are also other potential complications. Training budgets are in part dependent on departmental finances; sometimes they are generous, sometimes they are non-existent.

Also, reflecting the discussion above about the interpretation of what the bu has to offer, a number of team leaders made similar points. For example, one noted that:

> I would say there is a bit of snobbery involved. Folk would think: 'Mmm, bu, that's alright if I want basic PC [training], or if I want such and such.' But for somebody to learn Excel or something more advanced, they want to immediately go in at intermediate level. And so they would probably take themselves off to an external course. They might find out about who was doing it through the bu [but] they say: 'We want a fast track result given to us', and therefore they will pay a premium to get that fast track result externally. Staff sometimes want what they think is a Rolls-Royce product, and therefore would pay the premium to get that, because there's a whole set of beliefs about internal and external training that are very difficult to change. (bu team leader)

Another facet of this weaning of staff and their managers away from external courses and encouraging them to embark on the learning discovery within the bu is the 'hankering after' offsite training events:

> Culturally Barclays and Barclaycard is no different [from any other large organization] – it has had a culture of going on face-to-face training events. It's prestigious, we've got two hotels that we run them in, we go there and they offer you beers, you can put it on your company card – all that kind of stuff. So given the choice of two days out of work or two hours on a Learning Point [PC], it's not much of a contest. So the people who haven't necessarily embraced the e-based learning are probably still hankering after the off-site, face-to-face, nice hotel, yeah? (HR business partner)

Despite the ambiguities noted above and despite the lack of clear structures or even clear curricula, there was considerable support and commitment to the notion of the learning philosophy within Barclays – and especially in terms of its expression within the bu. One of the most memorable interviews was with one of the most junior members of staff interviewed. She was not new; she had been with the bank for a few years and had seen a number of initiatives come and go. However, she had been very impressed by one of the roadshows presented by the new CEO. She was impressed by his passion and sincerity and was convinced by his commitment to learning. She said:

> Matt Barrett came on board about three years ago and I think he's very much a people person. He is trying improve training, coaching, and people managing – all those soft skills that in the past have not been seen as beneficial. But I believe like him that they really, actually, are very important to the well-being of the staff, morale and ultimately to the business. You can get much more out of someone when they are happy and they are efficient … and I think that's what he is trying to do. He's trying very hard with the messages that he's sending out to support the idea of training, learning, coaching and managing people fairly. Over the last three years there has been much more emphasis on it.

This kind of deep down acceptance is of course a critical, arguably the crucial, test. The precise details of courses and the structures of CUs and who is represented or not on governing boards are all relatively irrelevant in comparison. An organization like Barclays, which can build on such a philosophical base, has the time to experiment with discovering the appropriate structures. But it does not have all the time in the world; the underpinning idea has to be acted upon in due course and staff and line managers have to find the learning opportunities relevant and worthwhile.

One team leader pointed out how actually gaining access to sufficient appropriate training can be difficult:

> It's a continual fight with directors and senior managers. They are interested in targets, targets, targets. You have to keep going back and saying: 'Yeah, we can do that, but we need the tools to do it. We need the coaching in place. We need the training in place. We need the support'. I see my role, in a way, as to continually remind [senior managers of this] – it's not something for the staff to worry about because they've got to worry about the customer. [Getting access to training] is a continuing battle that we have, but I will continually battle on for that because to me it is very, very important. It is a battle with management because they are into figures and targets and something tangible that they can see in money form, and all these other things like training seem to them soft – it is not money. (team leader)

Thus, even in an organization as committed to learning (in general) as Barclays, there can still be critical battles over its actual provision. For the bu to succeed it has to offer solutions to problems such as these.

Discussion and conclusions

The case described in this chapter reveals how a significant strategic learning initiative was launched on the back of a strong and compelling philosophy and yet without much initial drawing of the structural and operational elements. These latter have been discovered and invented over the past few years.

bu has successfully established a geographical spread of learning centres which have attracted some considerable endorsement from the staff who have come into contact with them.

On the other hand, bu operations do not reach through the whole company. Initial provision was of a mixed nature. Some of it was of the general life skills variety with very little direct immediate application to work. Other components were very carefully targeted indeed and bu staff jealously guarded the brand for training courses by vetting and filtering for suitable courses to include under its aegis while turning away other assignments. Thus, the bu has by no means been a catch-all, and yet, on the other hand, there has been some confusion about its character and the nature of its offering. In its early days it pitched its courses to staff below the managerial level. Staff perceptions were in consequence found to range from approval of the general commitment to learning which the Barclays Group demonstrated and yet some lack of clarity about just what remit the bu had. A further perception was, however, that in general the bu was targeted at 'lower level' staff tiers. Specialist senior staff we interviewed still very much preferred to sign up for courses at the more traditional external business and management schools such as Ashridge and Cranfield. If the new business school within the Barclays Group is to succeed, it will need to find a recognized, accepted and respected place within the total range of learning demand and this may or may not imply a substitution for the Ashridge and Cranfield courses.

Note

1. This was picked up on by bu staff; they then used the headline 'What's the catch?' on their publicity material to encourage people to use their personal budget.

7 The Centralization Dilemma (and a Balanced Solution)

Jean-Claude Nataf and Stacia Vigne

Introduction

Should training be centralized into a single consistent service, taking care of the global training needs of the company or should it be decentralized to allow individual business units to take care of own their specific needs? This is an important and all too common question faced by managers in many countries. There are arguments to support either view and the dilemma tends to be one of the more significant stumbling blocks for those people seeking to design and manage corporate universities (CUs). The purpose of this chapter is to help to demonstrate a practical way forward.

Multinational companies cannot operate without a global company culture, values and shared vision. It is also imperative to have common processes, tools and methodologies across the organization. In our own company, ST, this is what we call the 'corporate glue', holding the many diverse elements of our structure together. This 'glue' must exist in training (as well as in many other functions, such as communication, human resources (HR) and total quality management) in order to provide guidelines and reference points, to ensure the optimization of resources, and to act as a catalyst.

The corporate or central training team thus plays a key role in developing and disseminating ST culture, values and shared vision. This team also ensures that training strategy is aligned to the needs of the business as defined by top management, allowing us to identify the skills and knowledge required to meet corporate strategic goals. Strategic programmes are then tailored to achieve a competitive advantage for the company. An additional benefit of a centralized training organization is having a physical campus. This provides a place where managers can meet and create cross-functional and cross-cultural networks, a place where people feel at home.

Nevertheless, equally compelling arguments can be deployed in support of a decentralized approach, in which each business unit takes charge of its own training needs locally. Local organizations know best the training needs of their people and their site, and are able to respond quickly. So an effective training organization has to be close to those sites; close to the people it wants to develop, its internal customers. Also, because of time and cost considerations, not all employees can travel to a single, central location, especially considering the large number of sites in which ST operates worldwide, nor do we have the resources to send 'corporate trainers' to all company sites to train employees.

The obvious answer is to try to combine elements of both approaches; to try to secure the advantages of both centralization and decentralization. But is this really possible in practice –

or does one end up with the *dis*advantages of both approaches? What would a balanced and integrated approach look like?

This chapter explores this key issue based on the experience of the ST University (STU) whose approach, we believe, goes a long way towards combining the best of both models. The company is described in the box below. The next section describes the role and organization of STU. This is followed by an explanation of the principles that STU has evolved to tackle the centralization dilemma, setting out the way roles are defined and responsibilities allocated. The next section illustrates what this approach means in practice by describing the development and introduction of the curriculum for the School of Sales and Marketing. Finally, we offer some reflections on trends in the organization of CUs in the light of our experience.

ST – THE COMPANY

ST is a micro-electronics manufacturer and a French multinational company. It is a typical global company with resources and sales spread over the world in 17 main production sites, 12 advanced research and development centres, 32 design and application centres, and 74 direct sales offices in 27 countries. It employs 42 000 people.

Micro-electronics is one of the fastest growing and most strategic industries of our century. ST's products are in just about any electronic system or consumer goods you can imagine. The market in which the company operates is as large as the market for oil exports.

Continuous technology advances and new techniques mean that our reaction time must be very short in everything we do: designing a new product, launching production, introducing a new technology, and so on. This also applies to our training process, where we must be able to move quickly to update the skills and know-how of our employees.

Our key parameters for success are innovation, company culture and values, and cost management. But beyond our achievments in technology, our company strength depends on our workforce, and this makes education essential to the industry and to ST. In addition, training is a key tool to promote a common purpose and shared values within the company.

The ST University – principles and practices

ST is part of a value chain involving a variety of actors: design houses, suppliers, foundries, distributors, customers and others. In the same way, our CU, STU, has a service chain, which includes employees, managers, local training organizations, top management, suppliers, customers, and so on.

Service is at the heart of STU: service to employees, service to local management, service to senior management. But above all, STU serves our company vision and strategy. The service model we have put in place for ST training allows us to partner effectively with all of these different actors, in order to achieve our training vision:

To be the best in class for training processes and initiatives amongst the high tech companies in order to create a spirit of continuous learning to achieve the strategic goals of the corporation.

In this context, ST training is built on three guiding principles:

- **All training reflects a genuine need:** ST's training strategy is aligned to the business needs of the company, both at a corporate and individual level. Training programmes are tailored to meet corporate strategic goals and achieve strategic advantage for ST. In parallel, STU offers targeted career training, allowing ST employees to build competencies throughout their career.
- **ST trains ST:** To stimulate the sharing of knowledge and expertise within the company, ST has developed a trainer certification process to provide professional training skills to ST employees. This programme is the foundation for a dynamic and effective cadre of in-house trainers across all ST locations. Close to the reality of everyday life in the company, certified STU Associate Trainers and Speakers transfer, build and cascade the wealth of knowledge, experience and know-how present at all levels of the company.
- **Synergy, local and global:** STU, together with the corporate training function, coordinates the learning organization and the educational infrastructure across the company, ensuring that training is available when and where it is needed. They streamline training initiatives, methods and evaluation between local entities and the central organization, and optimize resources through shared training initiatives and experiences. In addition, ST fosters the use of efficient communication tools for training, such as the virtual ST Learning Campus, and deploys e-learning throughout the company.

These three principles are the foundation of ST training throughout the company. As in other companies, the creation of the STU was led by business drivers such as:

- globalization of the organization driving the need to bring common company culture, a shared mind set and values;
- the need to develop professional business management for the different levels within the company;
- the need to develop a strategic umbrella for job competency development.

In our case, the objective is to deploy the core competencies and cultural references through the development and the deployment of strategic programmes and other people development initiatives. In fact, the strategic role of STU is to reinforce, update and enhance our staff capabilities. This includes providing ST people with the skills, knowledge, and cultural adaptability the company needs in order to remain abreast of important changes, strengthening their sense of belonging and entrepreneurial spirit.

However, STU also has as part of its mission to serve the local training organizations by developing the training skills of local trainers through the STU Associate Trainer certification process and by helping sites build their own programmes based on clear pedagogical advice and guidelines. This is discussed further below.

The critical success factors for a corporate university are shown in Figure 7.1; these provide a convenient way of describing the way STU operates.

POSITIONING IN ORGANIZATION

STU is part of the Strategic Planning and HR organization, which ensures links with strategic goals, business objectives, job skills, behaviours and programmes developed.

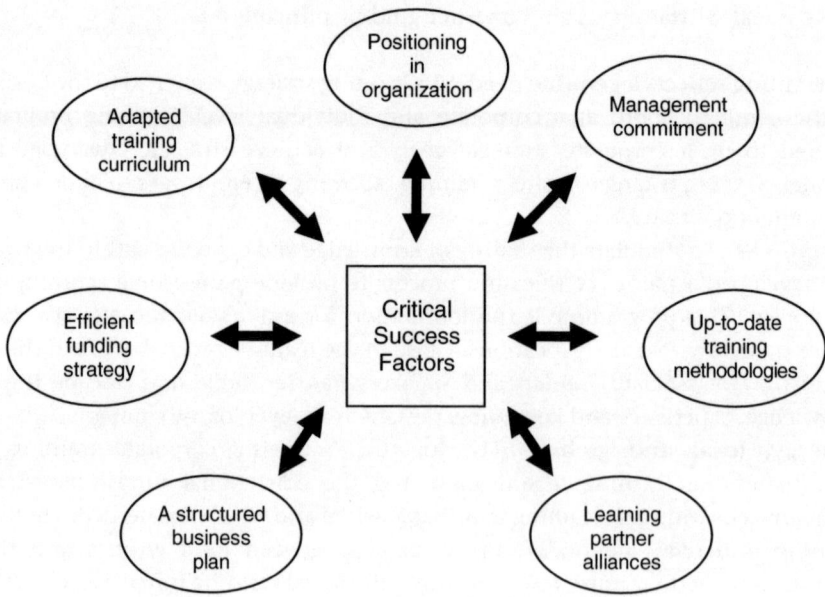

Figure 7.1   Key Ingredients for CU success

MANAGEMENT COMMITMENT

The CEO regularly acknowledges the STU role and senior managers participate in programmes to share their views, make speeches, answer questions, give advice and communicate on strategic ST directions. STU objectives are shared during a regular Executive Total Quality Council meeting involving our CEO and the company staff.

UP-TO-DATE TRAINING METHODOLOGIES

E-learning is more and more prevalent (15 per cent of our activity today) and we have adopted a blended learning approach for some of our programmes. The web is also used as a communication and sharing tool. A web-based learning campus is in use in ST, where you can find information related to learning for STU, sites and the outside world.

When we speak about a service model, it also means that the virtual ST Learning Campus (see Figure 7.2) is available to all actors of our learning chain, and includes data, suggestions and useful information:

• for managers, to help them define how to develop their people;
• for the training professionals to know what is available elsewhere in ST;
• for employees as our primary customers.

LEARNING PARTNER ALLIANCES

STU's learning alliance strategy focuses on building long-term, high-quality relationships with our external providers. Our experience shows that as our partners get to know our

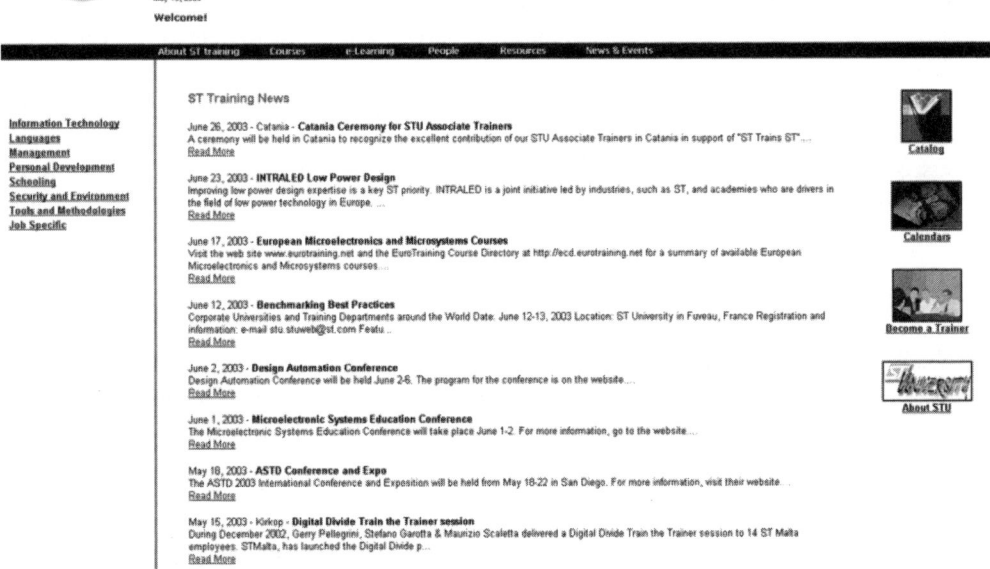

Figure 7.2   The ST Learning Campus

organization, their contribution is amplified, while at the same time they continue to provide an outsider's perspective to our business.

These partnerships allow us to offer ST people more and better learning opportunities; to further our reach in ST's value chain: customers (product training), suppliers (semiconductor training), shareholders (chip industry training), and community (environment training); and to generate revenues through increased external business. We also recommend our partners to site training teams for local initiatives.

A STRUCTURED BUSINESS PLAN

People development and achievement of the company's long-term goals (linked to our ST long-term vision) have to be supported and a five-year plan is necessary in terms of programmes, tools, budget, resources and promotion. This is what is done in ST on a yearly basis.

For example, promotion and internal/external marketing of STU is a key success factor. This is done widely through internal and external conferences and events, recognition ceremonies, publications, presentations and speeches, Internet/intranet sites and other areas, and is an important factor in motivating our service chain. In fact, STU received a Corporate University Excellence Award from Corporate University Xchange and the *Financial Times* in 1999 for developing and implementing innovative marketing techniques to encourage involvement in learning.

FUNDING STRATEGY

A balanced organization such as in our model requires a central budget guaranteed by the corporation to allow company-wide training initiatives and local budgets for local needs. While external fundings are targeted everywhere, our activity is more a cost centre than a profit centre in most of the cases or, as we prefer to call it, an 'investment centre'. This allows us not to be influenced in our learning choices by purely financial constraints and underscores management commitment to training. On the other hand, last minute cancellations are penalized to make sure everyone understands that training is a company investment to be taken seriously.

ADAPTED TRAINING CURRICULUM

Finally, it is obvious that our training curriculum is our top priority, both in terms of training content adapted to company strategic needs and in terms of quality. ST has an ongoing commitment to pragmatic training programmes, and they are all based on the same approach in terms of the development and diffusion process.

In summary, the STU has established a clear role within the company and is seen, both internally and externally, to be an effective operation. Nevertheless, STU staff understand the dangers of complacency and that circumstances may change. Figure 7.3 summarizes a SWOT analysis of STU's position within the company.

Strengths	Weaknesses
Part of Strategy group Management commitment Course quality ST trains ST Strategic alliances Marketing approach Fast reactivity	Influenced by downturn Cost centre
Opportunities	**Threats**
Company growth (Asia Pacific, …) New technologies Value chain evolution	Not reinvent ourselves Becoming a training department Not being able to answer needs Not being recognized as a corporate asset

Figure 7.3   STU SWOT analysis

ST's solution to the centralization dilemma: A mixed and balanced model

The training operations summarized in the previous section involve a mixed and balanced service model, combining a centralized, corporate training team and individual site training organizations flexible enough to pragmatically meet the training needs of ST. This section describes the key, complex relationship between centre and periphery in more detail.

In ST, the corporate training team is composed of STU, which focuses on both strategic training and company-wide training, and of a corporate training management function in charge of optimizing and cross-fertilizing training practices and guidelines throughout the company. Each of these is discussed in turn.

THE ROLE OF ST UNIVERSITY

STU delivers training centrally or at local STU branches, while the local site manages local training initiatives and its local training department, supported by STU trainers who travel to sites and 'STU ambassadors' present at sites. This requires:

- a strong corporate training team who can provide guidelines, support, materials and STU Associate Trainers;
- a strong local training organization supported by a network of internal trainers;
- a strong level of interaction between the two above entities.

In our model, we have defined the scope of training that falls under the full responsibility and lead of the corporate team, that which is managed locally, and that which is shared between the two. We have also defined which team defines training needs, selects training solutions, develops training content and decides on the deployment strategy.

We can summarize the role split using the acronym STU:

- **S**trategic training requires the full involvement of **S**TU. This includes programmes requested by top management; initiatives needed by several sites for which a common approach is essential; training requiring a company-culture approach; or training that a single site cannot tackle alone. Our concept of using our internal resources as much as possible to complement external resources also has to be considered strategic and we will see that STU plays a key role here.
- **T**actical training requires the involvement of **S**TU but is primarily a site or business unit responsibility. Here, the corporate function has the role of enabler and adviser.
- **U**rgent training is fully under the site responsibility and STU's role is to help local trainers build and improve their pedagogical skills.

THE CORPORATE TRAINING MANAGEMENT FUNCTION

Our central/local balance requires a coordination role, which is provided through the corporate training function. The corporate training mission is to identify the best practices and to define guidelines to be deployed and cross-fertilized across the corporation and to facilitate their deployment in order to ensure the effectiveness and consistency of the learning process and content.

This central role consists of managing and identifying the main training processes, such as training needs analyses, and the evaluation and certification processes. Below we look at these critical processes to see who does what in ST's model.

Training needs analysis (TNA)

Each site performs detailed needs analysis in order to elaborate their yearly training plan. The needs are also often defined through interviews with direct management and operational people when top management has identified the need. These interviews are conducted by STU and corporate training teams, involving both local training managers and HR departments, who are major actors in this process.

Consolidating the training needs to identify the required core competencies and cultural references is the role of the corporate training function. The role is also to define a consistent common timeline and to cross-fertilize best TNA practices within and outside ST.

Certification process

A key element of our model is to train internal speakers and experts to share their knowledge with colleagues. This allows fast, pragmatic and cost-efficient training to the different ST sites.

For this reason, in 1994 we implemented a certification process – outlined in Figure 7.4 – to provide professional training skills to part-time local trainers, who we call STU Associate Trainers. In addition to acquiring training skills, they also need to be locally supported. The role of the corporate training function is to ensure this, and to put into place a process of local recognition managed by the local training team.

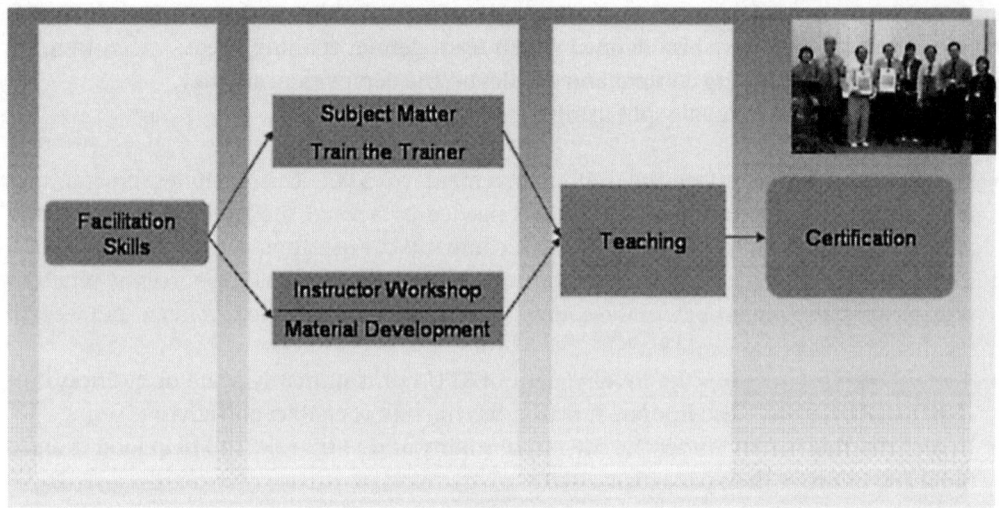

Figure 7.4   The STU Associate Trainer Certification Process

Evaluation

This is the last critical process to put in place. Each course has to be measured in terms of people satisfaction, efficiency and the impact on business or attitudes.

Other roles for this central function are to encourage exchanges of resources, human or material, to consolidate results, benchmark with the outside world, and establish training roadmaps by job area to be utilized locally as a standard framework to be adapted by sites.

When a site has a training need, corporate training can advise on the best way to meet it: to go through STU, to use material from another site or to recommend specific external consultants or solutions. The corporate training function also serves the organization in working with managers, experts or HR professionals to build an ideal training roadmap by job area. We will describe the Sales and Marketing roadmap as an example later.

Finally, the corporate training role is also to set standards to achieve world-class status and efficiency in the learning and education process, such as the quality level of courses, the minimum and average hours of training per employee, and so on. All of these standards are integrated in the company HR standards and are therefore very well known, displayed and measured.

Clearly, the corporate training function and STU have to work closely together and they share common objectives, which are:

- Build a learning organization by identifying and continuously improving the core capability of the company:
  - create and coordinate a dynamic forum of exchange among all ST management, customers, suppliers and training entities;
  - develop the necessary alliances with world-class institutions and internal and external experts worldwide to bring in the core competencies; in this area, STU received another Excellence Award from Corporate University Xchange in 2002, this time for innovation in developing strategic learning alliances;
  - support the local training organizations in the deployment of those strategic competencies and the development of their core competencies.
- Build ST and STU as a trademark in education and knowledge:
  - promote ST learning organization internally and externally;
  - continuously benchmark internally to identify best practices and cross fertilize throughout the organization;
  - support the local training organizations to improve the efficiency of the learning process by improving training materials and methods, enhancing the skills of trainers, and so on.

The ST balanced service model in practice – the case of the School of Sales and Marketing

A concrete example of our model in action will help ground the preceding discussion. The recent development of the STU School of Sales and Marketing provides illustrations of the key points.

ST training is split into eight training 'families':

- Management
- Job specific
- Schooling
- Tools and methodologies
- Personal development
- Information technologies
- Languages
- Security.

When we began STU back in 1994, our focus was on cross-functional programmes such as management, personal development and tools and methodologies. This was a key priority in building our common company language and culture. Since 2000, however, we have expanded our scope to create curricula by job function to foster specific competency development. Thus, within the 'job specific' family, we have created STU 'schools' dedicated to particular job functions, starting with the School of Sales and Marketing. Why start with the School of Sales and Marketing? ST has ambitious growth plans and challenging sales targets. This requires a high-performance sales force, which masters the technical complexity and market competition. The School of Sales and Marketing was created with the objective of increasing the performance, effectiveness and professionalism of our worldwide sales and marketing teams, from beginners to experienced professionals.

As per our global model, all major actors were mobilized: managers, local training organizations, experts, and the STU development team.

Our first step was to identify the global strategy and the precise needs. This is normally done on a global level through the Executive Total Quality Council, but we also decided to create a dedicated Sales and Marketing Council with a clear mission: validate STU directions for these specific programmes in relation to the global ST sales and marketing strategy and challenges and advise us on necessary adjustments and priorities.

This council is sponsored by a Sales and Marketing Vice President and is made up of senior staff and employees from Sales and Marketing, Operations, corporate and HR.

The needs and proposed solutions discussed during regular council reviews are the result of detailed needs analysis performed on sites or through interviewing by corporate teams, often with local training managers involved in the process. This gives us both a macro and a micro view of the company needs. We have broad knowledge of the corporate and staff objectives as well as the specific needs of a sales or marketing engineer.

The result of our analysis was that we needed to offer very pragmatic programmes taught by experienced ST professionals and top-level external consultants, providing the tools and processes needed to fulfill fundamental tasks, increase efficiency and effectiveness, develop customers' trust, and improve technical skills and application knowledge.

Next, the STU School of Sales and Marketing programme manager designed and developed the courses of the curricula together with a team of internal experts, using selected external partners when needed.

For each course, a pilot was then organized to get feedback from participants, experts and training managers to verify the course quality and outcomes. Once a course is validated, we often develop 'train the trainer' sessions and manuals for our internal network of STU Associate Trainers, so that they can cascade the teaching of the courses. Our STU Associate Trainers are carefully selected based on their skills, job experience and motivation, and are trained by STU following the certification process mentioned earlier.

The benefits of involving the complete chain are multiple:

- we have the buy-in of top management from the beginning, since we are in line with their macro objectives;
- we are fully supported by the sites as we answer their local needs;
- we have a perfect specification for what is expected as the course outcome;
- we can rely on a professional and motivated internal network of experts and STU Associate Trainers, allowing fast and effective deployment of the programme;
- we can rely on the advice and skills of experienced consultants in the field of sales and marketing when needed;

- our extensive analysis helps us build a theoretical training roadmap for sales and marketing people that can be split into programmes specific to the function (see Figure 7.5) and cross-functional programmes such as seminars for new hires, management cycles, and presentation skills.

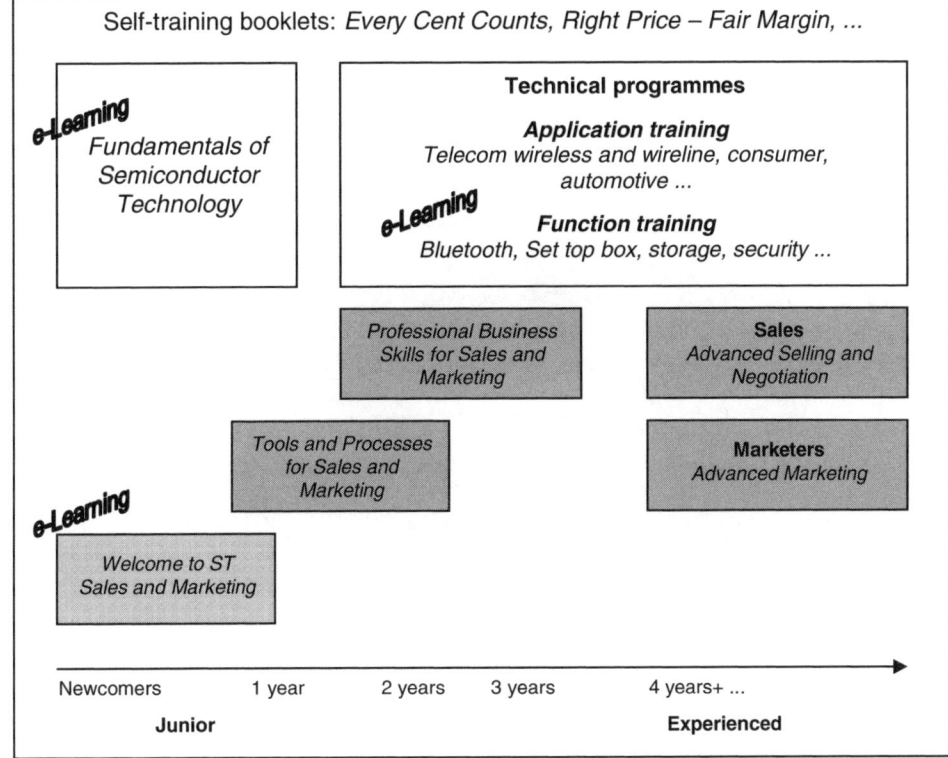

Figure 7.5   The ST Schools of Sales and Marketing curriculum

Conclusions

Many years ago, training was a function covered at each company site, locally. We were in the era of fully localized training. Then in the 1990s we saw a proliferation of CUs, first in the USA and then in Europe.

Apart from the large, well-known organizations such as Motorola University or GE, the term 'virtual university' was often used then to describe in flattering terms what were little more than low-budget organizations ('no-building' CUs) or, more rarely, full web-based virtual universities. In more recent years, we have seen the emergence of many physical sites in the form of modern buildings or 'Chateaux' in Europe. So we saw a move from fully decentralized training, to a virtual world, then to a centralized world.

Today, we believe companies are searching for ways in which a strong central organization can coordinate and work with many localized teams. This is the principle we decided to implement from the beginning in STU. This model avoids the pitfalls of a mammoth central organization, heavy to move, far from the field, yet gives us the benefit of an agile and flexible central team close to the company head and close to the sites, with a solid relationship with both training and operational managers. It allows programmes highly adapted to ST needs with easy and pragmatic implementation.

The network of STU Associate Trainers is an extra added value helping us to deploy large-scale programmes worldwide. They represent our 'virtual' university, delivering three times as many training hours as STU staff can deliver alone. They are the local arms of our company effort, with the training organization playing a facilitation role.

Another way to describe our model is using concentric circles, as shown in Figure 7.6.

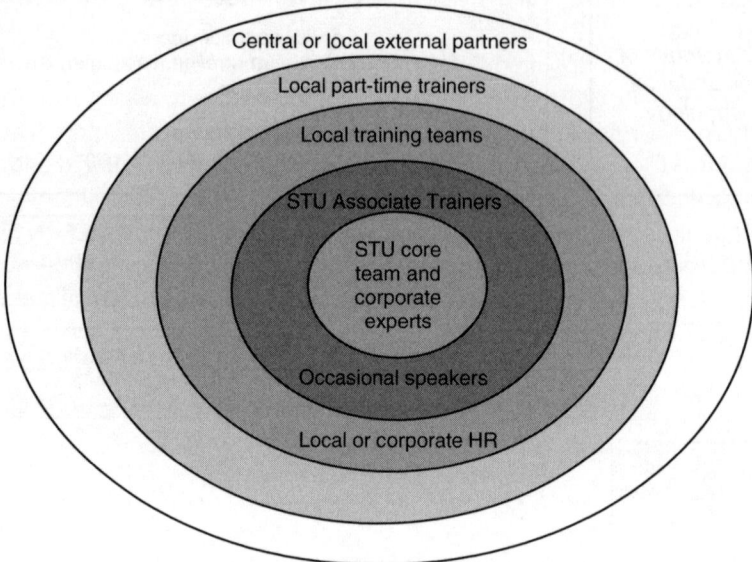

Figure 7.6   The expanding STU networks

Each layer has a specific role in the global scheme and interfaces with other actors in the global chain, from needs analysis to course impact.

As already described, STU core team and corporate training management gather training needs, define the ones to be covered by STU, develop and deliver programmes in some cases, help others to develop content in other situations, and develop the training skills of STU Associate Trainers and speakers.

Our occasional speakers are often senior managers participating in sessions to share experience, explain specific strategies and actions, and also to get direct feedback from participants on their perception of the business and of the current development of the company.

STU Associate Trainers, who are more formally trained and certified, are our ambassadors, deploying and organizing training sessions locally with the permanent support and coaching of local training organizations.

Local training and HR teams are our relays at local sites identifying local needs, entering into dialogue with us and local management, helping set priorities and selling company-wide programmes.

Some part-time trainers are not formally certified by STU. However, our objective is to work with local sites to give these trainers all the necessary tools to become STU Associate Trainers and improve their pedagogical skills.

Managers and experts are also key actors in the service chain. They are there both as support to define needs, as course participants, as speakers, as trainers, as coaches and as training promoters. They verify and give feedback on the course efficiency and effectiveness.

Finally, we work with external partners to maintain a balance between our insider view and outside one, mixing practice and theory. These partners are all fully integrated in our training process, and criteria for mutual benefits between them and ST have been set. We help them to increase their knowledge of ST, working closely with them to customize programmes to our business when needed. This gives them insider knowledge with an outsider perspective.

In conclusion, the service model we have put in place balances and integrates the concerns of the corporate centre and diverse local units. Within it, all actors in the learning chain have their own roles to guide ST to become a learning organization. The balanced service model suits ST – a large multi-site, multi-cultural corporation. Tailored to the business needs of ST, it gives us the necessary global vision thanks to a strong central function and the active participation of all members of our service chain. It promotes flexibility and pragmatism thanks to a strong local training team close to the field. It allows us to avoid bureaucracy, focus on speed of execution and efficiency, and reach our global audience.

8 *Doing Business with Business Schools*

Raymond Madden

Introduction

Almost every university now has a business school. Over 750 are listed on http:www.bschool. com and almost every week the *Financial Times* profiles a business school story. Business schools have three main activities: qualifications (for example Masters of Business Administration (MBAs)), research (which is probably the least well understood by outsiders) and executive education, which is mostly non-qualification in focus. It is important to recognize that research drives the agenda of most business school faculty members and their career structure. Research often goes unnoticed by corporates as it is promoted through highly specialized subject-specific journals and disseminated via academic libraries. Undertaking research and responding to corporate development needs creates real tensions in many schools, as they require very different skill sets. Sadly, relatively few faculty members are able to operate effectively in both markets.Those like Michael Porter, who have managed to transfer theory into corporate practice and sell their ideas, are highly successful. Corporates still find schools too academic and most faculty members have difficulty in making their research relevant to practitioners. This creates a real market opportunity for schools that can effectively run programmes for corporate executives and service their needs.

The business school executive education market and how it links to the corporate university (CU) is the focus of this chapter. In many spheres corporates are moving to partnerships – is this also happening with business schools or are relationships becoming more fluid and less formalized? If there were strong links between schools and corporates one might expect a significant cross-over in talent from one to the other. In this chapter we will look at how ABN AMRO currently manages it relationships with business schools. In the Netherlands ABN AMRO, the largest Dutch bank, established its Academy in the late 1990s and since then it has been joined by CenterParcs, Heineken and the ING Barings Business School.

The marketplace

Most corporates recognize the role that business schools play in training and developing MBAs. Whatever the market conditions, good graduates and MBAs will always be in demand. As Matt Barrett, CEO, of Barclays sees it, 'the quality of management – that is where sustainable advantage lies'[1]. The MBA market continues to grow, although the majority are focused around regional needs. In Europe only a handful of programmes are truly international, that is, where the majority of students originate from outside the country in which the school is located. This is not only a European phenomenon, as most US schools supply local demands with the exception of the elite schools like Harvard, Columbia and MIT.

Partnerships between traditional business school competitors now provide new courses for those that can afford it. Not one but two degrees are available in the case of the Executive MBA (EMBA) from London Business School and Columbia. New York University Stern School, London School of Economics and HEC in Paris have a three-way link via 'Trium'. These programmes are not cheap, not surprisingly, given their global reach. The EMBA from London Business School and Columbia costs US$112 000 and the Trium degree is available for US$92 000. However, both provide a unique learning experience with elements of the course being offered on different continents.

The tailored executive education market continues to burgeon. Most schools offer open enrolment programmes where corporates can send individuals for personal and professional development. Schools that operate in this market raise about 50 per cent of their executive development revenues in this way. The more lucrative market comes in the form of bespoke development for individual corporate needs. The extent of tailoring depends very much on the demands of the corporate and the flexibility of the school. Business schools charge from £9000 per day at Cranfield School of Management in the UK to £20 000 at London Business School and nearer €35 000 at INSEAD for a tailored programme. Other continental European business schools tend to charge less: ERASMUS in the Netherlands charges between €8000–14 000 per day depending on seniority of faculty members and has total revenues of €5 million per annum. IMD in Switzerland charges €23 000 per day and is probably the largest provider of tailored programmes in Europe. Programme development charges are extra and IMD requires corporates to join their learning network. *Business Week* estimated the traditional business schools' share of the executive market to be $800 million.[2] A general overview of how business schools operate is described by two UK journalists who interviewed a number of deans in the USA and Europe.[3] A recent benchmark study, undertaken by the Centre for Creative Leadership in the USA, estimated the entire training budget of 12 large European-based companies to be about €85 million. The Financial Services sector was one of the biggest spenders on training in recent years. The market size for leadership development alone for companies in the *Financial Times* 'European Top 500' list was estimated to be €105 million.[4]

Schools are attempting to differentiate themselves in the marketplace. The majority are university based, allowing faculty to generate additional income from teaching executives. Turnover from such activities is generally small as it is not core activity. Some schools now receive so little state funding that they have developed a significant executive education business. For example, London Business School receives only 15 per cent state funding and earns revenues of some £20 million from its executive education portfolio of open and customized business. About 20 per cent of the 100 faculty members are actively engaged in executive education activities, as research is the key driver for the school. In contrast, executive education is the main focus for Ashridge Management College in the UK, which has 80 full-time faculty members and 90 associates. All faculty are involved with teaching executives and the school's consultancy business is growing. The school has a well-established MBA, but does not have degree awarding powers or a large research capacity. The resulting annual turnover is in excess of £27 million making it one of the largest UK-based corporate suppliers.

With a market of this size you might expect a high level of sophistication over the purchasing decision. The reality is somewhat different. Not all corporates go to Columbia in the USA, which has been rated by *Business Week* as the top executive education provider over the last three years. There are now 105 business schools of varying quality in the UK alone and another 20 key players in Europe. The top five schools in Europe get regular requests for executive programmes from corporates but have to turn down a significant proportion of business. Requests are often viewed as being too mainstream or uninteresting to the faculty or demand simply exceeds supply. At the same time other schools are competing aggressively for work. Reputation matters when it comes to buying a bespoke programme for most companies. It is not unusual for corporates to ask up to five schools to pitch for a single programme. I once had to submit a proposal along with 14 other schools, consultancies and independents for a mainstream management development programme for a UK company.

One of the most effective suppliers of executive leadership programmes is not a business school at all. The Centre for Creative Leadership (CCL) in North Carolina has been so successful that it is the only non-business school to be ranked in the top 20 'schools' by *Business Week* magazine.[5] CCL offers a range of open and bespoke programmes that are world class in the area of leadership. The centre is recognized as having one of the most extensive research databases in the world of executive performance and is used by many corporates to benchmark staff.

Although business schools operate in a mature market, they provide a small proportion of corporate development needs. Many organizations send only senior managers or top teams to business schools. This leaves a large development market, which is currently filled by consultants or small training companies. If business schools had the flexibility to do more bespoke work they could increase their share of corporate training budgets considerably.

CUs see their role as commissioning work and managing suppliers in a cost-effective way. Business schools often see corporate universities as re-branded training departments. Although this may be the case for a minority, most are strategically positioned to enhance business performance through tailored development. The growth in CUs suggests they are here to stay and business schools will need to work creatively to add value to CU agendas.

Corporate universities in Europe

A significant number of CUs now exist in European-based companies with France appearing to have the largest number to date, which includes Alcatel, Axa, Bombardier, EADS, Schneider Electric, Suez, Thales and Vivendi Universal. The strong tradition of education in France provided by *grandes écoles* along with state-regulated training may explain why CUs appear to flourish.

In Germany BMW, DaimlerChrysler, and Siemens have formalized CUs and Deutsche Bank has recently established an operation in Frankfurt. Lufthansa used its CU as a major vehicle through which it successfully changed its corporate culture. Michael Hauser, head of the CU at Lufthansa, is a keen advocate of accrediting CUs along the lines of EQUIS (European Quality Improvement System) accreditation for business schools. The European Foundation for Management Development (*efmd*) in Belgium is developing formalized accreditation criteria for CUs/academies (see Chapter 12).

In the UK, BAE SYSTEMS had a very high-profile launch with the appointment of Geraldine Kennedy-Wallace as Vice Chancellor of its virtual university. Prior to her appointment she was Vice Chancellor of McMuster University in Canada. Barclays, BT, Egg, Lloyds TSB and Unilever have joined BAE SYSTEMS in establishing CUs. Both Barclays and

ING Barings in the Netherlands use the label 'business school' to describe their particular CU. Some facilities are virtual, while others, such as Unilever, have 27 training sites.

The focus at ING Barings is the top 500 senior executives of the bank, whilst the Barclays Business School is focused entirely on its retail operation, providing individual training budgets to all staff. The Barclays Business School is described in more detail in Chapter 6 by Scott Taylor, John Rogers and John Storey. A review of CUs across Europe can be found in 'Corporate Universities in Europe', by Renaud-Coulon.[6]

No dominant model exists between the many CUs in Europe typified by the senior management focus at ING Barings to the focus on all retail staff at Barclays. Multimedia helps Barclays offer a range of products to its staff through a small number of learning hubs located throughout the UK. Most CUs are still in their infancy but the profile is such that more and more, both real and virtual, are being established.

Who runs corporate universities?

With the relatively short history of CUs in Europe the question arises as to who runs the university: academics that understand pedagogy or experienced line managers who understand the nature of the business? The main driver for most CUs is the ability to transfer learning into having immediate business benefits. Ultimately their goal is to increase shareholder value by upgrading the skills of the staff in a more cost-effective manner than external training. Surprisingly few academics or business school faculty members choose to practice what they preach in the classroom. They prefer to act as independent consultants to corporates, rather than work for one particular company. In order to gain academic credibility, BAE SYSTEMS appointed Kennedy Wallace when they launched their virtual university. Similarly, General Motors appointed Tatsuhiko Yashimura, a former professor at Kyushi University in Japan, to the new post of quality professor at its reliability initiative in Detroit, though Yashimura is no stranger to car plants having spent 32 years with Toyota before retiring in 2000. Linda H. Lewis, who is the Senior Vice President of Learning and Education at Charles Schwab, has significant line expertise as well as having been for ten years a tenured professor at the University of Connecticut.

The trend of appointing academics appears less prevalent in Europe than in the United States, where CUs are more developed. The criticism laid by many business schools is that CUs are merely re-branded training departments and therefore most likely to be led by line managers. This may have some validity when the majority of staff employed by a CU provide purely administrative support. However, there is evidence that this is changing and that academics are being asked to lead CUs in Europe.

Royal Dutch Shell hired Michael Osbaldeston, formerly Director of Ashridge Management College in the UK to the newly created post of Global Head of Learning at the HR corporate centre at Shell International. After two years in the post Osbaldeston recently returned to a new academic post as Head of Cranfield School of Management. Recently Tom Cummings joined Unilever as Global Head of Learning having spent a number of years at IMD and as an independent consultant. On a personal note, I joined ABN AMRO as I wanted to see first hand how a European financial services organization undertaking radical restructuring would implement change. Key to this transformation is the introduction of a value-based management approach to enhancing shareholder value and how this can be achieved through learning and development.

Not surprisingly the talent exchange is two way, with a number of high profile company executives moving to universities and business schools. One of the most recent was John Thornton, former co-chief operating officer at Goldman Sachs, who joined Qinghua University in China. Goldman's hired Steven Kerr, former Dean of Faculty at the University of California, and more recently Chief Learning Officer and Vice President of Leadership Development at GE.

The exchange of talent is a signal that the CU market is starting to mature. Many corporates still have a preference for putting experienced line mangers in charge of running their educational operations. Bestowing academic titles on line staff appears more popular than hiring experienced educators who understand pedagogy. Corporates have to ask themselves whether they really are exploiting the power of learning and development as an enabler of strategic change by putting line managers in charge of learning.

CASE STUDY 8.1

ABN AMRO ACADEMY

ABN AMRO's Academy was established in 1997 sponsored by the managing board and, in particular, the late Michael Drabbe. Peter van den Acker, the first Academy director, recalls that funding was very easy to obtain from the managing board as the idea had such widespread support.

After restructuring in 2000 (see Figure 8.1), the bank re-focused what had been a group-wide Academy into two separate academies sharing the same facility. The retail bank training function delivers programmes in Dutch in the Netherlands, while the wholesale (WCS), – investment banking – provision operates on a global basis. This reflected the separation of the bank into three strategic business units (SBUs), each with its own profit and loss accounts. The Academy has a physical presence in South East of Amsterdam occupying 1500 square metres, which includes dedicated classrooms, breakouts and a trading simulator. The WCS Academy has six full time-dedicated faculty members with a mixture of line and business school expertise structured to offer advisory support and training to specific lines of business.

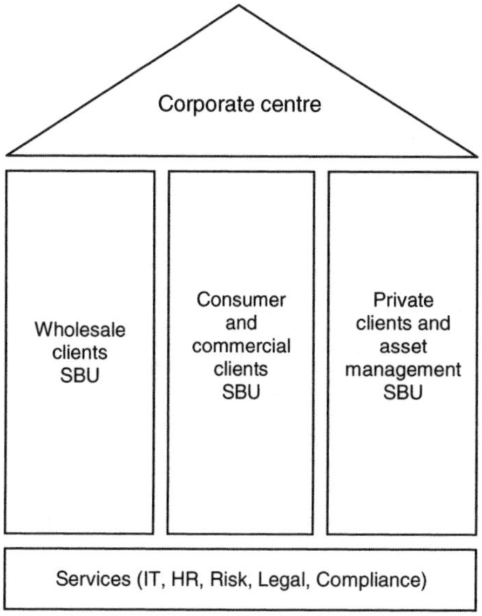

The WCS Academy is focused around business unit needs and offers:

- Needs analysis
- Programme design and development
- Delivery of tailored solutions by internal faculty
- Partnership and management of externals to deliver programmes
- Marketing of programmes internally
- Evaluation of programmes to Kirkpatrick levels 2 to 3
- Assessment and utilisation of technology-enabled solutions
- Client training and an International Banking Certificate.

Figure 8.1   ABN AMRO group structure

CASE STUDY 8.1 – *continued*

About 20 per cent of the total Academy training is spent on graduate development. A seven-week highly intensive programme for the wholesale business is designed to allow new hires to hit the ground running when they join the business. In its early days, the Academy had a strong technical finance focus. This broadened to include a portfolio of management development programmes tailored to business needs.

The Academy currently offers over 75 technical finance courses alongside 15 management skills/management development programmes. Each year, over 2000 WCS staff (about 12 per cent of the total) attend a programme. Numbers are rising as e-learning takes off and the portfolio of programmes expands to reflect business demands. In order to optimize alignment of advisory activities with the business, the Academy is structured as shown in Figure 8.2. The way we interface with human resources (HR) and line managers is depicted in Figure 8.3. The advisory role is key to influencing the development needs across WCS.

All the in-house trainers are experienced wholesale bankers who are also able to design, develop and teach on technical finance programmes. They are popular in the classroom as the 'war stories' and practical experience bring a session on bond maths or interest rate derivatives to life. This is an aspect business school faculty members often find difficult unless they have spent time in the industry. Due to the dynamics of the wholesale business, the lifecycle of a typical development programme is around 90 days, recognizing the rapidly changing landscape created by the financial markets.

Business unit relevant experience is crucial if internal faculty members are to gain credibility of senior management and colleagues in the classroom. The virtuous circle of line experience–teaching–advisory is key to our operating model. Some 60 per cent of programmes are outsourced to a small number of retained suppliers who develop tailored solutions to suit our business needs. Many have worked with the bank over a number of years. The ability to manage our suppliers and consultant faculty from business schools is a strength that we have developed. The relationship is beneficial for both sides: the bank gets leading edge thinking from the world's top schools at more competitive rates than going to the schools directly, while individual faculty members can use ABN AMRO as a possible research site. A longer-term aim is to write and develop ABN AMRO case studies, for use internally and to share the innovative approaches of WCS with MBA graduates through the European Case Clearing House, Cranfield University.

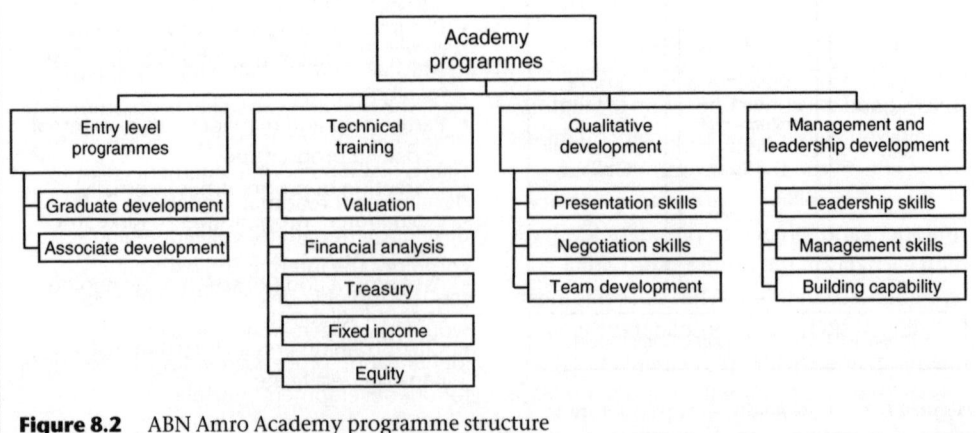

Figure 8.2   ABN Amro Academy programme structure

CASE STUDY 8.1 – *continued*

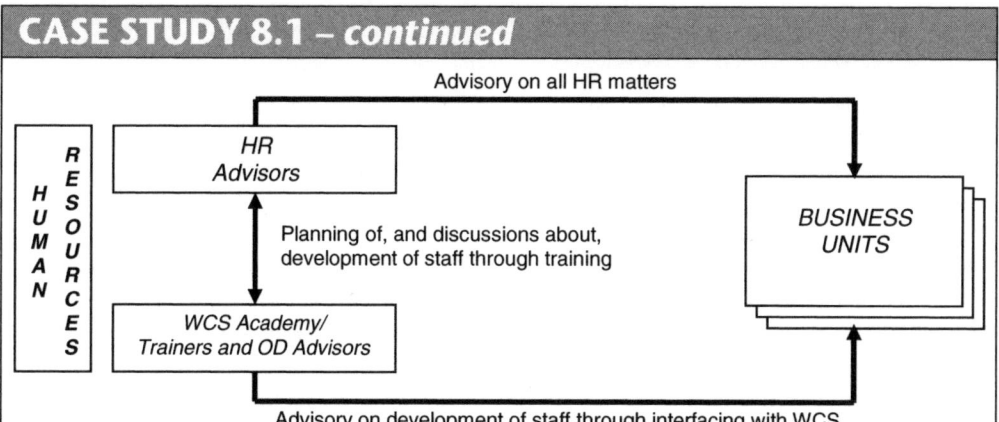

Figure 8.3   Structure of HR

The Academy is part of the HR function within the wholesale bank and has historically operated as a cost centre. However, by optimizing resources internally and utilizing resources externally we now operate as a profit centre even though our programme prices are a minimum of 50 per cent cheaper than the external marketplace. Aggressive cost management is partly responsible for this but our supplier-partners also recognize the challenging market conditions currently faced by investment banks and are keen to work with us to achieve a win–win relationship. An overview of operating CUs as a profit centre with Sun Microsystems as a case study is described elsewhere.[7]

Some of the best business school professors can be hired directly for US$ 5000 per day, about 25 per cent of the cost of going through the executive education departments of the schools directly. The key part of making this strategy work is that external faculty networks are required to select good executive education facilitators. Facilitation skills are key for faculty members to be effective in the classroom. On our Building Capability programme run at vice president and senior vice president level, we end each day of the programme with a workout session titled 'What does this mean for ABN AMRO?' This consolidates the learnings and enables participants to debate how we can use the ideas to increase our competitiveness in our chosen markets.

Our in-house faculty are in the learning and development business, so we require that they undertake some personal learning themselves. They also take a train-the-trainer course offered by Ed Jones – a US-based consultant – to help hone their facilitation skills. Being back in the classroom is useful in that it reminds faculty of what it is like to receive, rather than deliver, training and what works when it comes to learning and development.

A recent focus by the wholesale bank on management and leadership development has provided an opportunity to integrate thought leadership in the areas of market differentiation, strategic thinking, leadership and value creation. By using action learning, that is, business improvement projects, we can extend classroom learning to the workplace. We are building up a collection of business initiatives that have resulted from the building capability programmes to help create products and new solutions for clients first hand. A management development roadmap signals the development path for colleagues and combines the internal and external sequencing of courses, which historically would have been ad hoc. A talent identification process provides a better focus for our development portfolio.

CASE STUDY 8.1 – *concluded*

By engaging our clients in Academy programmes, we showcase ABN AMRO expertise and build a stronger bond. By canvassing the training needs of emerging market financial institution clients, we designed and developed a four-week international banking certificate with over 150 attendees in the first year of operation.

Client relationships have experienced measurable benefits and new business opportunities as a result of being in the classroom together. Clients, like colleagues, have access to http//www.abnamro training.com anywhere in the world to allow them to peruse the training catalogue, download readings or book online.

A new operating model

Typically, CUs draw up requests for proposal (RFP) and ask a number of business schools and suppliers to respond. RFPs are often ill-defined or use terms such as 'leadership' or 'change management' very loosely. Corporates are convinced that this approach invites a broad mix of ideas and recognizing the complexity of the market place helps them to make a more informed decision. School resources are very frequently constrained and respond by seeing which faculty members are available to act as programme director, and then assemble a group of faculty that will involve both experienced and inexperienced executive education facilitators. If a corporate wants a particular high-profile faculty member, they may be disappointed to find that a sabbatical is in progress, or they are already working with a competitor, or that they are simply unavailable due to other commitments. Business schools prefer to resource programmes with their own faculty to maintain their revenue streams. The reluctance of schools to outsource teaching to other business schools' faculty is due to their desire to maximize their own brand awareness. This is surprising since in a typical research-led school, only about 20 per cent of faculty members would be experienced executive education facilitators.

Many programmes that are run for corporates by business schools fulfil the basic development needs. After all, they are built around the corporates' RFPs. Recently, a friend who manages a training function at a UK company sent me an outline of a programme and list of faculty that had been put together by one of the world's top schools. She was asking me to critique the proposal and asked for my views regarding the faculty list. By going to one of the better schools, she is assured a level of quality control. In reality she is buying the brand name of the institution and the old adage 'no one got fired for buying IBM' comes to mind. My response was that the gurus were not included in the faculty list but my assumption was that she had not asked for them by name. About 25 per cent of the faculty listed were inexperienced executive educators but had a strong research record. Academia is the only field where experience in one area that is, research, is synonymous with being a good executive educator. In reality, the converse is often the case.

On the other hand, many schools provide corporates with leading-edge thinking and first-class executive educating facilitators. I can still recall the late Sumantra Ghoshal, formerly of INSEAD and then the London Business School, casting a spell over a group of executives when he compared the hot humidity of Calcutta during monsoon time to the fresh forest of Fontainebleau in spring, and related this metaphor to organizational change and to organizations having their *own* smell.

For the uninitiated, the following may help in getting a degree of clarity from a business school response to a corporate need:

- Who else are you working with in our sector?
- Why have you chosen this particular programme director?
- What cross-cultural and consulting experience do faculty have?
- What faculty have you sourced from other schools?
- I have read something by Professor X, will he/she be teaching on our programme?
- I have never heard of Professor Y, which other corporates is he/she working with?

These questions can help deepen the partnership between corporate and business schools if answered honestly.

The ability of in-house faculty at ABN AMRO's Academy to design and develop programmes provides the bank with development solutions that are: focused around the pressing needs of the business; cost effective, as we choose which external business school faculty and suppliers to work with; and opportunistic, as we are able to work with thought leaders and executive development professionals who are experts in their respective fields.

We do this by approaching faculty directly rather than by going to the executive education departments of business schools. Our core competence is the ability to source faculty and suppliers ourselves. Depending on seniority, faculty charge between £1500–5000 per day. This is clearly more cost effective than going to schools that charge from £4000 to 20 000. Additionally, our sourcing model allows us to attract a broad mix of faculty from a number of institutions globally. You might think that this sounds fine, but what happens if I am unsure which faculty to use? Academics are increasingly advertising themselves on the Internet, which can be a useful starting point.

Help may be at hand. Organizations like Management Centre Europe in Brussels and Clariant Corporation in Boston provide off-the-shelf faculty input through both open and customized formats. Another consultancy, Immersion Lab (http://www.immersionlab.com) operates a similar service in Canada and the Netherlands.

The Learning Partnership (http://www.tlp.org), run by John Sanders, develops executive programmes, leveraging off their access to faculty at the top schools built up through their speaker's bureau business. They offer a package that is more cost effective compared to going to the schools directly. A similar service is offered by Robert Dick, former Head of Executive Education at Judge in Cambridge, through Executive Education Europe (http://www.executive-education.eu.com), a small consultancy with design capability that can source top-flight faculty and other contributors though its virtual network. Dick has used his business school expertise to create an effective, alternative model for corporate custom programmes.

Some business school faculty operate as consultants. Gary Hamel, at Strategos, and Charles Handy are probably two of the most high-profile former faculty members at London Business School. Hamel's reputation means he can charge day rates that are significantly higher than leading consultants such as McKinsey.

Corporates are increasingly using independent consultants as programme directors of internally run development programmes. Both ABN AMRO and BAE SYSTEMS operate this model effectively. Increasingly, corporates are asking consultants to put together consortia of companies in non-competing sectors. For example, ABN AMRO partnered with ABB, BHP Billiton and Boeing in a global leadership programme. Eight senior managers from each organization were selected to attend. The similarities and dilemmas facing these companies post-September 11 are very similar and participants value highly the ability to share ideas with non-competitors through open dialogues. Using the geographical reach of the partner companies, the programme runs in three regions of the world, attracting faculty and industry speakers from Asia, Europe and the USA. Three one-week modules are held over a period of six months and include an action-learning project as an integral component of the programme. During the weeks together, participants spend time working on their company project supported by their respective company executive committees. Sponsorship from main board level reflects the strategic importance of the projects. Participants work within their groups to refine their ideas and present them to the partner companies at the start of the next module. The consortium plans to expand to its regional and sector breadth by including Benfield Group in the UK, PanAsia Paper in Singapore, Tata group in India, Unilever in the Netherlands and Standard Bank of South Africa. A number of other companies are asked to challenge and present ideas to the partner companies. These have included Johnson & Johnson, Cisco, Westpac, and PricewaterhouseCoopers, while PanAsia Paper described how a family-owned business manages its strategic challenges.

The idea of consortia is not unique but the model of using consultants to manage the operation on behalf of the corporate partners is. This provides an effective and flexible programme format. The interest of the companies is managed through an executive committee, which has an extensive network of faculty and speaker contacts. Business schools run a number of other consortia, with the school often dictating the content with relatively low levels of influence from the corporate partners.

An extension of the consortia concept would be to include clients with the view to better understand the drivers between supplier–client relationships. This would help break down the often formal relationship that exist and provide true business partnerships.

Business school deans are not particularly happy about these developments and some, such as IMD have imposed restrictions on faculty to preserve their 'competitive space'.[8] Peter Lorange, President of IMD, asks a key question facing schools today: 'What school can survive having its best faculty hired away?' As a result IMD now restricts the number of sessions individual faculty members can do privately for corporates. The governance of IMD allows for this to be a workable solution to cherry picking. However, although faculty elsewhere tolerate some restrictions, as they benefit from the branding that schools provide, the IMD approach is unlikely to be enforceable in most other schools. Experienced executive education educators are in demand and are mobile.

Conclusion

Success in revenue generation suggests that many business schools are doing most of what corporates want. Learning and development solutions are becoming increasingly sophisticated, having to respond, for example, to the development needs of intact teams in a particular business operating unit. The flexibility required by many corporates creates real tensions for individual faculty members. Business schools increasingly demand that faculty undertake research and publish annually, teach MBAs, supervise doctoral students, direct academic programmes, manage the school and allow time, usually 50 days per annum, to undertake private consulting. This creates an onerous burden on many faculty members.

Executive development revenues for schools have strong growth plans, with some expecting to quadruple revenues over the next five years. If this aspiration is to become a reality, schools must offer corporates first-class development rather than be beholden to their institution's revenue generating plans. If schools were more creative about the solutions they designed and developed, more business would come their way.

The onus is on corporates to work with business schools, to ask the right questions and provide the appropriate challenges to encourage faculty to be more customer focused. One business school dean commented that managing faculty is like herding cats, attempting to describe the competing demands on faculty time and their differing intellectual interests.

Schools need to educate corporates that faculty are engaged in research, teaching, consultancy, administration and management of the institution and that they are not available 24/7. Schools should continue to attract the best faculty and have a strong research focus with a view to generating new ideas that are intellectually rigorous but relevant to the needs of business.

Business schools will always be a source of talent and thought leadership for corporates. Charismatic presenters like Tom Peters, Charles Handy and Gary Hamel are not what business schools want to be known for. They see their role as generating research that will impact corporates in the long term rather than through short-term business dilemmas.

The traditional model of a custom-made one-week programme that comes from Columbia or INSEAD is rapidly disappearing. The challenge for schools is to be flexible, responsive to corporate needs and more open about where faculty input comes from. With this better executive education, corporate universities and business schools will result.

Notes

1. 'The quality of management – that is where sustainable advantage lies' says Matt Barrett, CEO, Barclays, in Peter Graham (2003), *Management development – making it work?* White paper, Cranfield University.
2. Schneider M. and Hindo, B. (2001) 'A mid career boost', *Business Week*, 15 October: 110–114.
3. Crainer, S. and Dearove, D. (1999) *Gravy Training: Inside the Business of Business Schools*, London: Jossey-Bass Wiley.
4. Centre for Creative Leadership (2001) 'The executive education market in Europe'. Available from <http://london.ccl.org/cclcommerce/index.aspx?catalog10=home>.
5. *Business Week* (2002) 'Recruiters like their grads' experience and language skills, which proved useful in a tough global climate', Special Report, 21 October.
6. Renaud-Coulon, A. (2002) 'Corporate universities in Europe', in M. Allen (ed.) *The Corporate University Handbook*. New York: AMACOM.
7. Moore, J. (2002) 'Running a corporate university like a business: A financial model', in M. Allen (ed.) *The Corporate University Handbook*. New York: AMACOM.
8. Lorange, P. (2002) *New Vision for Management Education – Leadership Challenges*. Oxford: Pergamon.

9 *Working with E-learning Suffpliers*

Perry Williams

Introduction

The publication of resources is a moment of truth for any e-learning programme. You can spend time, effort and money designing your strategy, establishing the information technology (IT) infrastructure, preparing people to accept the change and promoting e-learning – which are all vitally important things to do. But what will people find when they click on the 'e-learning' link? Will the resources be any good? Will they tell their colleagues to come too, or not to bother? Ultimately, an e-learning system is only as good as the learning it delivers.

So how do you make sure your e-learning resources work? This chapter draws on seven years' experience (both my own and that of colleagues at Learning Materials Design – LMD) of advising and developing e-learning resources for government departments, leading corporations, major charities and universities. In other words, it is written from the viewpoint of a specialist provider, with a good sense of what someone newly involved in commissioning e-learning resources might need to know.

The chapter starts from the point at which you have made the decision that e-learning resources – perhaps 'blended' with face-to-face training and computer-mediated communication (see Chapter 13) – will be the best way to deliver certain areas of training and development. The first section of the chapter is about the basic questions of aims and methods, the second section deals with managing the development process, and the third section gives some guidance on costs and timescales – and what you as a commissioner can do to keep them under control.

Aims and methods

THE BALANCE OF AIMS

Even if you think you know what you want, it is important to work through the implications as thoroughly as possible with everyone concerned, to make sure that when you get what you asked for you are not disappointed. To begin with, what do you want to achieve with the resources? It may be that your aim is a short-term one; perhaps some resources need to be put in place quickly, to prove the concept, to justify the investment, or to set a standard for resources to be developed later; or perhaps your organization has an immediate training need that it hopes to meet through e-learning. Perhaps your aim is a longer-term one, for example to shift the organization to an e-learning culture or to improve the quality of performance management. Or you may want to develop certain resources quickly to meet short-term needs, but in such a way that the collection can be expanded to fulfil a longer-term strategy.

Establishing this will help to clarify what kind of resources are most important to your organization and what will count as a successful resource in your particular case. It is also useful for clarifying how much, or how little, e-learning resources can do in themselves. For example, if the managerial aim is to effect a cultural change, you may need to remind other people and yourself of what any reputable developer will confirm: that e-learning resources can only *support* a change; they are not in themselves sufficient to create it.

DIFFERENT TIMES, DIFFERENT PRIORITIES

In the late 1990s, the UK Department for Education and Employment (as it then was) had just invested in an e-learning system that was intended to be something of a flagship among government departments. The Department was getting a good range of generic off-the-shelf e-learning resources from NETg, but it also wanted to show how e-learning could address the Department's specific needs and circumstances, so it commissioned LMD to develop a set of resources on performance management – which was a high profile issue internally at that time, as part of the 'modernizing government' agenda.

The initial aim, therefore, was to make a major impact. In view of this, it was agreed to use video clips of specially produced drama, which pushed the technology hard, requiring some ingenuity to make it work within the network constraints. The resources had the intended impact, and although the video playback involved download delays, this was an acceptable trade-off for what was going to be presented as an innovation. When the Department asked LMD to revise the resources in 2001, however, the priorities were different, and it was decided to replace the video with still photos and audio, grabbed from the screen image and audio track. It was now not so important that the resources be high-impact, but more important that they be robust.

See also Rob Watson (2002), 'Seeing the wow factor', *E-learning Age*, March: 20–22.

THE BALANCE OF COST, QUALITY AND TIME

In any development project, there is a balance to be struck between cost, quality and time. Put bluntly, you can probably get what you want with one or maybe two of these, but you need to be prepared to compromise on the other. If you want to develop e-learning resources really quickly, you should expect quality to suffer (because there is not time to make all the checks you would otherwise do) or the price to rise (because it is not possible to do it in the most cost-effective way). If you want something really high quality, you need to be prepared to pay and to spend a long time over it. And if you want something really cheap, you should not be surprised if it is not all that good and it takes a long time (because it may be difficult to persuade people to give it a high priority). What you *cannot* have is something that is 'cheap as chips', world class, and delivered tomorrow.

This balance between cost, quality and time is another issue to clarify as early as possible. It is likely that one or another of them will be fixed, but this actually makes planning easier because it introduces definiteness. If you yourself have no idea what balance you want, working with developers – internal or external – will be more difficult. Some of the most unhappy projects on which I have worked were those where the commissioner insisted on a tight timescale but could not appreciate the implications of this for quality; only towards the end of the development did they become nervous about what others might think of the resources, and so committed more time and money to reviewing and revision. In fact, quality was more important to them than time, though they could not see this at the outset.

Quality is often difficult to discuss, because it can have so many aspects. You can define it as 'fitness for purpose', of course, but that depends on your knowing what the purpose is – another reason for being clear about aims! There are at least five distinct kinds of quality, each of which may be more or less important to you.

- **Acceptability to users/trainees:** All too often this falls at the bottom of the list, especially in organizations that think in terms of 'telling' or 'sending messages to' their staff. However, there are many organizations in which training (including e-learning) is seen as an opportunity to engage people's hearts and minds, and developers will be expected to think about what people want to hear as well as what the organization wants to say. As an educationalist, I am going to add that I think this approach makes for more effective training.
- **Effectiveness:** Or, whether the trainees actually learn what they are supposed to learn from the resources and (a greater challenge) whether this actually makes a difference to their work. Again, traditionally this has come low on the list, because organizations have been more concerned about seeing that training was provided than about making sure it was effective. Happily, this is now changing, partly as a result of the larger financial investments required by e-learning; indeed some organizations are now quite insistent on having a return-on-investment business case for training.
- **Acceptability to the organization:** This can be a very serious matter in organizations with super-powerful communications departments, which insist on policing every corporate external and internal communication for conformity to a corporate message. Other organizations are more relaxed about training resources, unless they are covering a particularly sensitive subject.
- **Accuracy:** No-one will ever admit that accuracy is unimportant to them. The real question is: how much time and money are you willing to put into checking? How much checking will be 'good enough'? Mistakes of spelling and grammar may be irritating, but on the whole no-one is likely to lose their job as a result.
- **Production values:** Or, how good the resources look and feel. Professional work (writing, design, photography, audio recording, video recording, acting) on the whole looks better than amateur work; but for some purposes, amateur work (*good* amateur work) may be sufficient. It really depends on who is going to see the resources and what their expectations are.

THE BALANCE OF SOURCES

There are four basic ways you can get e-learning resources: you can buy them ready-made, off the shelf; you can adapt existing e-learning resources; you can transform the content of other modes of training delivery (for example, printed resources, face-to-face classes); or you can develop them from scratch. You will probably want some balance of the four.

Buying a copy of a resource that someone else has developed will almost certainly be cheaper than developing it yourself. The problem with off-the-shelf resources, of course, is that they are necessarily generic, so they cannot include a lot of organization-specific detail; they may use a different terminology to the one you use, or they may simply feel 'foreign' (for example, from a different industry sector). But before rejecting an off-the-shelf resource that suffers from these problems, it is worth considering whether it could still be used in conjunction with an explanatory resource or study guide. (Some examples: 'Work through Sections 1, 2 and 3.' 'Ignore Section 4, because it is irrelevant to our industry.' 'In Section 5, what they refer to as a *wimble*, we call a *dubrey*.' 'Section 6 includes a case from the Financial Services sector. What would be an equivalent case for our business?') It takes significant time to make a detailed review of an existing e-learning resource and to write a study guide; but even allowing for this, the cost is still likely to be much less than development from scratch.

Some generic e-learning resources are deliberately designed and built so that they are easy to adapt or customize to an individual organization's needs. Others are built in ultra-modular form, with the intention that the constituent 'learning objects' can be reused in different combinations, particular objects being added or subtracted according to need. This allows for customization of content, but is not much help if there is a particular overall message or vision that you want the resources to convey.

DESIGNING FOR CUSTOMIZATION

When environmental consultants Casella commissioned LMD to develop an e-learning resource on health and safety for Cassella to distribute to their own clients as part of their training services, it was vital that the resource be easy to adapt or customize to an individual organization's needs.

The resource that LMD produced allowed for easy 're-painting' in the client's corporate colours, changing of words on screen, and the addition of extra screens – though not radical alteration of the basic structure.

For a close fit to a specific organizational requirement, resources need to be tailor-made. As with clothing, bespoke development is a more expensive option, but you can expect to get something that will fit you precisely. If you already have a face-to-face training course that can be transformed or printed resources that can be adapted, this simplifies matters, of course. However, you should beware the temptation of jumping to the conclusion that 'there's not much more to do'.

- The transformation may be more difficult than you think; successful face-to-face training, subtly tailored to those present, may be hard to capture in a static resource, and even effective print resources may not work well on screen (again raising issues of quality).
- The existing material may be less complete than you think; casual estimates of how much content can be reused are always over-optimistic.
- The existing material may be less good than you think; or, more subtly, what was fine for a training course delivered face-to-face behind closed doors may *not* be fine when expressed in cold text for anyone in the organization (and possibly outside it) to see.

As a general rule, transforming or adapting existing material for e-learning always requires more development-from-scratch than anyone anticipates at first.

THE BALANCE OF PEOPLE

There are three kinds of people you can ask to develop the resources: subject matter experts or trainers, external e-learning developers, and in-house e-learning developers. In many cases, you will want to involve two or even three of these, and establishing and managing their roles will need to be part of the development process. You will want to involve subject matter experts when there needs to be specialist or technical content to the resource. The difficulty is that your experts may not have the skills to translate their subject knowledge into e-learning and write the content of the resource. The most difficult case is when they *think* they do (and they may indeed be good at writing briefing documents, lecturing to an audience or even conducting participatory training sessions), but in fact lack a sense of how to enable people to learn from a resource. Unless subject experts already know how to write learning resources, or are willing to learn extremely quickly, often the best thing is for them to provide raw source material to developers, be available to answer questions, and check the draft resource for accuracy – in other words, acting as quality assurance.

External developers will need to be involved if there are skills you cannot bring in any other way: for example, learning design, educational writing, design, coding, audio-visual production. External developers (or at least, some members of the team) will need to be able to grasp the subject matter and learn the organizational context, as well as to adjust quickly to your culture and ways of working.

In-house developers will almost certainly be cheaper than external ones, as well as probably more familiar with the organizational context and possibly the subject matter. You also have the management advantage of keeping lines of communication short. The disadvantage of in-house development is that you are limited in the skills, experience and breadth of vision you can call on, so what you are able to develop may also be limited. One way of getting the best of both worlds is to have external developers work alongside your in-house people initially, taking the opportunity to build your in-house skills, so that you are ready to take over maintenance and updating.

USING EXTERNAL DEVELOPERS TO BUILD IN-HOUSE SKILLS

When Oxford Brookes University was appointed by the UK Department for Education and Skills to deliver a national training programme for school coordinators of provision for gifted and talented children, the course team asked LMD to help them develop a way of teaching a master's-level course on what was for them an unprecedented scale. With the lecturers, LMD designed and built an e-learning website, incorporating course materials, conferencing in tutor groups, individual tutor email support, and an ever-expanding collection of resources. Having been supported through the development of the first materials and the initial population of the site, the course team now creates new resources and manages the website entirely themselves.

Whatever combination of in-house and external people you use, you are going to be putting together a team of people from different worlds and ways of working. Developers do not necessarily understand content, subject matter experts do not necessarily understand e-learning, and none of them – even if in-house – necessarily understand the context of use. All you can do is to choose people who have as much understanding of the other areas as possible, to minimise the possibility of conflict and misunderstanding between them, or quite simply to reduce the time necessary for them to learn and respect each others' way of thinking.

The development process

Different developers have different methodologies for project management, and so have different preferred processes. Many come out of the software industry and adapt the project management methodology used in software development – so, for example, there may be intensive specification and documentation, with many iterative loops for testing and refinement. Some developers with a multimedia or web-design background are happier with a looser methodology, and prefer to plan content around 'storyboards' showing roughly the relation of onscreen elements – essential for resources that are highly visual or graphical, although resources that are primarily verbal will probably still need a conventional editorial approach of planning and drafting text. Other developers (and I put myself in this category) have a background in education rather than IT, and their project management gives an important place to learning design and the specification of learning outcomes.

You and your developers will need to agree some kind of project management framework, based on what is usual in your organization and what is usual for them. If your organization normally uses a highly detailed methodology for large-scale commissioned work, you may find that you can abbreviate it somewhat. However, you will probably want to include all the aspects listed in here in some way, in some order.

SPECIFICATION

One benefit of working out a written specification as a first stage is that you and your developers have a shared document to which you can refer back later in the process, and against which you can record agreed changes to the plan (which will probably be necessary). Another benefit is that you have an opportunity to flush out and resolve tensions between stakeholders, rather than having them erupt later at an inconvenient moment. Effort expended in planning is never wasted; as when building a house, certain things (such as the number of storeys, the position of the toilets) need to be fixed early on, because they cannot be changed later without expensive alterations to the fundamental structure (the foundations, the drains).

Here are some of the things that it is important to include in a specification document or to record in some other way:

- the rationale for the resource (its overall aim and purpose, its position within the training strategy or e-learning strategy, relation to any other projects, the immediate and secondary uses of the resource, arrangements for updating);
- profile of learners/users (demographics, educational level, experience of IT and e-learning, how they will be directed to the resource, likely learning environment);
- learning outcomes (what you want the learners to be able to do, or to do better, after study of the resource);
- learning model, or instructional design (how the content is going to help the learners get to the outcomes – for example, through viewing presentations, through action and interaction, through reflection, through assessment);
- scope and outline content (in sufficient detail to establish what is in and what is out, perhaps including a draft structure);
- media (text, photographs, graphics, audio, video, interactivity) and estimated quantities (which is a fundamental determinant of cost);

- IT specification (including characteristics of both network and server, and end user machine);
- evaluation process (when and how you will evaluate the resource, and against what criteria);
- development process, with the people involved (for example, subject matter experts, reviewers, IT, corporate design, user representatives, trainers, senior managers for sign-off), and a view of the critical path;
- resources required (access to people, access to documents or collections, access to locations);
- schedule (including milestones and review stages);
- budget (or other system for cost allocation and control);
- risk analysis (what could go wrong and how the risk can be controlled – not everything can be anticipated, but the discussion is important for building trust and confidence that unanticipated problems will be resolved together).

You may find the biggest challenges come in discussing the scope, learning outcomes and media, because this requires everyone to imagine what the resource will be like on the basis of a plan. (This is at least as difficult as imagining what a film will be like on the basis of a script.)

SPECIFYING THE TRANSFORMATION OF A FACE-TO-FACE COURSE

BT commissioned LMD to develop a 15-minute online course about branding, based on their existing face-to-face workshop, which normally lasted half a day. Despite the disparity in the timings, both parties agreed that this was a workable specification: in the e-learning environment, the workshop content would actually be more effective and have greater impact with its users if boiled down to its essence, rather than being reproduced at full length. Even though the quantity of content was apparently reduced, the e-learning resource was judged equivalent to the face-to-face training, in terms of the learning outcomes achieved.

DEVELOPMENT AND REVIEW OF CONTENT

Except for the shortest of resources, it is wasteful of both time and effort to allow all the content to be written and assembled before it is reviewed. Here are some examples of better ways of developing content, which allow major changes to be made early before a mistaken direction is followed too far.

- **Lead module:** Developing one module or section of a resource first provides a model or template for the remainder.
- **Three-C process:** This applies mainly to text. The first draft is reviewed for Content or Coverage (is the right material present?), the second draft is reviewed for Communication (is the style and tone right?) and the third is reviewed for Completeness (is every detail correct?).
- **Key assets:** This can apply when a resource is organized around certain key assets – for example, learning activities, case studies, or scenarios. Developing and reviewing these first avoids wasting time on wrap-around material for assets that will never be used.

- **Point of no return:** Some types of content – notably video clips or interviews – are sufficiently expensive that their capture cannot be repeated, so marking a point of no return. The implication of this is that all aspects that can be reviewed in advance (for example, the video script, the interview protocol) need to be checked ultra-thoroughly.

If your developers have been through the specification stage together with you, what you receive from them should not be wildly different from what you were expecting. Those reviewing the content, however, if they have not been part of the early process, may misunderstand the nature of the resource, the status of the draft sent to them or what they are being asked to do. Whenever the briefing of reviewers is skimped (for anyone with significant involvement, I would say it should be done face to face), you are liable to receive review comments that are inappropriate to the resource (for example, they really want it to be about something else) or to the stage of the process (for example, suggesting a radically different learning model when they were only expected to make a final accuracy check). Such misunderstandings can, of course, be repaired, but usually only with embarrassment for the commissioner, who may have to disregard comments because there is no longer any way to incorporate them, and resentment for the reviewer, because they spent time writing comments which will not be used.

DEVELOPMENT AND REVIEW OF DESIGN AND TECHNICAL OPERATION

If you have an existing design and technical template in which to work, you can probably skip this stage of the chapter. If not, then you need to be aware that design and technical operation are so closely bound up with content that you will probably be developing them all roughly simultaneously. Content authors need an idea of what spaces they are aiming to fill and what technical functions will be available; and you will want an idea of how the resource will look and feel and work. All these are reasons why you will probably want design and technical development to start as soon as the designers and coders have sufficient exemplar content to work with.

As well as generally 'looking good', you may require the design to meet criteria such as:

- conformity to corporate design style, or any specific style for e-learning materials;
- usability – being easy to use, with a clear and intuitive interface and navigation devices;
- accessibility – being usable by people with disabilities, including visual impairment (now a legal requirement in the UK, unless alternative provision is made);
- technical inter-operability with other systems – for example, a learning management system, if you have one, or more simply the organisation's intranet.

Probably the biggest danger when developing design and technical operation is creeping ambition. It is easy to think, as a resource starts to take shape, 'let's have it visually rich', or 'wouldn't it be great if it could do this other technical thing' – and this is a temptation for developers as much as for commissioners! But extra graphics cost time and money, and technical additions may or may not be simple. This is a stage at which it is particularly critical to work out carefully the implications of extensions to the specification.

PROTOTYPES AND PILOTS

Unless your resources are being developed to an existing model, you will probably need to have specific stages at which you test technical aspects on a prototype version or check how learners will react to the resource (a pilot). There are just two rules for this kind of test:

- be clear about what aspects of the resource you want to check, so that your developers can make sure the prototype or pilot version actually includes them and you can brief your testers or pilot group accordingly;
- leave yourself enough time and resources to do something about any problems you discover!

You might want a prototype to test:

- navigation and interactive elements;
- interoperability (for example, with databases, learning management system, other online resources);
- streaming media;
- cross-platform compatibility;
- compatibility with assistive software (for example screen readers for the visually impaired).

You might hold a pilot to check:

- the product concept, perhaps including the learning model and media mix;
- accessibility, for standard and disabled users;
- acceptability (of content, expression, design);
- usability (for example, the clarity of navigation, interface, instructions);
- learning effectiveness.

A large pilot group may give complex or contradictory responses, and you will need to make decisions about which of them require action and what that action is to be. For example, it sometimes happens that a few piloters are completely hostile to the resource and you need to decide whether the resource is really fundamentally unsound, or whether their responses are just due to cynicism or misunderstanding. You may also want to consider what the responses would have been to comparable face-to-face training.

FINALIZING ASSETS AND BUILDING

At some stage, the developers will probably take away the 'assets' (text, graphics, any audio-visual material) into a (metaphorical) workshop to put them all together, and the next thing you see will be a complete product that hopefully needs only small-scale adjustments.

It is important to try to keep your hands off the resource during the 'build', to avoid confusion between different versions of the assets. The developers handling the assets at this stage may be excellent web designers and coders, but they are not necessarily excellent at keeping track of changes to content assets of which they may have no understanding and perhaps even no interest.

The ideal is to get all assets finalized and signed-off first, so that the build is just a matter of pouring approved content into approved designs. Where that is not possible, it is usually better to keep any further amendments on hold and not to try to implement them until after the build is complete.

CHECKING, TESTING AND INSTALLATION

The first built version of the complete resource ought to come as no surprise if your review of the content and design has been sufficiently thorough, but even so there will be many things to check, such as:

- implementation of the design (does material appear in the right place in the right style?);
- text accuracy (has any text been left out? Have any errors been introduced? is all punctuation, capitalization and so on in house style? – though this last should really have been checked before the build);
- interactivity (are all links correct? do all interactions work? do all media play?);
- interoperability (does it work on the server on which it will run? does it exchange information correctly with its database? does it work correctly with the learning management system?).

Some of these checks can only be made when the resource is installed in its final location and if it is at all complex there may need to be several technical adjustments before it works correctly.

Before handover is completed, you will want to have the developers document how the resource was built and archive the assets used. This will be helpful (perhaps essential) if you later want to update or modify the resource.

EVALUATION AND REVIEW

After the resource has been in use for a few weeks or months, you may want to evaluate it in some way. At the simplest level, you might find out how often the resource has been used, and by what kind of people. You may also have some kind of survey form attached to the resource, or delivered by the learning management system, to gather basic information about learner satisfaction.

Such forms – the equivalent of 'happy sheets' distributed after a face-to-face training session – should tell you if anything is seriously wrong with the resource; but response rates tend to be poor, and they can only provide the most basic measure of training effectiveness. If you really want to evaluate the effectiveness of the resource, you will need to have learners take some kind of post-study test to see how much training they have retained, or have their line managers report in some way on how much their training has improved their work.

After six months or a year, you may want to review the content of the resource to check that it is still relevant and to see whether any updating is needed. Minor changes to text should be simple; alterations to significant graphics or audio-visual assets are likely to be more difficult and expensive. Some of this can be avoided by careful attention at earlier review stages – for example, in video, avoiding references or images which date the material too precisely!

Costs and timescales

Enough of the why and how; you also want to know what it will all cost and when you can have it.

If you want an accurate quote, you will need to have a precise specification, or to work one out with your developer; you cannot expect to get a precise figure otherwise. But if you only want a very rough estimate of the cost, there are only two really significant variables: the size of the resource (that is, the quantity of material to develop) and its complexity (the media types, the interactivity, the extent to which the content is open-ended). Some developer companies publish costing guidelines based on just these two variables, and working from these, at the time of writing (early 2005) the industry standard seems to be:

	Cost range per study hour, for 3–5 study hours (not including taxes)
Simple resource – text and simple graphics on basic web-pages, no interactivity (except menus and links)	£6000–15 000
Interactive resource – complex graphics, complex content, simple audio, simple interactivity (for example a few standard types), including export of tracking and test data to an existing system	£20 000–30 000
Multimedia interactive resource, including audio and video, and more complex interactivity	£35 000–45 000

The above table needs a few words of explanation.

- 'Study hours' are one way of specifying quantity of material. The length of a resource, in study hours, is the time it would take an average learner (average, that is, for your target learner group) to work through all the material. Naturally learners may skip parts, or the resource itself may direct them to different sections; but the development cost will depend on the total quantity of material to be developed.
- With a resource that genuinely promotes learning, as distinct from simply providing information, the learner will be spending as much time thinking about the content as reading or viewing it; so, for example, in a text resource you might estimate the length in words as what can be read at an average speed in half the study time.
- Some developers prefer to cost in terms of 'numbers of screens' – which is fine for resources consisting of a large number of screens that are relatively similar, as long as you know how much material goes on one of these screens.
- Unless you are developing a new resource on an existing model, there will be initial start-up costs as you work out what one of these resources is going to look and feel like. For this reason, the first 'study hour' is more expensive to develop than subsequent ones – perhaps as much as double the cost. The figures above allow for that, and are average figures for around 3–5 study hours.

The single most expensive element of a resource, if you choose to use it, is likely to be video. A long-standing industry estimating guideline has been £1000 to produce a minute of finished video material. (For a standard television documentary, the cost per minute might be £3000; for television serial drama, it might be £8000; and for advertising, it might be £100 000 or more.) The actual cost will depend largely on the number of locations at which you film, the number of crew and cast (if you are using professional actors), the complexity of the material, the production quality at which you are aiming, and the total quantity of video material (a small number of minutes will inevitably cost proportionally more than a larger number).

How long does development take? Clearly, it can take as long as you like, although be aware that a development spread over time may cost more because of the costs associated with putting down and picking up the work. More relevant is the minimum time required. From my experience at LMD, I would say you should not expect to develop something from scratch in less than three months – unless the project is unusually small, simple and straightforward in some way.

Developers can only write, design and code so fast, but that is not usually the limiting factor. It is possible to save time by dividing the work among more people – although that introduces additional risks of quality, and more work is needed to make sure the various pieces are consistent. The limit is usually in the development process itself, and in particular the number of review cycles and (with the best will in the world) how fast commissioners can review, comment and approve material. With a minimum of four review stages (specification, first draft, second draft, complete build), and allowing one week for review at each (ambitious in most organizations) and a further week for meeting and deciding what action to take as a result of the review, that adds up to two months immediately, even before allowing any time to create the material!

Thinking about the e-learning development projects LMD has been involved with over the years, I would say that the four biggest risks to a project's cost and schedule are:

- unfocused ambitions, leading to poor initial specification and gradual creeping extension of the project – hence the need for regular careful review;
- source material proving to be unavailable or (more typically) not as useful as was anticipated, requiring time and labour to make good the shortfall – all you can do is to have this checked as early as possible;
- unavailability of key people at critical stages (for example subject matter experts or senior managers for review and sign-off) – precise advance scheduling may help, but the best intentions may not suffice if the schedule slips;
- too many stakeholders trying to control the project, especially those who come in late – hence the need for careful briefing and for limiting consultation to specific aspects at each stage.

All these are essentially the same risks to cost and schedule as you would find in any substantial project. They do not arise from the nature of e-learning. It should be reassuring to know that, whatever else may be new and strange, in this respect at least the challenges you are facing should be familiar!

Conclusion

What should be evident by now – if you were not already aware of it – is that developing e-learning resources is a significant investment of time and money. For that investment, you will want to be sure that you get what you want – and your best chance of getting this is being clear about what that is. Good developers, whether in-house or external, can help you achieve that clarity, by showing you options, exploring alternatives, working through implications. And that is what I have tried to do in this chapter, outlining the different aims you might have, the combinations of people and resources you might want to use, and the processes and problems you might go through to develop your resources.

I have aimed to summarize the range of possibilities and issues with sufficient detail to make them clear, which may have made this chapter feel complex. In your own situation, you will be able to concentrate on those that are relevant to you. As I hope has been amply illustrated, e-learning resources are not just one kind of thing. Successful development begins with working out which of the many possible alternatives will be right for you and your organization.

Acknowledgements

Thanks to Jane Wolfson and my colleagues at LMD, and to our clients over the years – from all of whom I have learned so much.

10 Reviewing and Reporting Results

Rob Paton

Introduction

> Training evaluation is a bit like eating five portions of fruit and vegetables a day; everyone knows that they are supposed to do it, everyone says they are planning to do better in the future and few people admit to having got it right.
>
> *(Tamkin et al., 2002: ix)*

As with any other unit or function, those responsible for a corporate university (CU) need information to help them manage staff and activities internally, and to report to the board or sponsoring directors externally. Three aspects of the CU context may make this more than normally challenging.

- The results of many training and development programmes are hard to measure and may arise only in the medium or longer term.
- CU activities are often a meeting place for a wide range of stakeholders with very distinct perspectives, concerns and professional languages (and national cultures, indeed). These may include the full range of business disciplines: practically all levels within the organization, from relatively junior staff in business units up to the corporate board; and various specialists, including e-learning technologists, trainers, academics, instructional designers.
- They operate in turbulent environments, so the goalposts are on casters.

Training evaluation is now a field of expertise in its own right represented by specialist consultants. This chapter will not attempt to summarize their know-how, in terms of the relative merits of different methods and instruments. It is not offering a recipe book or manual. Instead, it aims to provide some maps of the territory – a rapid overview highlighting key terms, approaches and debates, along with some pointers to resources. Hopefully the frameworks will assist newcomers to the field in thinking and talking with colleagues about the choices and challenges – and perhaps help clarify when, why and how one might usefully commission a consultant.

The chapter starts with approaches to the evaluation of particular programmes and then widens to broader issues of financial return, and the contribution of the CU as a whole. A running theme is both the importance of measurement and the huge costs and difficulties involved in capturing key dimensions of CU performance in a systematic way. A solution to this is to take measurement *seriously* – but not *literally*.

Evaluating courses and programmes: Kirkpatrick's levels and beyond

For nearly 50 years Kirkpatrick's four levels of evaluation have provided a fruitful and convenient starting point for anyone charged with evaluating a training programme (Kirkpatrick, 1959, 1996). This approach has been criticized and debated, to be sure. But other models are all additions, elaborations and alternatives to Kirkpatrick – no-one ignores this seminal contribution. The four levels are shown in Table 10.1.

Table 10.1   Kirkpatrick's four levels of evaluation

Level	What it refers to	How it might be measured
1. Reaction	What trainees think about the programme at the end, and perhaps during it	'Happy sheet'
2. Learning	What has been absorbed, in terms of new knowledge, skills and attitudes acquired	Individual performance test
3. Behaviour	Changes to workplace practice, resulting from the programme	Line manager's observation; self-reporting
4. Results	Business and organizational benefits arising from the new workplace behaviours	Relevant measures of business performance

Evaluations at levels 1 and 2 are commonplace and relatively straightforward. For obvious reasons, things get trickier at levels 3 and 4, and these are the areas where much recent effort has been directed. For example, if you want to be able to demonstrate that a course on 'people management' is leading to positive differences at level 3 (behaviour), you will probably need to carry out a focused, 360-degree appraisal of participants, preferably before the course as well as after it. This is administratively challenging, to say the least. For this reason, software and online services that will largely turn the gathering and processing of such data into a routine exercise are now becoming available (more generally, new information and communication technologies offer opportunities for cheaper, more convenient and often more reliable ways of obtaining and processing relevant data on all four levels).

To appreciate some of the criticisms and debate surrounding Kirkpatrick, it is helpful to view these 'levels' in terms of the underlying causal model (see Figure 10.1). One set of arguments points out that the model needs to be extended backwards and forwards – it takes

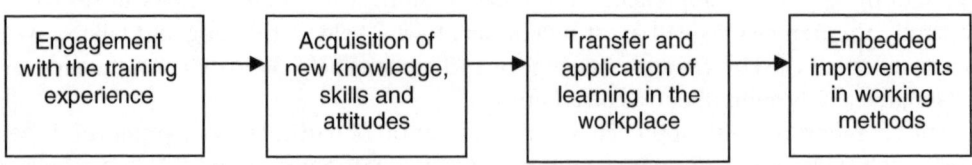

Figure 10.1   Kirkpatrick's levels as a causal model

too much for granted, and doesn't go far enough. Thus, it has been argued that training really starts with a business need and/or training needs analysis, or that one should assess the training inputs not just the process. Likewise, several authors, of whom Phillips (1994) is the best known, have argued that Kirkpatrick's approach needs a fifth level, concerned with the return on (training) investment (ROI).

A second set of concerns focuses on the crudity of the underlying model: it is pointed out that context matters and many other factors may intervene or influence whether, and to what extent, a training programme leads to the desired outcomes. For example, trainees may not like parts of a programme, although these are still necessary and effective. Likewise, a host of factors – often well beyond the control of the trainers – may prevent (successful) individual learning from becoming embedded in improved working methods (Tyler, 2004). These points are entirely correct, but whether they constitute a criticism of Kirkpatrick's levels is doubtful: arguably, the model implies that success at the preceding level/stage is *necessary* but does not claim it is *sufficient*. Indeed, one could turn the criticism on its head: the levels are useful precisely because they highlight where difficulties and failings may arise. Thus, for example, moving from level 2 to level 3 involves the application of generalized principles or techniques to the ambiguities and conflicting pressures of practice, and thus requires a great deal more *situated* learning (for which peer and trainer support may no longer be available).

Finally, Kirkpatrick's approach has been criticized for being narrow; it assumes a discrete, off-site, training intervention aimed at producing specific, testable outcomes. Such events have their place, of course. But it is not at all clear whether and how it might be applied to broader, longer-term, more developmental and workplace-based initiatives, such as action-learning, coaching, or extended leadership development programmes. These are now hugely important features of the training and development landscape, and one for which a distinction between levels 2 and 3 may not even arise (all the learning is within the context of use). Arguably, a more open-ended, reflective and participative approach, involving participants in a dialogue over time, is likely to provide more insight into the aspects of a programme that have lasting impact and the diverse ways in which benefits can arise.

Such criticisms cannot be ignored. They point towards useful embellishments and to important, if challenging, issues. Nevertheless, *if* training is being evaluated – and usually it is not – then the basic Kirkpatrick model is still by far the most widely used (see, for example, Bassi and Cheney, 1997). Apart from its undoubted simplicity, the key reason for this is probably the way the four levels relate directly to the different contexts in which decisions may need to be made about the efficacy of training activities. Information regarding levels 1 and 2 will always be required by those responsible for the design and delivery of training, in order to gauge, especially in its early 'runs', whether and how well a particular programme is working, and where modifications may be needed. Trainers will also be very concerned about level 3, because it is here that they stand or fall, as regards satisfying their customers – those who requested and sponsored the training for their staff. However, these customers – the line managers or those who express their requirements – are the ones who will be best placed to draw together information to judge and interpret the degree of success at levels 3 and 4. In other words, training evaluation is too important to leave to the trainers. Indeed, to be effective, trainers *require* well-informed customers.

The chimera of return on investment

The literature on the management of training is peppered with claims about the financial return on training expenditures. For example, Motorola University used to claim that every dollar it spent on training generated thirty dollars of productivity improvements over the following three years (for example, see the *Financial Times*, 3 April 2002). IBM was widely quoted as achieving a 2284 per cent ROI from its investments in e-learning (Nucleus Research, 2001). In the UK, BT calculated that £7 000 000 investment in training brought a £280 000 000 return over a six-year period (Bee and Bee, 1994). Because they involve making a large number of assumptions, such claims are always debatable (and some are simply specious). The principal difficulties fall in the following areas:

- Many of the strategic benefits sought through the training and development arranged by CUs – building a common culture, leadership development – are diffuse and will arise (if they do arise) in the longer term. Identifying these is hard enough, even without assigning monetary values.
- Establishing a meaningful benchmark – for example, what would have happened without the training? – often adds to the difficulty, though solutions are sometimes possible. The Boeing Leadership Centre was able to show that work groups with more Leadership Centre graduates showed statistically better ratings in a large-scale survey of employee attitudes and satisfaction (Mercer, 2001).
- Training is usually one element in a bundle of changes – new processes, new software, a new product, the creation of an ongoing community of practice, and so on. The financial benefits are therefore *co-produced* by a complicated combination of factors. Attributing them all to the training, however necessary and effective, is clearly misleading; but any 'share' will be arbitrary and contestable.
- The direct cost of training is the easy bit and often a small part of the whole. It is likely to be swamped by the cost of the time of participants, though this is often ignored. With more workplace-based forms of learning, 'training' and the job itself inter-penetrate, affecting the way it is carried out and interactions with managers and colleagues.

Given these difficulties, some major companies – of which GE is the best known – take the view that the whole idea of measuring learning and its benefits is misconceived and a distraction. Interestingly, according to Mercer (2001), the Boeing study referred to above was only possible because it was undertaken in the early years of the Leadership Centre when establishing its credibility was a priority for all involved. However, as an ex-GE man, he looked forward to the time when everyone at Boeing would, as at GE, 'just believe in it', and they would not have to divert resources into measurement.

Another way of looking at these difficulties is in terms of the distinction between routine management information and the findings of occasional research studies. Although formidable, none of the obstacles outlined above could not, *in principle*, be overcome by using a sufficiently sophisticated research methodology (not to mention a sufficiently large and long-lasting research budget). It is important, therefore, to distinguish between 'good enough', readily-accessed *information* that provides *support* or *evidence* for the business value of training, on the one hand; and *research* to *demonstrate* enduring outcomes in the workplace, or to *prove* the worth of a particular approach, on the other. Used selectively, research can make a unique contribution in settling controversies or moving practice forward. But if it is to be convincing, it may take years rather than months, and it tends to be intrusive and demanding of staff time, not to mention expensive. (Even the Boeing research is open to challenge – the association is impressive, but causation is not proven: perhaps the better managers chose or were chosen to go to the Leadership Centre? And how much were those improved satisfaction ratings really worth?)

The dilemma for many of those managing CUs, therefore, lies in the fact that they often feel under pressure to 'prove it': measurement is petty well synonymous with good management, ROI is a fundamental corporate commitment, and measurement experts can be relied on to berate training and development professionals for not doing more to show the monetary value of their activity (for example, Phillips, 1996; Kearns and Miller, 1997; Spitzer, 1999.). Yet at the same time, these grand schemes all involve practical difficulties, timescales, uncertainties, and costs (not least lots of senior management 'think time') that are all intimidating. As one recent report put it:

> The data demands of such an evaluation would defeat most organisations' data systems, and the rigour of analysis exceed the evaluation skills of most trainers and HR experts. The fact that so few organisations actually evaluate at level four, despite the urging of many, is probably testimony enough to its complexity.
>
> *(Tamkin et al. 2002: 45)*

Hence the pattern of 'perpetual good intentions' – neatly parodied in the opening quotation of this chapter – that marks much of the thinking and practice in this area.

But perhaps this is less a sign of weakness and more a mark of practical wisdom? An alternative view would be that, in the CU context, ROI is a metaphor or aspiration, a core value that has to be remembered and re-affirmed, *especially* when it cannot be easily demonstrated. It is rarely a meaningful and practical calculation, and it is a mistake to assume it should be. So senior executives are right, especially where established CUs operate in companies with strong measurement cultures, to *talk* of ROI and 'bottom lines', even while their reporting *practice* involves much more modest claims and pragmatic approaches. Typically, they rely on supporting evidence in one of four forms:

- **Demonstrating alignment:** Through information showing a direct contribution to the solution of a serious problem for an important 'customer'. Thus, in the BT case mentioned above, the training was (successfully) targeted on improving the decision making of junior managers where it had been established (through critical incident interviews with line managers) that costly mistakes were being made. It is these links, and the evidence that supports them, that makes it a convincing example of valuable training (the ROI calculations may have been useful as a rhetorical flourish, but are icing rather than cake). This is where companies like GE put their effort, treating the evaluation of training as an issue of quality and alignment to need, rather than trying to measure the value of learning outcomes.
- **Calculating savings:** Often these concern the direct costs of training against a previous way of achieving much the same. This is usually important whenever the introduction of e-learning or the rationalization of training provision is a priority.
- **Benchmarking externally:** Either through a benchmarking club, an award or accreditation process; or simply in terms of market prices (one very successful CU simply ensures that it charges its programmes out to business units at prices that are at least 25 per cent below the cost of equivalent provision through a credible business school).

- **Opportunistic measurements:** Seizing on available figures, anecdotes, events and testimonials to illustrate and ground reports on what has been achieved and why it matters (examples of such 'measures' occur in several of the chapters in this book – for example, website 'hits' at BAE SYSTEMS (Chapter 19); reduced turnover rates among alumni from Capgemini University (Chapter 17)).

Taken together, these are vitally important elements in evaluating and reporting on CU activities (which is not to say they are therefore unproblematic). Occasionally it may help to dress up the use of such measures with ROI type calculations; but even this should be done with caution because 'massive ROI … will only encourage financial directors to pick holes in your arguments' (Harrison, 2003). Besides, as knowledge management practitioners increasingly stress, it is stories at least as much as statistics that people notice, recall and learn from. For training evaluation contexts, Pulley (1994) draws on research to argue that even managers who call for hard data are likely to be strongly influenced by qualitative elements. In the end what matters in external reporting are *grounded narratives:* stories about success in meeting key requirements that are underpinned by telling anecdotes and available figures.

Scorecards for corporate universities

The discussion so far has concerned what CUs *do* – how to review and report the programmes and activities they provide. But for those running or sponsoring a CU some important questions also arise at the level of the CU as a whole: how are we, as a continuing entity or network within corporate space, doing? Are we well placed to help address the next shift in corporate strategy? What is our reputation among managers and staff? What dangers lie ahead? CU directors and managers have to consider both these levels – and they will need information to do so. As in any other business activity, it also helps to distinguish the different contexts within which information is used and decisions are made. Thus, regular operational review – are we on course, and doing things right? – requires certain sorts of largely routine and internal information. More intermittent but searching strategic appraisal – are we doing the right things? – is likely to need a wider range of information, including more that is external to the CU (benchmarking).

These two levels and two contexts for decision generate a simple framework for the sorts of information those responsible for a CU will need. These are shown in Table 10.2. Much of what is needed for boxes 1 and 2 has already been discussed. Kirkpatrick's levels 1 and 2 are relevant to Current Results (along with administrative and financial information, of course). Enquiries at Kirkpatrick's levels 3 and 4, along with benchmarking data, would help with judgements about the Underlying Performance of different programmes or services.

Shifting up to the level of CU as a whole, box 3 concerns the monitoring of key risks, the nature of which will vary widely according to circumstances. They might concern financial targets; or the successful introduction of a new e-learning platform; or the risk of breakdown in the relationship with a key business unit customer or course provider. Perhaps most interesting is box 4 where a raft of issues that affect a CU's ability to deliver *future* performance may need to be considered:

- Are physical and technological assets being maintained and upgraded?
- How strong is the internal brand of the CU – is it widely recognized and respected?

- What about its intellectual capital? – the expertise it can mobilize internally and through wider networks to meet new requirements and the shared (tacit) process knowledge of staff and associates in working together to run professional events and support workplace-based learning.
- What about relationships with key stakeholders and partners – are they being renewed and extended? Are new possibilities being identified?

Table 10.2   An architecture for corporate university 'dashboards'

	Context of use	
	Short-term/operational monitoring	*Longer-term/strategic review*
Programme level – what we *do*	**1. Current results** Indicators of current goal achievement and to assist continuous improvement	**2. Underlying performance** Information on how well programmes really work, and what else should be done, as well or instead
CU level – how we *are*	**3. Risks** Information on ways the CU may be at risk (avoiding nasty surprises)	**4. Assets and capabilities** Indicators of renewal or decline – are we building up our capabilities, or are they running down?

These are seldom matters that it is worth trying to capture in routine figures; but there is usually much relevant information to inform discussion within a company's records, or it can be sought in simple one-off exercises. Much will already lie in the minds and memories of those who work with and in the CU – although it may need a reflective occasion (an 'away-day') to recognize its significance and draw it together. Finally, more formal processes, like the Corporate Learning Improvement Process (CLIP; see Chapter 12), can be used to review capabilities (for further discussion of this overall reporting framework, see Paton, 2003 – Chapter 8).

Kaplan and Norton's 'balanced scorecard' may provide another, more familiar, approach to determining, in a structured fashion, the priorities for performance review and reporting. For CUs, this is interesting less for the particular measures a scorecard might involve – as usual, they will vary widely according to context – but for the question this approach immediately poses: what *perspective* on the CU takes pride of place? For companies, the 'top box' in the scorecard – the perspective in which final judgements about success and failure are made – is financial, as in the classic scorecard represented in Figure 10.2. Hence one obvious answer is to use this same pattern for the CU. This effectively makes the CU another profit centre within the company. Intentionally or not, this approach easily leads to the idea of selling spare course places externally and in due course to 'spinning off' the CU as a separate venture – a trajectory that has often been observed, most famously in the Arthur D. Little School of Management.

Doubtless there are contexts in which this has been appropriate and well executed. But it is certainly not the only or even the most likely way of structuring a CU's scorecard. Indeed, Kaplan and Norton (2001) have pointed out that many central service units are better understood and managed as *non-profit organizations operating within a for-profit environment.* Viewed in these terms, final judgements about the success of the CU should be made from

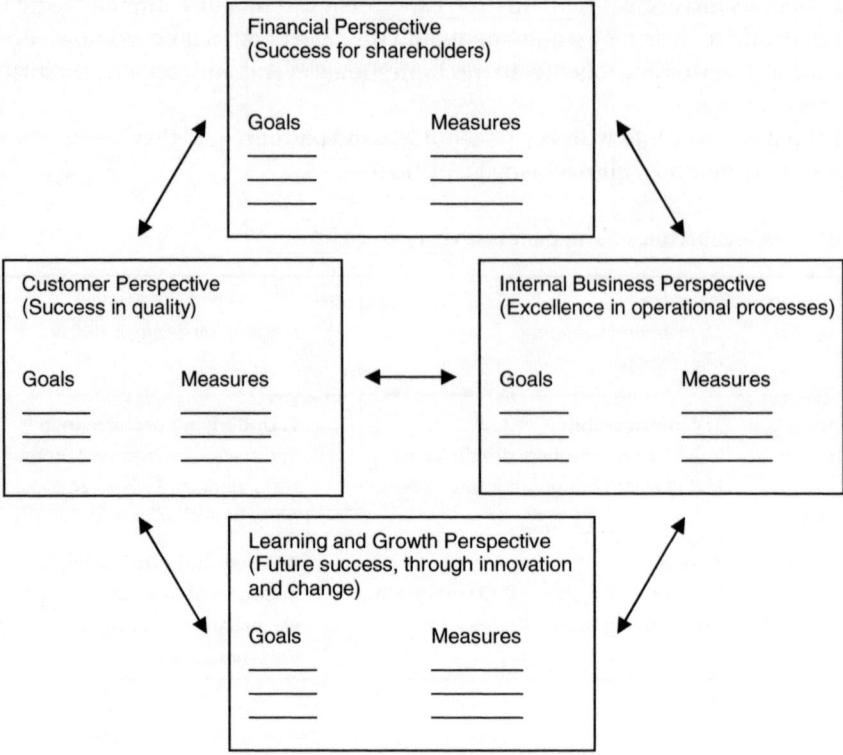

Figure 10.2   The balanced scorecard, after Kaplan and Norton (1996)

the perspective of customer service. This is not to say that the financial perspective and associated measures are unimportant (indeed, financial success can contribute to customer service). But they are not the *raison d'être* of the CU. It is the company's job to make money and the CU's job is to help it do that. Such arguments generate a scorecard on the lines of Figure 10.3. Interestingly, many of the management challenges of CUs – very disparate but demanding stakeholders, a largely professional staff, the separation of customers and clients, the lack of a clear and well-understood 'bottom line' – are immediately recognizable (not to say ominously familiar) to those with non-profit management experience elsewhere.

Conclusions: Taking measurement seriously, but not literally

This chapter has outlined some of the key issues and approaches used in monitoring, reviewing and reporting on the activities of CUs. To continue the theme of fruit and vegetables that started the chapter, evaluation can be likened to an onion. With each layer one needs to ask: why are we evaluating and for whose benefit? what were we trying to achieve? and how can that achievement be demonstrated? On the outer surface are straightforward issues about the evaluation of specific training sessions that have clear and measurable objectives, and where those inside the CU simply want to improve perceived quality. However, as the layers are peeled away and the heart of the corporate university becomes more exposed, the 'why', 'what' and the 'how' change markedly. The evidence needed to maintain a critical and reflective approach to development may be very different

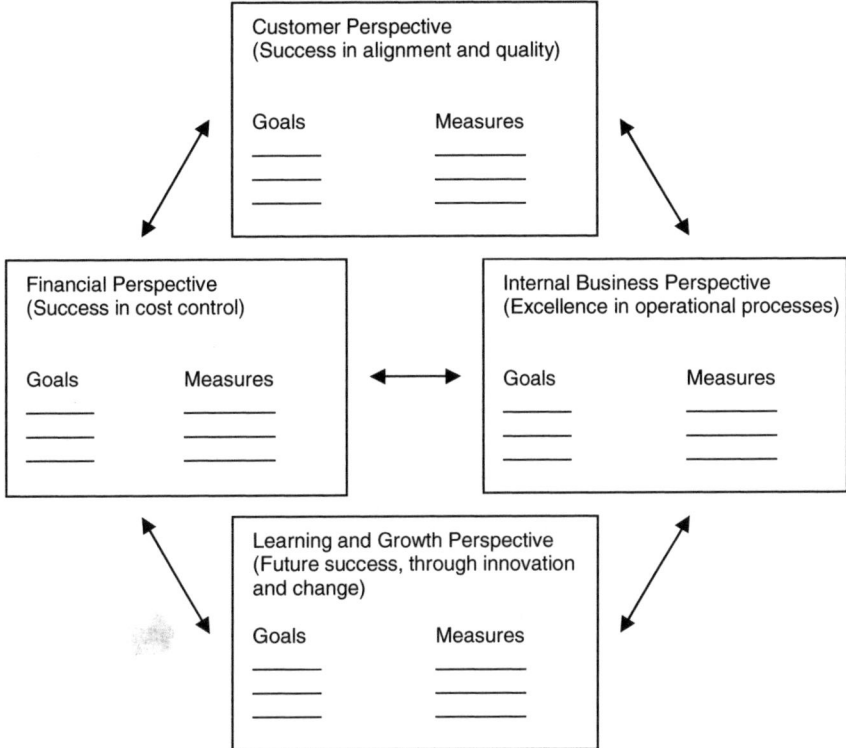

Figure 10.3   Scorecard for a service-focused corporate university

from the support that is required to ensure continued existence. If a CU is to survive and flourish then it needs to be able to maintain the support of its stakeholders, particularly the most influential ones.

The recurring themes presented here have concerned the need for those in CUs to stay close to key customers and sponsors – it is all about alignment. Their demands and expectations will almost certainly conflict as well as shift unpredictably – but that is precisely why these are the relationships that need to be negotiated and renegotiated in a continuing dialogue. For that is how confidence is built and maintained. In this context evidence is vital – and some corporate cultures will expect this to include systematic measurements and high-level indicators of performance. However, the practical difficulties and pace of change mean that those in charge of CUs should be wary of being drawn into grand, over-rational measurement exercises. Focusing attention on the things that matter is essential – and that is the contribution of the frameworks discussed – whether or not it makes sense to put in place formal measurement and reporting systems.

References

Bassi, L. J. and Cheney, S. (1997) 'Benchmarking the best', *Training and Development*, 51(11): 60–64.

Bee, F. and Bee, R. (1994) *Training Needs Analysis and Evaluation*. London: IPD.

Harrison, M. (2003) *Blended Learning in Practice*. Brighton: The Epic Group. Available from <http://www.epic.co.uk>.

Kaplan R.S. and Norton, D. (1996) *The Balanced Scorecard: Translating Strategy into Action*. Boston, MA: Harvard Business School Press.

Kaplan, R.S. and Norton, D. (2001) *The Strategy-focused Organization: How Balanced Scorecard Companies Thrive in the New Business Environment*. Boston, MA: Harvard Business School Press.

Kearns, P. and Miller, T. (1997) 'Measuring the impact of training and development on the bottom line', *FT Management Briefings*. London: Pitman Publishing.

Kirkpatrick, D. (1959) 'Techniques for evaluating training programs'. *Journal of the American Society of Training Directors*, 13(3–9): 21–26.

Kirkpatrick, D. (1996) 'Great ideas revisited: Revisiting Kirkpatrick's four-level model', *Training and Development*, 50(1): 54–57.

Mercer, S.R. (2001) 'Developing human capital and leadership through corporate universities: The Boeing Leadership Centre story'. In *Developing Human Capital through Corporate Universities*, proceedings of the Corporate Universities Conference, 29–30 October, Paris. London: Access Conferences International.

Nucleus Research (2001) *IBM ROI E-learning Case Study – Basic Blue*. Available from <http://www.nucleusresearch.com>.

Paton, R. (2003) *Managing and Measuring Social Enterprises*. London: Sage.

Phillips, J. (1994) *ROI: The Search for Best Practice*. Alexandria, VA: American Society for Training and Development.

Phillips, J. (1996) 'Measuring the results of training', in R. Craig (ed.) *The ASTD Training and Development Handbook* (4th edition). New York: McGraw Hill.

Pulley M.L. (1994) 'Navigating the evaluation rapids', *Training and Development*, 48(9) 19–24.

Spitzer, D.R. (1999) 'Embracing evaluation', *Training*, 36(6): 42–47.

Tamkin, P., Yarnall, J. and Kerrin, M. (2002) *Kirkpatrick and Beyond: A Review of Models of Training Evaluation*. Brighton: The Institute for Employment Studies.

Tyler, S. (2004) 'Making leadership and management development measure up', in J. Storey (ed.) *Leadership in Organizations*. London: Routledge.

11 Partnering Educational Providers in a Developing Country[1]

David Morris

Introduction

This chapter examines what happens after the decision has been taken to implement a corporate university (CU) – local educational provider partnership scheme as part of a strategic human resource management programme. Autoco, a multinational in the automobile manufacturing industry, has long been a leader in corporate citizenship activity, much of it in the field of education. This interest and progressive outlook has continued through the 100 years the company has been trading. Today's management and board remain committed to initiatives that involve workers, adults and secondary school students in a variety of collaborative programmes that always include a humanist component at the core of the curriculum. By humanism, the curriculum states up front that it is whole person oriented and value based, built on an intellectual framework that emphasizes respect for the individual person regardless of creed or gender, and that it seeks to unleash individual human potential. As this chapter outlines, despite this educational principle, the implementation of a partnership between a CU and local educational providers can encounter a variety of real-world obstacles. By analyzing the successes and difficulties involved in this process, a 'road map' of what to expect has been drawn up. Like early exploration maps, there are a number of spaces yet uncharted and areas where the navigator can only remark: 'Here be danger.'

Five years ago, Autoco decided that corporate activity in training and education could be expanded US-wide through a network of curriculum deliverers at secondary school level, using a detailed curriculum that incorporated English, maths, communication skills, economics and 'the world of work'. The curriculum begins from a holistic view of the work, based on classical concepts of the value of learning and work. The participating schools are seen as partners and the curriculum is offered free. Support is also free to the schools, many of which are located in working class or immigrant communities. This method of delivery to around 100 schools at any given time means that around 20 000 students are enrolled, with teachers and support staff committed to delivering the curriculum over a four-year period. There are two major kinds of delivery structure in the USA: 'embedded', into the government funded secondary school curriculum from grades 9–12; or as a weekend school with classes on Saturday or Sunday. Perhaps the greatest unintended consequence of the humanist orientation of the curriculum is the anecdotal evidence that many young people go on to post-graduate studies who might otherwise have chosen diminished career goals.

Senior Autoco managers came to perceive their programme to be a ladder into management and/or the middle class of the USA. Autoco itself does not publicize its support of the project, and the great majority of graduates from the curriculum do not seek employment with the company. The partnership structure, with the CU at its centre, extends through to local companies that offer internships. The learner thus has a wide variety of employment choices on completion and the tools to take advantage of them.

The experiment in internationalizing the corporate university

This chapter focuses on an experiment in the internationalization of this curriculum to an Asian country famous for its large population, large industrial base, poor infrastructure, delayed entry into the global marketplace, frustrating corruption and extremely large groupings of poverty. Although major strides in industrialization have taken place, the rapid growth of global capabilities in communication, transportation, infrastructure and business transaction have continued to leave countries like this one behind in absolute as well as relative terms. The net outcome of engagement there with globalization is that there is a 'creamy layer' of between 2–5 per cent of the population who enjoy the benefits, while the remainder of the population cannot. Those left behind number hundreds of millions of young people, who were thought to offer a natural constituency for the curriculum offered through Autoco.

This notion of bringing the CU and its core curriculum to the country was of great interest to managers working for Autoco for a number of reasons (not least the development of future employees and consumers); a proposal for an international experiment was accepted by the corporate headquarters. Limited seed funding and access to the curriculum was extended to the non-government organization (NGO) of which I am Executive Director. The partnership project was launched in 2000 and went through a series of stages.

STAGE 1: THE FUN OF CONCEPTUALIZATION

As those trained in organizational development know, the most fun in any process is often the 'sketching on a cocktail napkin' at the beginning. In this project, the fun was heightened by cross-cultural issues. Broadly speaking, these issues can be defined as two areas of tension. First, clashes between the values of the corporate entity, those of the local subsidiary and those of the chosen NGO – intra-project team issues. Second, those involving the community outside the factory walls (including language, history, and religion) – ex-project issues. Intra-project issues included all internal politics of the project and funding, while ex-project issues related to the processes of contextualization and implementation in the chosen context. To add to this complexity, intra-project conceptualization had two points of view: the meta-view of corporate management, with the sophistication and experiential breadth of strategic HR managers and the micro-view of the country subsidiary managers, concerned with local happenings.

The primary rule of thumb generated during the conceptualization phase, whether at corporate or local subsidiary level, relates to the intent behind the project and, specifically, the managerial experience of strategic human resource management (SHRM). Those with experience and commitment to SHRM, either through schooling or through experience, were quick to see the advantages of the project to both corporate and local subsidiary levels.

Their intra-project participation was universally helpful. Those who did not have such experience or expertise focused much more on issues of hiring, compensation and benefits, or managing headcount than on exploring the strategic implications of an innovative CU and HR development.

STAGE 2: IMPLEMENTATION

Here, as the popular phrase goes, 'the rubber meets the road'. With the necessary approvals from corporate headquarters, a budget and funding, the NGO for which I work began the process of implementation. With over 50 years of experience in grass-roots organizational development at local levels in a variety of countries, the construction of networks to recruit faculty, learners and partners was reasonably quick and built on the foundation of several other initiatives. There were some delays and challenges in contextualizing the curriculum, written primarily from a North American perspective, but nonetheless progress was rapid. Within three months, the curriculum had been adapted and teaching faculty recruited and readied – with the pace of preparations reflecting in part a sense that corporate support might not last. The cycle of transfers and promotions makes most large corporations highly unstable, especially in relation to long-term community base building.

It was accepted at all levels that the first year would be a pilot year. With this flexibility, faculty began translating the material both linguistically and conceptually, creating learning plans. An appropriate group of learners that had demonstrated willingness to engage was selected from a large number of candidates. Managers at corporate headquarters, within the local Autoco subsidiary and the NGO, all made contributions to the contextualization of the material. By the end of the first nine months, the essential dynamics and issues of such a project had been identified and policy created to deal with obstacles. The issues can be briefly summarized as:

- attempts to influence the management and aims of the initiative by local politicians and other influential individuals;
- maintaining quality in instruction by the faculty;
- coping with weaknesses in local schools in preparing learners to tackle such a curriculum;
- premature ownership by one partner at the expense of other partners.

By the beginning of the first full operational year, the experience gained enabled the creation of an administrative strategy that protected the project by expanding it beyond the range of influence of any one group. Several two-day workshops were held with staff and faculty to reflect on, and try to understand, each issue as it arose, and strategies developed largely through consensus.

STAGE 3: INSTITUTIONALIZATION

This is the stage where plans for standard operating procedures replace the innovation and creativity of the first two stages. The planned timeline for institutionalization was three years; this proved to be reasonable. Institutionalization also offered the opportunity to expand to partners beyond those involved in the pilot project. These included corporations who were interested in acquiring higher-quality workers and managers, governmental officers, and departments of the state educational bureaucracy. These partners were attracted by growing positive word of mouth concerning the project and its activity. By the end of the third year, we could show results that reflected strengths and weaknesses. The project grew to incorporate four partner schools, each with between 1000 and 4000 enrolled learners. This, all in a geographical area within 15 km of the Autoco factory, meant a tremendous boost for the public image of Autoco.

STAGE 4: WILDCARD

This stage is not inevitable or chronological, as any experienced implementers of SHRM initiatives can testify. Rather, it should be seen as a convergence of events. Managers not only have to cope with the wildcard event, but overcome any damage to transform the project into a stronger and more durable sustainable institution. Care was taken by the NGO management involved in the project to make it as robust as possible from the beginning. This project was protected by the following:

- allowing for use of double teams of faculty;
- personal interviews and testing of all potential faculty and staff;
- involvement of the senior management of the NGO as operational staff during the first three years;
- extensive documentation far beyond local requirements;
- high investment in relationship development and cultivation of all senior players, whether intra-project or ex-project;
- viewing and reviewing of successes and failures in similar ventures.

The management of the NGO understood from experience that in corporate and multinational institutions there would be issues relating to making sure the various levels of activity and reporting worked together. This was particularly complex because the project had to be constructed on a triangular structure: the NGO needed to report to, and be involved with, both the home office and the local subsidiary HR department. The NGO is experienced in dealing with such corporate initiatives locally and internationally.

One particular 'wildcard' during this project arose because the Vice President of HR in the local Autoco subsidiary was rotated back to headquarters at the end of her three-year term, during the pilot stage of the project. In stark contrast to her approach, the new HR Vice President began to ask questions of the entire project. She came from a recent acquisition in Europe, perhaps not sharing the values that had led the group managers to support the project initially. With a background of working in relatively hostile large manufacturing environments, she brought a very specific set of skills into a very different cultural and economic context. The previously collaborative approach to education was replaced by questions as to the more immediate and direct economic utility of the initiative. As the next section outlines, the project survived, mainly due to support from other managers within Autoco and active canvassing by local project managers.

STAGE 5: LEARNING TO SWIM

In this case, it might be argued that a number of key dynamics have helped to maintain this project. First, it is possible that much of the force of the change in managerial approach was absorbed by the robust structure of the project. Second, experience in dealing with wildcards helped in evolving tactics to create breathing space and the subsequent development of a strategy to contain and gradually eliminate the manager's ability to negatively impact the initiative. The tactics consisted of open sharing with partners, sympathetic champions at the corporate level, and staff, emphasizing the danger the entire project was in. Those committed to the initiative decided that the most effective route to take was to involve higher levels within Autoco. Third, and above all, we communicated to all supporters and participants that the project would continue, even if the corporate support were ended, through the resources of the NGO. This confidence stopped any erosion of support and the attendant lowering of morale of staff and learners.

Conclusions

From this experience of involving the CU of a multinational in bringing education and training to a host country, and the reflections on it of those involved, one primary conclusion seems to stand out: things will not go according to plan. Hence, the unpredictable conditions and inherent uncertainties should be mapped as far as possible from the beginning. Alternative routes, detours and bypasses may also be drawn on to the basic 'route map'. These will all cost more in time and resources to follow, but will also have the advantage of allowing flexibility, and capability to overcome setbacks. The following can be considered as essential:

- critical mass of people who believe in the efficacy of strategic initiatives in HR development and management;
- consensus and communication among staff within the project, so that the team is aware of all developments as they happen, negative as well as positive;
- experienced management;
- community support, and continual expansion of such support;
- belief in the value of the project;
- openness to creation of alliances, both temporary and permanent;
- opportunism;
- optimism.

As for the final verdict on the success of the initiative, we will have to wait and see, while continuing to do our utmost to ensure that it provides a means of leveraging the power contained within a CU for a broader social good. But it is a good sign that the initiative has been seen in corporate headquarters as a model capable of being replicated in other contexts in developing countries – and work to that end is being undertaken.

Note

1. Throughout this chapter, the company that sponsors and supports the CU initiative is called 'Autoco' and the country in which the initiative described has taken place remains anonymous. These conventions are followed to provide a measure of anonymity for the company and the individuals involved.

12 *Gaining Accreditation for a Corporate University*

Gordon Shenton, Peter Clist and Daniel Dirks

Introduction

Since 2002, efmd (European Foundation for Management Development) has been engaged in a major project to define an assessment and quality development scheme for corporate universities (CUs). From the beginning of this process, the Allianz Management Institute (AMI) has been closely involved as one of the principal partners at all stages, first as a member of the original working party that designed the system, subsequently as the first CU to go through the assessment process as a 'pilot', and currently as an active member of the steering committee that is monitoring the rollout of the project. The assessment system, known as the Corporate Learning Improvement Process (CLIP), is now well into its deployment phase. Following the initial testing of the process with AMI, four other CUs have been evaluated and have received the CLIP quality label. These are Universidad Corporativa Union Fenosa (UCUF), Alcatel University, Novartis Corporate Learning and Ergo Management Academy. A case study written by Peter Clist, Head of Succession Planning and Top Management Communication at Allianz AG and Daniel Dirks, formerly of Allianz Management Institute, but now a Senior Vice President of the Fireman's Fund Insurance Co, California, have written a case study outlining their involvement with CLIP. In the box later in the chapter they describe AMI's involvement with CLIP, and the issues and benefits from their perspective.

The efmd is a not-for-profit membership organization devoted to the improvement of management education in business schools and universities, and management development in companies. It is based in Brussels, entirely independent of the European Union or any external funding. Its mission is to provide the management development profession with a forum for networking, benchmarking and sharing good practice. The efmd has also come to play an important role in the field of standard setting for the profession through the highly successful EQUIS (European Quality Improvement System) initiative for the assessment of management education institutions in Europe and increasingly around the world. The more recent CLIP project has been derived methodologically from the experience acquired through EQUIS.

One of the specific and differentiating characteristics of efmd is that its membership is dual, including some 350 academic institutions and around 100 large European corporations. With EQUIS for management education institutions and CLIP for corporate learning centres, efmd is able to bring new perspectives for transferring best practices between its two constituencies, launching new initiatives to bridge the gap between the business school world and the world of corporate learning.

The development of CLIP

The partnership with AMI and the other companies that made up the founding working party has been particularly significant in tackling the basic questions that managers often pose about assessing CU initiatives: what can an assessment scheme deliver in the corporate environment? What is the added value for a corporate university in submitting itself to a time-consuming process of self-assessment and external review? What is the legitimacy of an external body such as the efmd to assess CUs and to award a quality label?

The efmd's own commitment to the project grew quite naturally out of its desire to provide corporate members with a quality improvement service comparable to the established EQUIS process for the assessment of business schools and university faculties of business and management. Contributing to the development of quality in the management development profession and helping its members to share experiences are central to the efmd's mission. CLIP, like EQUIS, is intended as a vehicle for achieving these goals. Furthermore, the work on CLIP was a natural extension of the experience within the Corporate University Learning Group, which for several years had been a forum for exchange and development among the participants.

In addressing the question from the corporate perspective, the first contribution of the CLIP project was to define an agreed framework of assessment criteria. The working party began with a series of brainstorming sessions to bring out the principal determinants of success in setting up and running a CU. The combined input of the members, reflecting the collective experience of eight companies, generated an exhaustive list of issues to be addressed, of choices to be made, of practical 'dos' and 'don'ts'. Through an iterative process, this raw material was refined into a nine-area structure covering the various factors to be taken into consideration when evaluating the effectiveness of a CU within a company:

- Appropriate design and positioning
- Clarity of strategic mission
- Definition of target markets
- Resources available to achieve the assigned learning objectives
- Quality of programmes offered
- Processes by which people are nominated or selected to participate in programmes
- Follow-up to participation
- Interface with other HR processes
- Capacity to innovate and anticipate strategic learning needs.

The essential point of this process was to produce criteria defined by members of the profession – active heads of corporate learning – who have pooled their individual experience to create a collective view of what constitutes quality in their activity. The ownership of the criteria framework is therefore located within the CU community. The role of the efmd is to provide a methodology and a locus for this process. The framework is, therefore, dynamic, in the sense that it is open to continuous refinement as the CLIP community expands and experience with participating CUs is gathered in the field. The original working party has taken on a more permanent role as a steering committee and has steadily brought in new members as interest has developed. It is now clearly understood by all members that a major outcome is the possibility to share experience within the group, to learn from each other, and to make progress together. It is important, therefore, that the committee should remain open to new members. The legitimacy of the system rests on the principle that it is grounded in the profession.

Self-assessment

The next level of added value for participating companies within the project is the self-assessment phase. Participating CU managers can use the criteria framework as a set of guidelines to conduct a detailed strategic audit and quality review of their operations. Managers can address the questions that are set out in the criteria checklist and make their own evaluation of the appropriateness of their organization and the effectiveness of their programmes. If it is conducted thoroughly, this process of measurement against the CLIP yardstick enables the CU team to draw up a critical and reflective picture of strengths and weaknesses. A demanding exercise of this kind is a valuable contribution to the internal strategic review that CUs often undertake periodically with their own advisory board.

However, in the CLIP experience to date, CU managers have often found self-assessment difficult to understand and execute effectively. Business schools and universities within the EQUIS scheme readily grasp the significance of self-assessment in delivering value to their institutions or customers, and have little difficulty in mobilizing resources to produce a substantial written report. However, within CUs, managers often lack the time and resources to draft a document that is sufficiently detailed and self-critical to be of value in itself. The experience with AMI showed that expectations regarding what can be produced at this stage must not be set too high, and that very explicit guidance must be given in the form of a detailed template for the production of the report.

Nonetheless, the steering committee and the CLIP management team within the efmd continue to look for the best way to help participating CUs to carry out this essential part of the process. Apart from providing an opportunity for rigorous self-analysis, it is also a necessary preparation for the work that will be carried out by the review team. A sufficient documentary base must be made available to the reviewers before the on-site visit. If the reviewing team does not have an adequate understanding of the organization and functioning of the initiative before it arrives, much time will be wasted in the early stages of the review digging out this basic information.

Peer review

The heart of the CLIP system is the peer review process, and it is undoubtedly here that the greatest value is added for the participating companies. The review team is composed of four or, exceptionally, five members, who are themselves actively involved in the management of CUs. In this sense, they are 'peers', equals in the profession who are freely giving their time on an unpaid volunteer basis as a contribution to the advancement of a common cause. Their expectation is that they will take as well as give, that they will learn from the assessment experience. Their role, then, is to take a critical, but fundamentally constructive, approach to the task of providing an unbiased external assessment. Critical, because they must challenge the assumptions and established practices in the unit that they are observing and engage in purposeful dialogue with the people they meet; constructive, because the overriding concern is to help the CU managers to make progress. The peer review team must have the courage to ask the hard questions and to probe when there is doubt, but they must also be courteous and understanding of the particular context in which they find themselves.

The process is also designed to put the review team under considerable pressure during the three days of the visit, because they must piece together a balanced assessment that will be fed back immediately to their hosts during the last meeting. One of the crucial lessons learned from the pilot review of the AMI was that this terminal feedback session is indispensable in focusing the review process and in giving closure to the event. The CU that is being assessed must hear some of the main conclusions immediately, otherwise there is a sense of incompleteness and unanswered expectations among those who have participated in the interviews. For this to be achieved, time must be set aside for the final debriefing with the CU team, and for preparation by the peer review team. This oral report, and later the final written report, will highlight first of all what was considered to be excellent or of high quality, and second what was found to be less convincing. The outcome is, therefore, both a confirmation of quality and an indication of where progress can be made.

In this spirit, the assessment is often accompanied by a certain number of cautious recommendations for possible future action. The process is in no sense normative or prescriptive, since it is not about making judgements against rigid standards, nor is it about establishing conformity to pre-established expectations about what a CU *should* be. It is an attempt to appreciate what is being done in a particular context and in the light of particular strategic choices that have been made (see Part 1 and especially Chapter 1). Above all, CLIP is designed to be supportive. Having said that, the process is by no means a toothless exercise of polite congratulation; for the participating CU, it is a unique occasion to receive a frank, uncompromising, unbiased, and carefully constructed opinion representing the combined reflection of four knowledgeable and independent people. The process has proved to be extremely powerful in revealing key issues and in bringing half-submerged problems fully to the surface. External confirmation of a half-recognized problem is frequently instrumental in getting the issue out into the open and on to the agenda for change. In many cases, the process can provide fresh impetus to strategic thinking internally and can strengthen the hand of the CU head in subsequent negotiations for maintenance of the CU.

CASE STUDY 12.1

MAINTAINING SUPPORT FOR THE CORPORATE UNIVERSITY: THE ALLIANZ MANAGEMENT INSTITUTE

The AMI came into existence in the late 1990s. The original intent was to pool the resources of three neighbouring German-speaking countries in management development. Initially, therefore, AMI covered Germany, Austria and Switzerland and was German-speaking. For the sake of convenience, it also included three programs in English that had been developed in a rather haphazard way: a high-potential program; a business simulation game (translated from German); and a business case program. These programs were also accessible, therefore, for non-German speaking members of the Allianz Group and provided the nucleus for the subsequently established AMI structure, with its global reach.

From these beginnings, the company decided to set up a full-scale 'management institute' working primarily in English, to serve an international group working in that common language. From the start, in a heavily decentralized company, the model

CASE STUDY 12.1 – *continued*

was very clear. AMI was not a brand for all training worldwide; it was not even a brand for all management training. All that properly belonged at a local level. AMI was to be executive training and development only for executives/managers/high potentials above a certain level in the hierarchy.

The start-up phase covered, in retrospect, four key decision stages. The first was the establishment of an AMI group board, including human resources (HR) directors from the five major subsidiary companies. This board agreed the curriculum and even, to push matters along quickly, agreed among themselves to find an academic supplier for each of the five key executive development topics: the USA found an information technology (IT) program (for non-IT executives); the UK, finance, and so on. This board ensured rapid start-up, support in the member companies and valuable feedback at all stages.

The second stage was staff recruitment. It would have been easiest to staff solely from the German parent, but this was to be an English-speaking institution relevant to a global organization. Two native English speakers (one British, one American), both with long experience in HR and training, were seconded from their parent companies to Munich. Together with existing links from the German AMI, this provided an instant international network.

The third issue was related to premises. There is an ongoing debate about CU initiatives owning expensive premises, or 'bricks and mortar', or taking a 'virtual' path. The Allianz answer to this debate was that a 'virtual' institution was not appropriate for the target group and that a prestigious institution needed prestigious premises. Further, those premises needed to be near the head office, so that board members could easily attend as sponsors and speakers. A small country house, on a lake near Munich, was found and purchased.

The fourth, and most important, stage was gaining support from the main Allianz AG board. Having agreed to fund AMI, and buy the premises near Munich, the board agreed curriculum proposals from AMI and its board, and agreed that board members would commit five days a year each to be speakers on and sponsors of programs. The result of this board support has been an unmistakable message to the whole organization that this initiative and its associated aims are important. Coupled with the other measures already described, it ensured solid internal support for AMI in the start-up phase.

Maintaining support has involved some old measures and some new. Clearly, some measures important during start-up are just as important in the next year or two. The main board continues to agree the AMI curriculum for the coming year and to provide speakers and sponsors. The process of staffing AMI, at least partly, from secondments from member companies continues. The premises at the small country house have been enlarged to allow more space for larger groups. However, maintaining support does not only involve continuing with the original thinking and measures. The AMI board, for example, is a different animal from at the beginning. As the group itself has grown, so the AMI board has expanded to include new major subsidiaries. Similarly, as AMI has become established, the AMI group board has developed its agenda. Checking program costs, raising potential curriculum needs, acting as a sounding board for program and project proposals are all now regular items at AMI board meetings.

In addition, the main Allianz AG board has itself gone a stage further. From agreeing to provide speakers, each board member is now committed to sponsoring one senior strategy-level program. The subject is, naturally, close to the director's heart and they attend the whole program. The effect,

CASE STUDY 12.1 – *continued*

clearly, is of Allianz´s most senior people worldwide understanding (and influencing) board thinking on a host of topics.

With board support of this sort, it has been relatively easy to encourage executives themselves to serve as speakers and sponsors. We believe a significantly smaller proportion of our speakers in comparison to most other CUs are external. We do use external experts, naturally, but we use many more internal experts. To achieve this, we are careful to use existing distribution networks as defined – all communications go to the CEO, with a copy to the HR Director, from whom all nominations must come.

We have also tried consciously to preserve the international nature of our group, as it has grown. Today, we are 14 people in total, representing 9 nationalities. This approach certainly helped when, for example, we received an enquiry from Shanghai in halting English and our Chinese staff member took the phone to deal with it. A further feature has been consciously and constantly to seek comparisons and expertise from peers. It is for this reason that we served on the efmd working party to develop a quality assurance process for CUs parallel to the EQUIS accreditation process for business schools. We learned a lot helping develop CLIP, volunteered to be a pilot company and were pleased to be the first company to receive the CLIP certificate. Lastly, here, we take every opportunity to raise the profile of AMI. We accept invitations as conference speakers whenever we can, take professional groups round our premises, contribute articles – whatever gets our name in the public domain.

So far, all of this seems to have worked. What next?

Well, there was one unintended development that has helped embed the AMI within the organization. In 2001, Allianz merged with Dresdner Bank. One outcome of this was the setting up of group centres in Munich. These group centres aim to

divorce departments with group-wide responsibilities from operating companies. They include, for example, corporate communications and mergers and acquisitions, both of which are handled at group level. One of these new group centres covered HR and AMI was incorporated into it. Suddenly, AMI was part of a wider offering from group HR covering succession planning, high-potential recruitment and worldwide marketing of an employee brand. That has helped significantly to spread a consistent message about good HR practice; it has also helped widen the potential pool for secondments into AMI, with the result that the number of staff on secondment has increased, spreading knowledge of AMI. A further aspect of this is that the board has asked group HR to work on some fundamental projects. One covers management development – trying to identify and codify best practice both within the group and outside, in order to spread it. A second is a group HR 'portal' (an electronic bulletin board and library), which will make widely accessible the best practice work from projects. These are projects complementary to AMI's core mission with executives.

As far as the future is concerned, many challenges doubtless lie in wait. Three are very much in our minds. The first and perhaps most important challenge is that within the current model AMI does not have mechanisms for identifying and addressing the 'hot' issue in management or the group in order to address it quickly. That is because topics for the following year are agreed annually with the board.

The second major challenge concerns something every trainer or management developer faces – does the return justify the cost? Our current answer is to look at proxy measurements of, admittedly, rather aspirational goals. The numbers of people attending AMI programs is a proxy for the goals concerning the alignment of senior people and the development of an

CASE STUDY 12.1 – *concluded*

international culture. Our impact on external reputation is harder to measure, but we believe that a well-founded, well-structured and high-quality set of programs for executives and high-potentials can only enhance our aim to be an employer of choice. The impact on our business results is even harder to measure, and this is something that many CUs are starting to address as a priority.

The third challenge is that if the work on management development is to be really worthwhile, it must aim to raise standards in local companies. Quite how this can be achieved, in a decentralized company with well-developed local independence, is again something that many CUs are incorporating as part of their remit.

Notwithstanding these issues, in general, the messages from our journey so far seem to be positive, taking into account that if you choose to take an approach involving a CU then you should:

- make sure the brief is clear, easy to understand and shared by major stakeholders;
- make every effort to get your stakeholders actively engaged so that the CU becomes their baby;
- take every opportunity to communicate, communicate, communicate.

These general messages were true for us in our start-up phase and seem to continue to be true as we mature.

Lessons learned about corporate universities and other managerial initiatives

The logic of CLIP is that the process does not necessarily end with the final report, but that it can be linked to the subsequent development of the CU. In almost all experience to date, the assessment has served as key input into a subsequent strategic review. In the case of AMI, two members of the peer review team were invited several months later to run a one-day meeting with the Advisory Board in order to identify strategic options, using the CLIP assessment as a starting point. The assessment function can, therefore, be extended into a formal or informal consultancy service if desired. This also occurred following the review of Novartis. A further extension of the peer review findings and recommendations beyond the final report is the discussion that can take place within the CLIP steering committee. It has now been agreed within the committee that the peer review reports, suitably edited in relation to sensitive material, will be shared among members.

What then are the lessons that have been learned within the efmd CLIP community about corporate universities? In the attempt to set up a viable assessment scheme, the pioneer group encountered a number of fundamental difficulties that had to be addressed. A first difficulty, of course, is the name itself, since the term 'corporate university' is problematic. Ironically, among the companies that have participated in the CLIP project, relatively few call their CU by the name 'corporate university' or even 'university'. Allianz speaks of its Management Institute; others prefer 'academy' or simply 'corporate learning centre'. A glance at the list of such entities in the corporate world will confirm that the term university is in reality rarely used. This is for a variety of reasons. In some European cultures, in which universities are revered institutions with a thousand year history of intellectual development, it would be considered a presumptuous misuse of the term to call a business training organization a university. In Germany, the word 'university' is a protected term that cannot legally be used outside of a regulated academic context (as was also the case in the UK until recently). On the other hand, the expression 'corporate university' is well accepted as a generic term designating a certain institutional concept in the corporate world of training and learning. This is no doubt due to the fact that the CU idea has been imported into Europe from the USA where it has long been established.

A key question is, therefore, how a particular corporate university distinguishes itself from a mere training centre or from the traditional training function within the company. How is the 'university' role for the training entity understood in the company? In fact, it turns out that the university as a model or analogy for the learning function within the company has, in most cases, little relevance beyond the symbolic. On the other hand, there is general agreement that what distinguishes a CU from previous approaches to training can be related to one or two key ideas. The most important of these is the understanding that learning is strategic, and that it must be planned and managed at the highest level. The company as a whole is seen as at least potentially a learning organization in which knowledge, skills, competences, behaviours, and corporate socialization can be nurtured in a systematic way.

Related to this is the notion that a corporate learning centre within the company must be fully aligned with corporate strategy. A CU is responsible for supporting the internal implementation of a strategy by disseminating key ideas and values, ensuring that investment in learning is targeted to the right people and geared to the acquisition of necessary competences. This function is particularly important when the company is striving to introduce cultural change or, as is so often the case, when the corporate headquarters is striving to bring together into a common culture a series of disparate business units that have their own established identities. This problem is often compounded by the fact that, through the process of industrial concentration and external growth, the company has made acquisitions outside its own national boundaries. This different conception of the learning and training function gives the CU a much more central role within the company. As a result, its formal positioning in the organization chart becomes a critical issue, since the training function is no longer seen as the exclusive domain of HR. The existence of a direct reporting line to board level, with the explicit support of the CEO, is a major concern. However, in all cases, the nature of the interface with HR processes will remain an important variable.

If there is some convergence of opinion on these common differentiating characteristics of a CU, in practice there are many contrasting situations. There are no pre-existing models that can easily be made to fit the needs of a particular organization. Each company must design its own tailored solution, taking into account the type of industry in which it is operating, the structure of the company, the strategic objectives being pursued and the historical and political constraints that are peculiar to the company. To the extent that a key success factor is the design and positioning of the CU within the larger organization to ensure maximum alignment with key strategic objectives and the sustained relevance of its programmes, it follows that each initiative will to some degree be different.

Another important issue is that of the scope of activities. Does the CU bring under its umbrella the entire training provision throughout the company, in all the business units, in all countries, and at all levels? Does the CU focus only on executive training at the higher levels of management? Does the CU exist alongside training centres in the business units and in other countries? In these cases, where does the remit of the CU end and where does that of the business unit training centres begin? Which programmes are to be designed and run centrally? Which programmes should be left to the responsibility of the local decentralized units? Following their initial success, both Allianz and Novartis, which have focused on top executive development at corporate level, are faced with the challenge of 'raising standards' in the local companies, as Peter Clist puts it; or 'driving the development processes deeper into the organization' as was said in Novartis. In other words, the issue of extending the scope of the CU arises quite naturally as time goes by.

From this point of view, the term 'corporate' can take on two quite different meanings. In the case of a CU designed to orchestrate the entire learning provision within the company, the term 'corporate' has the universal connotation of a common policy being implemented throughout the organization, across the dividing lines of geography and business unit identity. On the other hand, in the case of a CU focusing on top management and existing alongside decentralized training centres, the term 'corporate' refers to the inter-business unit level within the central headquarters. Alcatel University is a very interesting example of the CU as coordinator of a federation of autonomous training and learning centres within the different companies around the world. As part of this 'orchestrating' function, it provides a highly sophisticated quality control service in the form of accreditation of its participating training centres as well as a huge volume of training for external clients.

Implications for the development of CLIP

The obvious question to emerge from this is how we design the CLIP process to accommodate these and other complexities of CU management. When work began on CLIP, a common objection was that it would be difficult to define common standards to measure such disparate situations. The diversity of meaning attached to the term 'corporate university', the extreme variety of organizational solutions in their practical implementation, the large differences in mission and scope, and the absence of well-established models would appear to make comparison impossible. The argument went that the world of business schools was sufficiently homogeneous to make comparative assessment possible, but that in the corporate world this was not realistic. However, this was to miss the point. The assessment scheme has to start from the premise that diversity will be the norm and that any assessment must begin with a full understanding of the specific circumstances of the CU that is being observed. Each CU must be understood in its own terms, in relation to the assigned mission, the design choices that have been made, and the scope of its activities. The criteria for assessment are not conformity to a notion of standard practice, but rather notions such as the coherence of the chosen design model with the strategic goals, the relevance of the programme offering, and the effectiveness of training and learning.

Experience in the field with the CLIP assessment process has brought to light a further dimension of the issue of scope. For assessment purposes, there may not always be an easily definable unit with distinct boundaries. The object of the assessment is usually defined as an organizational entity devoted to the running of training programmes, because it is the CU that requests the audit. But, if the object is seen as corporate learning, a broader perspective is necessary. Learning takes place along a widely dispersed continuum that is not contained within organizational boundaries, and not limited to training programmes. The very fact that the emphasis, in managerial vocabulary and action, has shifted from training to learning is indicative of this difficulty. In the widest sense, learning is an activity to be managed at all levels and certainly by anybody in a position of responsibility. In particular, there are many HR processes that are more or less directly linked to corporate learning goals: people development, lifelong learning, management development, appraisal systems, competency management, succession planning, high potential management, coaching and mentoring, knowledge management, and so on. Whether or not the corporate learning centre is located within HR or reports directly and independently to board and CEO level, the organizational links between the training and learning function and the HR function in all its multiple dimensions will be a central concern.

Even in cases where boundaries and responsibilities are clear, the effective management of the interface between training and learning programmes on the one hand and these other strands of people development within HR on the other is, therefore, a crucial criterion for success. In most cases, there are ambiguities and tensions around these issues because of ownership disputes or territorial rivalry. It is not easy, nor perhaps desirable, for companies to integrate all the dimensions of corporate learning within the remit of a single organizational unit or under the responsibility of a single person. From what has been observed to date, defining the nature of this interface is a major challenge facing those CUs that are targeted at higher level executive learning. However, one encouraging aspect is that there would appear to be a growing awareness that such integration is necessary if the company is to achieve the strategic learning goals that are being set.

Certainly CLIP is positioned to look at the wider picture. From the beginning, people within the efmd envisioned a system that would not simply be focused on the training unit, but that would have a broad process focus and encompass corporate learning in all its ramifications. Uncertain definitions, absence of dominant organization models, variable scope – the field is remarkably open. In practical terms, much depends on the networking skills and the personal credibility of the person ultimately responsible for learning, who must work across departmental and territorial boundaries to bring things together.

A further element of uncertainty is the lack of institutional stability over time within the CU world. Companies that are constantly restructuring, expanding and contracting as fortunes change, cannot offer a stable environment for growth and development. CUs are set up in response to specific strategic needs at a given point in time under the auspices of a particular management team. When circumstances or key sponsors change, the CU may lose its support within the company and cease to be perceived as relevant. The death rate among CUs is regrettably high. There are relatively few CUs that have established themselves over time as enduring 'institutions' capable of surviving the ups and downs of corporate life. Most of the CUs that are associated with CLIP are quite recent creations and have yet to pass the hurdle of survival in a downturn of their fortunes. Even in the shorter run, and excluding the fate of closure, which may threaten some CUs, there is no certainty that the founding design and initial positioning choices will continue to be relevant. As new strategic issues emerge, there is almost always a need to periodically rethink the basic mission of the CU.

The role of senior management

The CLIP experience has revealed the considerable fragility and vulnerability of the CUs. Managers at the head of these units within the corporate structure are in exposed, even solitary positions where they must constantly strive to remain strategically relevant, and to be perceived to be relevant, to produce high-quality programmes, and to be perceived to be doing so. This is undoubtedly one of the reasons why an external, independent confirmation of the quality of what is being provided is so important. External recognition is one means to strengthen internal recognition and to ensure continuing support from decision leaders in the company. A key issue for the future is to build up a sufficient body of shared experience within the profession and to develop recognized models that can lead in the medium run to a stronger institutionalization of CUs within their companies. The challenge for CUs is to be able to survive both a change in the company's strategic priorities and a change in the leadership of the CU itself.

At a more operational level, the CLIP experience has highlighted a certain number of key issues in the mobilizing of resources for the company's learning programmes. It has become apparent that one of the success factors is the ability to involve senior management, at the board level and at the business unit CEO level, in the CU's learning projects – as the experience of Peter Clist at AMI illustrates. This commitment is often achieved by giving board members a sense of ownership of the CU itself, or by mobilizing individual board members as 'sponsors' or 'owners' of particular programmes. In the case of AMI, all its major programmes in the portfolio are proposed, designed and partly taught by the sponsoring board member. The idea is becoming embedded in many companies that a significant part of the leader's role is to facilitate learning and, therefore, to participate actively in the training unit's programmes. This is seen more and more, not just as a good deed comparable to an appearance at the Christmas party, but as a central responsibility for top management. It is an opportunity to transmit expertise and experience and to communicate with the different echelons of management throughout the company. Jack Welch, the former CEO of GE, participated regularly in the programmes of the GE CU in Crotonville. Spotting high-potential managers was one of his favourite activities.

However, senior management can only provide limited, although highly strategic, input into the CU's programmes. There remains the question of where the expertise is going to come from for the bulk of the offering. Here, the choice is between identifying managers and technical experts within the company or seeking expertise outside the company. A frequent solution, of course, is to subcontract the entire programme to a consulting company or a business school. An intermediate solution, unfortunately, is to cherry-pick the business schools' star performers on an individual basis, a practice that efmd does its best to discourage. It must be said that none of the CUs that have been reviewed to date within CLIP resort to this solution. Some outsource almost everything, while maintaining tight control over the programme design and evaluation; others prefer, as a matter of policy, to keep as much in-house as possible. The Union Fenosa CU, with its policy of considering the business units as faculties and their managers as faculty members, is almost entirely self-sufficient. This, of course, reflects the highly technical nature of much of the training within this utility company. In other cases, the choice of one or more prestigious business school partners guarantees that the programmes will be well regarded by nominees, especially if the venue is attractive.

However, from the CLIP experience, it appears that the relationship between CUs and business schools is not always an easy one. There is a backdrop of mutual lack of confidence and understanding, not expressed by all, of course, but often leading to quite vehement opinions of distrust. CU managers are not necessarily well informed about what business schools can offer and tend to remain within a small circle of the best known suppliers (see Chapter 8). Few have a systematic policy for supplier selection and partnership, with established criteria and processes. On the other hand, business schools have not always kept up with changing emphases and new learning requirements of companies. The schools are *perceived* to be slow to respond, somehow too academic in their approach and, at worst, behind the times in the relevance of what they can offer. Corporations are more oriented towards solutions and implementation than towards state-of-the-art formalization and conceptual rigour. They are more interested in research into cross-functional problems than in research within narrowly defined disciplinary fields. The efmd is concerned, despite this, to break down this distrust and encourage real partnership development between business schools and companies.

An important issue for the CUs is the size and profile of their permanent staff. Their missions tend to be not so much teaching or learning facilitation in the front line, as programme design, portfolio management, logistics, liaising with providers or monitoring of programme delivery. They tend not to have a strong formal background as educationalists or pedagogues, but to have acquired a talent, even a passion, for corporate learning through practical experience. The commitment and quality of individual staff members are often striking, but there are questions, in some cases, about the adequacy of the overall profile of the resources available to the CU. Operations are usually kept within fairly tight budgetary limits and CUs certainly must always avoid being perceived as overstaffed. The result is often that the team becomes overstretched as its success leads to expansion of its activities. For recently created CUs, the resourcing of growth is a major concern. Shortage of competent resources is also a significant constraint on innovation in educational methods and in the content of learning. Even when the budget will allow expansion of the core staff, it is not easy to find people with the requisite set of skills. There is as yet no recognized CU 'profession'; people find their way into training through HR backgrounds and do not necessarily expect to remain in this type of position for very long periods. CUs are often too small to offer career development and promotion opportunities. Replacement of a CU head or key staff members when they move on within the organization or out of the organization is no easy matter. It is for this reason that efmd decided to launch its LINK programme to help staff corporate learning departments with qualified educational staff.

Approaching dilemmas and towards the future

An important function of the CU is programme portfolio management to ensure an effective link with the HR planning cycle of staff appraisal, training needs analysis, and participant nomination. This militates for an extremely well-focused range of programmes that is communicated clearly and early throughout the company. In the CLIP experience to date, this is one of the strong points of the participating CUs. Most have worked hard to refine their offering, weeding out programmes that do not fit coherently and developing new strategically central programmes.

A difficult issue, however, for the CUs that have been involved in the CLIP process is to strike a balance between two partially conflicting roles. On the one hand, there is the essential function as disseminator and reinforcer of the target culture and the associated behaviours that have been defined in the context of the current corporate strategy. On the other hand, there is the 'university' function as vector for new ideas and challenges from outside the company. It is generally recognized that the CU should not just be a follower but should be in the forefront and even anticipate new trends; the reality is that this is hard to achieve. The portfolio of programmes tends to be set well in advance because of planning constraints and there is little room for short-term additions to the calendar. Nonetheless, there is definitely room for progress in this respect if institutions that aspire to become CUs are to live up to their names. Is there room in the corporate world for entities that can devote part of their time to environmental scanning, pedagogical innovation, new knowledge creation, development of new approaches to problem solving?

There are, of course, many other issues that remain unresolved, whatever the quality of the CUs. A worrying dilemma is the lack of instruments to measure the impact of the investment in learning on corporate performance; use of e-learning is also a recurrent debate, as indeed it is in the world of business schools (see Chapter 8). Certainly, in the future, 'blended' learning, associating different teaching and learning modes, will become more and more sophisticated. The CLIP peer review teams have already observed an innovative mix of action learning, project-based learning, experiential learning, personal assessment and development, coaching, alongside more traditional case studies and input by experts. The trend is clearly to place most of the knowledge acquisition into the (often electronically provided) pre-programme material. Classical teaching is becoming less popular, particularly with senior managers. This is one of the main reasons why companies feel that they are better able to provide learning solutions for their future leaders internally than by contracting out to the business schools. We at the efmd have sought to work with CUs, the managers involved with them, and the business schools that continue to be their main suppliers of high-level management development. The various processes that we have been through with them, underpinned by the peer review systems of EQUIS and now CLIP, indicate that CUs are and will remain a significant institution in the corporate learning field.

CASE STUDY – STOP PRESS: 18 MONTHS LATER

As we reread what we wrote a while ago, it is interesting to reflect on what has changed.

The completely unexpected development has been a major project on 'Leadership Values', aggressively driven by the CEO and main board. We have published our five key leadership values and run a worldwide survey of senior executives and their direct reports to see how well they are currently lived. That has led to considerable spin-off work in the areas of management development generally.

Partly as a result of the project, our programmes themselves have been reorganized to reflect three very clear objectives: campus (strategy development and communication); leadership (development of existing and future leaders); general management (skills development for current leaders).

One area for necessary improvement is the whole area of e-learning. We are looking at ways of marrying traditional classroom activities with modern concepts of blended learning. In truth, we have not yet found the 'magic bullet' to apply these methods to our target group of senior executives.

Our three-year initial funding period has come to an end. Most programmes are charged to participants at cost plus an administration mark-up. Of the three streams, only campus is still free of charge to participants. The AMI board itself has been extended beyond HR specialists – we now have 'line' representation from major lines of business.

Taking all of these developments together, one thing is clear. Throughout the life of AMI, the board has provided it with unwavering support. To us, this is perhaps the key lesson: the major success factor for the CU seems to be full and consistent support from the very top.

PART III

Learning Technologies and Processes

█ █ █ *Introduction*

A key challenge for professionals working in corporate universities (CUs) is the design, development and management of cost-effective learning processes. In an electronic era, this has often meant embracing new learning technologies and working out how to make best use of them, either alone, or in combination with other methods. Whether CU initiatives have started with a technology (e-learning) focus or have embraced it later, this has been, and will remain, a major challenge. Given the continuing pace of change – see Chapter 20 in the final part of the handbook – it is likely to become so again, intermittently, as major upgrades have to be engineered and assimilated.

Levis – in Chapter 13 – provides a comprehensive overview of the challenges to established practice in training and development that these technologies present. Many of the issues he introduces – concerning the active, social nature of workplace learning – are reinforced and developed in later chapters.

One common pattern for the development of CUs has been a progression through phases or waves, triggered by new technological possibilities. The first phase is inspired by the prospects and possibilities of e-learning but in practice is actually concerned with achieving technological mastery. This means putting an adequate infrastructure in place: the platforms or learning management systems (LMS) that will allow ready access, a suitable range of facilities for learners, easy housekeeping, and integration with a company's human resources (HR) systems. Technological perspectives and issues dominate the agenda, and provision is often supplier led. E-learning is seen as a way of reducing costs, and making training more timely, flexible and consistent – but in a fast-moving field, companies with limited experience can easily fall prey to the vendor's dazzling demo. All this was accentuated during the 'dot com' bubble. In our research, the one area where interviewees always fell awkwardly silent was on the details of their spending and experience with LMS; suffice to say that anyone who has felt let down by their LMS is in very good company.

Nevertheless, one way or another, this is a stage that has to be endured, and is one from which companies seem to emerge sadder but also much wiser. Stable and functional platforms take shape; the requirements for learning provision become incorporated in desktop specifications; a range of courses or modules is made available; a body of early adopters prepared to use and persist with e-learning emerges; supporting facilities – competence frameworks, diagnostics, catalogues and links for booking conventional courses – develop, along with realism about the limits and costs of e-learning. This is a sign that the second wave is now building.

The second wave is concerned with the *contexts, styles* and *preferences of learners*, and *what is needed to ensure a rich and effective learning experience*. This is 'pedagogy' (in Europe) or 'instructional design' (in the USA). All the talk is of 'blended learning'. At first the blends may be just online (e-moderating, online coaching, virtual learning sets …). But quickly it is recognized that, for example, online relationships work best if they build on and extend face-to-face contact. No longer is it just a matter of 'putting courses on the web'; the structure and style of the course has to be fundamentally rethought, using electronic delivery and communication when it is cost-effective and appropriate, in combination with face-to-face coaching, paper-based materials, workplace-based projects ... or whatever. Many trainers remain sceptical, not to say downright suspicious of the online elements, but again, there are early adopters – those training and development specialists who are interested in rethinking the way they work so as to incorporate technological enhancements.

The progression through these two phases is well captured in several of our chapters. Originally, the emphasis was on the 'e' of e-learning – now it is on the 'learning'. Bentley's account of the development of the Shell Open University (Chapter 16) illustrates these two stages well – and points forward to the third. Flood and Paton (Chapter 14) address the same issues through an examination of the currently potent notion of *blended learning*. It emerged as a reaction to the excessive emphasis on e-learning – and shifts the emphasis to learners' needs, preferences and situations. These central issues – what sort of learning, for whom, in what contexts, with what support – are always given sharp focus by the question of assessment: how will anyone know that learning has taken place? How can assessment be a useful developmental part of a programme, rather than a burden, a distraction, something that often misses the point – or even provides misleading indications of practical competence? Mason tackles these issues in Chapter 15, reinforcing important themes around the extent of control that will be appropriate in different settings, and 'whose learning is it anyway?'

As more training and development specialists become involved in supporting learners and devising new ways of using electronic facilities and resources, their importance as *intermediate users* is recognized. And so the third wave – concerned with *the assimilation and embedding of technologically-enabled learning* – begins to gather momentum. The initiative is no longer in the hands of experts at the centre; collaboration is now seen as unavoidable if high cost elements are to be widely and effectively used. Networked communities of practice start devising and asking for their own solutions, or coming up with unexpected ways of using existing resources. Learning is no longer being 'pushed' from the centre. New roles emerge, as 'learning advisers' help individuals recognize and track down suitable ways of continuing their development, and then support and coach them as they do so. This third wave is well represented in the accounts of networked communities of practice provided by Schaffer and Smith in Chapter 17, based on their experiences at Capgemini; and by Jackson, who in Chapter 18 describes networked learning communities for school leadership that are conceptualized and executed independently of any technological infrastructure. Finally, McCoy and West report their experience of blended *organizational* learning – where a virtual university has provided central coordination and infrastructure for a wide range of business improvement initiatives – in Chapter 19.

13 *What E-learning Has Taught Us*

Kieran Levis

Introduction

E-learning – or rather the cumulative experience of applying information and communications technology to training and education – has taught us some valuable lessons. We now understand a great deal more than we did at the height of the Internet boom about:

- why some investments have been highly successful – while so many have been dismal failures;
- the role, the potential – and the limitations – of different technologies to assist the learning process;
- the many different ways in which people learn – and do not learn.

The 'Business of (e)Learning' (a study carried out by Cortona Consulting, 2002) synthesized many of these lessons. This chapter summarizes these and offers answers to some of the strategic questions posed by the report:

- Just how large are the markets for e-learning?
- Why has the adoption of e-learning been so heavily skewed towards certain industries?
- Is technology leading to a revolution in the way people learn?
- How are e-learning markets likely to develop?

First, we should clarify what we mean by 'e-learning'. The term was originally applied to the use of Internet technologies in learning, which vendors claimed represented an entirely new paradigm. However, to the user, many web-based learning applications were virtually indistinguishable from tedious, page-turning computer based training (CBT), which pre-dates the PC as well as the Internet – they just happened to be conducted online. Indeed, due to bandwidth restrictions, some of these programs have often made less use of video and fancy graphics than media such as CD-ROM.

The Internet undoubtedly provided some major advances in what was possible, particularly in enabling groups of people to learn with and from each other, and in offering access to vastly more information than was possible before. However, the experience of earlier technologies and the work of pioneers like the UK's Open University, Ford and HP is still highly relevant to our overall understanding of what works and what does not. In any case, the term 'e-learning' has now become largely synonymous with virtually all applications of information and communications technologies to learning, and it is used in that broad sense here.

The success stories

The most successful implementations of e-learning, where there have been measurable improvements in learning effectiveness and savings in training costs, have been concentrated in four industries: information technology (IT) itself, telecommunications, financial services and large consulting groups. The outstanding practitioners include:

- Cisco, IBM, HP, Dell in IT
- BT, AT&T and Deutsche Telekom in telecommunications
- The Royal Bank of Scotland, Skandia, Merrill Lynch in financial services.
- Accenture, KPMG, PWC (now part of IBM) and virtually all the large international consulting groups.

The common factors in the successes of these companies are that in most cases they have:

- designed programmes that put the overall needs of learners first;
- developed engaging, relevant content, which enables learners to simulate real-work situations and to practice skills;
- drastically reduced, though rarely eliminated entirely, time spent in classrooms, supposedly absorbing information;
- provided social support for learners and opportunities to learn with others;
- integrated learning with everyday work and access to company information and knowledge;
- used technologies for what they are good at in an intelligent blend, not simply as a means of making savings in training cost, or throwing information at people.

This is a great deal easier said than done, and I enlarge on some of these themes when discussing the idea of a learning revolution.

Learning from failure

These companies, however, are the exception. Many experiments with e-learning have ended in disappointment and disillusionment. Many companies who invested in expensive learning management systems and large libraries of training content have seen little return on their investment – a common experience is that courses have simply not been completed.

The fundamental reason why so many initiatives, both pre- and post-Internet, have been disappointing has nothing to do with the limitations of any particular technology, but a poor understanding of how learning actually works:

- The mental model most people, including many teachers, have of learning is a crude one. We typically assume that it is about transmitting knowledge from teacher to learner, rather than learners constructing knowledge themselves. This is not a fanciful academic concept, but one born out by solid research. The only people who can ever learn – who convert information into knowledge – are active learners, not teachers or technology.

- Most technology and content suppliers come from the IT industry and know very little about how learning works. They have typically focused on improving the efficiency of the process, rather than the effectiveness of the learning. The underlying assumption is that technology is a kind of machine for inserting knowledge into passive learners more cost-effectively than classrooms; a substitute for other forms of learning, rather than simply a tool. Crucially, they under-estimate the importance of motivation, of learning-by-doing and of learning with and from other people.

One of educational technology's unintended consequences is that it has forced educationalists of various kinds to think hard about how learning actually works and to question some of their earlier assumptions. A number of clear lessons have emerged from the ferment of experimentation:

- Learning only happens if learners have a goal.
- All learners need encouragement, feedback and other social stimuli.
- Classrooms are just one of the places where learning can happen.
- Classrooms are poor places for transmitting information.
- Technology can transmit information very effectively, but not knowledge.
- Technology can also, though very few companies encourage it, enable valuable human interactions.
- Skills can only be learned from repeated doing, by applying knowledge.
- Learning is only ever done by learners, not by teachers or technology.

LEARNERS NEED A REASON

The single most important factor in the success of any learning activity is the motivation of the learner. If individuals do not want to learn, they probably will not, or only to a very limited extent. If they are highly motivated, the quality of the teaching and support materials can be almost irrelevant, as it is when a child learns to talk. Most learners fall somewhere between these extremes. They need guidance, positive motivation and reinforcement, and in particular, they need to see a reason why they should be learning what is being taught.

Most e-learning within corporations assumes that individuals will largely work on their own, and often in their own time. In many cases this results in courses simply not being completed.

Learning programmes that depend entirely on the motivation and self-discipline of the individual only really work for highly motivated, disciplined people. Most of us, without some external stimulus, are not. Any learning programme that depends on people organizing it for themselves, without any guidance, encouragement, criticism or feedback, is placing unrealistic demands on most mere mortals – even if there are sensible goals that the learner would like to attain.

PEOPLE NEED PEOPLE

The reason most people prefer learning in a classroom is that they need social stimulus, both from teachers and from fellow-learners. A classroom is not the only way of doing this, but it is the one we are all familiar with. It may not be very effective as a medium for transmitting information and it is certainly not very efficient, but it gives us something a crude CBT program never can.

THE GREAT TRANSMISSION FALLACY

The commonest fallacy about learning is that it is essentially about the transfer of knowledge from teacher to learner. This idea is particularly beguiling for the e-learning industry and most attempts to apply technology to learning, from satellite networks to the web, have concentrated on improving the efficiency of information transfer. Useful and efficient as this can be, it is only ever part of the solution.

Information systems can deliver information, but e-learning technologies and content cannot actually deliver learning. Only people can learn. And they learn most effectively by doing, and by learning with and through other people.

FOCUS ON COST CUTTING

Cutting costs is a perfectly legitimate reason for trying new approaches to learning and the single most important driver in the adoption of e-learning in corporate markets. However, learning programmes introduced solely in order to save costs, which leave all the responsibility to the learners, while giving them none of the help and support that might previously have come from a tutor in a classroom, have tended to work badly. Completion rates are generally less than 30 per cent. Companies that made big investments in learning management systems (LMS) and libraries of online content in the hope that this would mean big savings and more learning have been sadly disappointed.

ONE-WAY NETWORKING

The main drawback of most pre-Internet learning technologies was that they only allowed one-way communications. They assumed implicitly that they were filling empty vessels with knowledge. We now know that learning needs to be an active process and that passive recipients of information learn very little. Sadly, a great deal of web-based learning might as well be one-way for all the interaction that goes on. It is effectively reading from a computer screen, with periodic exercises to check whether the learner has got the 'right' answer.

Networks where participants can exchange information, on the other hand, have proved to be highly effective media for learning:

- individuals can share ideas and learn from each other;
- they can communicate in a variety of ways with tutors, obtaining guidance, encouragement, criticism and feedback.

However, the use of asynchronous collaborative learning has largely been confined to universities. Very few companies have even tried it. Indeed, in the corporate world, collaborative learning nearly always means synchronous – the virtual classroom. This is really a replication of traditional teacher-centred methods, with most of the information flowing one way. Like self-paced web learning, it has its uses, but a lot of limitations too.

LEARNING, DOING AND COACHING

For learning to be truly effective, it has to work in the real world; it has to be applied. The ultimate test of a training programme is how well people can do their job subsequently. Adult knowledge workers tend to spend:

- five per cent of their learning effort obtaining knowledge;
- 10–15 per cent of the overall effort gaining the basic skills;
- 80 per cent or more of the effort adapting and applying new skills and knowledge in their working life.

Most training programmes just deal with the first two – generally less than 20 per cent of the total. Most technology-based learning programmes have concentrated on the knowledge part alone. But the rare and really successful programmes ensure that human support and information are available to help during the adapt-and-apply phase as well. The human support does not have to be an instructor. More appropriate may be a coach, a subject matter expert or a colleague. Learners also need easy access to detailed information once in the nitty-gritty of the job. That cannot easily be extracted from a CBT program, but a well-designed portal can help enormously.

The most successful e-learning programmes, as practised by companies like Cisco and IBM, treat learning as an integral part of work, building as much doing as possible into the formal learning processes, and ensuring that the learning goes on both before and after the course. Interactive content encourages learners to acquire basic knowledge for themselves, to try out different approaches, to learn from something close to experience what happens in a range of scenarios. This is frequently cemented by remote, collaborative learning and some face-to-face sessions. This overall combination is frequently referred to as 'blended learning', although this term is often applied rather lazily to some rather mechanical mixes.

The key is to view technology not as a panacea or a machine for learning, but as a set of very useful tools that are only as effective as the way they are designed and used.

Measuring the markets for e-learning

Learning markets are difficult to define and segment, let alone quantify, and corporate markets are the most fragmented and problematical. Quite apart from the hype, the main reason that nobody knows with any precision how much companies spend on different forms of learning is that these are very diffused markets:

- The training industry is highly fragmented, with probably millions of mostly small suppliers worldwide.
- Although most businesses of any size do some training, markets of paid-for goods and services constitute only a small part of total learning activity. Most corporate training is still conducted in-house.
- Learning takes many forms, is intrinsically difficult to measure and informal learning can scarcely be measured at all.
- Paying customers are only rarely the consumers of the product or service in question.
- Many companies do not measure or know how much they spend on training. Virtually no sizeable company includes expenditure on training in its annual report.

In the case of e-learning, problems of definition and usage make the field even more complicated:

- Expenditure is frequently bundled with that on IT or knowledge management.
- The shift towards self-paced learning often means a drop in measured expenditure.
- In recent years, the picture has been confused by the deep recession in the IT industry.

Most published market research is based on small, statistically insignificant samples and biased towards suppliers' inflated estimates.

Cortona's estimates are much more modest than others. We started with an analysis of corporate e-learning markets in the USA, based primarily on what we know of the revenue figures of suppliers, other indirect evidence and informal discussions with suppliers, users and pundits. We have rounded them up fairly generously, because they are so much lower than the estimates commonly used. However, it is difficult to see how the totals could be much higher than those we have calculated (see Table 13.1).

Table 13.1   Estimates of US corporate e-learning markets, 2001

Category	Market size ($m)
Learning management	500
Collaborative platforms	150
Catalogue content	1500
Customised content	500
Consultants/integrators	1000
Total	3500

Source: Cortona Consulting
Note: Given the generous rounding up and the possibility of double counting, the true total is likely to be less than the sum of the five above. We will compromise at $3.5 billion.

These figures are not dissimilar to IDC's estimates for the total in 1999, which they expected to triple by 2003. They are also consistent with Gartner's estimate of $2.1 billion for 2001, which did not include consulting revenues. If we are correct, it represents about six per cent of total corporate expenditure on training. What these figures do not include is spending on IT infrastructure, where learning is a significant part of the cost, or activities such as building tailored portals, where learning is an important outcome but not the only one. These are certainly relevant and important contributors to e-learning, but would be very difficult both to measure and to allocate.

We know that European levels of expenditure are significantly less than US levels but have been growing faster recently, not least because of the greater severity of the economic recession in the USA. We therefore calculate the total European market to be worth a third the value of the US market, $1.2 million (see Table 13.2).

Table 13.2   Corporate e-learning, global estimates, 2001

Category	Market size ($m)
USA	3500
Europe	1200
Rest of world	300
Total	5000

Source: Cortona Consulting

The pattern of adoption

Our research suggests that the reasons why adoption is so skewed towards a few industries are:

- The market drivers for adoption of e-learning vary significantly in intensity between different market segments.
- There are two distinct forms of adoption – a radical, systematic approach, favoured by a few, and a more tactical approach typical of the vast majority.
- The radical approach is confined to early adopters, who are unlike other kinds of customers in several important respects.

Three main factors have driven the adoption of e-learning to date:

- The rapid growth in information that knowledge workers need to handle, particularly in relation to new products and processes.
- The rapid rate of change in knowledge and skills, especially in information and communications technology (ICT).
- The promise of savings in training costs.

Shortage of time to take conventional training, and competitive pressures to improve performance have also played a part, but it is these three that are present in nearly all large corporate implementations. Cost pressures are of course universal, but the information and knowledge explosion applies with particular force to a handful of industries, and it is precisely these that have invested most heavily in e-learning: IT and telecommunications, banking and financial services and the consulting industry.

What distinguishes these from other industries that have been fairly big adopters, such as automotive and energy, is that they are highly knowledge- and IT-intensive and have rapid product cycles. Manufacturing industries on the whole are much less likely to adopt.

- The ICT industries and the sectors that make intensive use of IT (notably financial services) have been under most pressure to update their IT skills more cost-effectively. They are also, of course, the companies that have the basic infrastructure in place (an important pre-condition).
- Industries with large dispersed sales forces and rapid rates of new product launches have a particular need for ways of rapidly updating people in the field. Both of these conditions apply to the ICT and financial services industries – and also to the automotive and pharmaceutical sectors.
- Industries that have automated large parts of their customer service operations with call centres and customer relationship management (CRM) systems are also receptive – telecommunications and financial services again, and also notably airlines.
- Industries for whom the systematic management of knowledge and intellectual capital is important have also been early adopters, notably consulting and, once again, financial services.

Radical versus tactical adoption

When we look a little closer at how companies have approached adoption of e-learning we find a major divide between those who take a systematic, strategic approach to learning and knowledge sharing, and the majority of corporate users who use e-learning tactically – two very different kinds of adoption.

Most large American companies now use e-learning in some way – typically by installing an LMS and putting self-paced learning programs online. However, for the most part, this is a tactical approach, driven by the need to solve a specific problem of time or cost. They want to reduce training costs, or train a lot more people more quickly, or both.

The systematic, strategic approach is really about a shift of mind, a different way of thinking about learning and knowledge. The distinction between what is e-learning, what is information dissemination and what is collaboration, becomes rather blurred. The kinds of companies that have most notably taken this approach are Cisco, Dell, HP, Merrill Lynch, Skandia and Shell. These companies have achieved not just savings in how they train people, but major productivity and performance improvements.

We have found the systematic approach only happens where:

- IT is mission-critical, and is used as a strategic weapon;
- knowledge sharing is critical to competitive success;
- large numbers of people need frequent briefings on new products and processes.

Even in those industries where all three conditions are present, most notably IT, financial services and consulting, the integrated approach is confined to early adopters. It is far from universal. However, a few old economy companies, like GM, Dow Chemical and Shell have taken a fairly systematic approach, and the competitive pressure to adopt it is going to be powerful in all industries where knowledge and intellectual capital are key strategic assets.

Early adopters and the mainstream

The radical approach is confined to early adopters, who normally make up less than 10 per cent of any eventual market. Early adopters are unlike other kinds of customers in several important respects. They identify benefits for themselves and are in much less need of references from others. It is generally difficult to 'cross the chasm' between adopters and the majority, because most customers take time and like to have the reassurance of seeing other customers like themselves taking the plunge first.

These principles clearly apply in e-learning markets, most strikingly in the case of life long learning. In the industry sectors where e-learning has seriously penetrated, the benefits of a systematic approach appear so strong that, in our view, it is likely to become the norm eventually, though it may not happen quickly. Given the enormous gains in productivity, speed of movement and accumulation of intellectual capital, companies in these sectors that do not operate in this way will be at a serious competitive disadvantage. This is also likely to be the case for businesses in other sectors where the key conditions apply.

Overall then, we can say that in the short term:

- The (addressable) market for strategic approaches is confined to a few hundred (mainly large) companies.

- There is a much broader, more diffuse market of companies that will make some use of e-learning.
- All these markets are still at an early stage of development.

Is it really a revolution?

Something close to a learning revolution is in its early stages in certain industries. Different technologies are playing a big part in it, but the revolution is only partly about technology.

The fundamental reason for a revolution is the need in a knowledge-based economy for vastly more learning, both formal and informal, than was required in an industrial society, and for a more systematic approach to the sharing of knowledge. Knowledge workers need to process enormous amounts of information and to tap into the knowledge of others and the collective knowledge of their organizations. They also need to acquire large amounts of knowledge and skills throughout their working lives. Classroom training is a very ineffective and expensive way of enabling people to acquire knowledge. Organizations and people clearly need approaches that are both more effective and more efficient.

The e-learning industry to date has focused much more on improving the efficiency of the learning process than on learning effectiveness. That has led to some big disappointments, particularly with off-the-shelf content that was scarcely ever used, and with LMSs that had little impact on learning outcomes.

However, valuable lessons have been learned from these and from the outstanding successes of organizations such as Cisco, IBM and Skandia in the corporate sector and the Open University and Phoenix among universities. These have taken an approach to learning which can be said to be revolutionary, and their example will undoubtedly be followed by many more.

The key elements in the learning revolution are:

- an integrated approach to learning and the management and sharing of knowledge;
- giving the main priority to learners and their needs;
- a broader and deeper understanding of how learning does and does not work – and an emphasis on measuring outcomes rather than attendance;
- the abandonment of classrooms as places where teachers or trainers try to 'transfer knowledge' to learners;
- learning, both formal and informal, becoming a continuous process, and part of normal working life;
- modularizing learning content so that it can be digested on a just-in-time basis at any time;
- much greater use of learning-by-doing and learning with, and through, other people.

Technology is the indispensable enabler of this revolution, not the instigator. All of the above approaches can improve learning effectiveness and some technological tools make a particularly useful contribution. Technology can also have a significant impact on the economics of learning, though not invariably.

The revolution is not about:

- The demise of the classroom. It remains an excellent forum for group learning, synthesizing knowledge and understanding and, occasionally, inspirational teaching.

- Across the board savings. Big improvements can be made in efficiency, but some solutions are inherently expensive and learners still need to invest significant time to acquire mastery of complex subjects.
- People learning on their own by reading from computer screens. Social interaction and practice are essential for most learning. Reading works better from paper.
- Transferring knowledge quickly by transmitting content. Only learners can acquire knowledge, and sometimes slowly means more effectively.
- Life-long learning for all. Serious continuous learning aimed at mastery of a subject will be the preserve of a (growing) minority of knowledge workers engaged in continuing professional development. Other adults have much less need and interest. Businesses will only invest in these where they can see a direct return in business performance. (In Europe, however, government bodies are investing significantly.)
- Companies outsourcing all their training. They may well outsource large amounts of it, but it is essential that they are the authors of their own learning and knowledge strategies. The most valuable content is not generic, and is frequently drawn from the company's own knowledge.
- The learning process being automated. Learning is an essentially human activity, like thinking and loving. Technology can make it much easier to do, in different ways, at different times and in different places, but only people can do the learning.

The model of e-learning as some kind of machine for delivering knowledge to learners needs to be ditched, along with the sterile, behaviourist view of humanity on which it is based. E-learning is a set of very useful tools and is only as effective as the way that the tools are designed and used. It is part of the solution – and sometimes part of the problem. It is never the whole story.

The conditions for the systematic approach to learning apply most strongly in the IT, financial services and consulting industries, which account for such a large part of adoption to date. Other industry sectors that have made significant use of e-learning are: automotive, energy and industries like airlines, which have automated much of their sales and customer service operations.

As IT and knowledge sharing attain strategic significance in more companies and more industries, the systematic approach is likely to spread and will include some old economy businesses too, as the examples of GM, Ford, Dow and Shell illustrate. The competitive pressures to adopt the systematic approach will be irresistible in industries where knowledge, IT and intellectual capital are of strategic importance.

The rationale for taking a more thoughtful approach to learning is so powerful in all industries – and the savings and other benefits in many cases so significant – that few sectors will be untouched. However, for many companies and industries, adoption will be much slower and more tactical. For them, e-learning will be a useful means of training more people more quickly and less expensively, rather than a transformational experience.

How learning markets will change

Learning markets will change in a number of ways over the next three to five years, but they will not coalesce:

- Learning and e-learning markets will continue to be made up of many segments with different characteristics. The market share of a few large suppliers will rise significantly, but these markets will continue to be 'fragmented.' It is unlikely that a small number of suppliers could dominate them.
- E-learning will cease to be seen as a distinct category and will often converge with knowledge management. An integrated knowledge and learning strategy will be a high priority for many companies. They will keep control of that strategy – and of mission-critical content – in-house, and increasingly distinct from IT management.
- One of the most visible changes will be the entry of skills development into the mainstream. Most e-learning to date has been about enabling people to acquire knowledge – many programs ostensibly about skills are really explaining concepts and testing understanding. Considerable progress has been made by suppliers like Cognitive Arts and Indeliq on programs that simulate how people acquire skills through discovery and repeated practice. Technologies like DVD are making these kinds of program more affordable.
- Companies will tend to outsource, and certainly to automate, learning wherever that is cost-effective. They will also outsource serious content development to competent specialists, and only develop simple presentation material in-house.
- Sales of 'complete' services will rise relative to sales of software licences. Enterprise-wide planning systems will converge with, and often absorb, LMSs. A growing proportion of e-learning will be conducted over the web rather than on corporate intranets and will be provided by specialist service providers.
- Buyers will become much more discriminating and seek to measure learning outcomes and effectiveness more than illusory savings. Many will demand performance-related deals with suppliers, rather than buying libraries of content.
- The role of corporate training departments will continue to evolve away from instruction and towards facilitation.
- IT training will continue to represent a large part of the total e-learning market, but its relative share will decline as companies use networked learning for skills development and company/product knowledge.
- Much of the market for off-the-shelf catalogue content will become commoditized – but there will be several attractive niches, such as those already developed for business schools. Overall this area will see less buoyant growth than custom content.
- Synchronous learning methods will continue to focus on front-line sales and service staff, notably in the USA.
- More interactive and collaborative methods will increasingly be deployed for knowledge workers engaged in continuing professional development. Asynchronous group learning has proved a highly effective and inexpensive technique in a university setting and more companies will surely start to make use of it for learning aimed at mastery.

Technology has massively expanded learning opportunities and will continue to transform the horizons of individual learners. The uniqueness of each learning pathway has been expressed most eloquently by Antonio Machado (1875–1939), a poet who knew nothing of computers or the Internet:

Wanderer, your footprints are
the path, and nothing more;
Wanderer, there is no path,
it is created as you walk.
By walking,
you make the path before you,
and when you look behind
you see the path which after you
will not be trod again.
Wanderer, there is no path,
but the ripples on the waters.

(Untraced translation)

References

Cortona Consulting (2002) *The Business of (e)Learning*, London: Screen Digest.

14 Designing for Blended Learning

Jim Flood and Rob Paton

Introduction

Blended learning has taken over from e-learning as the *mot du jour*, the phrase on the lips of practically everyone involved in training and development. But what does it amount to? Is it a solution, or a bit of jargon used to fudge the issues? Indeed, now that e-learning has been brought down to earth by the failure of its inflated promises, might it just be another, more acceptable word for the same sorts of products and systems that didn't work last time?

This chapter argues that blended learning should not be seen as an *answer* – but that it presents what has long been a centrally important *question* and does so in a useful new way: how best to combine different modes of learning? The advent of a range of electronic media greatly extends the combinations possible; and developments continue apace as new infrastructures and new software arrive, and learners become more familiar and proficient (and demanding). Everything is provisional in this field, but some useful frameworks and rules of thumb are emerging – and these are outlined. The analysis also suggests that blended learning may be exposing and accentuating some tensions that haunt much corporate training and development.

This chapter aims to:
- review the advantages, disadvantages and distinctive contribution of different learning modes and media;
- report some simple principles and frameworks for thinking about the sorts of blends that will work well for different purposes, people and contexts;
- highlight the significance of the shift to independent learning that a blended approach often enables and stimulates.

Two types of 'blend'

Occasionally, talk of blended learning refers to blended e-learning. That is to say, the resources, activities and discussion all take place and are available online. Table 14.1 summarizes the main components that are used in online blended learning. Clearly, there is a wide range of possibilities and these go well beyond what most people have in mind when they talk of e-learning (usually just the first two or three modes in Table 14.1). The table also contains comments on the advantages and limitations of these different components, deriving from our experience, our impression of current thinking in the field, and such research as there is.

Table 14.1 Blended online learning

Medium	Mode examples	Advantages	Disadvantages and limitations
	Basic e-learning – web pages with limited interactivity and structuring	Cheap, simple, quick to produce, easy to use, very accessible – can work well where the learning is essentially straightforward information transfer; and can be delivered through personal digital assistants (PDAs)	Unless the learner is already independent and/or highly motivated, completion rates are likely to be dismal (for example, 80 per cent drop-out or more)
	Multimedia e-learning – greater interactivity; video and animation; multiple pathways	Available on demand, when it suits More engaging Proves successful in focused skill training especially in technological fields	Completion rates may still be poor – needs protected time and support High volume may be needed to offset much higher initial costs Bandwidth limitation if delivered via the Internet
Online	E-mail advice, tutoring and coaching	Personalized and private support	Hardly sufficient on its own – but can be important
	Computer conferencing (asynchronous)	Provides a social dimension for distributed groups – can develop communities of practice Very low marginal cost	Much improved by skilful moderation – but this increases the cost Not to everyone's taste, but most value it even if only a minority are active
	Audio conferencing with shared whiteboard, and so on Voice over Internet Protocol ((VoIP), synchronous)	Some prefer this to video conferencing – excellent for virtual meetings in both the task and social dimensions	Investment cost to set up and learn Scheduling especially across time zones can be difficult
	Video conferencing and webcasts	Excellent for hot issues where the visual element is very important (for example, technological matters)	Ineffective (induces passivity) if used to deliver standard lectures, presentations, and so on Bandwidth limitation if delivered via the Internet

Table 14.2 Other media and modes of learning

Medium	Mode examples	Advantages	Disadvantages and limitations
Face-to-face	Presentations and instruction	Can be highly motivating and engaging, but very dependent on the quality of the presenter	Recall and retention from this mode alone is notoriously low Variable quality when scaled up High running costs and low throughput
	Workshops, discussions and action-learning	Can be highly motivating and engaging	High cost unless based on those who can meet easily anyway
	One-to-one coaching and mentoring	Tailored, private – suits those in senior positions who are already capable and experienced	High cost
Other resources, activities and media	Booklets and other printed materials	Flexible, robust, convenient and popular Develops independent learning skills Very cheap if appropriate resource available off-the-shelf Can be delivered online to an e-book or for printing out	Can be costly to produce your own from scratch – large print runs then required to lower costs
	Audio tapes/files	Low cost; wide access; can be convenient (for example, play in the car)	May encourage passivity if not linked to complementary activity
	Telephone conferences	Very useful for collaborative activities and maintaining the social dimension among distributed learners Very cheap and easy – much underrated?	Not 'sexy'. Scheduling may be difficult Should build on prior face-to-face contact if at all possible
	Workplace-based learning activities	Can be highly relevant	Requires the support of peers and line managers
	Videos/DVDs	Can be entertaining and stimulating Low marginal cost Can substitute for direct observation	Tend to be either expensive to produce – or less than inspiring
	Computer-aided learning on CD-ROM	Can provide feedback Allows different pathways through material Range of generic resources available	Purpose-built products are either expensive to produce – or less than inspiring

More generally, 'blended learning' refers to a mix of online and more traditional components, be they face-to-face events, books or workplace-based projects. In this context the electronic or online components may still make up much of the course or programme – or their contribution may be more limited. The main types of these other modes of learning are summarized in Table 14.2, along with, again, some comments on their advantages and disadvantages. Three points stand out from these tables:

1. The summary statements about advantages and limitations all proved controversial; as generalizations, they just about stand up, but those who commented on drafts could easily point to exceptions. In other words, it is all about *how* that mode and medium of learning is being used, and in what context.
2. Each and every one of these media and modes will be more effective if used in combination with others: no-one – as either learner or teacher – would want to rely solely on one, if others could also be used.
3. These different media and modes of learning can be combined in a vast number of different ways. The challenge for designers is to put together blends that are cost-effective for different sorts of learning, for different sorts of people, in different contexts.

Factors to consider in 'blending'

When it comes to picking and mixing different media or modes of learning, some of the relevant considerations – for example, concerning the costs and practicalities associated with the learning context – are pretty straightforward. If your learners are spread far and wide, then the blend is likely to be based around some form of distributed learning – either electronic or text-based. If timeliness and regular, rapid updating are essential, then elements of e-learning will be important to the blend. If you have large numbers of learners, then it is more likely that you can justify including multi-media resources, with their high development costs, in the blend. So long as the skills and know-how to be cultivated are largely *generic* (rather than company-specific), you may obtain excellent value by including off-the-shelf resources in your blend. And so on. Various tools for thinking through the practicalities, and for preparing a business case for proposals to shift to blended learning, are now available (for example, Clark, 2003; Harrison, 2003).

But the really interesting issues in blending are to do with the *sort* of learning required, and what this will involve. The range is huge. It starts with quite straightforward instances, such as acquiring further information (about a new product, say); or learning the latest systems or procedures (perhaps for a new computer system, or for a new company process). Learning of this sort – sometimes called *single-loop learning* – generally involves extensions to existing knowledge or elaborations and refinements of it. Often the learning can be formulated in terms of issues and questions for which answers can be authoritatively pronounced right or wrong. Indeed, sometimes much of the learning can be presented in terms of a series of progressively more challenging tests and puzzles that learners can rattle through in their own time and at their own paces. Also, computer-based tests can take account of prior learning and previous answers; by comparison, classroom or paper based tests are far more limited.

Now contrast this with another – classic – instance of learning, that involved when a technician, engineer, scientist or professional starts taking on responsibility for the team, section, project or department, and has to start learning *to be a manager*. Courses can help with this career and role transition by providing concepts and frameworks to assist reflection on issues in one's day–to-day work, and approaches to guide action (for example, in thinking through delegation, or concerning interpersonal skills, negotiation, leadership ...). Again, one can test whether such ideas have been correctly understood, but with this sort of learning that does not take anyone very far. What matters is whether and when and how those ideas are *used in practice*. And since that practice concerns 'soft' issues, use of the ideas cannot sensibly be approached in terms of the correct application of abstract rules. Context is all, and the newly appointed manager (or team or project leader ...) with all their pre-existing relationships that now need to be renegotiated, is a vital part of that context. So the person teaching the course will probably say, authoritatively, that they cannot offer right and wrong answers! Moreover, the managerial role may require embracing quite different concerns and ways of thinking, some of which sit uncomfortably with pre-existing values or professional commitments.

This sort of learning – *double-loop* learning – can at times be experienced as deeply frustrating and confusing (why don't they just tell us how to do it? why do they complicate everything? ...). One is not just adding in some more knowledge, but rethinking what one thought one knew. It involves un-learning as well as learning. It is about making personal *meaning*, rather than (or as well as) acquiring *information*. As two Harvard educators put it:

> When we solve a problem quickly, the one thing we can usually be certain of is that we ourselves are the same people coming out of the problem as we were going into it ... The point of the problem is not really that the students produce solutions. In fact, if the students too easily solve the problems, the teacher does not even regard them as good problems. The idea is not so much that the learners solve the problems as that the problems solve the learners. The good problems require the students to stretch and change their own ... understanding. Good teachers bother their students in useful ways. ... This collection of good problems for our learning is what is meant by a curriculum.

> For our learning as adults we are no less in need of a rich curriculum, a collection of good problems with which we can bear hanging out. But no clever educator need write our curriculum. It is waiting there in the text and tangle of our everyday experience ... *(Kegan and Lahey, 2001: 43–44)*

In short, double-loop learning increases our capacities; it changes us. But that involves us putting aside some familiar ways of thinking and experiencing, ways that served us well, and were perhaps so natural to us we were not even aware of them. It may not be fun.

Now consider a third instance of, or context for, learning – a multi-disciplinary team tackling a complex task involving scientific, technological, logistical, legal, financial and managerial dimensions. The task shares some features with others that various members of the team have tackled before in different settings, but is also unique. The learning in this case involves knowledge sharing, problem-solving and new knowledge creation. Whether the team is distributed or co-located (and if so for how much of the time), collaboration, investigation, and discussion will be central to the process. What's more, it is through involvement in such projects that recent graduates learn their trade, acquiring the experience and 'tacit knowledge' that cannot be taught, but that distinguishes the mature professional from the novice.

Three very different types of learning have been considered – the single-loop learning of, for example, new product information; the double-loop learning of a significant role transition; and the complex problem-solving of a multi-disciplinary team. Each of these could be technologically enhanced, that is, these could be instances of blended learning. However, they are entirely different, and what is needed for the learning to be reasonably successful is also very different. In the second instance, *support* is likely to be a key issue; and in the third the learning is inherently *investigative* and *collaborative*. In both, the learning has to be in different ways *self-directed* (either individually or collectively). It doesn't work if those outside the process try to control it at all closely – they are not in a position to 'know better', and any intervention may well be disruptive or demoralizing. In both instances, too, the *social dimension* of learning is clear. Very often we learn easily and naturally by watching and listening to others, by asking questions and by being shown how to do things by people who provide feedback on our actions and responses; or just by arguing passionately with people we respect, about things that matter to us.

Hence, if one of these more demanding forms of learning is needed, then, one way or another, the blend has to allow for support, investigation, collaboration, self-direction, and the formation and maintenance of social bonds. All of which may be obvious – but still easily overlooked when very broad terms like 'training', 'e-learning' and 'instructional design' are used casually. They carry over assumptions of straightforward information transfer and single-loop learning into contexts where something completely different is required.

Blending in practice

Call centres provide a context in which an e-rich blend of learning has been very successful. Call centre operatives need to be trained to use the call centre technology, to be able to deal with specific enquiries and to be polite and helpful – and all within a very short time. Much of this training can be delivered and assessed using CBT (computer based training), with some added face-to-face sessions based on simulations of dealing with difficult customers. Basic management training, once the preserve of conventional taught courses, now provides the opportunity for an e-component using the wide range of topics available online. Some of these are used as 'one shot', 'just in time' learning experiences available on demand (self-direction), others are structured to form a coherent package and linked to discussion groups (peer support), workplace-based assignments, and group projects (collaboration, social bonds). That is, the e-components are part of an ongoing learning process that can also take advantage of the fact that the staff are co-located.

Now consider the situation of workers on oil rigs – who may be spread all round the globe. In this case, e-learning is probably the only attractive proposition for training on a wide range of technical, procedural (health and safety) and management issues. However, this in itself does not mean it will work. The components that are likely to be critical in achieving completion, 'deep' learning, and effective transfer to the workplace, are the nature and quality of the online support available – in terms of structured activities promoting peer-to-peer interaction, conference moderation highlighting relevance, and the responsiveness of course leaders to individual difficulties.

In general, in terms of learning design, the components that combine particularly well together are face-to-face events, online access to resources and discussion, and workplace-based activities. A face-to-face session prior to the start of a supported online course reduces the anxiety of participants and increases participation. It can also provide a boost at mid points when the online activity might be flagging. For those already operating as independent learners, a residential seminar or workshop can be enriched, and the time better used, if it is preceded by an online forum that provides the opportunity for set reading, agenda-building, and the posting of biographical details. Workplace-based learning activities, in the form of assignments that require participants to investigate real issues and try out new approaches or techniques, are motivating, ensure relevance, and may provide the opportunity for demonstrating the achievement of learning outcomes. This type of assessment also provides a strong focus for collaborative working in a distributed set or cohort of online learners. Often, the groups of people at similar points in their careers and facing similar challenges who are brought together through such courses, continue to share challenges and to support each other afterwards, establishing ongoing communities of practice (see Chapters 17 and 18).

It's the pedagogy, stupid

The moral to the story is that any discussion of the choice of medium and blending has to start from the learners, the nature of the learning and what these require. It is about pedagogy first, technology-mix second. Happily, a broad consensus now exists, based on experience and research, about how adults learn and what they need for learning (these are not the same as for children – which is why some people talk of androgogy, rather than pedagogy). The adult learning model emphasizes the importance of:

- **Ensuring personal meaning and significance:** That is, explaining why what they are about to learn is important, and relating the topic to the learners' experiences.
- **Putting learners in control:** Enabling them to make choices and to find their own way through information and resources.
- **Preparation and support:** Ensuring the learner is (more or less) ready for the experience and providing support to overcome frustrations, or fixed beliefs about learning.

Following these principles, an appropriate model for teaching adults is based much more on the teacher as a 'facilitator of learning' rather than a 'transmitter of knowledge'. Likewise, the learner is less a 'receiver of wisdom' and more of a 'processor of information' or 'generator of insight' who is focused on dealing with an issue that matters.

Figure 14.1 suggests some of the ways in which these general principles can be translated into practice in e-rich courses and programmes. It shows four critical requirements for their success, and these are discussed below. The figure also highlights the two different sorts of learning outcome that will be involved in a well-designed programme: the 'know-how' that the programme was intended to bring about, but also the learning about learning, the increased ability to find, check, absorb and share new information and ideas concerning things that matter.

A MAP OF THE LEARNING JOURNEY

Sometimes called a 'course guide', this establishes an overview of the learning journey and

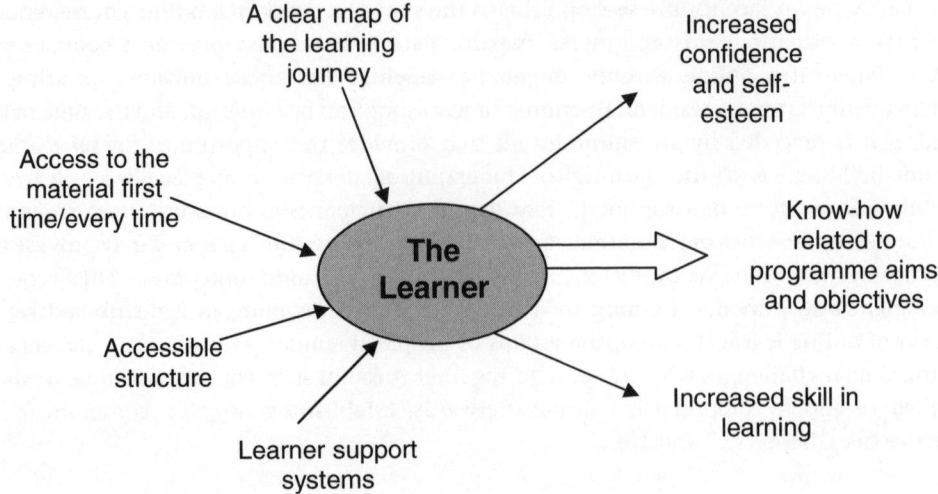

Figure 14.1   A schematic diagram of inputs and outputs for the learner

the outcomes to be achieved at various stages. It offers advice on strategies for tackling different sections and highlights deadlines. It also begins to establish the expectation that the learner is in charge, and expected to reflect and appraise their own progress. Learners are encouraged to use this resource regularly to ensure that they are literally 'on course'. Having such a 'map' reduces student anxieties about what is expected of them. It also helps them to become responsible for planning their own work schedule and establishing new patterns of learning behaviour.

ACCESS TO MATERIAL FIRST TIME/EVERY TIME

Research shows that learners who have difficulties accessing an online course experience high levels of frustration (much more so than if a lecturer fails to appear!) and tend to develop negative attitudes to online learning. The systems providing access need to be robust and reliable so that this potential barrier to learning is minimized.

ACCESSIBLE STRUCTURE

Good training is structured to provide key points as headlines for subsections. E-learning needs 'hard wiring' so that this feature is standard. Within an online course the 'key points' should also provide the basis for a learner to navigate in an exploratory manner (rather like flicking through a book) and also to move backwards and forwards to check their understanding when the point being made is not clear. Intuitive navigation is a common feature of good website design, yet is not always a feature of online learning. Good navigation provides further information and alternative explanations in the form of 'pop-up' windows so that learners can choose the depth they wish to delve into on the first reading. This provides for some of the differing learning requirements of learners.

LEARNER SUPPORT SYSTEMS

Four different forms of support may need to be available: pre-course preparation; support built in to the courseware (for example, help buttons); expert help when needed; and peer-to-peer help and emotional support. All four are likely to be necessary if an online learning environment is to be fully effective. Preparatory reading, diagnostic and study skills material all help to ensure a common starting point and reduce the feelings of inadequacy that many students bring to adult learning – especially if they have felt they were unsuccessful at school. Some of the functions of a face-to-face discussion or seminar group need to be replicated. Being able to ask questions of an expert by email, to be able to discuss issues in smaller groups, and to be able to work collaboratively are the key functions of an online support system that help to close the loops in a learning cycle. For all this the skill set of the course leaders ('e-moderators') in such an environment is, arguably, *more* crucial than in conventional face-to-face training sessions (Salmon, 2004).

THE LEARNER

Unless the course is insufficiently challenging, most students will lose confidence at one time or another. For some, this can be a big issue – arguably, our conventional education system tends to reinforce the sense of inadequacy because learners are encouraged to be dependent on 'experts' for what they learn and how they learn it. With the advent of online learning there is an opportunity to 'break the mould' and to develop learners who are confident in identifying their learning needs within a given framework, and of planning a route through it (and beyond) in a way that suits their available time and current disposition. However, the transition from dependent to independent learner is not an easy one. For many people computer-mediated learning has provided an inhospitable environment in which to engage in self-conscious learning. When they feel shut out because of software or hardware failure, or feel trapped by the system of navigation, they tend to locate the failure in themselves: 'I'm no good at this' is a common reaction – and they have little motivation to return to the scene of what is felt as humiliating.

So learners need to have the different expectations made clear; these need to be continually reinforced, and the 'psychological contract' that underpins them has to be delivered. The reality that students experience must reflect the principles. If this is done, then learners will become steadily more confident and independent – and as a result, *what is an appropriate blend changes*.

This is illustrated in Figure 14.2 showing a four module course. It begins with the learning being highly directive and dealing with the broad context. By module 4 the learning is becoming more self-directive and learners are beginning to identify the detail that is relevant to their own situation.

Whose blend is it anyway?

From the learners' perspective, the way in which components fit together is something they have to determine for themselves. To achieve this they need a confidence-building experience, followed by sufficient choice of components to enable them to determine what works best given their particular work challenges, learning styles, and situations. Figures 14.3 and 14.4 represent the blended learning experience of two individuals, using the convention that the relative distance of the element and the thickness of the lines depict the relative importance of different components in their learning experience. The point is that, in one

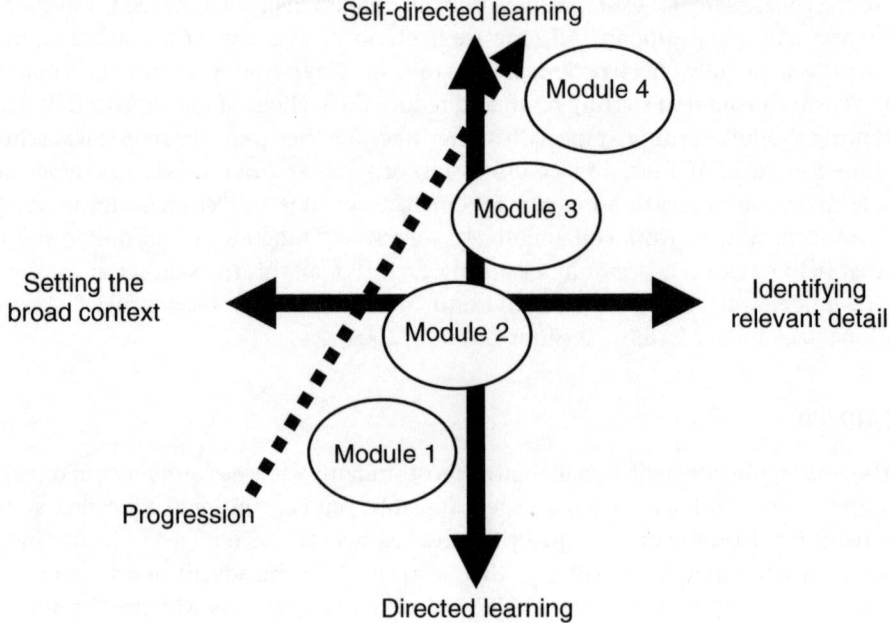

Figure 14.2   How 'learning to learn' can happen

sense, these two individuals are on 'the same' programme – the opportunities available to them are the same. At the same time, however, their programmes are very different: each has chosen to emphasize the modes of learning they find work best for them and that will make the best use of scarce time, in relation to the issues that are personally most relevant, in their

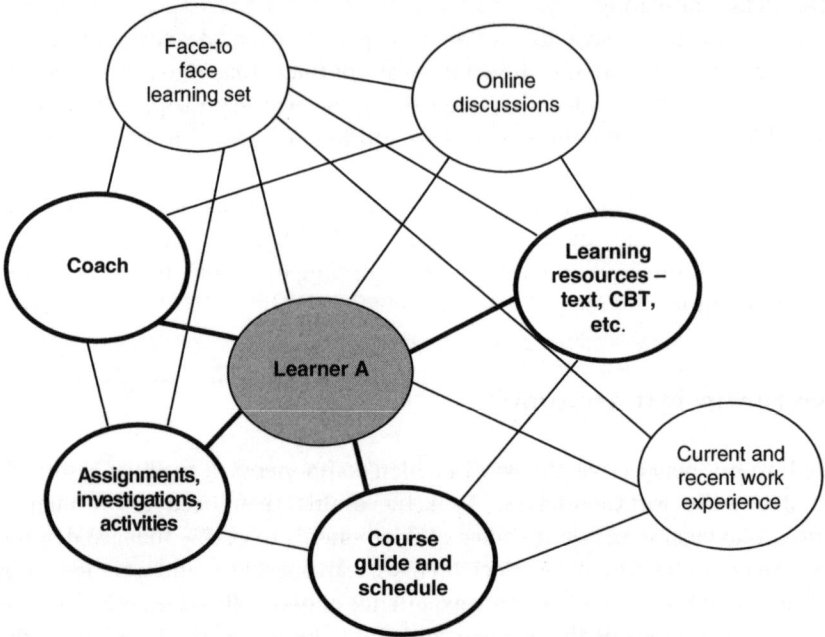

Figure 14.3   Learner A's blend – where A puts time and energy on programme x

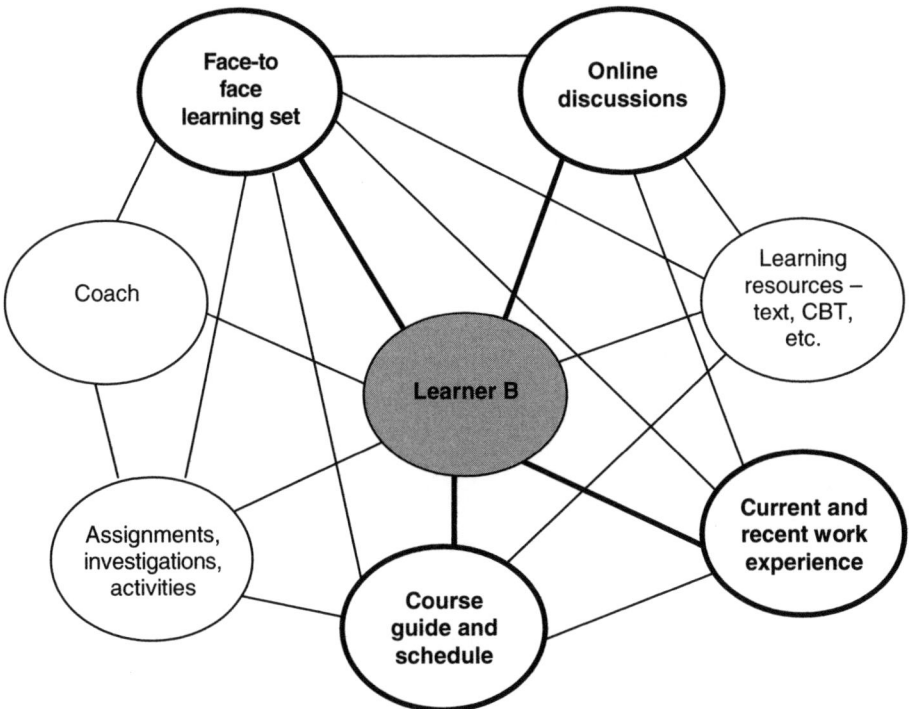

Figure 14.4   Learner B's blend on the same programme

particular situations.

Conclusions: E-learning revisited

The e-learning bubble was part of the froth of the 'dot com' era. The failures of the early forms of e-learning are now legendary – and quite well understood:

- In the rush to market the courseware tended to be adaptations of PowerPoint slides, originally designed as part of a presentation by a skilled trainer.
- Access to the courseware was often complicated, particularly when based within a learning management system (LMS).
- The organizational culture was not conducive to learning during working hours.
- The learning experience lacked a social dimension.

Nearly all technological developments are error driven: that is, improvements are made by analysing the failures in order to inform the changes needed to improve the success rates. On this basis, the analysis of the weaknesses and failures of e-learning have helped to inform the necessary attributes of successful approaches to designing blended learning. Even if standalone e-learning is rarely the answer, by providing additional elements in a mix, and introducing whole new sorts of mix, the online revolution offers transforming possibilities – greater accessibility, timeliness, cost reduction, customization and so on.

However, to make effective use of an e-learning environment, staff need to become independent – that is, more self-motivated, self-disciplined and taking responsibility for noticing where they have needs. For many this is an uncomfortable shift from the relative comfort zone of dependent learning to the uncomfortable, risky yet ultimately empowering zone of independent learning. But this is not just a challenge for staff. It presents an equal challenge to trainers, training managers and business leaders. The new approaches to staff development – that take advantage of the opportunities of blended learning – challenge the industrial (single-loop) assumptions underpinning so much training: the emphasis on control, standardization and predictability.

It takes a great deal of confidence on the part of senior management to set broad aims and then pass over control to individuals to learn how to implement policies that will achieve targets related to the broad aims. There are signs that the 'command and control' model of training is giving way to a more enlightened view of a learning organization constituted through self-organizing learning networks. Single-loop learning still has an important place, of course – but it is a part, not the whole.

References

Clark, D. (2003) *Media and media mix in e-learning*. Brighton: The Epic Group. Available from <http://www.epic.co.uk>.

Harrison, M. (2003) *Blended Learning in Practice*. Brighton: The Epic Group. Available from <http://www.epic.co.uk>.

Kegan, R. and Lahey, L.L. (2001) *How the Way we Talk can Change the Way we Work*. San Francisco: Jossey-Bass.

Salmon, G. (2004) *E-moderating: The Key to Teaching and Learning Online* (2nd edition). London: RoutledgeFalmer.

15 The Assessment of Workplace Learning: Issues and Approaches

Robin Mason

The assessment crisis

Assessment processes are known to be one of the most powerful influences on learning, yet most instructors treat assessment as a necessary evil, or at best, an add-on at the end of the training programme. This 'head in the sand' approach is not only ineffective and a waste of resources, but is actually damaging to learners. Research on assessment practices and the experience of trainers and learners confirm the fact that the negative side-effects of much assessment have long-lasting, counter productive outcomes. If learners perceive assessment as primarily to examine content knowledge, they will tend to do little more than rote learning. If course materials are over-burdened with factual content, a poor level of overall understanding usually results. Where learners feel anxious or threatened, they are more likely to adopt mechanical, surface approaches to tasks.

In this chapter, I examine current workplace assessment practices and consider a wide range of alternative methods and approaches for integrating learning and working.

The need to rethink assessment

There is a well-known tale about a person who has lost a key and goes looking for it under the light of a lamp-post. A friend comes along offering to help and asks where he lost the key. 'Well, I lost it way over there, but this is the only place light enough to look for it.'

Most current assessment practices fall into the same trap – we know they do not assess the real learning we think is taking place, but they are the only methods we have that promise high validity, reliability and ease of marking. Traditional assessments like multiple-choice questions are limited in their ability to evaluate complex thinking, deep understanding or skill in applying theoretical knowledge to real problems. Their strength typically lies in their ability to evaluate knowledge of facts and understanding of concepts. In order to assess learners' ability to use what they know to solve complex problems, to communicate their understanding or to work together cooperatively, different types of assessment must be used. A true test should engage the learner – in making judgements, interacting with others; in short, in doing something worth doing so that others can observe and evaluate it. 'A true test provides [the learner] with opportunities to apply their knowledge and skills to enduring and emerging issues and problems – ill-defined problems – and it requires the integration of discipline-based knowledge and general skills' (Huba and Freed, 2000: 221). Too often discussions of assessment in work-based learning are reduced to a discourse on measurement.

It has been argued that traditional assessment fails to provide opportunities for learners to learn the very thing they most need to know: how to assess their own learning. One of the aims of education must surely be to prepare learners for an increasingly unknowable future. There is a need for training programmes in which trainees reach not just immediate course-related goals but much wider learning and self-development goals.

Existing assessment practices frequently disempower learners and put the control and the judgement of learning in the hands of the assessors and tutors. For a learning society, it is the individual learner who needs to develop the skills to assess their own and others' materials, to make judgements about quality and value, to give and receive feedback. One of the most significant tasks of the tutor is to help students develop these lifelong learning skills.

Apart from the ineffectual and sometimes negative effects of many assessment processes, there are even more compelling reasons for rethinking assessment at this time. As organizations are increasingly realizing that their staff are their most important resource, it follows that improving the knowledge, skill and understanding of employees is the most important productivity investment that organizations can make. Lifelong learning has become the 'solution' to the problem created by the Information Age. The shelf-life of a degree is reckoned to be no more than about five years; employees need to take more responsibility for maintaining their employability throughout their working life, not once for life. In short, we can no longer afford to indulge in assessment practices that inhibit learning. Assessment can act as a vehicle for learning; it must not be a punishment, an after-thought or an accreditation mechanism.

Workplace learning

The typical workplace training programme is a response to senior level initiatives to:

- increase human capital;
- boost quality, efficiency or marketing success;
- improve technical skills;
- contribute to professional or managerial development.

Conventionally, programmes have been delivered to employees in the form of discrete courses, or workshops designed to cover gaps in the organization's capability. Organizations are increasingly finding this model to be unsatisfactory, especially as they face a competitive landscape that is characterized by global competition, complex and dynamic markets, rapid technological innovation, distributed workforces and rising stakeholder expectations. Formal courses that take experienced and knowledgeable employees away from the workplace, and rely upon a simple competence model of learning are seen as increasingly irrelevant. In conditions of frequent, often unpredictable change, learning is neither a luxury nor a secondary issue – it is one of the axes on which the future of the company will be decided.

The need for continual updating, re-training, or up-skilling is reflected in two associated phenomena:

- The rise of online learning
- A new focus on informal learning.

Employers, less and less willing to allow employees to go off on training courses away from the workplace for days at a time, are turning to online learning as a more flexible, cheaper and more appropriate medium for just-in-time learning. Online learning in its best form is not simply a set of page-turning computer-based training materials transferred to the web, but involves support from a tutor, interaction with other learners and content designed for the online environment.

Informal learning is intimately related to job performance; it may not be formally organized into a programme or curriculum by the employer, but it accounts for a good deal of the learning arising out of interactions between colleagues, ad hoc personal studies and the experience of work itself. The Education Development Center in Massachusetts has conducted substantial research on informal learning in manufacturing companies, and claims that 70 per cent of job-related learning takes place outside formal training events (Dobbs, 2000; Stamps, 1998).

What implications do these changes in workplace learning have for assessment of learning? It seems overly trite to say that if the nature of learning is changing, the nature of assessment should change as well. Nevertheless, as the opening anecdote illustrated, assessment has often not kept pace with changes in the nature and the processes of learning. In order to analyse how assessment should change, it is useful to break workplace learning into three separate categories described below.

LEARNING THROUGH WORK

This is the category that encompasses all kinds of informal learning and is defined as learning that occurs through direct work experience, individually or within teams or other collective groupings. Assessment of this kind of learning is relatively new and is the focus of much innovative practice. It is focused around reflection on work practices and the processes of reviewing and learning from experience. As the learning arises from ongoing projects and challenges, the knowledge that emerges is generally a shared and collective activity, one in which people discuss ideas and share problems and solutions. Online communities of practice, especially in geographically distributed companies, are one example of informal learning whose value is beginning to be recognized. Appropriate assessment of such a learning activity should reflect this collaborative origin.

LEARNING FOR WORK

Typically conducted at the beginning of a career, learning for work is defined as learning outside the workplace that is intended as preparatory or complementary to the work role. It has been referred to derogatorily as 'just in case' learning. A formal example might be a work placement as part of a sandwich degree programme. More broadly interpreted, it occurs through contact with professional bodies, interest groups and external boards and committees of all kinds.

Should this kind of work-based learning programme be assessed? There is a strong movement towards competency standards in the area of occupational and employment-related learning. Not only are courses defined in terms of outcomes to be achieved, but also the assessment is linked to the criteria expressed in the competency standards. 'To prove competency means having to demonstrate the attainment of skills and attitudes, not just having to write about them. Secondly, assessment becomes not merely a means of judging knowledge and performance, but an integral part of the learning process itself' (Gray, 2001: 6).

This implies the need for performance-based assessment that is criterion-referenced (judging outcomes against predefined standards), and directly related to the work situation.

LEARNING AT WORK

This category includes all company in-house training or learning opportunities that are offered by the employer or as a consequence of employment, which require work to be set aside in favour of activities that stimulate or simulate work tasks. This kind of learning is often assessed through multiple choice questions, especially when the content is delivered online. Managers like this form of assessment because they can be sure that all of the appropriate employees have met the standard set and can be considered trained on a particular issue or piece of software and so on.

Assessment in the workplace

The effect of the need for lifelong learning as well as the interest in informal learning, communities of practice and team working generally, is a noticeable blurring of the hitherto clear-cut categories of learning and working. Given this convergence, it is obvious that the processes for assessing learning should converge with existing processes for setting objectives, meeting targets, monitoring accountability, agreeing developmental plans and similar tacit forms of assessment.

Companies that take the human capital approach seriously are already innovating in the area of assessment. Examples of best practice in 'assessing for learning' can be categorized into three broad areas:

- Self-evaluation
- Peer evaluation
- Instructor evaluation.

SELF-EVALUATION

The driving force in lifelong learning is not the acquisition of knowledge in itself, but rather self-actualization of individuals themselves through the organizations where they work and live. A necessary condition of becoming a lifelong learner is to develop the ability to assess one's capabilities and learning needs. At one end of the scale, self-assessment can involve grading one's own work against a set of criteria given by a tutor. Brown and Knight (1994) quote research that shows this to be a relatively reliable method of grading and one that develops reflective, self-directed learners as well. Tutors still have an active role to play in helping learners to establish assessment criteria and in facilitating the reflective process.

Multiple choice questions with feedback on both right and wrong answers have been shown to be highly valued by learners, as a formative assessment tool. Learners can use such a test to evaluate their own process of mastery of content; they can retake the test following further study and can use the feedback to deepen their understanding.

Self-assessment does not have to involve grading; it may be about reflecting on the process of learning itself. Towler (2000) describes a career-long learning process that is based on self-evaluation methods:

> One of their first assignments is on 'Own Organization Monograph and Career Development' (OOMCD) in which they are asked to evaluate their career development in the context of their organization's requirements. This includes evaluating their past learning and identifying future learning aims. They are also required to develop specific learning objectives and create an action plan to achieve them.
>
> Their final assignment … takes the OOMCD a step further. This is usually completed somewhere between eighteen months and two years after starting their programme. They are asked to assess progress against the action plan from their OOMCD. They are asked to evaluate how the off-the-job learning has been transferred to their work and vice versa. They are also asked to update their learning plans by producing a new set of learning objectives for the following twelve months. (p. 220)

Learners may either be the harshest judges of themselves, or be inclined to inflated perceptions of their own capabilities. For this reason, the ability to reflect upon and assess one's own understanding or performance is as much a learning process as it is an assessment process. Learners are greatly assisted in developing the ability to assess themselves by the use of guidelines, criteria or standards. These can be provided by a tutor or trainer, or they can be jointly agreed with a line manager or developed in a group or team.

PEER EVALUATION

If learners are actively involved in decisions about how to learn and what to learn and why they are learning, it is equally appropriate to involve them in decisions about criteria for assessment and the process of judging their own and others' work. Furthermore, their engagement with the learning process will be qualitatively different from learners who are the recipients of teaching and the object of others' unilateral assessment. In collaborative assessment environments, learners work together to develop, review and assess each other's course work. It thus seeks to foster a learning approach to assessment.

Peer evaluation practices fall into two categories: those that involve individual work marked by peers, and those that involve group assignments as well as peer marking. The value of the former lies in the development of peer marking skills: judging the quality of work and preparing helpful feedback. In the latter case, the ability to work in teams is added to the mix of outcomes. The usual concern about peer assignments centres on the issue of uneven contribution of team members. This limitation can be turned into a learning opportunity as the following implementation exemplifies:

> In a self-managed learning environment, one way of approaching the issue of participation (and accountability to the group) is to ask each group to manage the process themselves. We are currently involving our students in forms of self- and peer assessment of individual participation, which is proving challenging for them but also surprisingly

useful too. We require each participant to review their contribution to the groups' work against a set of criteria, and then have their peers and tutor also present their review of that person's contribution against the criteria. The various reviews of those involved are shared within the group and become the basis for a discussion about the nature of participation. This open, reflective process helps each member communicate why they participated in the ways they did, and helps other members 'hear' those explanations while also providing their views on the nature of that person's participation. This has the beneficial effect of forcing discussion of the issue whilst reducing the possibility of a purely negative approach being taken: of people 'accusing' each other without knowing the particular background and circumstances of each person.

It also has the benefit of members approaching the issue as a learning event, one from which they can learn about the various ways in which people participate and the reasons for that. (*McConnell, 2002: 88*)

INSTRUCTOR EVALUATION

The practice of instructors (or trainers or line managers) carrying out the assessment of learners (or workers) is by far the most common form of evaluation both in education and the workplace. The limitations of this have often been noted:

I have long argued that an educated person is an aware, self-determining person, in the sense of being able to set objectives, to formulate standards of excellence for the work that realises these objectives, to assess work done in the light of those standards, and to be able to modify the objectives, the standards or the work programme in the light of experience and action; and all this in discussion and consultation with other relevant persons. If this is indeed a valid notion of what an educated person is, then it is clear that the educational process in all our main institutions of higher education does not prepare students to acquire such self-determining competence. For staff unilaterally determine student learning objectives, student work programmes, student assessment criteria, and unilaterally do the assessment of the students' work. (*Heron, 1981*)

Nevertheless, there are ways in which instructor assessment can be a learning experience. The elements of successful instructor-led assessment have been well rehearsed (though rarely practised in full). The following qualities are necessary components of exemplary practice:

- **Validity:** A valid assessment task must match the intended learning outcomes. In addition, the results of good assessment should predict performance in the workplace. Predictive validity is of particular importance to organizations that are sponsoring their staff through work-based learning programmes. For most organizations, and particularly those operating in a commercial environment, the financial 'bottom line' is paramount. Like any other activity, sponsorship of a work-based learning programme is seen as a means by which the skills and aptitudes of staff can be developed for the commercial benefit of the organization. It is important, then, when work-based learning assessment processes identify someone as a 'high performer', that this is translated into high performance activity in the workplace (Gray, 2001: 9).
- **Authenticity:** Devising assessments that invite students to apply course concepts to their own working context and that focus on the reality of ill-defined problems, are much more challenging and motivating than abstract problems with tidy solutions. Workplace

problems have the benefit of being complex and poorly structured, and so offer excellent opportunities for learners to demonstrate a blend of higher order skills, knowledge and attitudes in their response (Morgan and O'Reilly, 1999: 57).

- **Responsiveness:** Providing feedback on assignments that guides learners about how to improve their work is one of the prime ways of turning assessment into a learning experience. Even better are iterative procedures in which learners are offered the opportunity to refine and improve their assessed work on the basis of feedback from the instructor.
- **Transparency:** Explaining to learners the criteria against which their work will be judged is an essential feature of an assessment process that aims to promote learning. This means that the marking scheme, the key criteria, the level of mastery required, the quality of work expected, should all be made public. By making assessment standards public, a more trusting relationship is fostered between teacher and learners. The grading criteria are no longer a secret that only perceptive learners can discover. Fairness in judging learners' work is an obvious corollary to this, and openness about the marking scheme helps to achieve fairness:

A number of reasons are often cited for retaining 'objective' tests (the design of which is usually quite 'subjective'), among them: the unreliability of teacher-created tests and the subjectivity of human judgment. However, reliability is only a problem when judges operate in private and without shared criteria. In fact, multiple judges, when properly trained to assess actual student performance using agreed-upon criteria, display a high degree of inter-rater reliability. (*Wiggins, 1989: 710*)

Assessment methods

Assessment methods can be seen on a continuum from the highly individual, such as learning contracts, to the highly standardized, such as objective tests and exams that test content knowledge. In the middle, we find essays and other tasks that encourage learners to relate or apply specified issues and concepts to their own settings. The essence of choosing the right method is appropriateness – to the context, to the desired outcomes and to the nature of the learning material. The following list provides some examples of assessment methods that, if used appropriately, can provide a learning experience as well as a means of evaluating learning.

LEARNING CONTRACTS

Learning contracts are usually individually negotiated processes between the learner and the instructor, in which an individual programme of study to achieve specified outcomes is mutually agreed. The following elements are usual in the contract (Gray, 2001: 21):

- The learner's personal objectives
- Their professional objectives
- Work-based projects or initiatives they intend to pursue
- Any potential APEL (Accreditation of Prior Experiential Learning) claim
- The specification of a coherent body of knowledge to be mastered
- An agreed timetable

- Resources that can be accessed
- Support from the organization (sponsor, mentor or line manager).

Learning contracts are ideal for negotiating non-standard programmes of learning that reflect both personal and employer needs.

Brown and Knight (1994) describe four stages in learning contract development:

1. Constructing a profile of the skills, knowledge and understanding of the learner
2. Specifying the learning outcomes to be achieved
3. Devising an action plan either individually or in small groups or with a tutor, to identify timescales, resources and actions
4. Evaluation of how successfully the learning outcomes have been met.

PORTFOLIOS

One of the main benefits of using portfolios as an assessment method is that it promotes learners' ownership of their learning process. A portfolio usually consists of the learner's selection of evidence of their achievements. Within the workplace, this might consist of reports, correspondence, minutes of meetings, email communications, documents and presentations. Ideally, it should be accompanied by an overview document in which the learner draws together a coherent narrative about their achievements, using portfolio items as supporting evidence. Portfolios are the usual method used for submitted APEL evidence.

Another value of the portfolio method is the opportunity it provides learners to become more aware of their own learning processes – in short, to develop meta-cognitive skills.

Metacognition implies that the learner has knowledge of the private intellectual approaches and strategies that he or she employs in learning, as well as some awareness of how other learners' approaches may differ. These perspectives allow students to critique and evaluate their own effectiveness as learners, providing feedback to themselves to guide improvements. (*Huba and Freed, 2000: 244*)

Some form of written reflection is an important component of the process of developing meta-cognitive skills. This might take the form of a learning log, running commentary or journal, in order that the assessor can identify not only the degree of improvement, but also the way in which the learner has thought about their work.

Examples of the portfolio process applied to workplace learning might include:

- an accountability record in which the learner documents the targets met and provides a commentary on what they learned in the process of meeting the targets, developments in their views, attitudes, behaviours or work relationships;
- personal development portfolio that could document the evolution of a presentation, report or project from early notes through to final piece of work;
- annual learning record, documenting formal training as well as informal learning experiences accompanied by reflections on how the learning has been applied, examples of outcomes of the training;
- a work placement in which the learner keeps a learning log detailing events, attitudes and critical learning incidents.

PRESENTATIONS

Presentations are an ideal way of demonstrating the findings or recommendations of a project and can be assessed either by a tutor or by a peer group. It is important that the assessment criteria are defined beforehand, and that the content and process standards for the work are made clear to the learner. This method is applicable both to formative and summative assessment.

A modified version of a presentation might be a display, in which a team produces a poster display of their project outcomes. The value of this form of assessment is its focus on working collectively and constructively in teams. In addition, it helps develop skills in summarizing information succinctly and presenting it in a visually appealing way. The assessment process could include a presentation or defence orally to the judges.

PROJECTS

As a form of assessment, projects have to involve set goals. Participants should demonstrate a project plan, use of resources, anticipated and actual outcomes. It might involve the development of a product, in which case both the process and quality of reasoning that led to it, are evaluated. Projects can be carried out individually or through group work; they can be assessed by the instructor, the group or the individual. Applying criteria and making judgements are high-level learning activities, and the learning pay-off of self-assessing and/or peer assessing is often much higher than that of undertaking the assessed task on its own. Even more, when learners are involved in formulating and prioritizing assessment criteria to use in peer assessment, this activity in its own right has considerable learning pay-off relating to the learning outcomes being addressed by the assessment (Race, 2001: 21).

Online assessment

There are two distinct forms of online assessment: 'web-based assessment' (or sometimes computer-aided assessment), that is, various forms of multiple choice questions delivered via the web, and what is very loosely called 'online assessment', which usually refers to all those practices which involve web resources and/or communication with fellow learners. The pedagogy underlying these two categories is quite different: web-based assessment tends to be used in areas with a scientific, numeric or information technology (IT) basis and online assessment in areas of soft skills requiring analysis, reflection, teamwork or research.

While many forms of online assessment are simple copies of practices common in traditional, face-to-face teaching environments, others build on the unique properties of the web. Examples copied from traditional environments include:

- Assessment in the form of portfolios of work
- Research and critical review of resources
- Computer-marked quizzes
- Reflective journals
- Negotiated learning contracts.

All these have direct online equivalents, although they can be enhanced and improved through web delivery. Examples that have arisen because of the unique properties of the web include:

- Online debates
- Group discussions that form the basis of either individual or group assignments
- Individual and collaboratively produced websites
- Peers in remote locations commenting on assignments
- Repositories of student assignments for consulting and reuse.

The increased interactivity afforded by the web provides the most exciting area for innovative assessment, especially for distributed learners. The access to a wider range of resources, as well as to fellow learners, leads to a new set of skills and understandings that online courses are providing. These should be included in the course aims and objectives and also in the assessment of the course.

Networking presents new challenges for designers of assessment where accreditation is involved, because of the need to establish student identity and to ensure that students are aware of guidelines on plagiarism.

Electronic submission and marking of scripts lends itself to the use of a variety of formats in assignments, notably HTML. This opens up new opportunities for innovative assignments that encourage research beyond conventional course materials and caters for a variety of interests and levels of experience.

WEB-BASED ASSESSMENT

Web-based assessment offers much more scope for comprehensive testing of course objectives and student understanding than the old multiple choice systems (Brown et al., 1999). Examples include: fill-in-the-blanks, matching questions, multiple right answers, graphical hotspots, ranking, sequencing, assertion-reason, and so on. They are demanding and expensive to develop but are cost-effective with large numbers of learners and are particularly appropriate for multinational training. They are easy to quality assure, to 'deliver' and to mark and record. They require very little input from tutors.

The literature on web-based assessment, the software and support tools, and the availability of case studies from which to discover the pitfalls, are more extensive than the equivalent in the much broader category of online assessment. Software vendors maintain sites full of useful tips, case studies and practice sessions, for example:

- <http://www.questionmark.com/uk/home.htm>
- <http://www.i-assess.co.uk>.

Conferences on web-based assessment have websites with full text papers, for example:

- <http://www.lboro.ac.uk/service/ltd/flicaa/conf2001/pdfs/>
- <http://www.autc.gov.au/forum/papers.htm>.

Portals on the practice of web-based assessment are also a rich source of resources, tools, papers and frequently asked questions (FAQs), for example:

- <http://www.caacentre.ac.uk/>.

From these and other sources, it is possible to draw a number of conclusions. First of all, learners are generally positive about this type of assessment because of:

- the immediate feedback and grading (if applicable);
- the convenience and flexibility for part-time and remote learners;
- the clarity and objectivity of the procedures;
- the fact that they are less demanding than other forms of assessment.

However, there is growing evidence that the most useful application of web-based assessment is for formative and self-assessment strategies rather than as summative and graded assessment. Innovative practitioners are beginning to regard web-based assessment as part of the learning process, by building in extensive feedback, opportunities to go back and re-do the tests, especially as a revision exercise, and as an integrated activity with simulations and other interactive teaching materials.

Where instructors are using web-based assessment as a means of reducing their marking workload, the results are somewhat less positive. Many novices to the process have discovered that writing 'good' multiple choice questions is challenging and time-consuming. The use of multimedia – graphics, photos, audio clips and simulations – broadens considerably the type of question that can be set, but usually means the process of assessment design becomes a team production requiring IT support and even developmental testing.

Conclusion

From this list of alternative approaches, a tension is apparent between assessment processes that are too focused on skills development and hence miss the wider value of learning, and those that are too process oriented and hence miss the point of the original training objective. Finding the appropriate balance between these two extremes is always the aim.

A second tension lies in the balance between pedagogical effectiveness on the one hand and the practicalities of marking, providing reliability and assuring validity.

Implicit in this whole analysis is that the role of the instructor is even more vital than before:

- With web-based assessment, there is considerable skill needed to devise appropriate, challenging and workable questions.
- With most other assessment methods, the instructor needs to understand the relationship between course content, outcomes and assessment methods, and to identify real criteria for assessment.

However, with the convergence of learning and working, there needs to be a much wider ownership of learning. It can no longer be the preserve of the training department. The role of the manager must include an awareness of the learning needs and propensities of their staff. All employees must develop a sense of responsibility for their learning and learn to take time to learn.

There are numerous examples of reward systems that reinforce undesirable behaviours while ignoring those that are desirable:

- We hope for teamwork and collaboration, but we reward just the outstanding member.
- We hope for innovative thinking and risk taking, but we reward 'avoiding errors'.
- We hope for the development of people skills, but we reward technical advancements.
- We hope for employee involvement and empowerment, but we keep a tight control over operations and resources.

Assessment is the means by which learners judge what is important. It defines the de facto curriculum.

Learning for, through and at the workplace is necessary to create a dynamic, flexible workforce. Assessment tools require the delivery of outcomes of direct relevance to the workplace. Assessment processes are no longer the preserve of academic institutions. They should be a partnership between tutors, employers and learners.

References and further reading

Boud, D. (1986) *Implementing Student Self-assessment*, HERDSA Green Guide No. 5. Canberra: ACT.

Boud, D. (2000) 'Sustainable assessment: Rethinking assessment for the learning society', *Studies in Continuing Education*, 22(2): 151–167.

Brown, S. and Knight, P. (1994) *Assessing Learners in Higher Education*. London: Kogan Page.

Brown, S., Race, P. and Bull, J. (1999) *Computer Assisted Assessment in Higher Education*. London: Kogan Page.

Dobbs, K. (2000) 'Simple moments of learning', *Training*, 37(1): 52–54.

Gonczi, A. (1999) 'Competency-based learning: a dubious past – an assured future?', in D. Boud and J. Garrick (eds) *Understanding Learning at Work*. London: Routledge.

Gray, D. (2001) *A Briefing on Work-based Learning*. Learning and Teaching Support Network Briefing Series. Available from: <http://www.ltsn.ac.uk/search.asp?page=1&section=generic>.

Heron, J. (1981) 'Self and peer assessment' in T. Boydell and M. Pedler (eds) *Management Self-development*. Aldershot: Gower.

Huba, M. and Freed, J. (2000) *Learner-Centered Assessment on College Campuses*. Boston: Allyn and Bacon.

McConnell, D. (2002) 'The experience of collaborative assessment in e-learning', *Studies in Continuing Education*, 24(1): 73–92.

Morgan, C. and O'Reilly, M. (1999) *Assessing Open and Distance Learners*. London: Kogan Page.

Race, P. (2001) *A Briefing on Self, Peer and Group Assessment*. Learning and Teaching Support Network Briefing Series. Available from: <http://www.ltsn.ac.uk/search.asp?page=1&section=generic>.

Reynolds, J., Caley, L. and Mason, R. (2002) 'How do People Learn?' Research report for Chartered Institute of Personnel and Development (CIPD), London.

Stamps, D. (1998) 'Learning ecologies', *Training*, 35(1): 32–38.

Towler, D. (2000). 'Learning renewal: A manifesto for career-long development', in G. Prestoungrange, E. Sandelands, and R. Teare (eds) *The Virtual Learning Organization. Learning at the Workplace Campus*. London: Continuum.

Wiggins, G. (1989) 'A true test: Toward more authentic and equitable assessment', *Phi Delta Kappan*, May: 703–713.

16 *Developing an E-enabled Corporate Learning Strategy*

Peter Bentley

Introduction

The case for tutor-supported e-learning as an alternative learning delivery method – in terms of accessibility, timeliness, consistency, cost and so on – is simple. Indeed, it is pretty well 'case proven'. But working out *when* and *how* and *where* and *with whom* to make *effective use* of e-learning, in order to meet the disparate needs of a large multinational company, is quite another matter. That challenge is as complex and uncertain as the basic case is straightforward. For those of us involved in learning and development, tackling that challenge has itself been a learning process, tackled through the classic cycle of planning, doing, reviewing, and then planning anew. This chapter aims to show what that process is like – and to convey some of its excitement – based on the experience of the Shell Open University (SOU) within the Shell Group of companies (see below). It reports on a recent strategic review of learning, drawing on internal documents.

The chapter starts by describing how learning and development have historically been embedded in the Shell Group, and the origins and early years of the SOU. The reasons for undertaking a strategic review are then described – followed by an account of the review process. The key ideas in the new strategy are then summarized, followed by a discussion of the early stages of implementation. The chapter ends with some reflections on the key issues that large, multicultural organizations will need to address if they are to learn how to make the most of the new opportunities for learning provision.

Backdrop: The context and origins of the SOU

The majority of Shell employees are working in Exploration and Oil Products. In these two areas of the business, Exploration and Production (EP) learning is done on a cost neutral basis while Oil Products (OP) is done on a profit-based business model. In The Netherlands, both of these learning providers work together in the same location at our dedicated learning centre in Noordwijkerhout, about 25 km from The Hague, (where the Royal Dutch headquarters is located). However, as a result of decentralization some years ago, smaller training centres within many of the operating companies around the world have been created, to address local technician/operator needs, while the Dutch location addresses staff development (mostly technical) from a global perspective. Despite our considerable progress, there are still people today who regard personal development as 'training', and going on training courses as the solution to improving skills at work. Training tends to be perceived as a cost rather than an investment and often the operating company training budget is the first to be scrutinized for a reduction when the oil price falls. The reality is that this is a multi-cultural company, and most learners are not expatriates, but local people whose first language is not necessarily English.

THE SHELL GROUP

Shell is an Anglo-Dutch group of companies (more accurately a Dutch-Anglo company) consisting of two public parent companies Royal Dutch Petroleum Company (Royal Dutch) and The 'Shell' Transport and Trading Company, plc (Shell Transport). Royal Dutch has a 60 per cent interest in the group and Shell Transport has a 40 per cent interest. The Shell Group operates in over 145 countries employing more than 115 000 people, working in local operating companies. It has five areas of business, which are:

Exploration and Production
Shell's exploration and production companies have been finding and producing oil and gas around the world for over a century. Today, we have interests in ventures in over 40 countries.

Gas and Power
The Shell Group has pioneered the gas industry for more than 30 years. Our Gas and Power business stretches across 27 countries and, to meet demand, we are developing activities in a further 18 countries. Most of our operations are joint ventures with governments or local and international partners.

Oil Products
Worldwide, Shell has an interest in more than 50 refineries engaged in the manufacture of a range of crude oil and petroleum products. Through our global network of some 46 000 Shell retail outlets, we sell vehicle fuels, food, drinks, groceries, and other items. We are the world's single largest branded retailer.

Chemicals
We produce and sell petrochemical building blocks to industrial customers globally. These go into plastics, coatings and detergents used to make many modern products like fibres and textiles, insulation, medical equipment and components for lighter, more efficient vehicles.

Shell Trading
Formerly known as Shell Transport and Shipping Company (comprising both trading and shipping) Shell Trading trades enormous volumes of crude oil, refined products, natural gas, chemicals and electrical power every day.

New businesses
Renewables and Shell Hydrogen are small, but fast-growing businesses investing in making renewable and lower-carbon energy sources competitive for large-scale use.

Shell Consumer
This is a new business focused on understanding consumers as individuals and growing our consumer business.

Shell Global Solutions
This is a network of technology companies, set up for serving both internal Shell companies and external companies in a wide range of industries.

The virtual SOU was set up at the beginning of 2000. The underlying concept was to provide a 'learning proposition' to Shell people, using the latest available information technology (IT) and to make it accessible from the existing Shell intranet (Shell Wide Web or SWW). Virtual communication provides the possibility to communicate across geographical boundaries, across individual Shell operating companies and provide individual access to learning from people's desktops at their place of work. The SOU was built on a 'bought in' learning management system (LMS), which provided a course catalogue, a range of e-learning modules, and a simple competence gap analysis tool linked to possible learning solutions from the catalogue. It also included links to external learning partners and enabled a standardized approach to electronic enrolment for the individual. There is a tool for tracking learning progress and a billing system. It also required a small two-person back-up office to deal with email questions about courses and queries about how to use the system. All this remains in place today, somewhat enhanced, but the later discovery of the need for a digital learning platform has reduced the real need for an LMS. In the future it is envisaged that it may not be required at all, especially with the imminent introduction of a standard global SAP system across Shell operating companies worldwide.

To summarize the initial achievements:

- virtual SWW Shell Open University created;
- learning management system established;
- a range of unsupported e-learning modules provided;
- course catalogue and links to learning partners advertised;
- competence evaluation and gap analysis linked to learning opportunities;
- online enrolment and billing system introduced.

Our next step was to provide the portal to SOU on the SWW and use it as the first point of contact for any learning enquiry. New competence frameworks and a gap analysis tool are on the verge of being made available via the SWW. For ease of access to any online learning event we now use the worldwide web (WWW), which not only provides employees with access to learning from their desks, but also from home, from mobile drilling rigs, cyber cafes, their vehicles – in fact anywhere that they have access to a computer and the Internet (though accessing the SWW and crossing its security firewalls is only possible from a Shell-compatible computer). Enrolment for an online learning event is done using the learning platform administration that may in future be linked directly to the global SAP system. This will take care of internal billings where required and in the new learning organization it is believed learning progress and evidence of success will become the responsibility of the learner.

During this period, too, we evolved to support online learning events as it became obvious that unsupported online modules were not effective – a drop-out rate as high as 60 per cent recorded in some instances. Furthermore, a mixture of learning experiences (virtual and face-to-face) based on both the learner's needs and the delivery requirements of each specific subject has been seen as the way forward ('blended learning').

Our initial experience was very positive, and by 2002 we had developed:

- WWW digital learning delivery platform acquired from Twente University – called 'TeleTOP';
- continuing classroom teaching in Noordwijkerhout, the regions and the operating companies;

- action learning workshops and consultancy;
- e-learning online programmes and online coaching;
- blended learning – combing the advantages of all the above designed to suit the desired learning outcomes for the learner.

In that year the Learning Centre at Noordwijkerhout provided over 300 facilitated courses, 30 new blended programmes and approximately 400 free online modules to over 9000 participants from 229 operating companies. In total around 40 000 facilitated learning days were provided to our EP and OP people.

The strategic review

At the end of 2002 we commenced developing an improved learning strategy. One of the reasons for this lay in the changing landscape of the oil industry at the time and the resultant need to develop and build on existing skill sets.

Our research indicated that, on a global basis, more than $100 million was being spent on training within EP alone and that we had over 160 classrooms and specialist learning spaces available. Yet there was still a growing skills gap in the business. Clearly existing learning resources had to be harnessed and, jointly with the operating companies, better value for the businesses had to be provided. Global thinking, acting regionally and delivering locally was required. It was from a business perspective that the question was asked: 'So what are the true problems for the businesses?'

There was a concern that the marketplace was not providing the right skills to meet today's industry needs. Although the universities offer technical degrees, they increasingly include additional subjects to attract potential students, but the resulting degrees seem to lack the depth of technical knowledge required by the industry.

We also have a problem with what we call 'the big crew change'. Recent research has identified that within the oil industry, 50 per cent of the current workforce, contractors included, will retire before 2010. Recruitment, and in particular graduate intake, was and still is less than required to meet the needs. People in the industry today are being asked to embrace an increasing amount of emerging new technology, to work as integrated teams, become more widely skilled and all within an ever-changing business environment that is managed by targets, scorecards and bottom-line dollar results.

Clearly, a learning strategy was needed that would close the widening capability gap in the businesses and, at the same time, foster a change in the corporate culture towards people wanting to learn. In other words, a learning organization where learning is an every day occurrence and seen as an investment, not a cost.

At about this time a new director of learning was appointed to the SOU who had an in-depth appreciation of the value of learning and development. As a result, a team was put together to develop an improved learning strategy, with a target of completing the project within four months.

From the start we avoided the corporate tendency to devote endless time to focusing on 'the process'! In a divergent creative activity we felt that worrying about the process was of little value and indeed could be restrictive. Instead it worked well to devise a process to meet the natural needs of the team after the needs had been identified.

First, an attempt to define 'what success might look like' was made. The subsequent ideas focused around:

- competent, capable, motivated people, developing in the business;
- developing professionals' skills on the job – driven by the business need;
- sharing our successes and failures and learning from them – globally;
- learning is based on validated information and relevant to the business;
- learning content is captured in a knowledge database and available to all anywhere, anytime;
- learning becoming a daily habit (which creates a 'learning organization');
- learning reflecting the needs of the group competence frameworks.

Success was seen as an evolution from pushing learning at the business to integrating with the business. This would encourage the pull of learning into the business, based on the business's and the individual's needs. Learning would become the catalyst to add value to the business. It would address the short-term business needs and the development of our people for the business needs in the future.

Next, we thought it a good idea to find out why adults learn and our research led us to the work done by Malcolm Knowles (Knowles et al., 1998).

He suggests there are four characteristics of adult learners:

1 Self-directive, **prefer to be in control of what and how they learn.**
2 Experienced, **recognize that they can draw from their experience when they learn.**
3 Ready to learn, **more interested in learning things that seem urgent or relevant.**
4 Problem-centred, **more interested in learning in situations in which they want to understand better or behave differently.**

Based on the individual's learning experiences in the team, this made sense – so these four characteristics for reflecting the needs of our future learners were adopted.

The following stage was to create some guiding principles against which the ideas that surfaced in our future strategic thinking could be evaluated – see below. They were written from the perspective of being important to us rather than definitive in their own right, and were in no particular order.

GUIDING PRINCIPLES FOR THE NEW STRATEGY

1 We should address the needs of the people in the business today and prepare people for their future roles in the business tomorrow.
   Benefits: A value proposition for recruitment and retention of people for the business. Job satisfaction now, career satisfaction in the future for our people. Competent people for the business today and tomorrow.
2 Jointly with the business, the SOU should deliver capable people.
   Benefits: Motivation for our people. Everyone capable of doing their job for the business.
3 Learning should be integrated within the business.
   Benefits: Learning becomes a habit for our people. Performance improvement for the business.
4 The business should have one clear learning identity.
   Benefits: Open access for our people. Speed of access for the business.
5 Learning should not be affected by short-term falls in $/barrel selling price.
   Benefits: Supports consistent and continuous learning culture for our people. Retains people's trust in the business commitment to learning.
6 The SOU should do what it is good at (add value – not just cost) and create partnerships with those parties who are good at what we need.
   Benefits: More learning opportunities for people. Cost-effective learning for the business.

7 Learning should be provided as close as possible to the learner, culturally and learning styles sensitive.
   Benefits: Accessible anywhere, anytime for our people. Cost-effective and timely for the business.
8 Designed learning outcomes should address competence frameworks.
   Benefits: Relevant learning for our people. Competent people for the business.
9 Jointly with the business the SOU should assess learning provided and workplace capability.
   Benefits: Internal portable qualification for our people. Consistent standards for the business.
10 Integrated IT learning technology should be a tool, not a driver.
   Benefits: Consistent, robust appropriate tools for our people. Cost-effective for the business.
11 Learning should be based on the use of small reusable knowledge objects, 'nuggets' (right time – right place).
   Benefits: Flexible learning for our people; cost-effective and timely learning application for the business.
12 The SOU should maintain and ensure its own internal learning quality standards.
   Benefits: Consistent quality for our people; consistent quality for the business.

It seemed sensible to then have a look at what the SOU was doing on the basis of 'what was it good at', 'what was it not so good at', 'where did it add value to learning and development' and, therefore, by deduction, where should the SOU use other more cost-effective 'value adders'. This was a tough exercise with some surprising results.

Rather than thinking that the entire existing course content was unique to Shell, it was realized that over 90 per cent was in the public domain and not unique at all. There was a shift from thinking that doing it in isolation was always adding value to realizing that there were comparable learning events available from the external marketplace, sometimes at less cost. It was also discovered that uptake of existing courses was not a function of price but one of promotional techniques – the quality and appropriateness of the event did not seem important to the learner! In addition, the existing competence frameworks were lacking in some skills areas, while there was insufficient learning content to address other areas.

Some time was spent addressing the issue of sharing failures and learning from them – on a global basis. A *Shell Planners* newsletter recently made the point that most corporate planning focuses on avoiding errors. In an era of uncertainty an improvised approach allowing for continuous adjustment and tolerance of mistakes will be more beneficial. Over time, the making of policy by the organization has resulted in a culture emphasis of 'over-control' of the individual (avoiding errors) and while creating a strong desire to perform successfully through scorecards (reward) it has become unacceptable to fail (fear).

This culture requires a change towards one where people feel free to admit their lack of knowledge, able to experiment knowing that the outcome may be unsuccessful, and feel secure that management will not criticize any possible failure as long as employees learn from their mistakes. A secure learning environment goes some way to meeting this.

Those activities that the SOU wanted to keep were parked for future challenge and the rest became the basis of thinking how they might be done better in the new learning strategy.

The team was now in 'divergent' creative mode and this is where the ideas for the strategy emerged. It required some effort to balance the creativity with realism – and ultimately lead the team back into 'converge' mode with a timely outcome. The pressure of a delivery date was invaluable!

The new strategy

The central idea of the strategy became: 'Move learning into the business'.
    This was supported by two tactical drivers:

- **'Providing learning for today'**: The response to an immediate business need.
- **'Developing people for tomorrow'**: The response to anticipated future needs of the business and the development needs of our employees.

The diagram shown in Figure 16.1 was used to illustrate the main elements of the strategy and how they all fitted together. The two vertical columns are the tactical drivers and the seven horizontal bars are key platforms supporting them both.

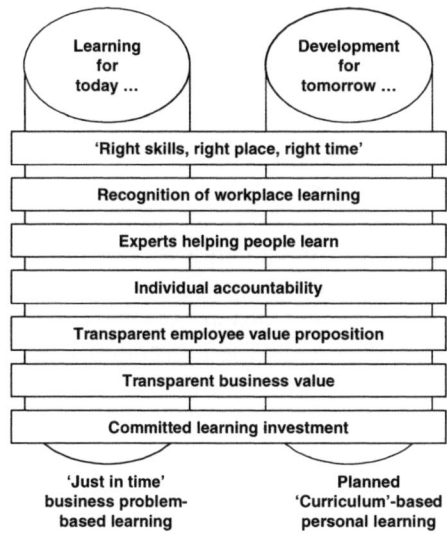

Figure 16.1   The main elements of the strategy

The 'platforms' are essential elements of the strategy, and summarized as follows:

- **Right skills, right place, right time:** Enables delivery of business performance today and prepares people for their future roles in the business tomorrow (optimizes the learning investment in our people).
- **Recognition of workplace learning:** Creates time for flexible/blended learning using appropriate learning methods and content.
- **Experts helping people learn:** Ensures knowledge transfer from more experienced people to less experienced people (50 per cent of our workforce retires within the next eight years).
- **Individual accountability:** Creates 'pull' from the business and provides an incentive for skills development, job satisfaction and individual recognition.
- **Transparent employee value proposition:** Ensures the value of learning experiences and enhances attraction and retention of our people in the business.
- **Transparent business value:** Ensures learning aligned with business needs, allows proactive monitoring of knowledge assessment and performance in the workplace.

- **Committed learning investment:** Ensures alignment between supply (people) and demand (business performance). Ensures business ownership – poor budgeting practices do not negatively impact business learning.

'Move learning into the business' is designed to build on the strengths around the group learning organizations, while eliminating non-value adding internal competition and the wasteful use of precious resources. It requires the adoption of the virtual SOU as the first 'portal of call' for learning and development support and its web-based learning platform, 'TeleTOP'. The SOU came to recognize that possession of the content on its own does not constitute adding value for a learning organization, that is, how it is applied and the designed learning outcomes required for the learner is what adds the value. The learning content among the various operating companies will be evaluated and the best made available through TeleTOP, in nugget format, free of charge for use by tutors and facilitators wherever they happen to be located in the group.

From this concept the SOU is evolving a business model proposal (not yet agreed) that says:

- Negotiated annual SOU enrollment fee payable by the business regions based on number of employees and their recognized learning needs
  Benefits:
  – SOU costs/overheads recovered through annual enrollment fee – business regions see investment (cost) per person.
  – All online-based learning will be provided free of charge to our people – 'pre-paid' from the enrollment fee (no non-value adding administration costs).
- Workshops/courses wherever delivered charged at cost to the business – no SOU profit margins included.
  Benefits:
  – Transparency of costs to the business – builds trust.
  – External competitiveness can be measured by the business.
- Learning research and development funded 'centrally by and for the group'.
  Benefits:
  – Demonstrates leadership and commitment from 'the centre' towards building an open learning organization.

The strategy also means that people in the business who have a passion for learning and coaching others, whatever the role in which they work, will be invited to come forward and provide the initial cadre of online and workplace coaches. Figure 16.2 explains in more detail the supporting roles and resources required for delivering the two tactical drivers in the business.

The strategy of moving learning into the business means that 'workplace learning' must be recognized for the value it adds – both in learning for today and development for tomorrow. It is the basis of task-based learning 'on the job' – which is also part of a blended learning design for phase 1 and 2 programmes. Courses and workshops similarly apply to task-based learning 'on the job' and structured 'curriculum-based' programmes delivered locally or regionally. The foundation for all this is the reusable 'learning nuggets' (content), which can be appropriately moved around digitally from within the TeleTOP database into learning or coaching events. The nuggets are continuously created, refreshed and reused as a

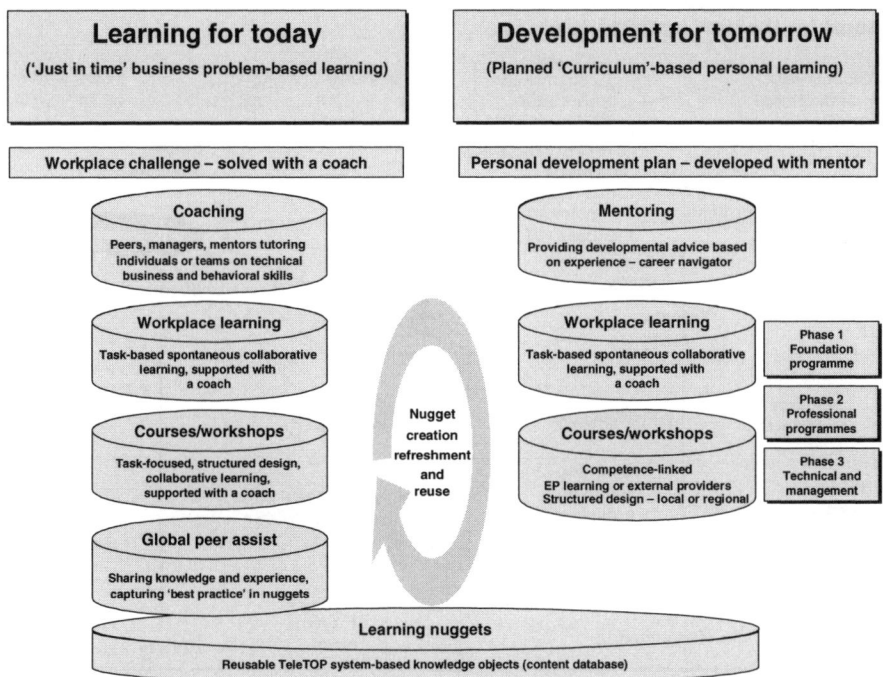

Figure 16.2   The supporting roles and resources required for delivery

result of their application to the learning process – and tracked using a user-friendly Sharable Content Object Reference Model (SCORM) tagging system.

Concurrent with developing these concepts, we quickly recognized the need for engaging the stakeholders. Creating something, however good, in isolation and then announcing it as a 'tablet of stone' to a cost-focused suspicious business was clearly not going to achieve very much in the short term, let alone the long term.

We identified all the stakeholders who could influence the strategy and positioned them using a four-quadrant matrix, the vertical axis being degree of strength of support, the horizontal axis being degree of strength of influence. A simplified version is given in Figure 16.3.

Some stakeholders obviously deserved more attention than others so we decided on four methods of approach – engage, lobby, inform and align – and allocated the most appropriate to each. The desire was to move many of them to the upper right learning strategy 'aspiration' – which in the end we managed to do.

Although at times time consuming, and not always of major benefit to the thinking of the learning strategy team, the process realized immediate and obvious benefits in gaining their input (checking and modifying our concepts) and providing us with the opportunity to demonstrate the adoption of it or, on occasions, discussing why it had not been adopted (gaining wider ownership). Best of all we generated enthusiasm, support and commitment as we developed the strategy, which is now proving invaluable during the implementation phase. Indeed, some stakeholders are now our best ambassadors and managing their enthusiasm can be challenging at times. Allocating time and resource to stakeholder engagement proved to be crucial and of much more benefit than we imagined at the time of implementing the process.

Support for the new learning strategy

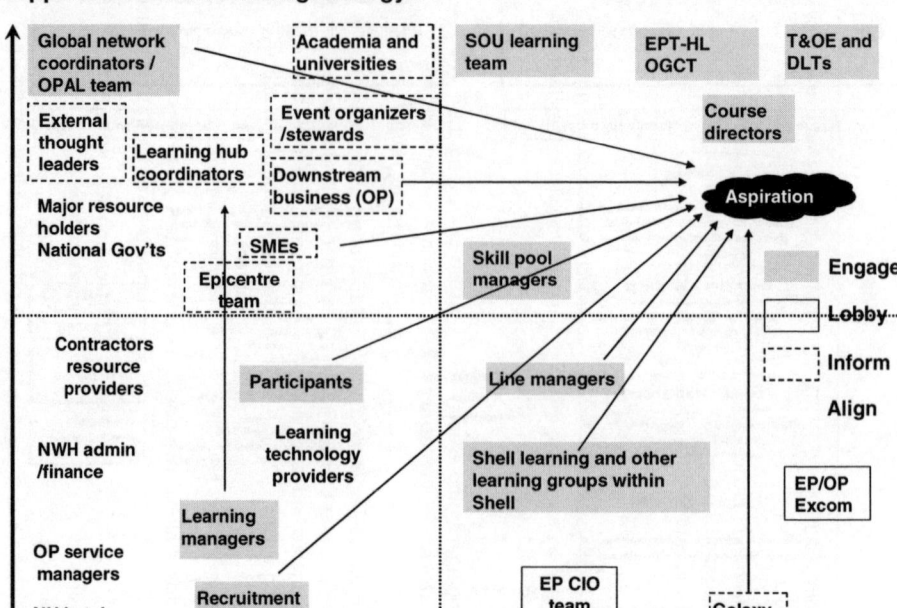

Figure 16.3   Stakeholder strength and influence

Towards implementation

In considering how to implement the strategy, the first step was to clarify the roles and responsibilities of the SOU and its customers in the regional businesses (see Table 16.1).

Table 16.1   Roles and responsibilities of the SOU and the regional businesses

	Responsible for	*Accountable to*	*Custodian of*
The regional businesses	Regional learning and development	SOU for regional learning and development	Local best learning practice
The Shell Open University	Group learning and development	Directors	Competence frameworks SOU websites Standards Assessment process Pedagogy Learning technology Learning resources

The SOU team then looked at what the new focus, responsibilities, accountabilities and tasks for people working within the virtual SOU could be (see Table 16.2). Some of the roles are evolutions from existing ones, others are new. These roles need not all be co-located in a training centre (they could be anywhere in the world) and, in some cases, they could be part

Table 16.2 The different roles and functions within the SOU

	Focus	Responsibility	Accountability	Task
Head of faculty	The business regions	The SOU faculty	Learning solutions	Manages the learning interfaces with the business regions
Knowledge, innovation and design	Pedagogy Delivery Design Innovation Networks	Creative excellence Knowledge management	Best learning practice Links to global networks, academia and SMEs	Networking academia, industry, IT and influencing SOU best practice
Tutor/coach	Learning delivery	Design and delivery of appropriate learning to meet the learner's needs (externally accredited)	Best teaching practice Provision of learning to meet agreed outcomes	Coaching individuals, groups in the workplace, the classroom and online
Event facilitator	Supporting learning events	Learner care before, during and after the learning event Assists tutor/coach	Arranging learning events Pastoral care for the learner	Assists in creating the learning environment and supporting the learner
Subject matter expert (SME)	Learning content	Relevant learning content to meet the needs of the Competence frameworks	Up-to-date, relevant, re-usable learning content for use in spontaneous and curriculum learning events	Monitoring global networks, Internet, Shell and external companies, academia and peer group for best practice content Learning outcomes
Assessor	The learners Curriculum-based events	Evidence of knowledge assessment	Consistent global assessment standards	Assessment of learners to a standard agreed with the businesses
Services	SOU	SOU support services	IT Websites Accounting Resources	Managing SOU website, IT infrastructure Standards Competence frameworks Accounting Resources

time. The transition will require careful management as the task of learning provision will require maintaining throughout. These were only concepts at this stage but designed to ensure the evolving SOU will be able to deliver its promise to the business. However, it is interesting to note that during the current implementation these ideas have been adopted and have become the basis upon which the SOU is being structured.

Having completed the divergent thinking, the SOU then had to turn the ideas into something that would demonstrate to senior management how the SOU could impact on business value.

Human resources (HR) in EP was approached, as well as a technical director, in order to seek sponsorship support and advice on how to present the strategy. It was agreed the SOU needed to do this in terms of answers to the questions 'so what's different', 'what's in it for the business' and 'what will it cost'.

Another data gathering phase was entered – looking both externally at best practice and internally at what was going on in the existing learning organizations. The results of this work are summarized under the three challenge questions described below.

WHAT'S DIFFERENT?

- The linking of learning to the Shell global networks, which will require the taking of published 'best practice' from the networks and creating TeleTOP-based reusable learning nuggets with the intervention of a subject matter expert (SME).
- Reinstating and providing motivation for mentors to apply their experience to advising younger people on their career development both for them and the future business need.
- Reinstating and providing motivation for people who have a passion for learning to become tutor/coaches, supported by coaching techniques from the SOU and freely available, verified reusable learning nuggets.
- The provision of a safe learning environment in the workplace, disconnected from the business performance and scorecard focus, where people can feel free to admit their lack of knowledge and learn with guidance from a professional tutor/coach.
- Using the demographic issue to our advantage by encouraging experienced staff close to retirement to become tutor/coaches for their last few years in the company, and to continue, for the two or three years after their retirement, to provide home-based online assistance.

WHAT'S IN IT FOR THE BUSINESS?

- Opportunities for continuous development for potential new graduate recruits becomes an employee value proposition that will attract and retain quality people. (The single most important employee retention factor is the opportunity to learn new skills – Hay Group survey of 0.5 million employees in 300 companies, see <http://www.haygroup. co.uk>.)
- The application of spontaneous business problem-based learning will provide clear and immediate evidence of the value of learning through visible problem solving successes.
- It speeds up 'time to skill' as it is no longer necessary to wait for a specific course.
- The SOU becomes the catalyst for improving staff development, staff planning and the matching of the requisite skills to the future business needs; this is achieved through

mentors for career guidance, skill pool managers for monitoring the skills pools and budgetary planning input for staff development from the businesses.
- The use of retiree volunteers for tutoring/coaching softens the impact of the exit of nearly half of our experienced employees in less than ten years and also assists their knowledge transfer to younger staff.

WHAT WILL IT COST?

- Recent research done by *Training Magazine* (see <http://www.trainingmag.com>) told us that a global pan-industry learning and development leader spends 15 per cent of technical payroll on learning. An upper quartile industry benchmark exercise suggested 6 per cent of technical payroll and an estimate for the Shell Group was roughly 8 per cent of technical payroll. Current expenditure on learning and development in the group is therefore not excessive, but behind the global pan-industry leader.
- The adoption of a new SOU business model of a negotiated annual enrolment fee payable by the business regions based on number of employees and their recognized learning needs means the SOU becomes transparently accountable for delivering quality learning solutions. The introduction of knowledge assessment on the curriculum-based programmes and the introduction of skills assessment in the business further highlights the accountability of the SOU for knowledge transfer. Lack of skills improvement on the job can therefore be related to the quality/validity of the learning provided.
- An analysis of how the existing worldwide learning budgets were being spent highlighted duplication of effort, excessive administrative support and, in Europe, overheads for four training centres within that business region. Careful review of all the available data meant it was possible to state in the management proposal that the strategy will be delivered by better use of new and existing resources, including new learning delivery technologies currently in use in the SOU.
- The possibility of future, upfront investment, cost-negotiated between the business regions and the SOU, is directly linked to their declared business learning needs and it becomes a question not of cost, but of investment in people. Through our internal research, it has been estimated that the cost of *not* investing money in learning and development was too great to contemplate!

Conclusions

The SOU now understands 'the what' of the new strategy, and the business is beginning to understand 'the why' it is required. The EP management committee (EXCOM) has endorsed the strategy without reservation; the OP EXCOM is to be approached shortly. However the greater task of addressing 'the how' (implementation) is still being undertaken. The business, the learning strategy and the development of a learning organization depend on people, their behaviours, attitudes, personal motivations and their perceptions of 'what's in it for them'. Without the learners' and the organization's recognition of their respective responsibilities towards learning, and a true understanding of the benefits to the business of becoming a learning organization, the strategy will ultimately be unsuccessful! Creating a learning culture and motivating the learner to learn is now key. 'No one can help develop anyone else apart from him/herself. The door to development is locked from the inside' (Chris Argyris, 1962).

The Shell Group has to discover how we can motivate mature employees to want to become mentors for young people. Dormant coaching skills exist at all levels in the organization, but how are they found and how are the people with these skills motivated to help others to learn? Improved learning technology is an exciting enabler for the business but can still be a barrier to many. Learning from shared experiences gained of unsuccessful outcomes is an important part of ensuring we only have to learn once rather than repeating the failure globally. However, publishing lack of success is very sensitive in some cultures and even where it isn't, it is hardly likely to succeed in a business measured on scorecard performance and where employees bonuses depend on successfully meeting their targets.

Motivating the learner is related to ensuring the emerging learning organization addresses the climate for learning, the physical environment in which the learning takes place and individual learning styles. Some people prefer learning online, and form strong collaborative groups, others prefer learning in a classroom environment away from the pressures of work and in a social environment. Both these ends of the learning spectrum can, of course, be addressed through the principles of blended learning, but how does the SOU overcome people's perceptions, which are often based on past experience, both good and bad? Early attempts at unsupported e-learning did not help the introduction of coaching online today.

A new team will be set up to address these issues. In collaboration with academic research, identifying best practices in the corporate universities and discovering some model examples of learning organizations, the team will be accountable for developing a programme to evolve a new learning culture in support of the SOU learning strategy. Perhaps the SOU is already beginning to show the business the way forward?

References

Argyris, C. (1962) *Interpersonal Competence and Organizational Effectiveness*. Homewood, IL: Dorsey.
Knowles, M.S., Holton, E.F. and Swanson, R.A. (1998) *The Adult Learner: A Neglected Species*. Houston, TX: Gulf Professional.

17 Communities of Value: Harnessing the Power of Networked Learning

Crystal Schaffer and Steven Smith

It's a sad fact of life, but the shelf life of a Twinkie[1] is usually a whole lot longer than the shelf life of today's corporate knowledge. (The Heller Report, June 2001, <http://www.hellerreport.com>)

Introduction

It is a sad fact of life that most businesses have not been able to harness the power of their own knowledge. It is hard to disagree with the authors of the Heller Report, among others, that in most instances where businesses have tried to cultivate information, ideas, and innovation they have failed to translate these into bottom-line value. The limited success rates have led to some backlash against concepts like 'knowledge management', 'communities of practice' and 'information capture' in general, particularly in these uncertain economic times.

Nevertheless, collective corporate knowledge remains a critical business asset. So rather than abandon these efforts to harness it, the challenge has to be approached in a less traditional way. The opportunity exists for an alternative approach to connecting people with people, combining this with innovative methods in learning. With available technologies it is possible to leapfrog barriers to the flow of information, knowledge, and ideas. Those possibilities are at the heart of the aspiration for 'communities of practice' and 'knowledge management' and they orient our own learning-based approach to these issues that we've come to call 'networked learning'. This learning process is enabled by appropriate technologies and sustained by contributions among widely distributed participants. It succeeds because its *purpose* is to deliver bottom-line value to an organization and its *premise* is to build the strength of the collective knowledge and community of all participants.

This chapter reports the experience out of which the idea of networked learning has taken shape, and sets out its guiding principles. It is based on our experience over the last five years developing programmes for the Capgemini University (see overleaf), as well as the many other organizations we've connected with and consulted to in the process.

CAPGEMINI AND ITS UNIVERSITY

Capgemini is one of the world's largest providers of consulting, technology and outsourcing services formed from the merger of Cap Gemini, Gemini Consulting and Ernst & Young consulting in May 2000. Building upon its global strength and multicultural heritage, Capgemini's mission is to help businesses implement growth strategies, leveraging technology.

Traded on the Paris Stock Exchange, the organization employs approximately 50 000 people worldwide and reported 2002 global revenues of €7047 billion. The group offers its local and international clients in more than 30 countries services in:

- Management and technology consulting
- Systems transformation
- Systems management (outsourcing)
- Local professional services (via its Sogeti division).

Global strategic alliances with the top technology companies in the world (for example, Microsoft, Cisco) help Capgemini to provide clients with solutions tailored to their unique business needs.

Capgemini prides itself on a truly multicultural environment in which flexibility and freedom of thought are encouraged, with initiative, growth and client service prized above all.

The company founded its university in 1989, basing it in a chateau outside of Paris with an initial charter to strengthen cohesion within the company and provide professionals with a place to develop the skills needed to advance their careers. It has since evolved into an award-winning state-of-the-art corporate learning centre, now relocated in the company's international business learning forum at Les Fontaines (http://www.les-fontaines-community.com), where the university team continues to serve employees worldwide as well as key clients and partners.

Connecting people to people with the bottom line as the measure

Victor Hugo once remarked that we have gone from a world in which everything was divided, disconnected, and static to a world in which everything is alive, related, and connected. His observations referred to the impact of railroads, but could as easily apply to the modern age. What's different now is that we are not physically constrained. It's not the flow of exotic spices or the best linens from afar – what flow now are information, knowledge, service and innovation. And for this the Internet is critical. It is a means of facilitating powerful human connections with the potential to create and destroy ideas, companies and markets. The authors of *The Cluetrain Manifesto* speculate that this power rests in the ability to connect people freely to 'indulge their curiosity, to debate, to disagree, to laugh at themselves, to compare visions, to learn, to create new art, new knowledge' (Levine et al., 1999). This suggests an approach to knowledge management based far less on collecting documents, creating storage repositories or even websites where information can be housed, and more about connecting people to people and allowing them to exchange with, enjoy and learn from one other.

Numerous models of networks and communities exist simply for the sake of exchange (think: teenage chat rooms). Far more dramatically, network-based collaboration – such as the development that led to the Linux operating system – have taken these basic concepts far further to create value rather than mere conversation. When a group of independent programmers came together over the Internet to test theories and exchange code that would later become famous as the Linux operating system, what was so remarkable about it was not that this group of like-minded technologists wanted to exchange new thinking, but that the community they formed created a market-making product.

Often held up as the gold standard in distributed development and almost as frequently disregarded as merely a happy accident, Linux emerged from the collective wisdom and actions of up to 40 000 networked participants who, together, built a product with significant market share (estimates have ranged from 8 per cent to 30 per cent) within just a few years. The Linux initiative is responsible for the term 'open source' because the operating system's source code, basically its recipe, is open and available for free. Open source in this sense not only means free access, but also implies open collaboration. Many companies are clamouring to figure out how they can harness this kind of open collaborative power.

If innovation occurs when sets of ideas and experiences recombine, a network with contributions from a large set of distributed participants can be its engine. But one could certainly argue that several peculiarities converged in order to rouse tens of thousands of hackers to volunteer their time to develop software that is distributed for free. As inspiring as it is to imagine individuals from around the world coming together virtually to create an economically viable product in an ad hoc manner, results are generally generated with a greater degree of structure than is apparent in a first glance at 'open source' (see <http://world.std.com/~rkarash/>), and bear little resemblance to a Richard Karash's fictive 'open sauce' – where a restaurant is not the better for letting everyone simply dump in their own ingredients.

Meaningful products of networked learning, we find, emerge from some sense of community – whether this community is based on a type of governance, a particular technology, or a sense of affinity. When these innovations and member contributions are channelled toward solving problems, building new knowledge, and increasing productivity, corporations can begin to take advantage of a new learning model. 'Networked learning' is about taking such advantage. Done right, it can bring good ideas to marketable life, and derive innovation and market value in the process.

Capgemini University has indeed evolved a networked learning programme to drive bottom-line business benefits across its international organization. The company's first networked learning programme, International Business School (IBS), has already delivered more than €300 million worth of client business to Capgemini over the course of the past three years, driven a number of innovations in business operations, and created lasting managerial networks that enable fast navigation across its 50 000-person organization. The company's other networked learning programmes – from its Architects and Engagement Managers programmes to its innovative GuruSchool and new MasterClass offerings – have been similarly designed to create communities of learners that can create value within the organizations and 'bubbles of excellence' that they operate. We discuss each in turn.

The International Business School: Cementing lasting business networks

Capgemini's longest-running and most successful networked learning programme, the IBS, asks high-potential managers to put themselves in the shoes of an executive committee member and work in transnational teams to address a real business issue over the course of a six-month working partnership.

Leveraging a blended approach that combines relatively simple e-based network tools and methods of communication, learning, and knowledge sharing with out-of-the-box live sessions, IBS creates results by establishing and cementing lasting business networks that drive toward the accomplishment of real business goals. The programme's success lies not in its ability to employ whiz-bang technologies, but to successfully leverage the early lessons of network dynamics and value creation in the Internet age.

IBS teaches participants to apply what they learn to real business issues within the company and asks them the question: 'How do you see the future?' This ensures that participants both understand the content of the programme and apply this within the organization. The programme is constructed to allow the participants to actively benefit from each other's professional experience within the project. This allows them to apply both content delivered via subject matter experts and their own experience. During this recombination phase, the participants can use their field experience to ameliorate methods and contribute to Capgemini's knowledge systems.

The programme uniquely fosters multiple cross-community relationships – some tied to traditional lines of business and others designed to foster new 'grassroots' networks. Participants are put into teams designed to provide the most heterogeneous environment possible: business expertise, nationality and team profiles. Each of these teams will be made an owner of a different business issue. During the six months of the programme the participants will receive both appropriately timed content inputs and coaching within four main content streams: business results, teams of leaders, delivery excellence and communicating critical messages.

Each team is also given a team process coach to ensure that the teams are actively applying the content to their dynamics as well as challenging them on how they are leveraging tools that are available for them to work more effectively: knowledge bases, discussion forums, email, conference calls, physical meetings, classroom sessions.

Does it work? The proof is in the returns. The career progression of the individuals following the programme is followed with over 90 per cent of the alumni being promoted or taking on significantly more responsibilities within a year of finishing the programme. So, as an executive-proving ground, the programme more than meets its objectives. But that is only the tip of the proverbial benefits iceberg.

Ultimately, the members of the IBS communities use their networks for both business and personal purposes. For business purposes the participants have leveraged their connections, learning and knowledge from the programme to win, facilitate and deliver over €300 million in real business for the company. Examples of this include developing business in Asia based on client relations in Europe, the staffing of key positions within an international information technology (IT) outsourcing contract, the transfer of innovative customer relationship management (CRM) approaches from Spain to Sweden, and the development and launch of one of Capgemini's most successful new service offerings.

The networked approaches have yielded additional benefits as well, including an attrition rate of less than 10 per cent annually. Further network members who have left the company have been re-recruited via their business friends to both re-join the company and pursue new business opportunities. Thus, the network not only facilitates learning and develops business, but it cements lasting, networked relationships between colleagues that ultimately continue to attract key employees to the firm long term.

Similar networked learning theories have been applied to learning for more traditional 'practice communities' as well.

Traditional communities, innovative methods

Capgemini's systems architects community numbers more than1200 people and serves as a core foundation of the company's technology consulting practice. With the support of targeted learning programmes, this team has created a networked community that continuously improves and builds up their knowledge bases, methods and learning.

The architects use their learning programme as the key network-building cornerstone of their community. The programme is designed to run over a week with both core sessions attended by all and specialists' tracks. The specialists' tracks are run in parallel and participants are self-selected based on their development and business priorities. The tracks are taught by the top-level Capgemini architects who have developed the methods and contributed to the knowledge bases of the community. During these same learning events, master class streams will be run. In these streams the specialists come together to compare notes from the field, ameliorate existing knowledge and methods as well as create new content streams based on market and technological demands. These new ideas are then tested in the field and validated at the next master class meeting where they can become the new methods and collateral for the knowledge bases – taking the entire community to the next level.

Again, the value of the networked experience extends beyond the classroom and actively produces impact in the field. The learning events have a high relationship-building component that fosters trust and exchange between the participants. After events, participants continue to use their relationships and contacts to resolve business challenges and become more efficient via fast and high-quality delivery. Examples include the use of the network for highly specialized staffing purposes related to specific technical platforms or winning a financial services business deal in France based on projects delivered in Sweden.

The architects community and their networked learning approach is a main contributing factor in keeping Capgemini in what the market analysts at Gartner (see <http://www4. gartner.com/Init>) call the 'magic quadrant' for IT strategy, planning and architecture. In 2000, Gartner praised Capgemini for having a recognized, active process for 'building competencies to sustain their leadership position in the market'.

Communities of gurus and masters

Capgemini have further tested the boundaries of networked learning and value creation through community via innovative external offerings, including the three-year-old open-enrolment programme GuruSchool and the emerging MasterClass programme.

GuruSchool has applied networked learning to thought leadership. The programme invites participants to discover what it takes to get a new idea, product or service noticed in the battle for mindshare among clients, investors, media, and colleagues and teaches participants how to gain a competitive advantage in the race to commercialize new thinking by teaching information marketing, personal branding and critical selling communications strategies. It is an ideal programme for people taking new or innovative products or services to market.

The programme combines e-based modules with live-action classroom sessions and an ongoing alumni network of services to deliver a small group of participants both personalized and targeted coaching in key aspects of branding, marketing, communication and selling, as well as network connections to a variety of 'guru' services, colleagues and techniques that can facilitate their continued growth.

Opportunities to meet and network with successful market gurus and experts in relationship development, publishing, marketing, branding, and selling over the Internet (IP) are combined with one-to-one and small group coaching in idea 'productization' and 360-degree marketing. Ongoing development opportunities to develop pitches and test concepts are also offered for top idea-makers through GuruSchool's awards and network programmes.

The connection of the individuals enrolled in the programme with professional gurus and programme alumni has produced key connections for participants that have helped them expand their skills and reach into the marketplace. Several have used the experience as a launch pad for publishing, business development and new IP creation. For example, over a 12-month period Capgemini's Dutch organization successively sent members of the Microsoft.Net (MSDN) team to GuruSchool to develop and refine its offer. At the end of the period the team launched its offer, Jaggle. The team's success was not only validated by the market, but also got it recognition from its partners at Microsoft. Team members were featured on Microsoft's home page and received a personal 'thank you' and gift (a coveted early edition X-box!) from Bill Gates.

Based on the early success of the GuruSchool programme, Capgemini University's external business-learning forum group, Les Fontaines, sought to create a similar high-level networked learning programme to facilitate senior leadership development. The MasterClass programme is an exclusive learning event where business leaders learn from life's masters. The programme builds on the belief that today's greatest leaders must not only be skilled in business but must be multi-dimensional in their professional, perceptive and personal development.

MasterClass offers a unique networked learning experience and opportunity to jump the learning curve through exposure to masters from multiple disciplines and other business leaders from diverse backgrounds, combining small-group and personal coaching with networked classroom and e-based sessions to create a one-of-a-kind learning experience for emerging senior leaders. By creating the right mix of participants by level in combination with a diverse set of qualified experts, the programme cements a peer-level community learning experience that can be sustained beyond the in-person sessions. Capgemini has designed the programme with the long-term results of IBS in mind and anticipates the creation of a highly cohesive business network that can continue to add value to the participants long after their initial meeting.

Lessons learned: Creating your own revolution

By its very nature, this brand of networked learning breaks the mould of classic training and goes beyond conventional e-learning to drive innovation and value creation. Neither content (the information) nor connectivity (the channel) alone is sufficient for learning.

Optimum networked learning solutions like these marry the soul of the classroom with the speed and freedom of e-learning technologies. They include face-to-face interaction that provides people with the opportunity to explore with one another in a safe environment, while simultaneously facilitating rapid access to, and transfer of, information and helping to develop long-term connections. Most importantly, they will improve business impact as well as build capabilities. This combination of attributes and drive towards tangible outcomes is at the heart of the networked learning revolution.

To begin to create that kind of value, a learning organization should also do five things – we discuss these in turn below.

CREATE THE RIGHT CONDITIONS AND MOTIVATIONS FOR ALL STAKEHOLDERS

Both the motivation of the participants and the context in which they are brought together must converge in order to yield real results. Learning is inexorably linked to the conditions in which it takes place.

Linux didn't just happen; it would not have occurred without the right conditions (the Internet, for a start) and would not have succeeded without the motivation on the part of the participants (to beat Unix). Developers of networked programmes need to start with setting the right parameters to encourage collaboration – considerations, from ownership to feedback to results, are at the core of creating the motives needed to create a successful networked programme. Creating context requires clear stewardship and objectives for a start, a common end-goal and a transparent process. With these basic needs met, more sophisticated objectives can begin to be achieved.

Research by Peter Senge's Society for Organizational Learning (see <http://www.solonline.org/>) – which aims to discover, integrate, and implement learning theories and practices for the development of people and their institutions – builds on the understanding that all human beings possess an innate, lifelong desire and ability to learn, which can be enhanced by all organizations to yield value. This research as well as other studies (for example, Raymond, 1999; Markus et al., 2000) suggests five steps in particular that an organization should address to create the drive for learning:

1 **Recognize that learning is social:** People learn best from and with one another, and participation in learning communities is vital to their effectiveness, well-being and happiness in any work setting.
2 **Establish learning communities:** The capacities and accomplishments of organizations are inseparable from, and dependent on, the capacities of the learning communities that they foster.
3 **Align with nature:** It is essential that organizations evolve to be in greater harmony with human nature and with the natural world.
4 **Focus on core learning capabilities:** Organizations must develop individual and collective capabilities to understand complex, interdependent issues; engage in reflective, generative conversation; and nurture personal and shared aspirations.
5 **Create cross-organizational collaboration opportunities:** Learning communities that connect multiple organizations can significantly enhance the capacity for profound individual and organizational change.

Additionally, in harnessing the powers of collaborative development, it is important to note that both the motivation of the developers and the context in which they work must converge for a result – see Figure 17.1.

Motivation	*Context*
1 Scratching your own itch What better way to ensure a demand curve than by letting the customers solve their own product development?	**1 Serendipity** Leverage tools, and physical and virtual 'spaces' to increase the probability of recombining information, ideas, and experiences.
2 Ownership A sense of ownership is part of the ongoing exchange in distributed collaboration. No one 'owns' Linux or, actually, everyone does.	**2 Redundancy** Multiple sets of eyes will put all ideas on the table and to the test. The winners are the ones that are adopted against the most stringent tests of feasibility: the public at large and the marketplace.
3 Real-time feedback Everyone loves positive feedback, especially when it involves money or prestige. 'Release early, release often' was the Linux modus operandi dictating that patches to the code would be incorporated up to several times a day. Developers eager for this kind of acceptance remained loyal.	**3 Clear leadership and objectives** Linux hackers didn't just code and see what came of it – the objectives were clear: Make something like UNIX, but better. This single-mindedness and clear leadership in the style of Linus Torvalds are necessary to command the attention of such a wide constituency of stakeholders.
4 Reputation Clear attribution is an important incentive for further contribution – whether for a sense of acceptance from the community or for economic gains resulting from a good reputation.	**4 Transparent and distributed progress** Constructive laziness in Eric Raymond's terms: If a good partial solution is out there, why not build on it? This involves a large element of transparency and accessibility so that people can build upon progress and solve problems.
5 Reciprocity Individual contributions are accessible to everyone so that community give-and-take is reciprocal rather than focused on a quid pro quo for each exchange.	**5 Universal tools** Learning is more a human than a technical experience. All the whiz-bang gadgetry isn't worth the chips it's stored on if human beings cannot or will not use it. Yes, delight your users, but don't let the technology that's meant to facilitate their success hamper it instead.

Source: Capgemini, 2002

Figure 17.1 Embedded learning through motivation and context (after Schaffer et al., 2001)

CONSTANTLY GO BEYOND THE BUSINESS CASE: DEFINE AND DRIVE ACTIONS TOWARD PRACTICAL BUSINESS VALUE

Networked learning methods make a fundamental shift away from traditional learning paradigms built on the 'parent–child' principles of 'Me, teacher; you, student'. In a networked learning model, teachers and students learn from one another. This type of appreciation for the content and knowledge of all the participants is a critical success factor, but it alone is not enough to ensure success. Too often corporate learning doesn't 'stick' in organizations because it lacks connection to the day-to-day operation of the business.

In his 1998 study of refrigeration repair technicians, for example, Phil Henning writes that students showed markedly different capacities for learning about the intricacies of refrigeration repair. Among those who learned the most in a classroom setting, one commonality existed: Individuals who had some experience working with technicians in the field – no matter how brief – regularly performed better than those who had not. Their exposure to the community of technicians, according to Henning, increased their capacity to learn (Henning, 1998).

Networked models of learning start with experiences that are quickly tied to clear objectives that impact the bottom line of the business. Goals are well defined from the start and drive toward real business outcomes and provide, at minimum, a triple series of benefits offering clear return to the participants, their management, and the clients they serve. For networked learning to gain this traction, executive support is a key requirement (think: Crotonville). In addition, tying the learning to the core of the business is critical. Participants shouldn't get the sense they are ticking boxes on the way to the next promotion, but learning something that is immediately applicable to the drive toward results.

To achieve this, you must ensure your learning is intimately connected not only to your management review processes, but also to bottom-line measures of your business, such as sales targets, new product development or even retention of key staff. Ensuring these fundamental connections are present will better enable you to deliver practical value to the business you support.

LEVERAGE THE 'EMOTION FIRST, LOGIC SECOND' FACTORS TO DRAW PEOPLE OUT OF THEIR COMFORT ZONES AND FULLY ENGAGE THEM

Whether we are buying a new car, entering a relationship, or making a life decision, most of us make choices based on emotion first and logic second. Similarly, to draw individuals into a community starts with an emotional connection to a defined goal or objective – whether it is to beat the competition, drive new products and innovations, or simply meet this year's plan, people need to get a bit jazzed about it to commit. Once the buy-in is there, logic comes into play. People want key questions answered – 'why are we doing this?' and 'what's in it for me?' are often the first two. Successful networked models emotionally connect people to one another through a shared sense of the end-game immediately and keep them engaged by continuing to add value to them as individuals.

How can you do this? Start by creating networks that match individuals of like level and skill based on common interest or expertise, and then provide them with an environment (physical and/or virtual) that is a free and creative one. To keep the dialogue moving, you will want to provide incentives for participants in the form of opportunities or awards based on group and individual outputs. Appeal to what motivates people in your organization.

We have seen it work with complex contests and reward mechanisms as well as far more simply, with bottles of champagne and a mountain-bike auction. To prevent 'mob mentality' or insular thinking, involve external partners or experts in the work at various stages, continually pushing the group to take a market-focused approach toward new solutions. When the emotional 'me' needs are met first, the more logical 'business' benefits are more easily reinforced and achieved.

REMEMBER THAT WHAT'S MEASURED GETS DONE … AND RECOGNIZED

Networked learning models have altered the way companies measure the results of their training efforts. When the classroom model gives way to alternatives that are less structured, and more integrated with the way people work, a number of conventions are challenged – from training hours to testing. More relevant measures for community learning experiences include:

- establishing individual and team goals, so that both are rewarded;
- developing a feedback process for collaborative work in performance management such that real 360-degree development is possible;
- triggering corrective action at a given performance level to keep boundaries open, but ensuring outputs are aligned with what's 'real world' within your organization;
- measuring performance within a time factor for a goal, that is, based on real-time achievement of key objectives;
- rating the process, not just the product, recognizing the journey can be as important as the destination;
- tying results to organizational goals ensuring you have built on the most solid of foundations;
- benchmarking continuously, outside as well as inside your organization;
- sharing best practices, again both internally and externally, to continuously innovate and expand your impact.

LEAD WITH PEOPLE FIRST, TECHNOLOGY AND PROCESS A JOINT SECOND

In our many discussions about networked learning, the questions we are most often asked at the outset are about the technologies that should be employed and the project plans to be implemented. These are interesting and necessary discussions in the long run, but efforts that begin here are doomed to fail. Community-based learning is about human interaction and experience first and facilitated technologies and processes second.

As with the design of any learning programme, it is important to distinguish between business objectives and tools and methods. Often it can be tempting to lead with the whiz-bang tactics and solutions, but before getting there, designers of programmes need to first think of objectives and strategies.

Capgemini University, for example, has established a networked learning system that is founded on the ability to connect learners long after any e-based or live classroom session takes place. It is founded on basic Internet technologies, with the focus on the ease of connecting the user to the people who have the knowledge not with six degrees of separation, but one mouse click.

Once the move is made toward implementation, it is important to put the right support in place. Implementation of a networked learning solution is a shared responsibility among organizers, business leaders, and the participants involved. As a prerequisite, it requires the ability of people to work outside the boundaries of a hierarchy. Everyone involved must accept responsibility for both the process and the results of the interaction. For participants and corporate educators, this means stepping out of the traditional comfort zone of adult education. For the business sponsoring the initiative, it means accepting and working to profit from the consequences of an open and free-forming interaction. Despite the challenges, it is clear the bottom-line results for doing so are well worth the risks.

Note

1.   Twinkie – legendary US snack cake.

References

Henning, P. (1998) 'Ways of learning: An ethnographic study of the work and situated learning of a group of refrigeration service technicians', *Journal of Contemporary Ethnography*, 27(1): 85–136.

Levine, R., Locke, C. Searls, D. and Weinberger, D. (1999) *The Cluetrain Manifesto*. Cambridge, MA: Perseus Books.

Markus, M.L., Manville, B. and Agres, C.E. (2000) 'What makes a virtual organization work?', *Sloan Management Review*, 42(1): 13–26.

Raymond, E.S. (1999) *The Cathedral and the Bazaar: Musings on Linux and Open Source by an Accidental Revolutionary*. Sebastopol, CA: O'Reilly & Associates.

Schaffer, C., Funk, K. and Cothnel, J. (2001) *Learning to Innovate*. Capgemini Center for Business Innovation.

18 Networked Learning in the Public Sector: The Case of NCSL

David Jackson

The characteristics of network-based learning systems are paradigmatically different from the prevailing orthodoxies of the past. Achieving such radical change will require a fundamental shift in thinking at all levels of the system – and the challenges are that we have to do it in practice as well as in theory, and to do it to scale. The introductory quotation from Dr Rick Foster below frames this challenge.

> It isn't about knowing, but about continuous learning; not about hierarchy, but about relationships; not about seeking stability, but about encouraging dynamic interplay; not about being self-contained, but about being connected; not about singular solutions, but about multiple opportunities; not about control, but about positioning for innovation and creativity; not about competition, but about collaboration; not about the parts, but about the 'multiple wholes' that can be made by continuous integration and disintegration. (Dr Rick Foster, Vice President at the W.K. Kellogg Foundation)

In our work, we are seeking to understand more about the contribution that the Networked Learning Communities programme can make to learning about how this challenge might be met.

Introduction

This chapter describes the opportunities and challenges of a large-scale educational development and research project. The English National College for School Leadership's (NCSL) Networked Learning Communities (NLC) programme was designed to improve learning outcomes for children in individual schools. The programme models alternative system configurations, based around school-to-school networks. Such a network-based system offers opportunities for self-regenerative learning, lateral knowledge transfer and for schools and teachers to take active control of transformation.

The NLC programme did not set out to be such a large-scale operation. It began as a relatively small development and research project, of between five and ten networks, which would be funded modestly to explore possibilities for interdependent working and learning relationships:

- **within schools**, for example, department–department – within school variation is a particular challenge;
- **between schools**, whose organizational structures do not traditionally accommodate institutional collaboration – for instance, timetables and arrangements for teacher continuing professional development (CPD) are usually individual to each school;
- **and between groups of schools and their partners**, most often Local Education Authorities (LEAs), but also Higher Education partners in the case of CPD and Initial Teacher Training (ITT) or community partners. In some authorities, moves towards multi-agency working practices mean that schools' partners may also include Social Services, the Police Authority and Heath Service Providers.

As a result of extensive co-design with practitioners to build ownership of, and support for, the project, an unexpected sense of energy and urgency grew around the design, raising its profile significantly higher than had originally been anticipated. Equally, the work was serendipitous (or propitious) in that senior policy makers were seeking to move from the era of 'informed prescription' to a period of 'informed professionalism'. It appeared both to fit the policy mood, and to capture a moment in time for the profession. We were initially concerned about whether the target of ten NLCs would be reached. In the event, more than 150 submissions were received for the first cohort! Eighty-four were accepted.

The success of the programme was due in no small part to the groundswell of support for the idea of collaboration from a profession tired of competing for pupils and resources and constantly battling in the theatre of league tables, parental choice and a complex policy environment within which they were both visible and vulnerable. One of the characteristics of the NLC programme is its unashamedly moral dimension – caring about all children. NLCs make a commitment to improving learning opportunities for *all* children, not just those in a single school or catchment area. This dimension struck a chord for teachers and school leaders and has proved to be a sustained theme, highly motivating for participants, and of significant interest to policy makers serving a centre-left UK government.

In less than two years, from the initial idea grew a national programme involving 1564 schools (approximately 6 per cent of all schools in England) in 93 LEAs (62 per cent of all LEAs). This represents 32 474 teachers and 577 513 pupils working and learning in NLC schools.

The explosion in scale presented huge challenges to the thinking about the kinds of support that schools might need to change their organizations, their leadership and their CPD to accommodate collaborative arrangements. The knowledge-management solutions for the programme necessarily increased in sophistication, and innovation in research and enquiry methods, communication strategies, resource development and information architecture became the most fertile and hotly contested arenas in the programme.

Resource followed demand and a team of experienced educationalists comprising practitioners – classroom teachers and headteachers – LEA officers, OfSTED inspectors, academics and other researchers was assembled both to support and learn about network development and its implications for schools. This team was diverse, geographically dispersed and many members were on fractional appointments or working in consultancy arrangements. All were appointed for the fixed term of the programme. The leadership and management issues presented by this dynamic and challenging group were complex and constantly changing as the programme unfolded.

All these complexities also posed organizational challenges for NCSL and for the Research Group within it that spawned the NLC programme. Once the first cohort figure of 84 NLCs had been agreed with the Department for Education and Skills (DfES), it was apparent that dedicated organizational arrangements would be required for this team of facilitators, researchers, writers and corporate support staff recruited to ensure the effective implementation and facilitation of the programme – and to garner the learning from it. The decision was made to establish a dedicated unit for the newly formed Networked Learning Group on the campus of the University of Cranfield – close to the M1 motorway, to Milton Keynes, and on the site of a university itself well networked into non-educational fields of knowledge and expertise.

Now two years old at the time of writing – half way through the programme for the first cohort – it is a useful point to reflect upon how NCSL came to design the programme, the fertile policy context that spawned it, some of the characteristics that it is developing and the emergent learning.

Context, development and design

THE ESTABLISHMENT OF NCSL

The NCSL was established in England in November 2000. At that time – and still, at the time of writing – it was the only national leadership development provider of its kind in the world. The prospectus for the new National Leadership College described the aspirations for the impact of the college as being to provide a 'coherent national framework for headship' for England's 24 000 schools.

The college inherited three national training programmes for prospective and existing headteachers:

- the National Professional Qualification for Headteachers (NPQH), established in 1996;
- the Headteachers Leadership and Management Programme (HEADLAMP), which was introduced in 1995 to address the training needs of newly appointed heads, providing all with an entitlement to induction training;
- the Leadership Programme for Serving Headteachers (LPSH), a residential training programme designed in partnership with Hay, McBer Business Consultants, which was introduced in 1998.

While the direction and strategic vision of the College were at that point yet to be defined in practice, the government's agenda was clearly set out in the prospectus. The tasks included:

- developing further NPQH and making this qualification mandatory for headteacher applicants;
- a national induction programme for newly appointed headteachers, including annual national induction events;
- the refinement and expansion of the LPSH;
- a nationwide network of links with LEAs and universities, possibly in the form of regional centres of the NCSL;
- research into leadership and leadership development;
- designing an evaluation strategy for the college's work and its impact;

- building leadership capacity and the system's capacity for self-improvement;
- developing strategic programmes of work to support the drive to raise standards and improve achievement.

The final two items in this list provide the obvious impetus for the evolution of the NLC programme, but its roots also lie in the early work of the Research Group of the NCSL – and the frustrations inherent in the dissemination of educational research findings to schools and to school leaders.

THE INCEPTION OF NETWORKED LEARNING COMMUNITIES

In the fields of both knowledge management and the utilization of research evidence, education has a long road to travel. Michael Fullan recently commented that 'it is one of life's great ironies: schools are in the business of teaching and learning, yet they are terrible at learning from each other. If they ever discover how to do this, their future is assured' (Fullan, 2001). If we sense that this is true, then it is unsurprising that in the Organisation for Economic Cooperation and Development (OECD) research entitled *Knowledge Management in the Learning Society* (OECD, 2000), education did not fare well against comparable knowledge intensive professions. Table 18.1 (a distillation of the original) suggests that we have some way to go if we are to become accustomed users of research knowledge.

Table 18.1   Differences between sectors

Dimension	High Technology	Medicine	Education
Pressure for knowledge creation, mediation and use	Very high	Medium	Low
Structures and resources for knowledge creation, mediation and use	High	Medium	Low to very low
Outcomes of knowledge creation	Very high to high	High to variable	Low

Source: OECD, 2000

In many ways, it is this valuing of, and receptiveness to, knowledge – both professional knowledge, or the knowledge from practice, and the knowledge available out there from theory and research – that the NLC programme is seeking to address. The two questions that we asked ourselves were:

1 What would the educational system look like if it was configured for learning?
2 How could we design a programme that would help both the college and policymakers to learn more about how to develop and support such a system?

The NLC programme was introduced in September 2002 as a means both of applying what, in England and abroad, had been learned about successful school-to-school networks, and in order to provide a source of learning and knowledge flow for future policy extension. Its design and implementation followed an intense period of research and analysis.

There is nothing particularly new about networking, of course. Teachers, headteachers and schools have long engaged with one another in forms of collaborative activity. However, there is something fundamentally more challenging about the idea of 'collaborative capacity' and 'networked learning'. It represents a shift away from market-oriented competition, a new emphasis on capacity building and learning conceived as being a part of a collaborative innovation and knowledge-management architecture for the future school system.

NCSL set out to take the challenges seriously of building from and applying what is known from the international literature to the design of the NLC programme. While generating the NLC design between January and April 2002, the programme team drew upon five inter-related areas of knowledge:

- **Theory and research:** Through the study of previous initiatives within the UK and internationally.
- **Prior policy learning:** By commissioning a study of previous network-based policy initiatives.
- **Messages from 'best practice':** By visiting sites of interesting practice around the world.
- **Expert knowledge:** By connecting with those with experience and understanding, using think tanks, knowledge seminars and critical friendship relationships.
- **Practitioner understanding:** Utilizing the grounded wisdoms of programme leaders, network facilitators and other practitioners.

During the early design and development period, NCSL commissioned an extensive desk study of literature relating to network-based school development programmes in the UK and abroad (Kerr, et al., 2003), together with a study of fields of theory underpinning the proposed NLC design (McCormick, 2003). A large-scale study was also commissioned into the published evaluation reports of both successful and less successful network reform initiatives of the past decade (Bentley et al., 2002). This research, entitled 'Learning the Lessons', proved to be a rich source of practical wisdom, drawing from the recent history of UK reform and also from key initiatives abroad. We also commissioned focused research on some areas of specific interest, such as: communities of practice (Thorpe et al., 2003), action learning sets (Fielding and Webster, 2003) and online learning communities (Open University, 2003) – and we undertook our own research on what was known about network leadership (NCSL, 2002).

Prior to embarking upon the initiative, the NCSL Research Group arranged a programme of international study visits (using enquiry partnerships involving both academics and school leaders) to 14 locations around the world – eight in the USA and Canada, others in New Zealand, Australia, Sweden, South Africa and Singapore. These visits focused both on leadership development centres, and on the relationships between these centres and networks of partner schools (Bush and Jackson, 2001; West and Jackson, 2002).

We attended the OECD international seminar in Lisbon designed to draw learning from the world's most advanced school-to-school networks (CERI/OECD, 2000; OECD, 2003). Throughout the development phase, both in England and abroad, a systematic programme of think tank opportunities and invited seminars was instituted, initially to provide ongoing critique of the design and then subsequently to subject the principles and practical strategies of the programme to critical scrutiny and to draw out the evolving learning.

The development team also read widely from related literature and visited evaluation studies of other programmes (for example, Canter, 1994; Church et al., 2000; Clarke, 2000); Copland, 2002; Hopkins et al., 1996; Kahne et al., 2001; Kerr et al., 2003; Lieberman and Grolnick, 1996; Lieberman and Wood, 2003; Mandell, 1999; Newmann and Sconzert, 2000; Sarason and Lorentz, 1988; Southworth and Sebba, 1997; Supovitz et al., 2001; Wohlstetter and Smith, 2000; Wohlstetter et al., 2003). We involved national and international experts as critical friends and partners; and we built enquiry, research and learning into our evolving work. Before we started, we felt that we knew some things about design – although less about the implementation and support of such a large-scale, systemically significant programme.

CONTEXT – THE POLICY ENVIRONMENT

Much thought about system reform in education, in the UK and around the world, is focused upon how a transition might be effected from one reform paradigm to another. In England, the reform agenda of the last decade of the twentieth century was characterized by the application of uniform national strategies (albeit based upon informed understandings from past change efforts); by sequenced and delivered 'outside-in' solutions; and by the application of external accountabilities and associated data collection, to measure pupil and school performance. This approach served well to lever up attainment levels in the short term. As a strategy, it made targets and outcome expectations clear. It identified and addressed problem environments, provided for an important and specific platform of knowledge and skills and served to mobilize and focus the profession.

It did not, however, prove to be a capacity-building model, as identified in the external evaluation of the National Literacy and Numeracy Strategies (Earl et al., 2003), which stated:

Continuing improvement will require not only greater individual capacity in headteachers and teachers, but also greater organizational capacity in schools and LEAs. In the long run, we believe that the commitment to collective capacity building is the most promising direction for addressing the challenges of the future.

It was perhaps unsurprising, therefore, that pupil attainment trajectories in the UK, having risen sharply initially, levelled off, or that professional morale became strained, or that schools felt little sense of ownership over the direction of the educational agenda.

National strategies, which apply existing knowledge across the system, can and have produced short-term gains. However, top-down, outside-in change approaches are unlikely to continue to work well in the medium to long term without an emphasis upon capacity building within the system – at middle tier, school, leader and teacher levels. Beyond a lowest common factor, national education development is about learning which, as with student learning, depends upon building on what diverse individuals, groups and systems know and can do already; a task of continuous adaptation and diversification. It is no longer efficient or appropriate to use hierarchical models of control or dissemination in this context. One-to-many modes of reform work best when there are relatively simple, constant, universal priorities. Contemporary change needs are too rapid, knowledge is too transient and distributed, and contexts of knowledge application are too diverse. Outside-in strategies are unlikely to be sensitive to the unique challenges of increasingly diverse school contexts, nor to stimulate and thus utilize practitioner innovation and ownership.

It is also importantly the case that the improvements already achieved have not closed the gap in educational achievement between the most and least advantaged. In fact, they have widened it – between the highest and lowest performing children, and between the best and worst performing schools. The diversity of context mentioned above is a natural system characteristic but it is also one that has been exacerbated by the accountability framework utilized in recent times – in particular the combined effects of publicly available inspection data, league tables of results and parental choice of schools.

We have, then, both a diverse system, and also one in which government is seeking to replace outside-in delivery strategies with more lateral, more collaborative and more capacity-building learning and change models. Some of the underpinning components of such a capacity-building strategy are discussed by Hopkins and Jackson (2002). One is the importance of people – the leaders, educational professionals and students, and the dynamic expansion of their collaborative contributions through the development of professional learning communities within and between schools. A second relates to the alignment and synergies created when internal processes and teams are working optimally. A third corresponds to the organizational arrangements (the 'programme coherence' and the 'networks') that support capacity development. A fourth is the 'higher order' territory of shared values, moral purpose, social capital and trust-based relationships – all essential for collaborative and network-based activity between both people and organizations to be successful.

New forms of joint work engagement – those that enable effective practice to be developed and tested through collaboration within and between institutions – offer a more effective method of integration and adaptation, and have been shown to be effective in many different organizational settings. Learning or knowledge about what works in one setting is infectious when potential users can ask questions, see the practice in context and thus have the information they need to adapt it to meet the needs in their own context. In those sectors that have been through the most profound organizational restructuring over the last generation, 'task groups', 'project-based teams' and collaborative relationships with others are essential to maintaining organizational coherence and collective purpose amid the multiple complexities and insecurities of contemporary organizational life (Bentley, 2003).

For some years prior to and since the launch of NLCs, the UK government has viewed the incentivization of school-to-school networks as one way of responding to these concerns. Successive policy strands, particularly those focusing upon the most challenging schools and upon the most successful (the two ends of the achievement spectrum), have promoted networking and collaboration – through Education Action Zones, Excellence in Cities, Beacon Schools and Specialists Schools in particular (Demos/NCSL, 2002). More recently, collaborative imperatives within Leadership Incentive Grant funding and Leading Edge Partnerships in 2003 and 2004, and the statement within *Excellence and Enjoyment* (DfES, 2003) that every primary school should have the opportunity to be a member of a network from September 2004, have further extended this commitment. These policy strands encompass a range of models of the nature and function of effective collaboration.

Such a rapidly evolving policy commitment to school-to-school networks has the potential either to release school-level energy or to reinforce the existing, unhelpful patterns of 'victimhood' – based on concerns about initiative overload coupled with unremitting, public and relatively crude accountability measures. Ensuring that networking efforts are part of the solution requires robust and rapidly acquired knowledge about what works and what does not for what purposes in a range of areas. The focus or aims of networks and the nature of effective approaches to structure, process and governance all need to be designed early in the life of a network and are matters that funders need to understand in order to make sense of the initiative and their contribution to it.

The NLC programme was specifically designed to provide one source for this policy learning in relation to network size and type, facilitation and leadership, formation processes and growth states, brokerage, system support, incentivization – and evidence about how and under what conditions networks can make a contribution, both to system learning and to the raising of student achievement. It set out to inform policy learning, both through illustration of what is possible and the creation of living experiments that others can visit or encounter through case studies, artefacts and research reports. It aimed to do this by finding ways of representing for those beyond the programme, lessons being learned across the networks through, for example, 'what we are learning about' documents that draw upon both enquiry-oriented learning and more traditional forms of commissioned research and action research.

The NLC programme was introduced, then, as a means both of applying what, in this country and abroad, had been learned about successful school-to-school networks, and in order to provide a source of learning and knowledge flow for future policy extension and to this end followed an intense period of research and analysis.

NETWORKED LEARNING COMMUNITIES – WHAT ARE THEY?

The programme

An NLC is a cluster of schools working in partnership to enhance the quality of pupil learning, professional development, and school-to-school learning through enquiry-oriented learning approaches. Initial aspirations were embodied thus:

> In Networked Learning Communities, schools and teachers will create and exchange knowledge collaboratively, continuously and systematically. By ensuring that adults learn, and that schools learn from one another, we can help children to become powerful learners.

The programme was designed to improve learning opportunities for pupils and to support the development of schools as interdependent professional learning communities. For example, it

- placed teachers, leaders and schools at the heart of innovation and knowledge creation within the profession;
- encouraged the development of local, context-specific practices and solutions;
- encouraged schools in other contexts to interpret and adapt solutions from one context to their own needs;
- required NLCs to act as critical friends to one another – network-to-network learning, across the system, is one of the key opportunities offered by the initiative;
- required networks to have at least one external partner, which could be a Higher Education Institution (HEI), LEA or community group – and most have more than one.

The programme itself was developed as a partnership initiative involving the NCSL, the DfES, and, increasingly, the recently established Innovation Unit (IU). Additionally, the General Teaching Council (GTC) and the Teacher Training Agency (TTA) offered consultancy support. NCSL acts as the facilitator of learning and knowledge transfer between networks and takes responsibility also for spreading good practice from the programme to the wider audience within both practice and policy.

Specifically, each NLC (and by April 2004 there were 137, involving over 1564 schools) comprises a group or network of schools committed to partnership and interdependence. Learning networks are thus being promoted as a means of enriching professional practice while creating and exchanging practitioner knowledge to support improvement in teaching and learning and organizational restructuring. In achieving these goals, schools within NLCs aspire to:

- collaborate around the study of teaching and learning – within and between schools;
- promote practitioner enquiry – co-creating knowledge;
- engage with theory and research, in support of enquiry processes, so expanding learning about what works;
- utilize a wide variety of approaches to CPD including: coaching/mentoring, induction programmes, lesson study, pupil feedback, intervisitations and internal and external programmes of learning that qualify for accreditation;
- draw grounded theory from the collaborative study of practice with a view both to implementing the learning from this process, and to generating artefacts that can be shared with other schools and networks.

The programme supports NLCs to improve the learning of pupils and staff through school-to-school learning and to build capacity for growth and continuous improvement (and knowledge about the process). It provides a supportive context for risk-taking and creativity, and the confidence to 'turn and face the danger' – to take charge of innovation and change and thrive. The programme also wrestles with the complexities of learning from this large-scale and widespread activity in what we call 'real time' and for multiple audiences – practitioners, programme, 'middle tier' and policy-makers.

The NLC design

There are six strands to the basic framework of the NLCs' design, and four non-negotiable principles. The six strands are:

- **Pupil learning** (a pedagogic focus)
- **Adult learning** (with professional learning communities as the aspiration)
- **Leadership learning** (at all levels, but particularly collaborative headteacher learning)
- **Organizational learning** (progressive redesign around learning principles)
- **School-to-school learning** (between 'communities of practice')
- **Network-to-network learning** (a programme priority).

The four non-negotiable principles are:

- **Moral purpose** – a commitment to success for all children ('raising the bar and closing the gap' is a social justice representation of the same theme)
- **Shared leadership** (for example, co-leadership and distributed leadership)
- **Enquiry-based practice** (evidence and data-driven learning)
- Systematic engagement with the **three fields of knowledge**.

Both collaborative engagement and generosity of spirit are involved – hence two key mantras within the initiative. The one for collaboration is: 'working smarter together, rather than harder alone' and for the critical moral purpose dimension: 'learning *from*, *with* and *on behalf* of one another'.

The NLC model of learning

There are many elements to the learning models within NLCs. At its heart lies recognition of the importance of:

- the social construction of learning;
- the role of enquiry processes in taking learning for practice forward; and
- an emphasis on the importance of focusing on learning over specific curriculum contexts or teaching as transmission.

We also explicitly emphasize the importance of drawing equally upon three fields of knowledge. These are:

1 **Practitioner knowledge** (we start from what people know, the knowledge that people bring to the learning table)
2 **Publicly available knowledge** (the publicly available theory research and case practise to be drawn into learning environments)
3 **The new knowledge that we are able to create together** through collaborative working and enquiry.

These three fields are identified as being in an interdependent relationship with each other as shown in Figure 18.1. A key dimension of the model, as indicated, is the integration of the three knowledge fields through network-based activity and use within classrooms – represented by the connecting ring of the model. The model is consistent with what we know

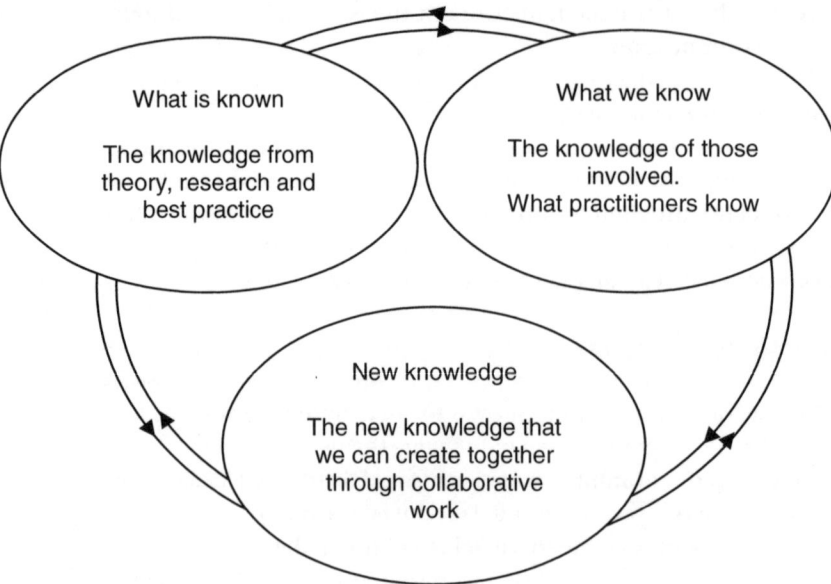

Figure 18.1   Three fields of knowledge

about knowledge use in networks. Lieberman and Wood (2003) state in their recent publication on the American Writing Project: 'Linking school knowledge and university knowledge, they (networks) … find ways for "inside knowledge" (the knowledge that teachers create on the job) to inform "outside knowledge" (the knowledge of reformers, researchers and policy-makers), and vice versa'. This is a goal that Huberman (1993) identified as a proper goal for action research, but one observed more in the breach than in the practice. It also features as a well-established challenge for an increasingly knowledge-based era of government. This emphasis on the three fields of knowledge also echoes the need that Senge highlights of identifying new ways of learning that involve leveraging diverse perspectives into collective or shared group intelligence and integrating theory, new capacities, and practice with one another (Senge et al., 1994).

The NLC learning focus

Core to the design of NLCs was the idea of the 'learning focus'. Each network was asked to identify a pedagogically grounded learning focus to develop a unifying theme, around which 'networked learning' could be located and to ensure that activity undertaken between schools could be acted out in classrooms. The intention was for this to act as an initial vehicle through which schools within NLCs would begin to change organizational processes in support of new ways of working together. It was also intended that, through the shared values and the discipline of the six strands of learning, a clearly articulated learning focus could also be related to the learning foci of other networks, in order to facilitate wider transfer of knowledge. Learning foci selected ranged from improving literacy, through generic processes such as thinking skills and assessment for learning, through to community-based goals.

Development work within and around the learning focus provides a detailed snapshot not only of how a fundamental component of the programme is being acted out in schools and classrooms, but also of how the design of the programme as a whole is working to connect learning between networks.

This development of learning foci has proved to be an important determinant of – and springboard for – network development. In reporting on the first year, it became clear that it was important that the pupil learning focus in particular was acting as a strong driver for development in networks where progress was perceived by participants as strong and effective across a critical mass of participants. In particular, the pupil learning focus is seen as impacting upon network design:

> The importance of a clearly defined and widely shared pupil learning focus emerged as a key issue in network design as well as a key part of the enquiry processes. Identifying a particular NLC pupil learning focus is highlighted in 52 per cent of network enquiry reports as important for the structure and organization of networked learning. (*CUREE/NCSL, 2003*)

and upon the adult and leadership learning dimensions:

> Where the adult and leadership learning foci were well articulated with the pupil learning focus, (for example if assessment was the focus both for enhancing pupil learning, and for adult learning), there was a stronger perception of shared understanding of and commitment to the aims and goals of the network. In such reports, the articulation

between learning foci at different levels through the work of the network was also seen as a strategy for achieving synergy across multiple initiatives. (*CUREE/NCSL, 2003*)

A cross-programme working group was convened in Summer 2003 to explore this evidence in more depth and to establish enquiries into:

- the strategies that are proving effective in refining pupil learning foci so that they act as a driver for networked learning; and
- the ways in which learning foci that explore thinking skills, assessment for learning and emotional intelligence can or should inform each other in order to identify progression paths for networks and tools for facilitating such progression.

The first part of the Pupil Learning Focus (PLF) programme was seen as short-term and instrumental and has generated learning instruments and audit tools.

The second strand of PLF activity is working to a longer-term, enquiry-oriented timescale. It flowed from a perception amongst facilitators and researchers that well advanced networks, working with either thinking skills (TS) or assessment for learning (AFL) as a focus, were sometimes hitting a glass ceiling in terms of progress and enthusiasm. Widening the focus to encompass TS or AFL, whichever had not been on the agenda previously, had proved instrumental in creating a new surge of energy for work which was complementary to what had gone before. At the same time, much of the work on both TS and AFL had raised the importance of effective relationships between students and teachers. Facilitators and researchers were noticing that pedagogic responses to this had much in common with those emerging in networks with emotional intelligence as a learning focus. An enquiry group involving a leading edge researcher in his field, several facilitators and researchers and a small cohort of networks was convened with a view to eliciting common concepts and strategies for each learning focus, and to using these to develop tools and instruments that others might test and use.

NETWORKED LEARNING COMMUNITIES – DEVELOPING 'NETWORKED LEARNING' STRATEGIES

NLC is a 'development and research programme' – we apply the learning model that we promote for pupils, adults, teachers, schools and networks to the programme-level work we do together. Learning from such work is a core programme value, as can be seen in the development of the PLF work already described. It is implicit in the annual enquiries and reviews, in the research we commission from others and undertake ourselves, and in the day-to-day work of the Networked Learning Group (NLG). In the NLG we use the terms 'the work' and 'the programme' to signify learning from networked learning and our own role in connecting learning across the programme. The work is what networks do. It goes on both without our support and with it. The programme, on the other hand, is the ways in which the project team adds value to the work of networks and seeks to gather together a body of knowledge about 'networked learning'.

In doing this, we ask our network consultancy team to perform four roles simultaneously or interchangeably. In their interactions with networks and with network co-leaders, they are asked to be:

- **consultants** whose role is to ask good questions;
- **networkers** whose role is to connect networks to one another;
- **sense-makers and interpreters** whose role is to enquire into network practices and processes and to connect the learning with learning going on elsewhere in the programme;
- **reporters and writers**, whose role is to find ways of representing what they are learning through process, events and in the products.

Through the adaptive use of this model of facilitation, the programme seeks to support good work in networks and to learn both from what they do and from how we engage with them. We try to ask good questions and make connections; to guide and prompt; to act as critical friend – we are committed also to holding the networks to account against their own aspirations and the values of the programme through programme-wide enquiries and annual reviews and through ongoing dialogue facilitator-to-network and network-to-network. Simultaneously, network consultancy involves developing insights – understanding, observing, analysing, drawing learning from the work of networks – making the connections that will enable network-to-network learning.

This transfer of knowledge requires collective sense-making and representation or 'reification' processes, (Wenger, 1998; Wenger et al., 2002). The reflective sessions that we have – a two-day residential each month for all facilitators, researchers and writers – offer a programme-based opportunity to make sense of what we are learning and to turn it into usable materials such as protocols, processes and artefacts. (For example, a recent residential took the theme of 'reach' as its focus. The team used the development of evidence-based conjectural statements in sub-groups of facilitators, supported by researcher/writers, as a tool for exploring common patterns in the networks' approaches to extending network activity beyond natural enthusiasts.)

Organizationally, the NLG needed to adapt. It required its own network structure. The establishment of Development and Enquiry (D&E) groups, Programme groups and Theme groups in the summer of 2003, in response to issues emerging from the Spring 2003 enquiry (CUREE/NCSL, 2003), represents one response to this challenge. These multi-disciplinary groups have become a key way in which the work is studied and the learning represented. The groups also ensure that enquiry-generated learning from the pattern of work across networks takes place in collaborative learning relationships with them.

In addition, the construction of artefacts to represent programme learning and facilitate its transfer is increasingly undertaken in partnership with the NLCs, too. While most school-based co-leaders of NLCs are headteachers (68 per cent), the D&E programmes explicitly recruit from other groups within network schools such as 'theme champions', 'activists', 'action learners', 'lead learners', 'ICT champions' and 'teacher enquirers'.

For example, the seven Development and Enquiry Groups operating in April 2004 were as shown in Table 18.2.

Adopting, as has been outlined, structures and processes for enquiry-based learning between the schools within the networks and simultaneously in the interstices of the programme (or the spaces between the networks), a complex 'net' for the capture of learning has been fashioned. This 'learning exchange' function provides a complex challenge to the programme – just as it will for a network-based learning and exchange system.

Table 18.2   D&E groups as at April 2004

	Number of networks	Number of schools
Teachers as researchers	13	183
Research lesson study	22	104
Networked learning walks	3	21
Collaborative leadership learning	11	133
Developing capacity	3	24
Pupil participation	27	223
Transforming learning	12	152
Total number of networks and schools participating in D&E programmes	**91**	**840**

Conclusion

The challenges and the learning for NCSL have been significant. Not long after the NLG moved to Cranfield, the DfES also asked the college to establish and lead the National Workforce Remodelling programme, based in London. Functioning as a distributed (and networked) organization has posed its own challenges, not least because these new patterns of organization have had to be adopted hand-in-hand with the significant challenges of scale and speed of implementation for both NLCs and Workforce Remodelling.

At the time of writing, the NLC programme still has more than two years to run until the end of cohort 2. Already, the learning from the work is beginning to inform emerging education policy. Similarly, it is having its influence upon the ways in which many LEAs are beginning to broker new kinds of relationships between groups of schools – and with those groups of schools. The networks have provided a 'laboratory' environment for some of NCSL's work – and learning from them further feeds into the college's understandings of how distributed leadership and lateral learning can help to drive system improvement.

Where will it travel and how will it end? Who knows! However, current indications might suggest that it will not so much be an ending of the programme as integration into a system that has travelled in a similar direction, and where networks in education are as necessary to professional learning and knowledge transfer as they are in business and commerce and biology!

References and further reading

Allen, K.E. and Cherrey, C. (2000) *Systemic Leadership: Enriching the Meaning of Our Work*. Boston, MD: University Press of America.

Bentley, T. (2003) 'The purposes of networks and their contribution to collaborative capacity', unpublished policy discussion paper, Demos.

Bentley, T. Crane, H. Horne, M. Stasinopoulou, K. and Skidmore, P. (2002) 'Learning the Lessons: How past policy initiatives can help practitioners in the Networked Learning Communities programme', NCSL commissioned research paper, Demos.

Bush, T. and Jackson, D. (2001) 'Preparation for school leadership: International perspectives', paper presented at the University Council for Educational Administration Annual Conference, Cincinnati, USA, November.

Church, M., Bitel, M., Armstrong, K., Fernando, P., Gould, H., Joss, S., Marwaha-Diedrich, M., De La Torre, A-L. and Vouhe, C. (2002) *Participation, Relationships and Dynamic Change: New Thinking on Evaluating the Work of International Networks*. London: University College London.

Clarke, P. (2000) *Learning Schools, Learning Systems*. London: Continuum.

Copland, M. (2002) *Leadership of Enquiry: Building and Sustaining Capacity for School Improvement in the Bay Area School Reform Collaborative*. Stanford, CA: Centre for Research on the Context of Teaching.

CUREE/NLC (2003) 'Early messages from the Networked Learning Communities: Some implications for policy', report commissioned for DfES Innovation Unit 'Developing Strategic Networking and Collaboration Project', September.

Demos/NCSL (2002) 'Learning from experience: A literature review designed to help those establishing and running Networked Learning Communities', paper presented at the Networked Learning Communities Launch Conference, June.

DfES (2003) *Excellence and Enjoyment: A Strategy for Primary Schools*. Nottingham: The DfES Publications Centre.

Earl, L., Watson, N., Levin, B., Leithwood, K. and Fullan, M. (2003) *Final Report of the External Evaluation of England's National Literacy and Numeracy Strategies*, Nottingham: The DfES Publications Centre.

Fielding, M. and Webber, T. (2003) 'Action learning: Tackling practical challenges', an NCSL commissioned research report.

Fullan, M. (2001) *Leadership in a Culture of Change*. San Francisco, CA: Jossey Bass.

Hopkins, D. (2000) 'Schooling for tomorrow: Innovation and networks', paper presented at the CERI/OECD seminar, 14–15 September, Lisbon.

Hopkins, D. and Jackson, D. (2002) *Networked Learning Communities – Capacity-building, Networking & Leadership for Learning*. Nottingham: NCSL.

Hopkins, D., West, M. and Ainscow, M. (1996) *Improving the Quality of Education for All: Progress and Change*. London: David Fulton.

Huberman, M. (1993) 'Changing minds: The dissemination of research and its effects on practice and theory', in C. Day et al. (eds) *Research in Teacher Thinking: Understanding Professional Development*. London: Falmer.

Kahne, J., O'Brien, J., Brown, A. and Quinn, T. (2001) 'Leverage, social capital and school improvement: The case of a school network and a comprehensive community initiative', *Educational Administration Quarterly*, 37(4): 429–461.

Kanter, R.M. (1994) 'Collaborative advantage: The art of alliances', *Harvard Business Review*, July–August: 96–108.

Kerr, D., Aiston, S., White, K., Holland, M. and Grayson, H. (2003) 'Literature Review of Networked Learning Communities', NFER, NCSL commissioned research.

Lieberman, A. and Grolnick, M. (1996) 'Networks and reform in American education', *Teachers College Record*, 98(1): 7–45.

Lieberman, A. and McLaughlin, M.W. (1992) 'Networks for educational change: Powerful and problematic', *Phi Delta Kappan*, 73(9): 673–677.

Lieberman, A. and Wood, D. (2003) *Inside the National Writing Project: Connecting Network Learning and Classroom Teaching*, New York and London: Teachers College Press.

McCormick, R. (2003) 'Theoretical perspectives of relevance to Networked Learning Communities', Open University, NLC commissioned paper.

McLaughlin, M., Talbert, J. et al. (2000) *Assessing Results: The Bay Area School Reform Collaborative, Year Four*. Stanford, CA: Center for Research on the Context of Teaching.

Mandell, M.P. (1999) 'The impact of collaborative efforts: Changing the face of public policy through networks and network structures', *Policy Studies Review*, 16(1): 4–17.

NCSL (2002) *Why Networked Learning Communities?* Nottingham: NCSL.

Newmann, F.M. and Sconzert, K. (2000) *School Improvement with External Partners*. Chicago: Consortium on Chicago School Research.

OECD (2000) *Knowledge Management in the Learning Society*. Paris: OECD.

OECD (2003) *Networks of Innovation: Towards new models for managing schools and systems*. Paris: OECD.

Sarason, S. and Lorentz, E. (1988) *Challenge of the Resource Exchange Network: From Concept to Action*. Cambridge, MA: Brookline Books.

Senge, P., Kleiner, A., Rovarts, C., Ross, R. and Smith, B. (1994) *The Fifth Discipline Fieldbook: Strategies and Tools for Building a Learning Organization*. New York: Doubleday.

Southworth, G. and Sebba, J. (1997) 'Increasing the LEA's capacity to support schools as they seek to improve', paper presented to the BERA Conference, September, York.

Supovitz, J., Poglinco, S. and Snyder, B. (2001) *Moving Mountains: Successes and Challenges of the America's Choice Comprehensive School Reform Design*. Philadelphia, PA: CPRE.

Thorpe, M. (2003) 'Communities of practice and other frameworks for conceptualising, developing and evaluating NCSL's Networked Learning Communities', NCSL commissioned paper.

Wenger, E. (1998) *Communities of Practice: Learning, Meaning and Identity*. Cambridge: Cambridge University Press.

Wenger, E., McDermott, R. and Snyder, W.M. (2002) *Cultivating Communities of Practice: A Guide to Managing Knowledge*. Boston, MA: Harvard Business School Press.

West, M. and Jackson, D. (2002) 'Developing school leaders: A comparative study of leader preparation programmes', paper presented at the American Educational Research Association annual conference, April 1–5, New Orleans.

Wohlstetter, P., Malloy, C.L., Chau, D. and Polhemus, J. (2003) 'Improving schools through networks: A new approach to urban school reform', *Educational Policy*, 17(4): 399–430.

Wohlstetter, P. and Smith, A.K. (2000) 'A different approach to systemic reform: Network structures in Los Angeles'. *Phi Delta Kappan*, 81(7): 508–515.

19 Delivering Business Benefit through Organizational Learning

Paul McCoy and Richard West

Introduction

Organizational learning has been a vogue term for at least the last decade; that it has remained current for so long is a sign that the issue it highlights remains vital. But the subject of organizational learning can prompt more questions than answers. How do you do it? What does it look like? How do you ensure that it delivers to its full potential while continuing to meet the changing needs of the business? This chapter reports on one way of answering such questions, based on five years' sustained pursuit of organizational learning in BAE SYSTEMS (formerly British Aerospace), a large multinational defence systems and aerospace company. The company is outlined in the box below. Throughout the period described, BAE SYSTEMS has been faced with significant business challenges resulting from the consolidation and restructuring of the European defence marketplace, and other dramatic changes to the global market for defence systems and commercial aerospace. This period also involved significant organizational change, including the amalgamation in 1999 of British Aerospace and Marconi Electronic Systems.

Our aim in the chapter is to outline the approaches and practices that have been used to stimulate, enable, nurture and deliver organizational learning at individual, team and business levels. This work has been the continuing central focus of BAE SYSTEMS' corporate university, known as the Virtual University (VU). Two features of the VU approach are fundamental. First, a constant *alignment* to business needs, and second, the *integration* of a wide range of practices. Hence, the focus on individual and organizational learning for performance improvement has remained constant, even as the mix of approaches and tools has evolved on the basis of experience, need, and technological advances.

We start by describing the VU, by locating it within the BAE SYSTEMS corporate landscape, and by explaining the model of organizational learning that has informed our approach. With this ground prepared, we then review our experience of organizational learning at the business unit and team levels, outlining the range of tools that have been used at different times. Then we report on our efforts to enable the individual learning that is needed to underpin and complement organizational changes. Finally we reflect on where we have reached at this time, and what seem to be priorities for the future.

BAE SYSTEMS (FORMERLY BRITISH AEROSPACE)

- A global systems company innovating for a safer world.
- Dedicated to making the intelligent connections needed to deliver innovative solutions to customers with technologically challenging requirements.
- Prime contractor and systems integrator in air, sea, land and space.
- Order book of £42.5 billion (year-end 2003).
- Sales of £12.6 billion (year-end 2003).
- Presence across all five continents.
- Over 100 000 employees worldwide.
- Wide breadth of activities.

Within the UK, employees (including those in joint ventures and Airbus UK) are working in a variety of roles from leading-edge, innovative scientists in the company's Advanced Technology Centres, to fitters and welders building the next generation of nuclear submarines or the Eurofighter Typhoon. The vision is: 'To be the leading Systems Company, innovating for a safer world.'

Supporting this vision are five core values, which guide the way the company plans and operates its business. These values are:

- **Customers** – our top priority: We will delight all our customers, both internal and external, by understanding and exceeding their expectations.
- **People** – our greatest strength: All our people will be encouraged to realize their full potential as valued members of the team.
- **Performance** – our key to winning: We will set targets to be the best, continually challenging and improving the way we do things, both as individuals and as members of our teams.
- **Partnering** – our future: We will strive to be the partner of choice, respected by everyone for our cooperation and openness.
- **Innovation and technology** – our competitive edge: We will encourage a hunger for new ideas, new technologies and new ways of working, to secure sustained competitive advantage for our company.

The rapid pace of market and technological developments in the defence and aerospace industries have required the development of new capabilities and partnerships, new innovative ways of working, and greater organizational agility in responding to the needs of customers and marketplace. A cornerstone of the company's approach to addressing these challenges has been its ongoing investment in organizational learning and the development of its people, as reflected in the 'People' value above, and the investment made in the company's Virtual University. The Human Resources (HR) strategy clearly reflects these challenges by focusing on ensuring we have the necessary talent, that we create and sustain a performance culture, and that the company is organized in the most effective way.

The Virtual University within BAE SYSTEMS: Its remit and approach

The VU was established in April 1998 to champion the company's intent to improve the capabilities of the organization through the development of its people, its processes and its technology. The organizational structure of BAE SYSTEMS has changed significantly since then. However, it has been characterized throughout by having a significant number of operating units, geographically dispersed, and large business groups each with clear business objectives and goals. A comparatively small, central headquarters function is responsible for the coordination of corporate strategy, and the delivery of a limited number of core corporate-wide services (including business planning and other activities required by UK plc status). The VU has since its formation been part of that central headquarters function. Since founding it has been sponsored by senior members of staff, initially reporting to the CEO. More recently, it has reported into three senior directors who provide leadership for the VU's activities in the areas of Organizational Learning and Leadership Development, Engineering Capability Development, and External University Research and Partnerships.

As a focus for organizational learning, it was imperative that the services provided by the VU were driven by business needs. In this context benchmarking (managed within the VU by a Benchmarking and Best Practice Centre team) was seen as a critical 'front-end' analysis tool for the business in order to establish the capability and performance gaps within core business areas. Hence, organizational learning within the VU included carrying out benchmarking projects on internal areas of the business in order to establish both capability and performance gaps with world-class companies. Awareness of the capability gaps was then used to inform priorities for the VU and for the business on the development solutions required by individuals, teams and businesses, as illustrated in Figure 19.1.

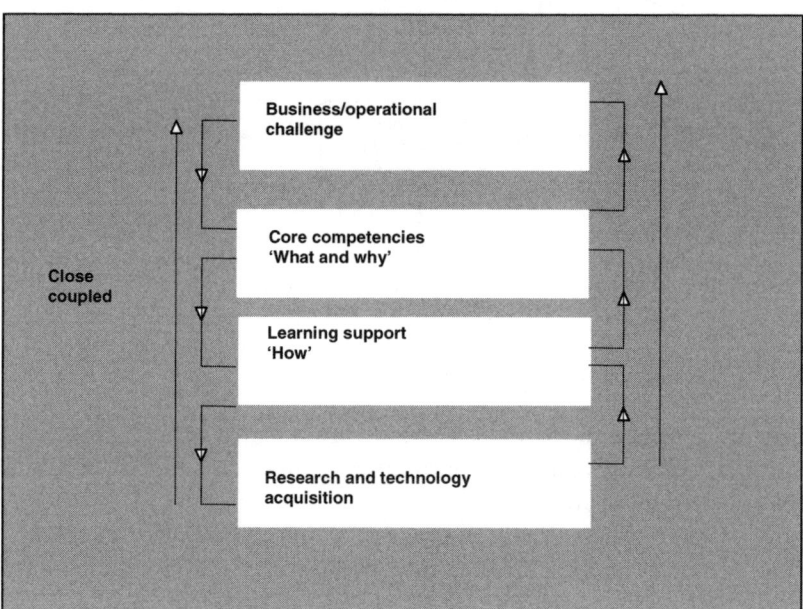

Figure 19.1   Business alignment at BAE SYSTEMS VU

The VU activities thus aimed for a 'close coupling' between the business/operational challenges (identified through the company-wide strategy and business planning cycles), and the identification of core organizational capabilities and competencies required to support these challenges. Clarity on what these capabilities were enabled learning support to be defined and deployed (at an individual, team and business level). The VU's role also included directing and sponsoring technology research and acquisition (both in terms of product technologies and those relating to manufacturing and business processes). Finally, part of the remit of the VU, particularly in its early years, was to develop and exploit leading-edge technologies for the transfer of learning and knowledge across the company on a global basis. This remit resulted in the development of a number of key tools and partnerships, which form the basis of the VU's current e-learning strategy and capabilities, described later in this chapter.

Another way of describing the VU's role and contribution is in terms of the learning and change cycle shown in Figure 19.2.

While the overall objective of the VU was to enable and support effective organizational learning within the company, the learning and change cycle shown below was primarily managed by the VU's Organizational Learning team. This cycle is at the heart of organizational learning and change both at a company level, and in relation to the support and services provided by the VU. This is the thinking behind it:

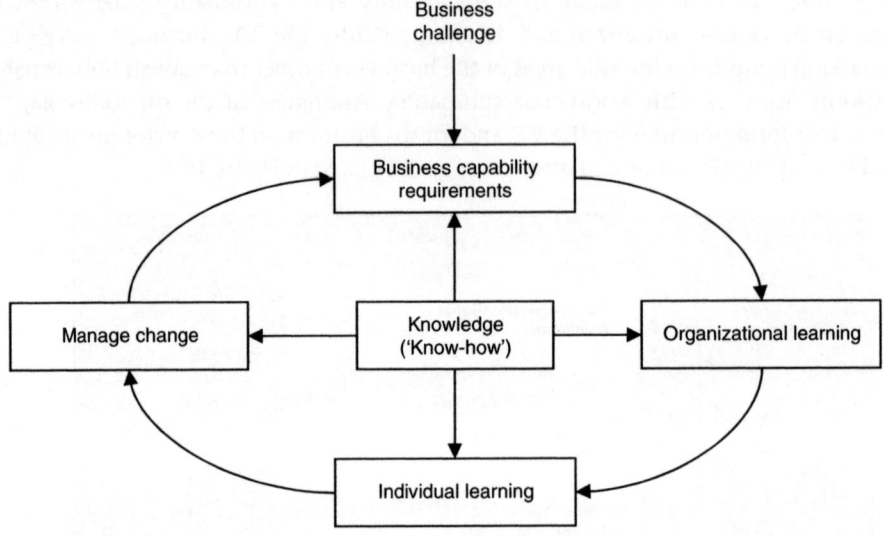

Figure 19.2   The VU's learning and change cycle

- Any change or learning is most effectively undertaken with a clear understanding of the business or local challenges and/or opportunities – this is why we link our cycle closely into our business planning process.
- With clarity of the business drivers for change, gaining an understanding of *how* the organization needs to change – the organizational learning that is required – is the next step.
- Having identified the type of change required and the new capabilities that need to be established, team and individual learning objectives and plans can be defined.
- The other critical element of the cycle is the management of the change itself, which draws on project management tools and capabilities. Individual and team learning continues through this stage, both in relation to acquiring new skills required to support new business processes and ways of working, and also to help individuals and teams to manage through the change process itself.
- Central to understanding the business drivers for change, for delivering organization and individual learning and for effecting the change itself, is access to knowledge and experience ('know-how') – hence its place in the middle of the diagram.
- A final step in any change is to review the learning and achievements, which have been secured through the process.

The cycle shown in Figure 19.2 not only illustrates a potential sequence for approaching organizational change; it also reflects the way in which the VU and company aim to integrate individual and organization learning.

Figures 19.1 and 19.2 describe the general approach and intention of the VU. They provide a high-level map within which particular activities and services can be located. It is to these that we now turn, starting with those that support the organizational learning phase of the learning and change cycle.

Organizational learning in practice

The concept of the VU emerged as part of a major change programme within British Aerospace, known as Benchmark BAe. This programme established a single company vision, mission and values and 17 core actions (one being the establishment of the VU). A number of the other actions related to innovation and performance, which collectively supported the creation of a culture of learning and sharing across the company. Clearly, creating an effective learning environment within an organization such as BAE SYSTEMS requires significant and sustained commitment from the top of the organization. It takes time for new practices to become the normal way that people work day-to-day, and normally a range of initiatives will be needed to promote and embed different aspects of an overall culture change.

The diagram in Figure 19.3 summarizes a number of key programmes linked to the VU and to the company's 'Innovation' and 'Performance' values, which were important in the early years of the VU's life. In different ways the programmes were all important to organizational learning and the sharing and transfer of best practice across the company. The diagram shows the degree to which individual programmes either supported cultural or

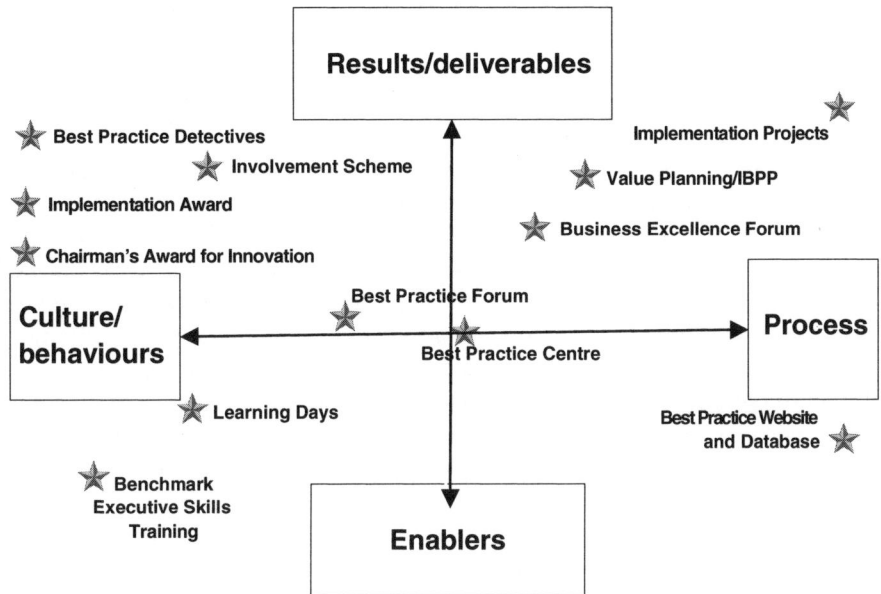

Figure 19.3   The variety of VU programmes

behavioural change within the business, or the introduction of harder business processes for sharing and learning. The programmes are also placed relative to the vertical axis according to whether they were large-scale enabling activities, likely to require significant time before results were seen (lower part of diagram), or more tactical programmes (top of diagram), where results were more local and more immediate.

Figure 19.3 does not show all the relevant initiatives supporting organizational learning – although some might view even those shown as being too many. In our experience, however, it is important to adopt a broad and balanced set of activities, in which some change the way people feel about learning and sharing best practice, and others change the business processes and infrastructure that supports the transfer and management of know-how within the organization.

The most significant of these programmes from the perspective of benchmarking and best practice (know-how) exchange were:

- **Best Practice Detectives:** A cultural programme, giving volunteers from across the company the opportunity to act as local 'detectives', searching out best practices and sharing them across the company. Volunteers received training and were provided with support to act in this role. Within the first nine months of operation, these volunteers had identified over £1 million of benefit opportunities at a local level within the company. As well as having a serious outcome and business benefit, there was a significant element of fun and enthusiasm with the programme, including a 'Sherlock Holmes' themed launch event in Baker Street, London.
- **Chairman's Award for Innovation/Implementation Award:** A high-profile company award scheme recognizing exceptional innovation achievements in relation to products or working practices. Within this scheme a special category known as the Implementation Award promoted the importance of sharing best practices and specifically the successful implementation of best practices from elsewhere in the business or from an external partner. The award ceremony was a prestigious event hosted by well-known media presenters, and there was widespread communication of the event and the winning innovations and best practice transfers across the company.
- **Best Practice Forum, Best Practice Centre and Learning Days:** A more formal means of promoting benchmarking and best practice was the establishment of a cross-company Best Practice Forum. The Forum was a community of practitioners and experts who met both online and in physical meetings to understand the different business issues and challenges and to share best practice as potential solutions. The forum's website was open to all employees and provided virtual notice boards and other facilities to allow people to post requests for, and offer best practice in, a wide range of business disciplines. A physical Best Practice Forum meeting was held on a quarterly basis for members representing different areas of the business. These meetings would review the progress of the various activities to promote the sharing of best practice, review local approaches to organizational learning, and identify what further corporate coordinated work would be beneficial.

The Best Practice Centre comprised a small team based within the VU, who supported the Best Practice Forum, and provided expert advice and support on carrying out benchmarking projects and in the adaptation and implementation of best practice from other companies, or parts of the organization. The Centre also supported the extensive web-based facilities, which provided support to employees across the globe. To focus learning and sharing around particular categories of best practice, the Best Practice Centre coordinated Learning Days based on different criteria from the Business Excellence model and the company's five values, such as Performance. The days were normally held for around 200–300 people and representatives from all parts of the company would be involved in both sharing their best practice and learning from others.

- **Best Practice website and database:** The Best Practice Forum website, as mentioned already, was an extensive resource available to all employees containing over 1000 examples of best practice and numerous links to both internal and external services to support benchmarking and the identification of best practice. An example of the original website is shown in Figure 19.4.

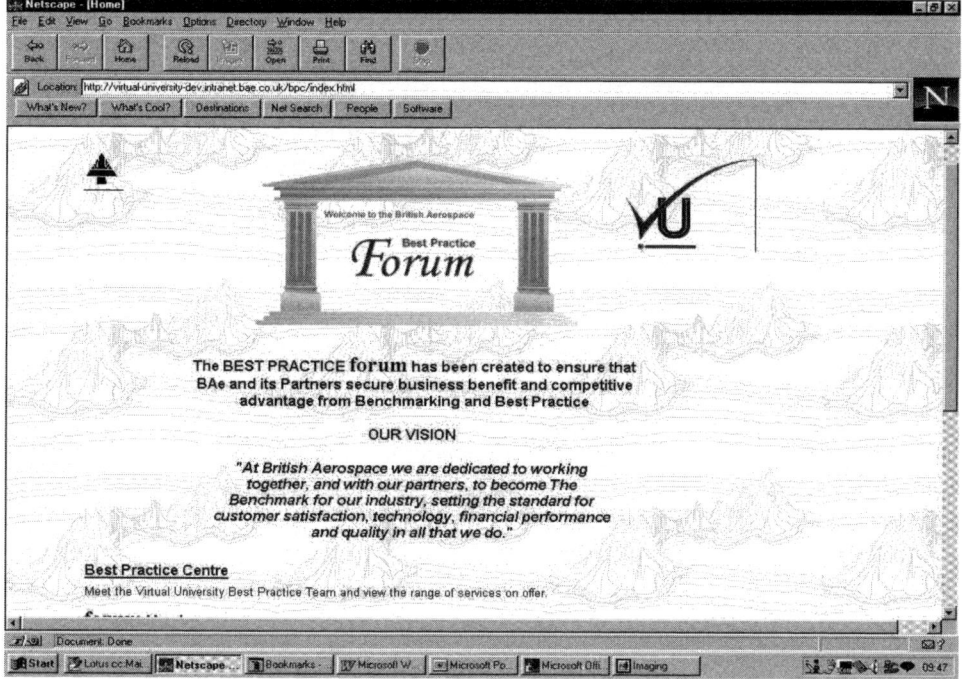

Courtesy of BAE SYSTEMS

Figure 19.4   Best Practice Forum website

All of the activities and programmes shown contributed to the overall environment within the company of the importance of learning and of sharing best practices and know-how. However, care was needed continually to ensure that the messages given in connection with these programmes reinforced the importance of best practice and know-how management as part of normal working, and not as something separate to the 'day job'.

The benchmarking of business capabilities and performance across the company was also central to the pursuit of organizational learning. This was carried out over a period ranging from 1995 onwards, using a number of high-level benchmarking frameworks. In this period, the Business Excellence Model was important within the company, as was becoming a benchmark company (that is, one that others see as setting the standards). The Business Excellence model was also used within each business area to help drive improvements, identifying improvement priorities and in the process of identifying best practice that could be shared.

The importance of common reference models is illustrated in the framework in Figure 19.5. Using Business Excellence, PROBE[1] and other benchmarking tools allowed performance and capabilities/practices to be identified within and outside the company using common terminology and context. This was important for collecting know-how, and for linking the benchmarking and best-practice sharing activities.

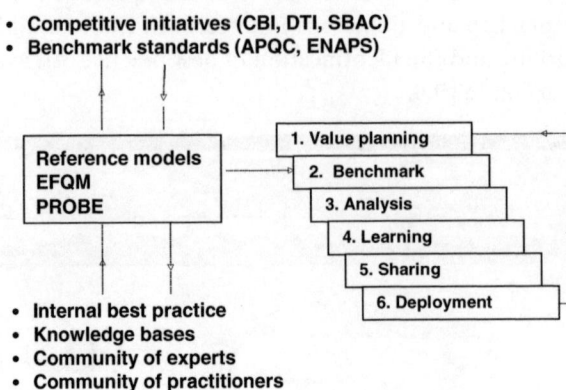

Figure 19.5   The benchmarking and best-practice framework

This simple framework and six-step process encouraged individuals and teams to understand the challenges contained within their business strategy and business plans. It enabled key areas of the business to carry out benchmarking activities to understand both internal capabilities and performance, and to identify where to go to find best practices that could be adapted for local needs.

While the Excellence model provided a valuable goal and reference model for improvement at an enterprise level, more tactical tools such as PROBE were used extensively to identify gaps in operational capabilities and performance both in relation to external world-class companies and internal operations.

The diagram in Figure 19.6 shows one example of the information that the benchmarking tool PROBE provided on capabilities and performance across the company. The

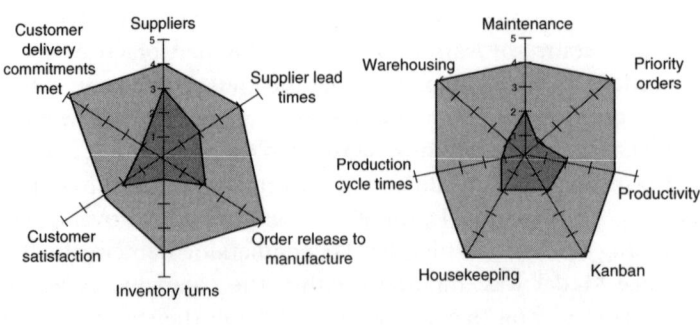

Figure 19.6   Using PROBE to present information on the improvement opportunities in lean manufacturing

inner areas of the radar plots indicated the lower performing areas of the business, and/or where capabilities are less mature, the outer area, indicating business areas with high performance and mature capabilities. The light-grey shaded section between outer and inner lines therefore represents the capability and performance gaps between different areas of the business, and hence the learning potential available within the company.

The potential benefits of closing these capability and performance gaps across the company were significant, and are illustrated by Figure 19.7.

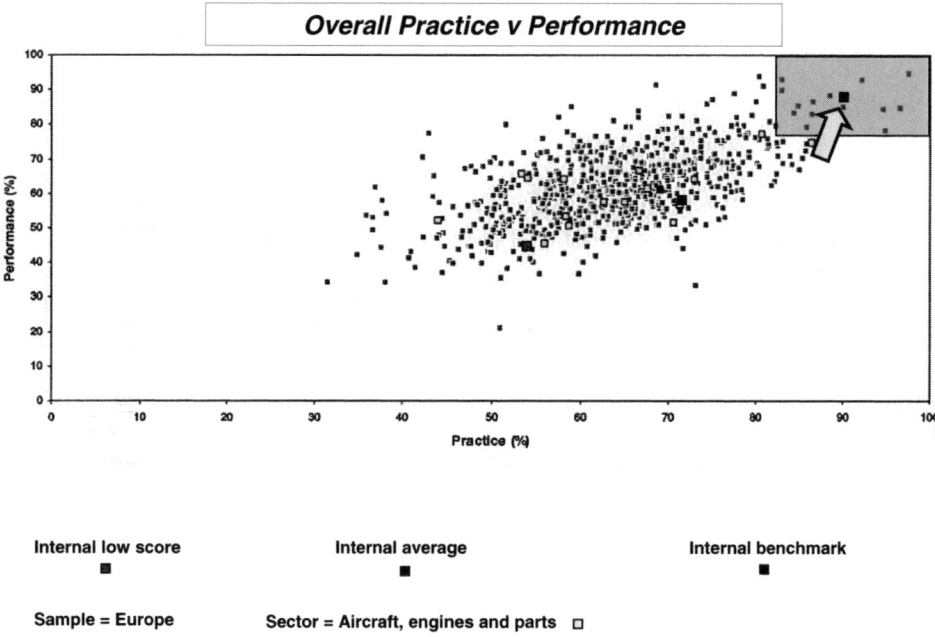

Figure 19.7   Performance benchmarking – an example

The scatter diagram is another example of output from using PROBE and presents the benchmark scores from a wide sample of companies in the aerospace sector. The diagram is helpful for organizations to compare their journeys to world-class performance as they move toward the top right-hand corner of the chart reflecting mature capabilities and world-class performance.

The PROBE model was also used within the company to illustrate the potential of discrete elements of best practice and high performance that existed in different parts of the organization. By inputting these higher scores on capability and performance into the model as if the scores were all located in one part of the business, the organization was given a 'virtual' picture of where BAE SYSTEMS could be (see arrow at top-right corner in Figure 19.7) if it could effectively share its best practices throughout the organization.

In one sense this provided a 'wake-up call' for the organization on the importance of benchmarking and best-practice exploitation. However, the challenge on the VU was how to spread such know-how – hence the focus on organizational learning services.

Individual learning and the development of professional capability

From an organizational perspective, the recruitment, development and retention of high-calibre professional staff, particularly in the areas of engineering and systems, is critical to the future of the company. Where professional development needs to be provided on the basis of a common, corporate approach, the VU has a key role. Given the recent growth of the company through mergers, with the companies involved all having their own disparate terminologies, frameworks, programmes and course providers, this has been a significant challenge. Essentially, the VU contributes in two ways: first, where a consistent approach is needed in the *content* of programmes; second, where a company-wide *infrastructure* for learning is needed. Each of these is discussed in turn below – although the two areas of content and delivery platform are usually linked in practice.

The VU was involved in the definition of an engineering competency framework against which engineers across the company can compare their knowledge and understanding at each stage in an engineering career. This framework enables the company to have an overview of engineering competency, skills and expertise/talent management across the company. Underpinning the framework, the 35 000 engineers receive online and formal support in career planning and with managing training for both task and career development needs.

This project, named Engineering Developing You (EDY), provides access to a rich and diverse portfolio of suitable development options, in an online environment. EDY will also provide the engineer with assistance in recommending the best-fit learning solutions, registering for chosen courses and initiating a standard delegate management process in the case of off-site or residential programmes. However, e-learning is not sufficient as a standalone media for delivering learning. Stimulating peer group interactions and work-based projects will also support creative thinking. Only through blended learning can BAE SYSTEMS provide its engineers with the right range of approved solutions catering for individual learning styles and, of course, the need for a collaborative learning environment.

In a more recent timeframe, as part of the drive to establish a performance culture in BAE SYSTEMS, an approach called Performance Centred Leadership (PCL) has been established. This is currently applicable to the top 600 senior leaders, but with the potential to roll out further in the organization depending on the requirements of the business group. This approach provides a framework for the review and appraisal of individual performance and development needs and determines the way the company rewards, develops and manages the careers of its leaders. Appraisal draws on a variety of measures including peer reviews, 360-degree feedback, employee opinion survey, with much of the process provided online through the company's intranet. This online access also enables the integration of tools that support both individual annual appraisals and reviews, and the identification of appropriate development options via the VU's online development portfolio.

VU online learning infrastructure

Underpinning the VU strategy is a scalable information technology (IT) infrastructure designed to deliver organizational learning and know-how company-wide and cope with numerous legacy computer systems and complex networks. It was clear from the VU's launch that if the company intranet had not already been in place, the VU would have had to create it.

E-learning and web technology were the only rational solution to creating affordable access to a continuous learning environment for over 100 000 employees, working at over 60 sites across the UK alone, and many more abroad.

Mergers and acquisitions had left the organization with a legacy of learning contracts and supporting IT systems that did not provide value for money nor provide individuals with a consistent, high-quality level of learning content. The learning material was, in the main, CD-ROM based and only available at the Learning Resource Centres (LRCs) due to the restriction on desktop PCs and CD drive lock-down. Also, from an individual's perspective there was a lack of visibility of 'best fit' learning solutions across the organization and it was not uncommon for business units to source external training solutions directly, at a significant cost, albeit that another site had a learning intervention that was fit for the purpose.

An initial cost reduction of over £1.5 million in the provision of computer based training (CBT) was achieved through rationalizing content suppliers across the company and establishing a corporate online learning service along with a network of site-based LRCs (providing CBT and other development support).

The online learning service available on both company intranet and the Internet now offers over 500 courses and currently has over 23 000 registered users, with 27 000 online courses undertaken last year, and an average of 6000 training hours per month delivered by on-line means. In parallel, across the UK sites, an estimated 12 000 people use LRCs to access the CBT and other employee development services. The LRC network has now grown to include 59 centres worldwide, covering UK, USA, France, Germany, Sweden, Australia and Saudi Arabia. A Mobile and Family Learning capability has attracted, to-date, over 1200 family members to take up the VU's learning service at home.

An increasing proportion of online learning content is being developed specifically for in-house purposes, supporting key processes and tools where clear business requirement and benefits have been identified. Greater use of online systems are also being made through improved approaches to blended learning, particularly where online courses can be supplied as pre-work for delegates prior to attending off-site development courses.

To ensure the VU provided employees with clear visibility of all the potential development solutions, the 'Learning and Development (L&D) Guide' was launched on the intranet in 1999, a 'one-stop shop' for learning support, development opportunities and career guidance. It offered web-based search tools to allow individuals to search for 'best fit' development from open learning courses, online courses, formal training and placements linked to personal development plan requirements. A learning styles guide allows individuals to assess their preferred learning style before embarking on specific development. Only courses and programmes listed in the 'L&D Guide' were officially approved. By late 1999, over 3000 courses, many for accreditation, were listed on the 'L&D Guide', including the 500 online learning courses from beginner to expert, recognized and accredited professional development programmes, certificate to degree courses, and personal effectiveness courses ranging from presentation skills to teamwork.

Every employee now has access to the intranet VU 'L&D Guide' and to e-based services from a desktop computer or by visiting the nearest LRC, where a manager will also offer support, a library of reference materials, and advice on best-fit solutions. The 'L&D Guide' and its Integrated Development Portfolio receives over 12 000 hits a day and remains the most popular site on the intranet.

Though important, courses are not enough. The VU's thinking was that to truly drive competitiveness through learning, access to wider sources of learning – such as best practice, know-how, research and even expertise, personalized to an individual's or team's needs, available at the right time – would be needed. Such thinking was reinforced by a significant drive from the CEO to get more return on the investment the company had made in its intranet. The intranet had been growing organically and was fast becoming impenetrable. It was a potential goldmine, but users faced information overload, unstructured information, timeliness issues, and the complete inadequacy of the keyword search engine to locate the requisite information.

Autonomy: A key supporting technology for organizational learning

The management of knowledge in this twenty-first century is the competitive edge, but how many large global organizations have successfully addressed this issue? Corporate intranets and databases explode with information and hundreds of returns are typically retrieved in response to single but too broad keyword searches. A considerable degree of what appears on an employee's screen is generally irrelevant to business needs because of accidental links or coincidences of natural language and contemporary context. For example, 'AIDS' can show up as a medical condition, a United Nation foreign aid poverty programme, and a UK government launch aid repayable business loan programme.

In May 1998, the VU proposed a trial of two leading products, Autonomy and Excalibur Retrieval-ware to address the business information problem. The trial lasted three months, with over 350 users across the business and extended enterprise, and led to the implementation of Autonomy's technology to power the VUs online strategy. The Autonomy engine worked by accurately understanding key document themes rather than searching with keywords. Importantly, it was able to filter the correct learning to the right people and communities – that is, to those who wanted and needed it.

The VU aim was to provide employees with the learning, know-how or information that they sought, and where they could simultaneously be offered a customized opportunity, to be alerted in the future to what they did not know but would want to know. The VU and Autonomy worked together to build this 'killer application' that is now deployed on the 'L&D Guide' and website, following pilots integrated into the professional development programmes in manufacturing and engineering. This proved a remarkable enhancement of the learning environment, and a tool for senior executives and technical specialists.

The VU has now pioneered the deployment of Autonomy (VuFinder) via a three-tiered approach. First, employees can search across organizational sources such as the intranet, shared drives, learning and best practice databases as well as premium news sources and people sources. This intelligent search and retrieval receives over 6000 web hits a day.

Second, individuals can enter a particular website centre of excellence (such as manu-facturing, engineering, customer solutions) and be networked immediately into relevant opportunities for educational development, potential mentors and links to complementary centres of business excellence and job placements across the company.

Third, the ability to create a virtual and global network of people who, as 'colleagues', ask the same questions or seek a common answer. These are all potential knowledge brokers. The full integration, exploitation, and leverage of the selected databases, along with the know-how emerging from individual's local and global experiences in diverse businesses, are the strategic goals of the VU in its knowledge brokering role. Utilizing this smart retrieval technology has been a quantum step forward. But achieving the ultimate business performance requires can-do attitudes and willingness to share best practices, to overcome the barrier of any 'not-invented-here' syndromes.

The VU's leading-edge technology implementation directly supports the VU's overall strategic direction and through this blend of technology, and supporting processes such as Best Practice Detectives, Chairman's Award for Innovation and the Best Practice Forum, the company can already point to over £50 million pounds worth of savings.

Where are we now?

Over the past five years we have created a number of robust capabilities within the organization to support organizational learning. These include the ability to carry out performance benchmarking, and business and team diagnostics in order to understand potential performance and capability gaps. A broad range of development options are available to individuals and teams within the VU's development portfolio, and this is supported by online learning courses. We can map all these tools and resources onto the learning and change cycle shown earlier (see Figure 19.8).

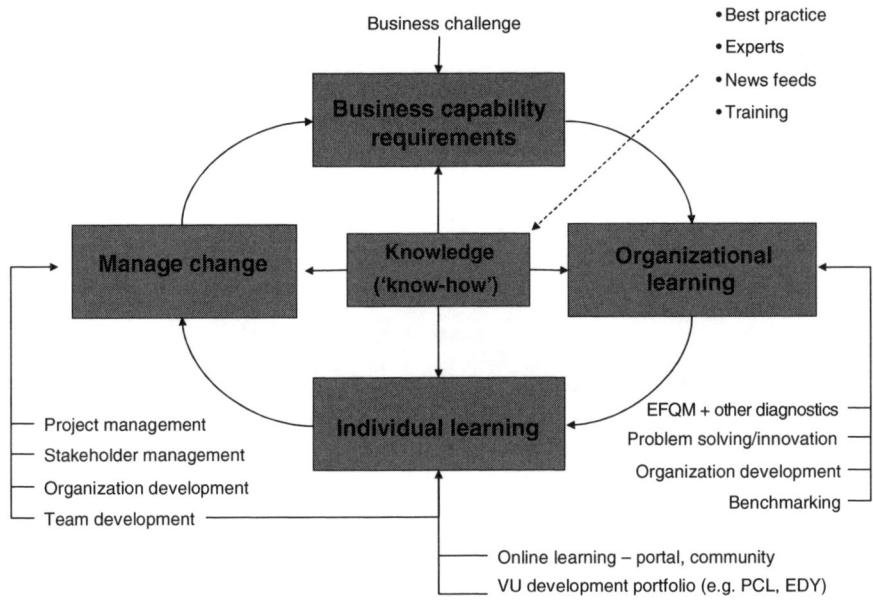

Figure 19.8 The VU's learning and change cycle

As our experiences with benchmarking and sharing know-how have matured both within the VU and across the company, three significant things have happened. First, the importance of best practice has been recognized by the business, and is a prerequisite for any review or effort to improve how we operate the business. Second, the Best Practice Forum, and specific activities to promote best practice, are no longer needed. They are not seen as adding value, since identifying and adopting best practice is now an accepted approach in everyday working.

Third, and building on previous work in adapting and applying best practices, there has been an increasing demand from the business for better tools and approaches for managing *change* rather than simply finding best practice or managing know-how. As a result, over the past year, the organizational learning team has developed and applied an overall process, known as the Wizard Process, which supports teams and businesses in managing improvement and change programmes, and incorporates tools for benchmarking, best practice adoption and innovative problem solving. The Wizard Process is illustrated in Figure 19.9. In its complete form, it is not only a business support tool used by VU 'Consultants' working with business teams, it is also a framework which generates and retrieves best practice and performance metric information, which can be shared across the company, as shown in the middle of the diagram.

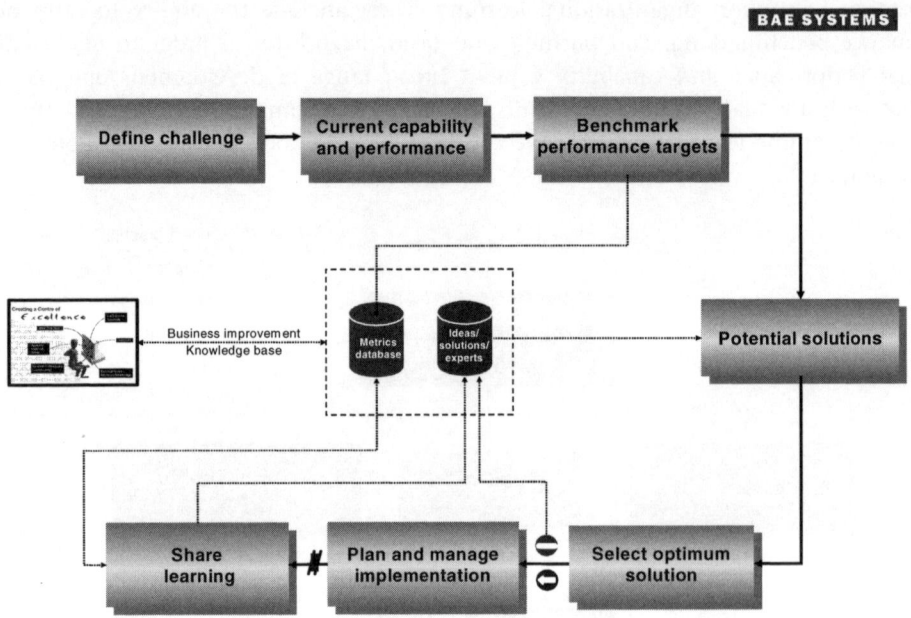

Figure 19.9   The Wizard Process

Increasingly, the VU's resources and expertise in organizational learning are being used in supporting particular areas of the business, or particular functional areas within the company, to improve capabilities or performance.

For those individuals and teams who are part of a community of interest or who wish to sponsor and support a centre of excellence in a particular business topic, the VU's capabilities to support community-specific web portals are now well established. A fundamental element of these portals is the ability to define what access is required to external information feeds and internal best practice. The number of prospective portal developments being requested from the VU is steadily increasing. The coming year will provide the real challenge of whether the scaleable approach to configuring and supporting individual requirements using a generic design of web application fully meets its requirements.

The future of e-learning within BAE SYSTEMS lies in taking this holistic view of learning and in supporting projects, teams and communities with access to everyday learning. However, achieving the highest levels of business performance is as much about culture and people's behaviours as the technology. True global learning organizations require can-do attitudes and willingness to share best practices, to overcome the barriers of 'not-invented-here' and 'knowledge is power'.

As the e-learning services continue to evolve and grow, user support becomes increasingly important. In order to offer the users the right pedagogical and technical support, many of the transactional level services such as advice, delegate management and online learning content delivery is being transferred into a joint venture company with Xchanging (which provides human resources services to the organization). Much of the joint venture service utilizes web-based technology for course availability and booking/delegate management, with the advantage that these systems can be linked seamlessly with the VU and other web-based learning and development resources.

In conclusion: Looking ahead

If we view organizational learning as the means by which organizations and their employees continually challenge current capabilities and performance, identify the need for change, and acquire and apply the necessary know-how to support such change – then organizational learning will continue to be a key focus for organizations for many years to come. Within BAE SYSTEMS, the future of organizational learning means an integrated approach to knowledge management and change management services, exploiting all forms of learning, and continuing to deliver e-learning with a shared service focus.

Technology solutions will continue to play an important role in delivering consistent, quality interactive training where this is appropriate – for example, where geographical separation and size of organization makes other methods impractical, ineffective or too costly. Hence the emphasis will be on exploiting technology where it can have most impact. At the same time, learning and development must be driven by business needs/imperatives (such as capabilities). Know-how sharing and e-learning must also focus on key areas of the business such as our engineering, and project management capabilities.

The activities will be further strengthened by stronger levels of sponsorship from the business, providing approval for investment and resources before individual projects are started and ensuring adequate levels of business take-up once services are available. As e-learning capabilities and facilities are better understood, it will be easier for the future evolution of online based training to be planned and implemented as part of a holistic approach to learning and development at all levels of the organization. In practical terms, this means the VU needs to review and renew the partnership between corporate and local management of learning and development. A corporate lead is valuable where large investment in shared infrastructure/technology is required; local direction and management is best, for example in defining local business content requirements.

Developing and diffusing an understanding of blended learning will also be an important challenge. Once online infrastructure is established, there is a danger that online delivery is considered as the preferred delivery approach. But care is needed to establish end-user training requirements and the acceptability of online delivery to specific audiences before such choices are made. Cost savings and time effectiveness, of 'anytime, anywhere' learning via the intranet and Internet is likely to mean the current baseline of online services continues to be provided for all employees. However, significant scope exists to improve how these services are provided, and by whom. There is much to be discovered about when different learning blends are appropriate and cost-effective.

Note

1. PROBE stands for Promoting Business Excellence and is the title used to describe a series of business benchmarking tools that were developed and marketed by the Confederation of British Industry, London Business School and IBM.

PART IV

Prospects and Possibilities for Corporate Universities

Conventional universities have a history in Europe that dates back more than 800 years. In that time, they have changed and evolved to meet the needs of the time; new ones have been created and others have long since disappeared. In comparison, corporate universities (CUs) may seem like shooting stars that dash across the sky. But in comparison with universities, companies and legislatures are recent arrivals too. So what is the future for CUs? They could, of course, be a very temporary phenomenon – in the sense that the current predilection for the use of academic-related labels will pass. What seems far less likely – indeed far-fetched – is that large organizations in turbulent environments will decide that they no longer have any need for strategic learning initiatives. As was said in Chapter 1, CUs are a response to a confluence of factors related to the knowledge economy, the state of flux of corporate structures, the prevalence of communications technology and the changing face of education. There seems little prospect that any of this turbulence in the corporate environment will abate. Certainly there are few commentators who predict that the relationships between corporations and their partners and customers, let alone their dealings with nation states and regulators, are likely to become simpler and more stable. Equally, the very late twentieth century technological change that provided a networked PC on each desk and thus the infrastructure for company-wide e-learning, was already dated before that millennium ended.

Part IV of the handbook brings together two renowned exponents of CUs and e-learning to frame what they see as the issues for the immediate future and beyond. Jeanne Meister has long been an advocate of CUs and through her books and in person she has held the hand of many as they started down the CU road. In Chapter 21, along with her colleagues Jonathan Andrews and Thomas Kraack, she paints a picture in which CUs come of age in the adult world of tough decisions about business priorities and profit centres.

Before that, in Chapter 20, a leading scientist from the Knowledge Media Institute, who has helped companies devise the means to achieve their learning and knowledge transfer aims, offers his informed insights on the technological possibilities for our children's life-long learning. Peter Scott skips quickly through the impact of the hard technologies of ubiquitous mobile technology infrastructure and grid computing, before opening up the prospect of the higher-level technologies of knowledge systems, rich media, and presence systems.

Taking these two chapters together with the diversity of the earlier ones, it is clear that the need for CUs is likely to remain strong, whatever their name and focus; but the forms they take look set to go on evolving. Learning will continue to surprise us.

20 *The Emerging Technologies*

Peter Scott

Introduction

Tracking emerging technologies and speculating on future uptake and influence is a risky business. Consider, for example, 'digital paper'. The idea that you could interact with a 'sheet of paper-like' computer screen that would be robust, but thin enough to roll up or even fold, while also perhaps touch sensitive, and even without wires – has been a seductive vision for many years, (Negroponte, 1995). Arguably, it is inevitable that this sort of innovation will happen at some point, but predicting *when* it will be available as a consumer product is too hard to call.

To help us to picture the growth of our technical world Dana Moore (2000) has characterized the development of new technologies for what he terms the 'infosphere' along four main 'V' axes: volume, velocity, variety and value. As he notes, the first three measures increase with the steady march of technology on an almost daily basis, whilst the fourth, 'value' is much more debatable. This view of the expanding infosphere is extremely apt to the growth of the corporate university concept. The increasing 'volume' of activity and the increasing 'velocity' of change is everywhere evident, so much so that for the corporate university (CU), it is tempting to add 'volatility' to Moore's list of critical technology 'V's.

By 'variety' Moore intends 'variety of format', and in the 'infosphere' he can point to technical leaps in mobility, such as Personal Digital Assistants (PDAs) and even mobile telephony extensions into the online. However, a measure for 'variety' in corporate learning is less easy. The thousands of courses that have so rapidly come to fill CU portals over recent years still seem to be strongly attached to the learning models that come along with the animated digital book. Reading a large volume of text on your desktop PC, walking around with those pages of text on a PDA, or even reading it in the bath on some form of 'digital paper' still evokes basically the same interaction with the same social device – 'the book'. In this way, while it is clear that hardware developments will have significant impacts, their *value* to CUs is very hard to guess.

Some easy wins for future-prediction pundits include communication leaps such as Bluetooth, WiFi, mobile devices like 3G telephones, radio frequency identification (RFID) tagging, and even grid computing. The first three of these are part of a general trend towards increasing ubiquity in computing devices, such that one can bring the network to everywhere. The first, 'Bluetooth' is a low-power, short-range wireless technology suited to wirelessly connecting any device with any other (http://www.bluetooth.com). So high-street shops now stock Bluetooth-enabled mice, cameras, games, printers, phones, and so on. This allows for the creation of 'personal networks' of interesting devices. The second technology, 'WiFi', extends the range and bandwidth of the wireless network connection to a local-area network for higher-powered devices such as laptops and PDAs. Many travelling business folk now seek out WiFi public 'hot-spots' where they can connect without plugging in. Mobile phones are getting to be more like PDAs and laptops so that computing power is getting more pocket-sized and hand-held. The use of 3G 'digital' mobile phone networks greatly improves the amount of data such devices can use.

At the other end of the spectrum, RFID is another low-power, short-range wireless technology. RFID devices listen for an appropriate and authenticated radio query and respond by transmitting a unique ID code. These devices are typically very low power – the tags, for example, can typically respond using only the power from the radio signal that is trying to read them. Without a power supply, the tags themselves can be very long lived, cheap and tiny – at the moment manufacturers are making the chips smaller than a grain of sand, and perhaps even washable (although frequently they are attached to larger articles such as key-rings or cards, to incorporate an aerial, see for example, http://www.rfidjournal.com). In principle, they could become cheap enough to 'powerlessly' tag anything in a networked world. They do not carry much data, unlike the other network technologies, but enough so that, for instance, all the boxes in the warehouse can 'call out' to the inventory computer to say what they contain and where they are at the moment.

The final hardware flavour-of-the-moment, 'grid computing', leverages the interesting potential of peer-to-peer networking (http://gridcomputing.com). The peer-to-peer concept is that computers can transfer data directly to each other instead of via servers. Where the 'peers' are themselves significant servers, then 'supercomputers' can become 'emergent properties' of many computers acting together in concert and sharing processing out among each other in vast 'grid' systems.

As we have argued with the digital paper example, it is highly likely that all of these will happen – indeed most are happening now. Unfortunately, some of the merely 'technical' advances will, at best, only allow us to do more of the same thing, do it more easily, or do it faster. Looking for the technologies that will have valuable transformational effects on a business such as the CU is much, much harder. What counts as 'value'?

While 'value' is essential in the corporate learning sphere, it is less relevant for the conventional campus-based universities. The latter, with an affinity for both books and lecturing, can 'put their lectures online' as a low-cost marginal add-on to their core business. Some have even invested in a substantial automation of the process to reduce the costs even further, such as the eClass lecture-recording project at Georgia Tech (Pimentel et al., 2001). However, none have yet seriously challenged the lecture-based, synchronous-classroom, timetable-driven didactic models that are still by far the dominant mode for their learners (see, for example, the challenging critique by Laurillard, 1993).

So it is interesting (even in attempting to pay homage to the conventions of the traditional university) that it is the opportunity (and threat) in the e-learning value equation that is driving the CUs to question the models themselves. It is 'killer' emerging soft technologies that have the potential to transform the learning models and thereby add real value.

In this chapter, there will be no speculation without real evidence of 'current value', and this will inevitably shift the focus to the nearer term – within the next ten years. If a technology can work today then it might really be in general use in ten years time. Therefore, we will examine working examples of three 'killer' soft technologies that will have a significant impact on the CU in the medium term, near term and immediate future. These will be *knowledge systems, rich media, and presence systems*, respectively. The argument will be that knowledge systems, and, in particular agents and the semantic web, will influence the medium-term future of the CU (that is, within the next five to ten years). Rich media systems will have a significant impact within the next five years, and presence systems will be of immediate 'emerging' significance (say one to three years). These technologies are already demonstrably significant – but it is worth looking in some more detail at examples that may highlight how they might change the value equation in corporate learning.

The semantic web and intelligent agency

THE IMPORTANCE OF SEMANTICS

The recent emergence of standards for the semantic web will have a medium- to longer-term impact on all business conducted on the net (Berners-Lee, 2000). The **semantic web** is based around a set of standards for representing the semantic relationships between objects in what are known as 'ontologies', that is, structures for knowledge.

The extensible mark-up language XML seeks to move beyond the document hypertext mark-up language of the conventional web (HTML) with its 'dressing tags' such as <b> meaning 'bold' and <p> meaning 'put a paragraph here'. So XML allows you to define more meaningful tags like <person> to indicate that some piece of text is 'the name of a person' or <date> to intend 'this is the date of something'. This more 'semantic-oriented-view' can actually do some work for you once you add an agreed dictionary to standardize and compare different tags and a structure of these tags to show how they can be related to each other. The former can be called a resource description framework (RDF) while the latter is something like an ontology (see for example, Klein, 2001). So, for example, in the semantic web you could (trivially) define <birthday> using the <person> and <date> tags. More significantly, you can also start to make 'inferences' from this data using rules to deduce new information!

As the semantic web is of longer-term impact, it is difficult to find working examples that will highlight the strengths and weaknesses of this technical development. We will focus here on one innovative form of semantic inferencing system that, while it does not depend upon semantic sources, will be particularly well suited to exploit the semantic web as it emerges – the intelligent agent.

Intelligent agents are software systems that can act autonomously on your behalf. Sometimes, a user can delegate substantial authority to such a system. Typical examples crowding the research literature are systems that perform searches for you. For instance, you might give your software agent a product name and perhaps a few other constraints (such as price boundaries) and it should try to seek out the best deal. However, trying to function without the semantic web to help them makes it very hard for such agents to function – so most of this work remains experimental. Indeed the only sign of such 'shopping agency' systems that you can actually use is via portal sites such as RoboShopper (http://roboshopper. com) and MySimon (http://www.mySimon.com), where the portal runs the searches on your behalf. Alternatively, you may want an agent to trawl through various sources of news and use a simple set of heuristics (or 'rules of thumb') to construct a personalized newspaper for you containing only the stories in which you are likely to be most interested. These research systems have not yet made it into mainstream public production, but the concept is a strong one and will certainly have a medium- to long-term impact. A few companies have already started to deploy corporate systems using the simplest 'search agent' concept (for example, http://www.autonomy.com), and some are even offering interactive online-assistant systems (for example, http://www.artificial-life.com).

EXAMPLE: AN INTELLIGENT AGENT

A critical future development for the CU lies in the integration of the training function with a company's knowledge management process. If future workers must be 'knowledge workers', then part of their learning process should involve exploring, and contributing to, the memory of the organization. The 'Sentinel' system is a good example of an attempt to leverage knowledge for organizational memory (Moreale and Watt, 2002). Sentinel came out of early research at the Knowledge Media Institute on the concept of a 'Virtual Participant' in online-communication (Masterton and Watt, 2000). The virtual participant (VP) was an agent that tried to take part, as an independent and autonomous third party, in online asynchronous forums in the Open University. These forums are where the online students discuss their assignments and generally work cooperatively with each other by posting to shared message spaces. The VP agent sought to interject into their conversations to assist the progress of their discussions and problem solving.

The system designers noted that after each presentation of a course, filled with large quantities of 'email-like' forum discussion (by students and mentors), this would all get archived. Then a new batch of students would come along and start by saying very similar things, all over again. The VP agent compiled 'stories' out of the older public forum correspondence by looking for patterns over many years. It could then try to spot evidence of these patterns emerging as similar 'stories' in the current live forum. Its most challenging task was finally to take an 'appropriate next' segment of the old 'compiled' story and interject as a 'virtual participant' itself into the current forum discussion – the critical concept being to help the discussion to move along. This idea was very compelling, but the VP agent has not yet made it into the mainstream course system for a variety of reasons: it is hard to know when to interject constructively into a student debate; it is hard to spot fragments of the story worth interjecting; and it is very hard to interject to both help the students to progress in their own debate, and yet not preempt it; and, of course, one critical issue is getting users to accept, and make use of, semi-autonomous, slightly intelligent systems.

In contrast, Sentinel took the concept out of the university and into a large multi-national oil company whose use of Microsoft Exchange™ forums was for working engineers and managers. As a technology, Sentinel has succeeded where the VP fails, because of one critical side effect of its work. In processing past and present stories, the agent effectively takes and composites snapshots of what workers across the company are talking to each other about at any one time. Where the VP still has problems seeking to interject into the debate, the Sentinel can step back from it and merely log its compiled view of company discussion to web pages. Just like the classic concept of an 'answer garden' for organizational memory (Ackerman and McDonald, 1996), the Sentinel pages find a very keen readership. In this way, the Sentinel provides a powerful set of technologies to help companies to create and then surf their own agent-assisted knowledge base.

THE IMPACT OF THE SEMANTIC WEB

It is already clear that standards are critical to brokerage and the trading of learning objects for the future of e-learning. The semantic web offers a real opportunity for future corporate portals to draw intelligently upon a wide base of new content via this brokerage (Nejdl, 2001). The e-learning industry has already started to develop its own sets of standards – the first of which, supported by the US aviation industry, has already established a respectable batch of 'compliant' systems (http://www.aicc.org/) and others are already offering ambitious XML based templates and development guidance (http://www.ims.org/). The development of these standards into semantic web systems is very promising, (for example, Stojanovic et al, 2001).

So, where are intelligent agents going to fit into a company's online learning strategy? The history of artificial intelligence research runs alongside the history of intelligent tutoring systems – ever since we have tried to make machines smart, we have also tried to produce software architectures that aim to empower the human learner without tying up other (expensive or rare) humans in the process (Wenger, 1987). Serious commercial versions of intelligent 'teaching agents' have not come out of this research just yet, but the emergence of the semantic web coupled with learning object standards may change this within the next ten years (for example, Johnson et al., 1998). Even if the influence is slower than this, it is clear from the example discussed that intelligent agency will help companies to manage a range of their knowledge effectively – and this should be brought into the corporate training sphere.

Working with rich media

THE IMPORTANCE OF RICH MEDIA

Some chronic problems for learning systems have remained pretty intractable over the years. The production of quality rich-media content has been one of these. One argument is that CUs have tended to keep with a book-driven model and conventional universities, with the lecture-driven model because they are easy and cheap to produce. While interaction greatly enriches the learner's experience, it is expensive.

Recent developments in digital video have meant that reasonable quality recordings can be made and easily digitized. It is now possible to integrate web-based video economically with other media into much richer and more interactive content. A wide range of systems have been developed to assist in this process. For example, the Microsoft prototype MRAS system (Bargeron et al., 1999) produces streaming-video-driven presentation for on-demand training. Students can view synchronized slides with audio and video and can also make notes and even log questions. When MRAS allows students to annotate dynamically a multimedia presentation, it also allows them to share these notes with others.

Other interesting approaches have sought to design 'live' rich-media events for 'online only' users. The Stadium project (Scott and Eisenstadt, 1998) has explored the impact of live telepresence on learning in a range of experimental studies (http://stadium.open.ac.uk). While many companies already deploy webcast technologies and systems, they are usually considered to be mechanisms for leaders to routinely use simple online (one-way) broadcasts to get a message out to their staff; they are typically viewed as a variant of 'business television' with a talking head to camera; and rarely deploy rich media or interactivity. Stadium experimental webcasts are distinct from the broadcast of a rock-concert or new-product launch, in that the participant must 'interact' with both the material of the event and with other participants (Scott and Eisenstadt, 1998).

EXAMPLE – LIVE, RICH-MEDIA WEBCASTING

Consider a simple business example of rich-media webcasting working (experimentally) within a company. On 25 March 1999, the Stadium webcasting technologies enabled a project team from a British Petroleum (BP) oilfield facility in Dorset (UK), to achieve a key learning goal. They were able to share valuable technical knowledge about specialized oilfield equipment with a large and distributed community of practice. In two webcasts lasting 40 minutes each, three oilfield engineers spoke live from a working field stores shed, over the BP intranet, to over 50 colleagues seated at their desks around the world: from Bogota, through Houston to London and Aberdeen. It had to be two events to reach the 'awake' parts of the world at their desks. Remote participants were able to see the presenters, interact with them via text chat, and interact with their presentation by clicking on animations and virtual-reality views. All this within a page of a web-browser on a standard desktop or laptop machine.

The client computers accessed the webcast via an applet (a Macromedia Shockwave™ web page plug-in) embedded in a web page. They received the streaming video and audio, together with the presenter's slides. Additionally, they could send text messages via the web page applet to all connected computers, including the presenter. All remote users were directed to a local URL on the BP intranet web server. The live event page gave them some details of the timing and nature of the scheduled event. Near to the time of the event, they could click a link on this page to get access to the webcast client applet.

Figure 20.1 shows the client applet that brings together and fully integrates controls, slides, text chat etc. It also shows some of the rich-media synchronized slides that appeared in the slide pane of the interface for users to interact with. Beneath the slide area is the text chat input where users could talk to each other and send in questions to the presenter or support team. Where the BP rich media event can be considered a success for the cohort of workers who were interested in learning about the 'piece of pipe' that could impact on their work, it may be instructive to push back a couple of years to a different rich-media learning event which failed.

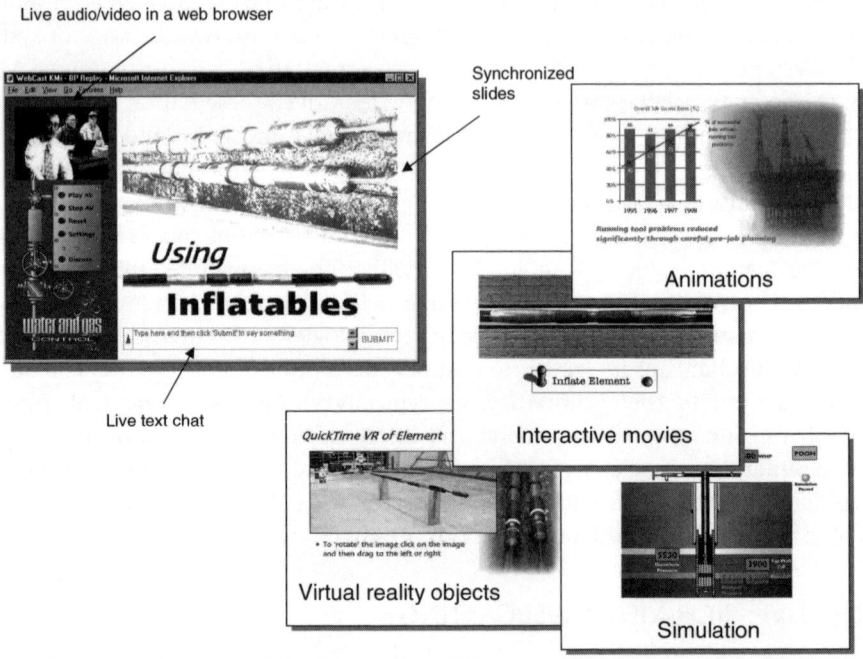

Figure 20.1   The rich-media Inflatables webcast

This second group of workers were managers in the IBM Corporation (Europe) and were all taking a post-graduate university level business administration course. The webcast event was conducted live on 11 April 1997 and made extensive use of a metaphor intended to help motivate the students. It transpired that the use of this metaphor was a large part of the problem.

As is typical with students studying with the Open University, these individuals were working remotely, but were provided with a physical tutor whose job was to facilitate regular group meetings at a convenient physical location for each co-located 'tutor group' (in this case eight to ten students in groups around Europe). The students were studying for an examination on an introductory Master of Business Administration (MBA) course. Instead of flying to a central site in the UK or continental Europe to attend a large-group revision seminar, this particular cohort of IBM-sponsored managers went to a local IBM Technology Learning Centre to participate in a world-wide exam revision session run by central faculty members at the Open University headquarters in the UK. The live revision session was designed as a mix of 'broadcast', 'interaction' and 'game' sessions. The game was designed to use the metaphor of a British 'pub quiz'.

The 'pub quiz' concept may require some explanation outside the UK. A pub quiz is typically a 'bar-based' team game that is conducted with general knowledge questions in a traditional British pub setting – and the prize is usually more British beer. Questions are 'called out' to the teams, who may discuss possible answers among themselves before recording their team response on an answer form. At the end of the event, the team's answer forms are marked, and a prize (typically alcoholic) is awarded to the winning team.

In our event, students in each geographical location – the IBM resource centres across Europe – each registered as teams in their existing tutor groups (a typical grouping comprised six or seven sharing a single PC with a projection screen, and a designated 'team captain' to type in the responses; we had also allowed for virtual teams of isolated home-bound individuals to be created; but while some observed, none registered to 'play'). Live streaming audio from the tutors provided running commentary and feedback, and a sequence of questions appeared in a custom browser frame that challenged the students to think about their coursework. A special scoring interface enabled the central academics (sitting in Milton Keynes in the UK) to score the team's answers at the end of each round. The instantly updated team scoreboard inspired some friendly competitiveness. The scoring mechanism could have been made automatic and therefore large scale, but it was kept open and personal to allow participants to be creative and expressive in their 'free text' responses. The scoring interface simply allowed tutors to turn around a large number of 'free text' questions and answers very efficiently.

The pub-quiz web-page interface (see Figure 20.2) was designed to reflect the concepts of a British pub scene. The main controls are present on the 'bar' at the bottom: an 'ashtray' icon resets the user to the current state of the quiz; a 'beer mat' depicting a map shows the live location of other players; the comments and questions 'bar towel' provides an interface for the user to participate in the live text chat; the quiz 'beer mat' is used in the replay to start the quiz; and the 'pint of beer' is a live indication of where you are in the quiz – when you are out of beer, the quiz is over! The interface was deliberately cute.

The 'specials blackboard' to the left of the window reflects the current scores of all registered players (note that the link shown at the bottom of the indicated figure was not available in the live version – it is for replay users to see how the marking happened; also note that whilst the live stream was carried by Bamba™ the replay version was executed with

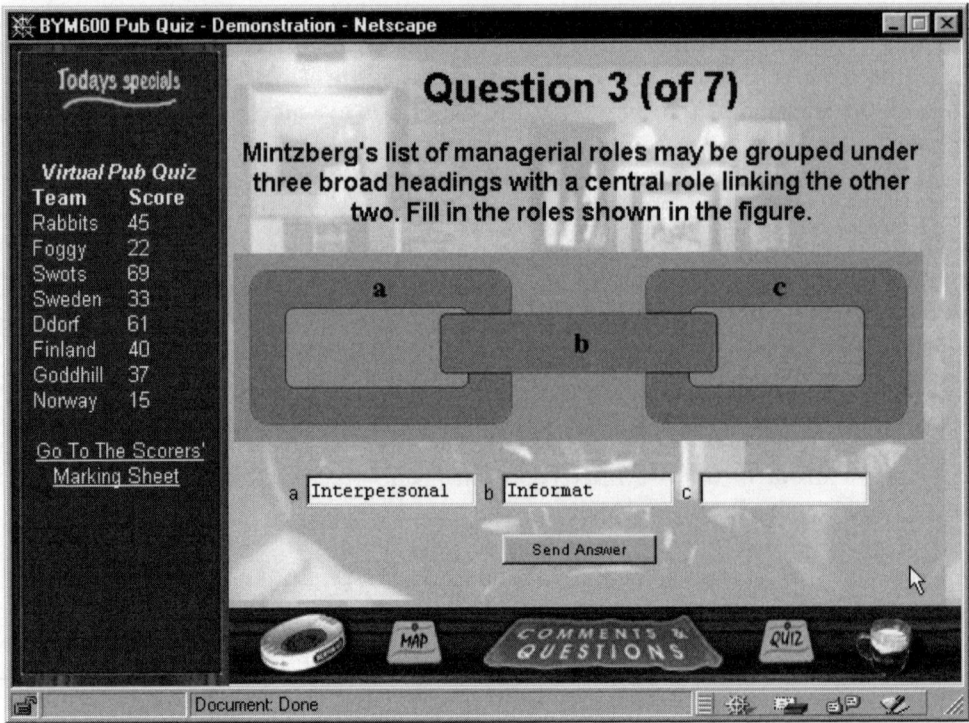

Figure 20.2 A question screen in the pub quiz

RealAudio™, now part of the RealNetworks™ toolset). Note that this was well before the days of reliable, quality and low-bandwidth streamed video.

When the player registers and enters the pub they are connected to the live audio stream carrying the discussion and questions. The area above the bar is the activity area – showing the current state of the session. As the quiz game progressed, the teams were led through a series of questions (presented in free text entry forms as in Figure 20.2) and were given a specific time to return an answer. The answers were logged in the pub-quiz database, which was then accessed by the markers. The sample question shown in Figure 20.2 is a simple 'free text' choice entry – but other questions required a few lines or short paragraph as an answer. The questions were carefully produced to ensure that some (at least) would require team members to actively discuss an answer before submitting it.

The marker view of the pub-quiz database is shown in Figure 20.3. The marker in the figure is currently reviewing the team that has called itself 'rabbits' and their responses to some questions in Round 1. The call to the database server to view a team's entries generates a web-page form around the answers submitted so far (with any marks already given). When the marker has finished marking what has been submitted so far, they can submit the marks back to the database, which will then be reflected – live in the students' interface – on the scoring blackboard (shown in Figure 20.2). Between the three 'game' quiz rounds, we ran slide-based revision sessions and 'question-and-answer' pieces based on the issues raised in the text chat interface.

Not including technical assistance and the central team, the event was attended by eight 'playing' groups and a further nine individuals worldwide. The location of the teams is

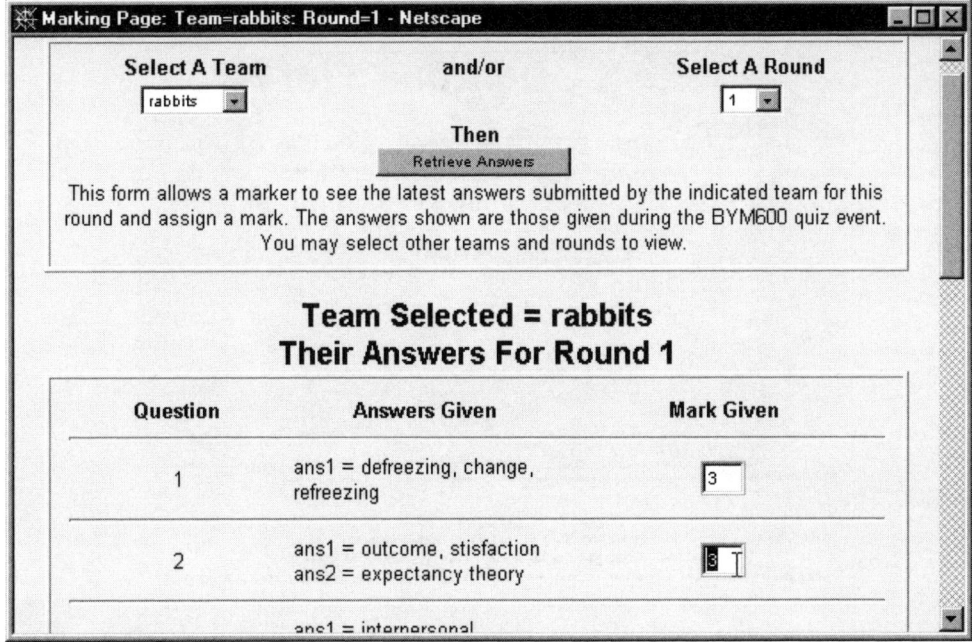

Figure 20.3   The Marker interface to the pub quiz

indicated by Figure 20.4, which shows the result of clicking on the 'map' beer-mat. All teams who registered to play the game were able to participate to some extent.

Figure 20.4 shows the geographical distribution of this group of students. This collection of learners particularly valued the ability to see the 'dots on the map' light up to indicate the activity of their colleagues around the world. This *presence* technology is addressed in the next section.

This 1997 event has many interesting features – most particularly that it represents an attempt to rethink a conventional model (the revision lecture) in a novel format – a made-for-the-web interactive, synchronous and distributed team game. Alas, as already indicated the event was a failure in three ways.

First, it was dogged by minor technical glitches. The second and most critical problem was that its wide international audience seemed to find the concept of a British pub-game pretty alien! Finally, for a large audience of non-native English speaking professionals to keep up with a time-based competition such as this – filled with British pub colloquialisms – was too much of a challenge!

THE IMPACT OF ENRICHING CONTENT

Quality content is complex to produce, maintain and manage. So it will be highly valuable if the new technologies, especially those for managing digital video can make this significantly easier and cheaper in the next few years. Live webcast management systems will dramatically improve in usability to allow the simplest of presentations and meetings to be more effectively shared and to be more usefully interactive. A number of services are now available to help integrate live media with rich presentations (see for example Centra, WebSymposia, and WebEx).

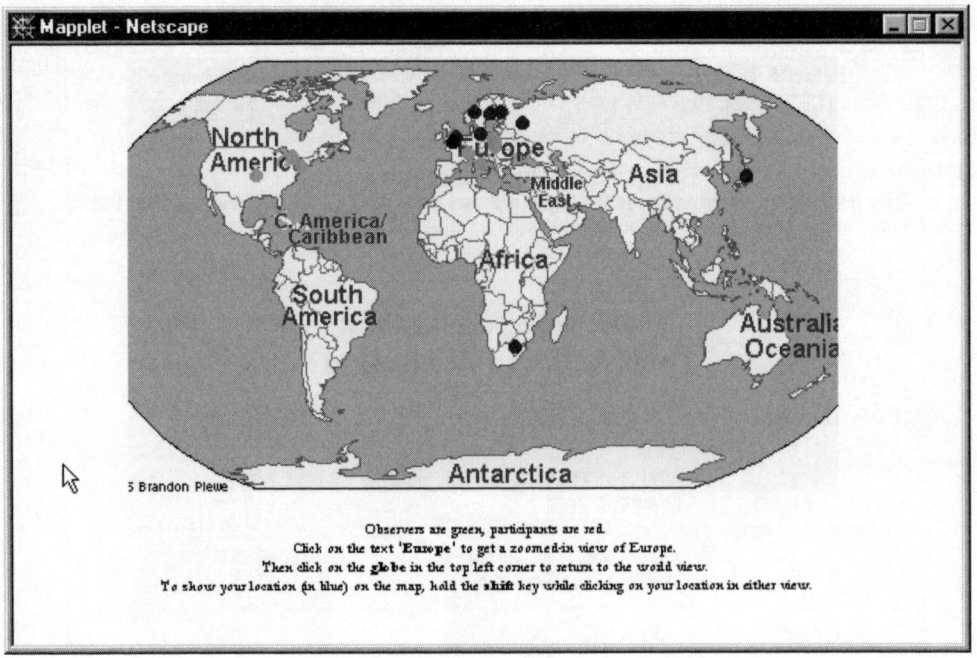

Figure 20.4   The world map view of live pub-quiz participants

However, as the pub-quiz example shows, even the most innovative of events, carefully designed with the remote user in mind must match the user's expectations and needs in an appropriate social context.

Presence

THE IMPORTANCE OF PRESENCE

The concept of presence is about sharing information about the current state of members of a community. The classic example of a presence-based application is an instant messenger (IM). An IM client will allow you to say something about your state at the moment (for example, 'I am busy', 'I am away', and 'I am available') and to observe and monitor those states in a remote, online community. Instant messaging applications such as ICQ, MSN Messenger, Yahoo! Messenger, AIM, Odigo and Jabber are very popular tools in dial-up communities where people want to know who else is online when they sit at their computer. It allows them to have an instant text chat with their family and friends, which is much more immediate and synchronous than email.

The most widely used of desktop IM applications share a very similar set of basic features, such as showing who is online, with some indication of their self-labelled 'state'. The handling of the different states differs superficially in most IM systems, but in essentials, users are invited to say that they are 'online', 'available for chat', 'busy', and so on. Some include more advanced communication capabilities, such as voice chat and file exchange, while the most sophisticated provide powerful community visualization features such as interactive maps.

EXAMPLE – VISUALIZING A LEARNING COMMUNITY

The BuddySpace system (Eisenstadt and Dzbor, 2002), for example, builds upon the Jabber standard for IM interchanges. It uses the concept of 'lights' distributed over maps to show location and state of 'buddies' or co-workers (see Figure 20.5). In BuddySpace, users can share maps of their groups of users with live dot annotations. For example, green dots light up 'available' users, yellow dots indicate 'away' users, while the red dots are currently offline.

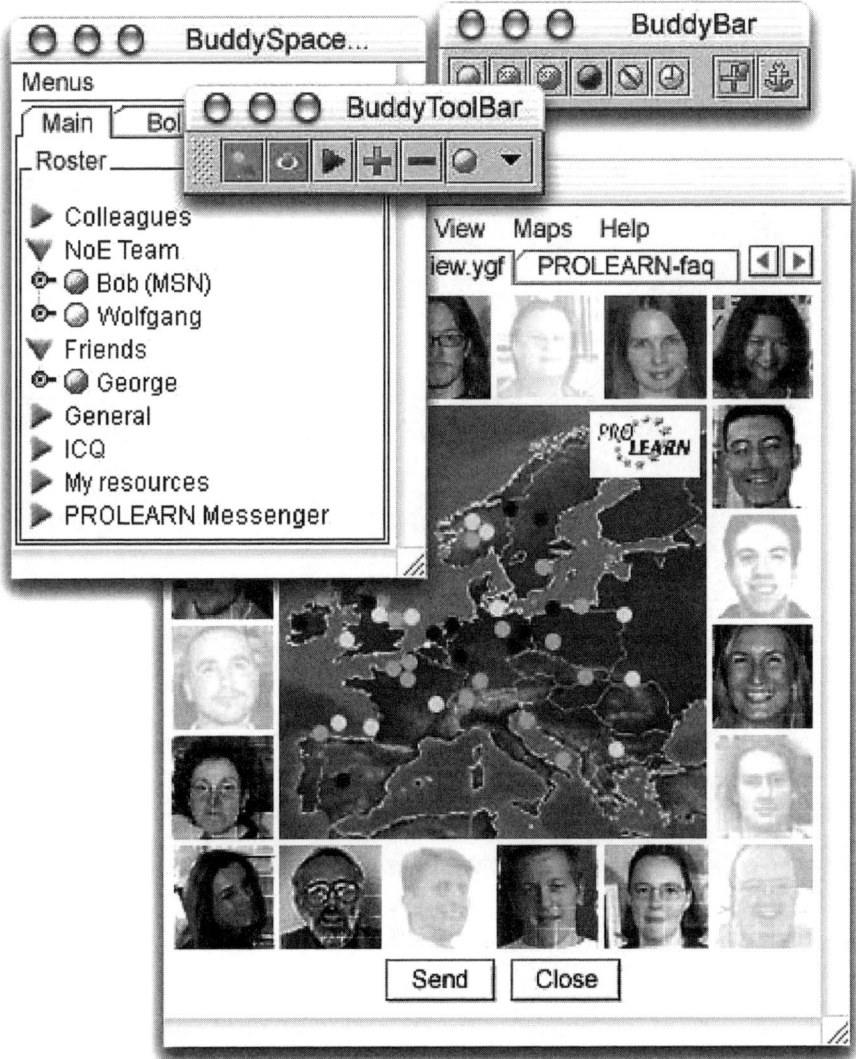

Figure 20.5   A community view in Buddy Space

This ability to see 'at a glance' the status of those around you in your 'virtual community' and to have a short and easy interaction with them is potentially very powerful, even if it is only a 'water cooler' or 'passing in the virtual corridor' text chat. A logical extension of the visualization concept is to add the use of webcams into presence clients. Studies have reported on the use of video webcams to help establish the availability of other users for communication (Johnson and Greenberg, 1999), and some innovative systems have already started to implement experimental 'presence' systems. Hexagon for example (see http://cnm.open.ac.uk/projects/hexagon/) allows a community of users to use a web application to share a configurable collection of web-camera views. The community can see a large and updating view from the cameras of all members from within a web browser (Figure 20.6). Each user can move any of the images of 'buddies' around the screen, click to have an IM text chat with them and can even have an 'open microphone' live audio chat in a space that they have designated the 'coffee room'.

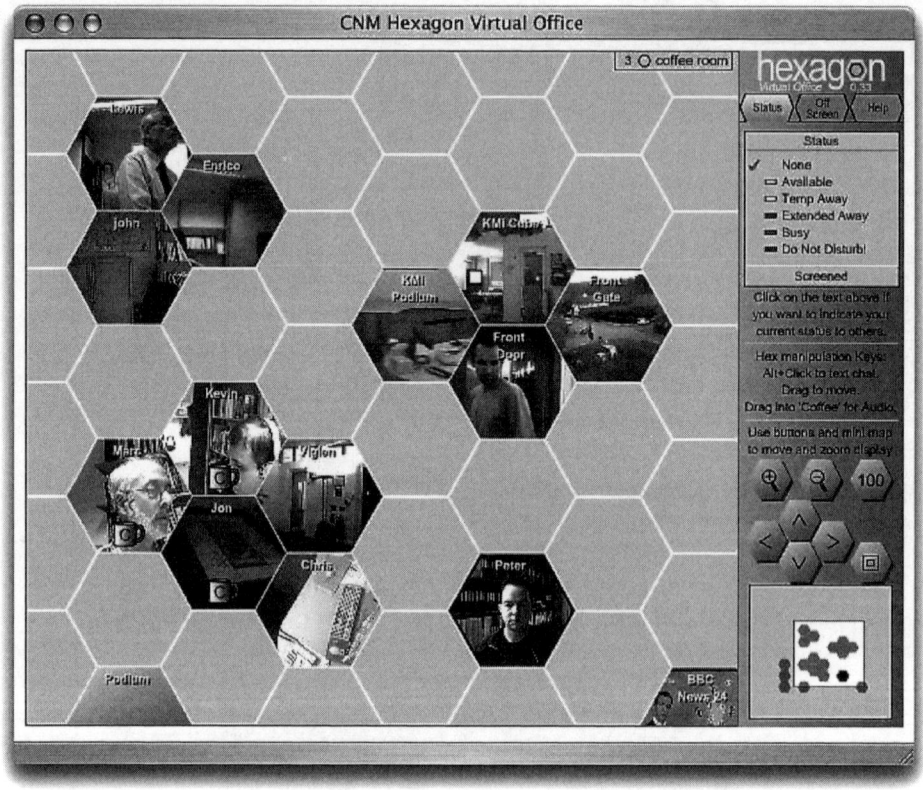

Figure 20.6   A 'video wall' Hexagon community

In a corporate study of implementing the IM tool 'Rear View Mirror' in a multi-site multinational company, Herbsleb et al. (2002) noted the huge impact of 'at that moment' contact over very different company locations to trigger an effective opportunistic team communication. Note, however, that the Hexagon prototype with its mix of casual interactions and constant video awareness is fairly extreme. After a little use, the Hex experience is that many users tend to point their cameras at anything else other than their faces – keyboards are a favourite compromise; as fingers moving over keys are a very strong 'presence and activity' indicator without revealing too much personally, which some users are clearly very concerned about.

THE IMPACT OF PRESENCE

According to Gaudin (2002), IBM has about 270 000 people using IM already as a critical business tool. In a business context, effective presence means that one need never try to call a colleague who is not ready to pick up the phone. If you can 'see' that they are not 'available' at their desk, then you may use presence technologies to find out where they are or to seek an alternative contact that may be able to help. The concept for the corporate learner is one of ready and 'visualized' access to a learning community. If you are currently struggling with learning about X, then presence technologies offer the opportunity to readily 'see' who in your community may be able to help you. This may be a 'currently online tutor' or 'X expert' or even another student who is also currently struggling with X too!

Conclusion

In the introduction to this chapter, it was suggested that conventional universities were not seriously challenging their own role and business models against the emerging technologies (Laurillard, 1993). However, some of the newer forms of university can be seen to be embracing change. Daniel (1999) discusses the emergence of the 'mega-university' from the newer correspondence, television and distance higher education institutions. For these university operations it is the power of 'scale' that is the critical metric. Daniel asserts that it is knowledge-media that will help the mega-university to succeed. Essentially, the emerging technologies discussed here effectively define what he meant by that. So, while the typical CU may be closer to 'micro' than the mega-university that Daniel had in mind, it seems that the value equation has some very similar drivers.

The creative cross-fertilization between these emerging technologies is very striking. Some researchers are already bringing together the hardware radio frequency tags mentioned in passing in the introduction with ideas such as 'presence'. One group (Salber et al., 1999) presents a toolkit for RFID tags that can contribute to a range of interactive systems including presence ones – such as a live in/out board application and a 'meeting display' tool. Some projects are even more strongly integrative, for instance, the CoAKTing system. Bachler et al. (2003) have reported integrating webcast meetings conducted with shared collaborative environments based on grid computing! Their system also uses input from ontology about 'meeting semantics' to help users to structure and search the replay of the meeting.

It has been argued that all these knowledge-media technologies will have a significant impact upon the future direction of the CU. The critical topics that unite them are *ubiquity*, *standards* and *integration*. The basic agreements of standards for all these new systems are helping them to work together in an integrated way. New devices and the increasing reach of networks are making them all more accessible from very different locations and very different devices. However, whether mega-university, micro-university or CU, it is the very different learning models that these technologies can support that may make something of real value, in the future.

Acknowledgement

All images are originals of the Knowledge Media Institute copyright the Open University.

References and further reading

Ackerman, M. S. and McDonald, D.W. (1996) 'Answer Garden 2: Merging organizational memory with collaborative help', in *Proceedings of the ACM Conference of Computer-supported Cooperative Work*, New York: ACM.

Bachler, M., Buckingham Shum, S., De Roure, D., Michaelides, D. and Page, K. (2003) 'Ontological mediation of meeting structure: Argumentation, annotation, and navigation', First International Workshop on Hypermedia and the Semantic Web, 30 August, Nottingham, UK.

Bargeron, D.M., Gupta, A., Grudin, J., Sanocki, E. and Li, F. (1999) 'Asynchronous collaboration around multimedia and its application to on-demand training', Microsoft Research Technical Report 99–66. Available from <http://research.microsoft.com/research/coet/MRAS/ww8/paper.htm>.

Berners-Lee, T. (2000) *Weaving the Web*. New York: HarperCollins.

Brin, D. (1998) *The Transparent Society: Will Technology Force Us to Choose Between Privacy and Freedom?* New York: Perseus Books.

Daniel, J.S. (1999) *Mega-Universities and Knowledge Media*. London: Kogan Page.

Domingue, J. and Scott, P. (1998) 'KMi Planet: Putting the knowledge back into media', in M. Eisenstadt and T. Vincent (eds). *The Knowledge Web*. London: Kogan Page.

Eisenstadt, M. and Dzbor, M. (2002) 'BuddySpace: Enhanced presence management for collaborative learning, working, gaming and beyond', JabberConf2002 Europe, June 2002, Munich.

Gaudin, S. (2002) 'IBM Manager: IM muscles up for corporate users', *Datamation*, 16 August. Available from <http://itmanagement.earthweb.com/secu/article.php/1448271>.

Herbsleb, J., Atkins, D., Boyer, D., Handel, M. and Finholt, T. (2002) 'Introducing instant messaging and chat in the workplace', in *Proceedings of the SIGCHI Conference on Human Factors in Computing Systems: Changing our World, Changing Ourselves*. New York: ACM.

Johnson, B. and Greenberg, S. (1999) 'Judging people's availability for interaction from video snapshots', Proceedings of the IEEE International Conference on System Sciences, 5–8 January, Maui, Hawaii. Available from GroupLab papers: <http://www.cpsc.ucalgary.ca/grouplab/papers>.

Johnson, W.L., Rickel, J., Stiles, R., and Munro, A. (1998) 'Integrating pedagogical agents into virtual environments', *Presence: Teleoperators and virtual environments*, 7(6): 523–546.

Klein, M. (2001) 'XML, RDF & Relatives', *IEEE Intelligent Systems*, 16(2): 26–28.

Laurillard, D. (1993) *Rethinking University Teaching: A Framework for the effective Use of Educational Technology*. Routledge: London.

Masterton, S. and Watt, S. (2000) 'Oracles, bards and village gossips, or social roles and meta knowledge management', *Information Systems Frontiers*, 2(3–4): 299–315.

Moore, D. (2000) 'The Changing face of the infosphere', *IEEE Internet Computing*, 4(1). Available from <http://www.computer.org/internet/v4n1/moore.htm>.

Moreale, E. and Watt, S. (2002) 'Organizational information management and knowledge discovery in email within mailing lists', Intelligent Data Engineering and Automated Learning – IDEAL 2002: Third International Conference, 12–14 August, Manchester. Proceedings, *87, Lecture Notes in Computer Science, Volume 2412*. Heidelberg: Springer-Verlag.

Negroponte, N. (1995) *Being Digital*. New York: Knopf.

Nejdl, W. (2001) 'Learning repositories – technologies and context', Proceedings of ED-MEDIA 2001 World Conference on Educational Multimedia, Hypermedia and Telecommunications, 27–29 June, Tampere, Finland.

Pimentel, M. da Graca, Ishiguro, Y., Abowd, G.D., Kerimbaev, B. and Guzdial, M. (2001) 'Supporting educational activities through dynamic web interfaces', *Interacting with Computers*, 13(3): 353–374.

Salber, D., Dey, A.K. and Abowd, G.D. (1999) 'The context toolkit: aiding the development of context-enabled applications'. *Proceedings of the SIGCHI Conference on Human Factors in Computing Systems: Changing our World, Changing Ourselves*. New York: ACM.

Scott, P. and Eisenstadt, M. (1998) 'Exploring telepresence on the Internet: The KMi Stadium webcast experience', in M. Eisenstadt and T. Vincent (eds). *The Knowledge Web*. London: Kogan Page.

Scott, P. and Quick, K. (2003) 'Technologies for electronically assisting nursing communication', *IADIS International Journal of WWW/Internet*, 1(1): 15–28.

Stojanovic, L., Staab, S. and Studer, R. (2001) 'eLearning based on the semantic web', proceedings of WebNet2001 – World Conference on the WWW and Internet, 23–27 October. Orlando, FL.

Vogiazou, Y. (2002) 'Wireless presence and instant messaging', Technology and Standards Watch Reports, Joint Information Systems Committee. Available from <http://www.jisc.ac.uk/index.cfm?name=techwatch_report_0207>.

Wenger, E. (1987) *Intelligent Tutoring Systems* . Menlo Park, CA: Morgan Kaufmann.

21 Increasing the Business Impact of Learning: Lessons from High-Performance Learning Organizations

Jeanne Meister, Jonathan Andrews and Thomas Kraack, Accenture

Introduction

THE GROWING IMPORTANCE OF ENTERPRISE LEARNING IN ACHIEVING HIGH PERFORMANCE

How much is the enterprise learning function valued these days? Ed Betof, chief learning officer – BD University, tells of a recent gathering of the top global executives of Becton Dickinson where the company's CEO kicked off the meeting with a discussion of the importance of BD University to the company's mission and goals. That says a lot about the transformation of enterprise learning that has been taking place over the last few years. The learning function is now enjoying respect and high visibility both in business and in government. But this visibility means top executives are looking at learning with new lenses: 'You're important to my business,' they are saying, 'Therefore, we're going to treat you like a business.' That is the opportunity and the challenge facing enterprise learning today.

This chapter shows what this means for companies and public organizations. In particular, by examining the most successful among corporate learning organizations, we identify three trends that look set to shape future developments in this era of new opportunities and raised expectations. Throughout, the discussion draws on two things: first, our experiences consulting with major clients and providing outsourced learning services to them; second, on several Accenture research initiatives. These include ongoing research into the characteristics of high-performance businesses, as well as two specific studies: the Accenture *High-Performance Workforce Study*[1] (based on a survey of 244 global CEOs and COOs); and the Accenture Learning *Survey of Learning Executives*[2], conducted with 285 chief learning officers.

That learning executives face a combination of opportunity and challenge comes through again and again in this work. For example, one in five CEOs and COOs rate training and development – hitherto a notoriously poor relation among business disciplines – as one of the top three functions in importance for their entire organizations. In fact, more CEOs than HR managers rated training that high in importance. In the Accenture Learning study, enterprise learning departments and professionals were found to face heightened expectations to deliver value, and, at the same time, to deepen and enrich the roles and competencies of the learning staff.

The most-cited challenges of learning executives all speak to the business impact of learning:

- To align their activities with the most pressing and important business or operational needs.
- To measure their effectiveness and their impact on the performance of the business or agency as a whole.
- To proactively communicate their value to all stakeholders.
- To earn acceptance of the learning function across the leadership of the entire enterprise.
- To provide training to their learning staff so the learning organization can meet the increased expectations of the enterprise as a whole.

These learning executives were also keenly aware that they must overcome a number of legacy restrictions: processes, metrics and techniques that were fine for an approach to learning a decade or two ago, but which are no longer adequate to an environment where executives are looking for measurement-rich reports about the impact of learning on the business, or on the performance of citizen-centric services in government.

If, as a consequence of these challenges, learning executives sense an underlying feeling of discontent among their fellow leaders, they are probably right. Our research makes this clear as well: only 17 percent of executives surveyed report that they are 'very satisfied' with the performance of their training organizations.

Yet the best-performing businesses and government agencies today know of the potential lying latent in their workforces. Our research on high-performance businesses has found that these companies have a distinctive 'performance anatomy.' They are better than their competitors at exploiting the collective intelligence and motivation of their workforces. With more highly attuned people development capabilities, these companies create a 'talent multiplier' – achieving superior business results versus their peers per dollar of investment in their workforces.

WHAT THE HIGH-PERFORMANCE LEARNING ORGANIZATIONS KNOW

About 10 percent of the learning departments or learning organizations studied in the Accenture Learning research have enabled their companies to 'multiply their talent' and achieve measurably higher levels of performance. Analysis of survey data, coupled with additional financial data from other publicly available sources, demonstrates that companies with these high-performance learning organizations returned better revenue and profit growth compared to their competitors and industry peers:

- Productivity (as measured by sales per employee) was 27 percent greater.
- Revenue growth was 40 percent higher.
- Net income growth was 50 percent greater.

Seven capabilities in particular were key to the higher performance of these learning organizations:

1 Alignment of learning initiatives to the business goals of the organization.
2 Measurement of the overall business impact of the learning function.
3 Movement of learning outside the 'four walls' of the organization to include other members of the overall value chain such as customers and channel partners.
4 A focus on competency development of the organization's most critical job families.
5 Integration of learning with other human performance systems and functions such as knowledge management, performance support and talent management.
6 Blended delivery approaches that include classroom as well as both synchronous and asynchronous electronic learning.
7 Mature design and delivery of leadership development courses.

With these capabilities as a backdrop, we want to focus on three major trends that we believe will be increasingly important to the success of learning organizations over the next decade:

- *Delivering and measuring business impact.* Organizational structures, processes and metrics that keep a learning organization aligned with the business, and that ensure that the learning function is run like a business.
- *Customer and channel partner education.* Programs outside the traditional constituencies of training departments that increase the business impact of learning.
- *Technologies that merge learning, knowledge management, collaboration and performance support.* New technologies that increasingly blur the distinction between learning and knowledge management, enabling companies to get people performing at higher levels faster, which enables them to collaborate, and which contributes to growth and innovation.

Trend 1: Managing learning to deliver business impact

DELIVERING MEASURABLE IMPACT

A number of companies today are truly pioneers when it comes to measuring the business impact of learning. For example, when Avaya – a global company in business communications software, systems and services – prepared to embark on an aggressive schedule of new product launches, a key success factor was making training programs immediately available to help *customers* promptly realize efficiency, performance and business benefits. It became clear, however, that Avaya's geographically fragmented learning organization was not positioned to meet the accelerated training needs that would enable rapid market uptake. To cope with the increased learning demands, Avaya outsourced its entire learning function. According to Avaya's Suellen Roth, one of the key benefits of this arrangement has been 'using learning to transform the business proposition.' However, this meant introducing a new sales certification program which was piloted and evaluated *for its business impact*. It demonstrated that the company could increase flow into the sales funnel by about 10 percent and improve its close rate by about five points.

Yet, not all companies are being as successful as Avaya at measuring the business impact of learning. According to the learning executives we surveyed, measuring the effectiveness of learning is the number one challenge of learning professionals today – more challenging, even, than dealing with budget constraints. Executives were also less than satisfied with their ability to communicate the value of learning across the organization. Although this result is hardly surprising, it underscores how far the learning profession still needs to go to apply the same sort of rigor in measurement and efficiency of knowledge work that has been attained in a more mature field such as manufacturing. Underlying reasons for the inability to measure and demonstrate the business impact of learning are complex, to be sure. Yet the research points to at least a few causes.

First, most learning executives measure effectiveness in terms of the learning function (course completion rates, budget spent on learning or learner satisfaction rates) rather than in terms that can be translated into business impacts, such as increases in revenue or decreases in costs or in employee turnover. Although statistics such as enrollments, student satisfaction, completions and hours delivered are the easiest to compile, they do not track the impact of those courses on the performance or people or the company.

Second, executives of learning organizations that have not yet achieved high performance place less value on such capabilities as financial planning, the business of the organization and marketing/communications capabilities as key competencies for chief learning officers.

Finally, many learning organizations – in fact, one in four of the organizations in our research – fail to measure the financial return of learning in any way.

Striking differences in measuring and communicating the business impact of learning can be seen when we compare high-performance learning organizations with the rest of the pack. High-performance learning organizations are generally more sophisticated and in terms meaningful to the business, such as improved satisfaction and retention of customers, improved product and service quality, and better safety scores.

High-performance learning organizations are also more likely to have their future funding and growth tied to their ability to measure success. That is, these companies appear, quite simply, to get more from their learning departments because they demand more. High-performance learning organizations are, indeed, having an effect on the business.

SOME SPECIFIC MEASURES

What specific learning measures are needed in order to make the link to business results and upside value creation? Companies do well to focus first on the following set of measures to link learning to business outcomes.

1 *Time to competency*. Reducing the time it takes a new employee to attain a competent level of performance delivers financial value in two ways. First, it reduces the amount of training spend (for example, from 12 weeks of upfront spend to eight weeks). Second, it means you have a worker who is being more productive faster. If you have a sales person, for example, who is bringing in higher revenues faster, that obviously shows up on the bottom line.

2 *Turnover management*. Increasing a company's retention rates results in several financial benefits. Less upfront training is required for fewer people, a higher percentage of the workforce stays with you long enough to move to higher levels of productivity; and knowledge and experience remain within the organization for longer periods of time.

3 *Resource leverage*. If companies can decrease the time employees spend away from the 'front lines' of job performance (in training, locating needed information and coaching others) they can increase productivity. And if less coaching time is needed, that also frees up the time of more senior level workers.

4 *Productivity*. The specific metrics employed for this measurement will depend on the type of industry and workforce involved. But, whether the metric is in calls handled per hour, sales figures or widgets manufactured per day, productivity is a direct measurement of value that must be benchmarked.

5 *Quality*. Quality of service rendered or product manufactured is measured in financial terms in less rework and higher levels of customer satisfaction and retention.

6 *Risk management*. In the wake of recent corporate scandals, companies are acutely aware of the costs of failing to anticipate and manage risk. Risk comes in many forms: operational, safety, financial and strategic. Increasing the capacity to assess and mitigate risk has high value in producing value and in protecting a brand. Maturity of risk management capabilities can be measured in terms such as reduced rework, on-time and on-budget delivery of projects, and reduced costs of compliance.

SECRETS TO SUCCESS

What are some keys to the success enjoyed by high-performance learning organizations in creating and implementing effective measurement programs? Notes Dan Gorski, Avaya's Director of Global Learning, 'We have moved beyond defining our value as "amount of training delivered." Now we have broad acceptance throughout Avaya University – and throughout Avaya itself – that value will be defined as "results enabled through effective training." We develop solid business cases, we identify the anticipated ROI and then we selectively measure investment versus value delivered.'

One important tactic not to overlook is the employee survey. At the Midland Company – a provider of specialty insurance products and services – Elisabeth Baldock, vice president of human resources and learning, has used surveys to assess the confidence of associates in their supervisors as well as in their ability to do their jobs. 'We had gone through a period several years ago when people felt as though they didn't have enough training to keep their skills up to date, and didn't understand their career paths or how they could better themselves to take on additional responsibilities.' She notes that some of the skills shortages had to do with project management. 'So for the last three or four years we have really focused on helping our associates get up to speed not only from a soft skills perspective, but also for the harder skills, focusing pretty heavily on supervisory training and project management.' The work paid off: the most recent survey Midland conducted showed a dramatic 50-plus percent increase in the favorability ratings used to assess employee self-confidence in their skills.

The key to effective measurement is balance between metrical rigor and human relationships. Kevin Wilde, Vice President and Chief Learning Officer at General Mills, Inc., has been resolute in getting his training organization to, as he says, 'speak the language of the business,' which in the consumer products industry is heavily survey oriented. 'All members of my team are charged with monitoring the follow-through and impact of their programs,' says Wilde. At the same time, however, he cautions that measurement should be seen as the means of understanding the impact and effectiveness of the learning effort, and not primarily to prove the worth of learning. 'Proving value means linking what you do with strategy, and then establishing credibility through strong relationships. Measurement is simply the pro's way of doing the job well. Through relationships, you build credibility with senior leaders, and then you link what you are doing to the strategy. Then senior management just gets it.'

MANAGING LEARNING LIKE A HIGH PERFORMING BUSINESS UNIT

Learning executives are increasingly measured in terms of how well they manage the business side of learning. For example, the top three performance criteria by which executives in our research are measured are 'ability to prove business impact for learning and development' (73 percent), 'ability to demonstrate improvements in the satisfaction of business unit heads with learning department executives' (70 percent) and 'managing budget to business plan' (69 percent). Also important was 'ability of learning department to increase access of learning while reducing costs' (57 percent).

Managing the learning function as a business involves three primary elements:

1 *Governance.* Putting in place the governance structures and decision-making mechanisms that enable you to understand the business well enough to direct the learning outcomes that affect business results, and then to manage relationships with key decision makers, making sure you are included in their agenda from a planning and business management perspective.
2 *Upside value creation.* Determining the particular value objectives (using financial measures such as shareholder value, book or market value, employee and customer value, and so on) most closely linked to the learning investments.
3 *Efficiency planning and management.* Using the best cost management techniques to drive business results with the most efficient use of resources.

GOVERNANCE

Close collaboration between those responsible for the development and delivery of learning content and the company's senior management responsible for establishing the business goals and objectives is too important to be left to chance, or to simply 'keeping management informed.' Companies need a more formal organizational structure and system of governance to ensure that strategy and workforce enablement are in lockstep. In our work, we actually call this 'Business Interlock' – a formal business function with services, interactions, metrics and application capabilities that link learning outcomes to business objectives.

While strong visible top management support is a critical factor in the overall success of a learning organization, a network of business unit managers is also needed to give the effort sufficient mass in its early stages. At Avaya, this governance system includes not only a steering committee of top executive leaders but also another eight to 12 business unit managers – called the Learning Council – who come together to develop a shared vision for the corporate university.

LEARNING AS A COMPONENT OF THE VALUE CREATION AGENDA

Properly conceived, learning investments are some of the most critical drivers within a company's overall value creation plan. When we work with our client companies, we begin with an overall value planning process, using benchmarking to help them identify value creation opportunities and to articulate their strategic objectives in terms of concrete and measurable interventions.

A learning diagnostic is often an important first step in this overall analysis. The learning diagnostic permits an organization to:

- document the scope, operating model and costs of their company's learning organization;
- identify learning organization goals, issues and priorities;
- benchmark the major components of the current costs and service levels;
- confirm the major areas of value creating opportunities;
- articulate a business case for moving forward, and
- develop the initial guidelines for the potential learning design and development project.

COST MANAGEMENT

At its most basic level, cost management in any endeavor can be thought of as a 'Goldilocks' issue; not too much investment and not too little, but a 'just right' level of spending to get maximum value without either waste or insufficiency. Understanding what 'just right' means, however, entails understanding the principal cost management drivers. For large-scale training delivery, four drivers account for approximately 80 percent of the variability around the proper leveraging of resources.

1 *Migration to e-learning.* Cost savings from e-learning are well documented and manifest themselves in a number of ways. The first is a decrease in direct costs – lower program tuitions as well as the reduction or elimination of items such as facilities and travel costs, instructor fees and travel costs and a great percentage of publishing and printing costs.

For most companies, the relative percentage of student days delivered via technology-enabled means is still far from optimized. This phenomenon is particularly true in some industries, such as financial services, retail and health care where many of the right elements are in place to justify large-scale migration to e-learning. But even in less likely situations, such as in manufacturing and resources companies, examples exist of aggressive programs of e-learning migration. Overall, dramatic breakthroughs in cost leverage can result from challenging traditional assumptions of user acceptance, technical barriers and near-term investments.

2 *More effective vendor management.* In enterprise training today, it is not unusual for vendors to account for as much as 30 to 50 percent of the total cost of the solution. As a result, procurement and vendor management become big opportunities for cost reduction. Vendor consolidation can result in significant savings. In most companies, some 10 percent of their vendors provide approximately half of their training programs. Clearly, such companies need to target their vendor discounting activities. But what about that other 90 percent of the vendors who provide the other half of the programs? That's where consolidation (followed by discounting) can again yield impressive savings. The value of such consolidation also goes beyond cost; by decreasing the number of suppliers, companies can build stronger relationships with a smaller number of organizations, increasing the capacity of both sides to work together creatively.

3 *Common learning design.* Another consequence of decentralized training is redundancy in course design and development. Some companies have as many as 100 different training and development groups, each providing non-strategic and non-proprietary programs. Companies with multiple versions of content obviously multiply their maintenance costs when they update that content. Consolidating learning design activities, therefore, can

create more consistent learning experiences and increase a company's ability to maintain content at significantly lower cost.

4 *Process reengineering.* One of the most important truths about learning management today is that updating technology without updating processes likely means a company is under-leveraging new technologies. But restructuring processes to refocus the roles and capabilities of training staff, which in turn provides greater strategic value to the organization, can be a critical source of both value and cost savings. In some companies, as much as 25 percent of all training staff time is spent in administration – getting people registered, dealing with cancellations, getting the training facility ready, and so on.

Trend 2: Customer and channel partner education[3]

Although most learning organizations today serve primarily their own employees, about half of the organizations from our research study are attempting to improve the business impact of learning by expanding offerings beyond their four walls to customers and channel partners.

High-performance learning organizations are more likely to affirm the importance of channel partner education programs. For example, 81 percent of high performers offer either customer or channel partner education programs, or both; with their peers, that number drops to 44 percent. Over the next three years, more high-performance learning organizations plan to launch customer education programs (71 percent, compared to 28 percent of their peers).

THE VALUE OF CUSTOMER AND CHANNEL PARTNER EDUCATION

Why should the issue of education across the value chain be of concern to learning executives? Because such programs are a way to increase customer satisfaction and build loyalty and, by extension, to increase revenue and shareholder value. Customer and channel partner programs can also create an enduring point of competitive differentiation in the marketplace.

For example, consider Nielsen University (Nielsen U), which supports Nielsen Media Research, the leading provider of television audience measurement and related services, worldwide. Customers of Nielsen – which include television networks and affiliates, independent stations, syndicators, cable networks, agencies and advertisers – need to be able to use Nielsen's software applications efficiently in order to get the full value of the service. NielsenU offers a combination of tutorials, synchronous online classes and classroom offerings, allowing clients to choose the method of training that best suits their learning preferences. Convenient scheduling suits the requirements of busy clients. Customers can register through NielsenU for training programs and individual learning activities on how to use various Nielsen software applications and services. NielsenU provides Nielsen Media Research clients with a way to maintain their level of proficiency with Nielsen's software products. Not only does this learning program increase customer satisfaction, it also helps decrease the number of calls that clients make to Nielsen's client support helpline for assistance.

Another reason for extending the reach of the learning organization is that large numbers of companies are now using channel partners to increase sales. To make that strategy work, companies need to differentiate their products in the minds of the partners doing the selling and education is the best way to accomplish this.

Consider the new channel partner education programs being developed by Hitachi Data Systems (HDS). According to Nick Howe, vice president–HDS Academy, 95 percent of the company's channel partners are also selling products from Hitachi's competitors. Therefore, 'the relationship these partners have with our educational programs is a fundamental part of their entire relationship with HDS.' The company has been proactive in surveying its partners to develop a business case to transform its channel partner education programs.

High-performance learning organizations know that effective customer and channel partner education programs can not only cut costs, but can also grow revenue. HDS is focusing in particular on channel partners' revenue and satisfaction. Currently, satisfaction levels with partner education are just over 60 percent, and HDS has plans to move those up over 90 percent quickly. They are also targeting up to a 20 percent increase in total revenues from the partner channel as a direct consequence of the new and better training experience.

FINAL DESTINATION: AN INTEGRATED APPROACH

Where are these trends in channel partner and customer education headed? Ultimately, companies are moving toward a fully integrated approach to embedding intellectual property and experience into their products and services for maximum impact at the best price. One way of embedding experience, after all, is simply through the functions and features of a product. Effective feedback from customers and channel partners means better design and better kinds of service. In other cases, bundling coaching, mentoring and/or training within an overall solution is the right answer. And, the coming days of ubiquitous broadband will certainly revolutionize all aspects of learning, including customer education. Online learning promises to be the dominant mode of differentiating products and services through education and support.

It may also be that, one day, a discussion of channel partner and customer education will be dominated by how great it is for generating revenue, but that time isn't now. Learning executives are certainly interested in breaking even some day, but their real goals are somewhat loftier. They know that channel partner and customer education are important tools for increasing brand awareness, building customer loyalty and gaining competitive differentiation in the marketplace.

Trend 3: Learning that looks like knowledge management, collaboration and performance support[4]

Traditional boundaries between learning and other related functions – such as knowledge management, performance support and talent management – are blurring. High percentages of learning organizations from our research are incorporating (or have immediate plans to incorporate) learning with:

- knowledge management (61 percent)
- performance support (59 percent)
- talent management (56 percent).

Executives of high-performance learning organizations lead the way here, more likely to have incorporated many of these key areas:

- performance support (77 percent of high-performance organizations compared to 57 percent of their peers)
- talent management (65 percent to 55 percent)
- change management (50 percent to 45 percent).

Why is this trend significant? A central issue for enterprise learning organizations is how to capture and deliver relevant knowledge and experience to the workforce at the point of need. This cannot be done optimally with a classroom-type structure alone. It is crucial to build an environment that encourages and rewards knowledge sharing. In today's knowledge worker environment new performance challenges arise too quickly to be met by the traditional methods of curriculum development. It is vital in those environments to establish platforms and infrastructures for real-time collaboration and contact with experts, wherever they are located inside or outside the company. Learning organizations are becoming a key focal point for taking the knowledge created through experience and collaboration and then putting it into formats that can be delivered to everyone to optimize the performance of a company as a whole.

TRENDS IN CONTENT MANAGEMENT

Probably the most important of relevant trends involve the area of content management. Traditionally, content reflected the needs of a particular function within an organization; the training function developed its own content, as did product development engineers, the help desk, and so on. As a consequence, when one spoke of delivering 'content' to someone, it was never clear which 'content' was meant. The employee taking a course about selling new products might not have the same information as the help desk employee responding to inquiries about those products.

The internet changed all that. The design constraints of web content creation fundamentally altered the way we deliver content and that change has rippled through companies' main architectures. Today, content is not only web based, it has become more granular or modular so it can be updated more quickly. This, in turn, has driven object frameworks for content, allowing companies to separate text from images, images from audio or video, audio or video from customer information, and so on.

By detaching content development, management and delivery from each other, this enables the ability to (1) perform search and retrieval on knowledge repositories, (2) manage information centrally, and (3) push fresh and relevant content via whatever delivery mechanism we want, wherever we want- learning, help desk, sales brochures, web content, and so on.

And, because the knowledge is more granular, companies can now use technology to deliver bits of content to workers to aid their performance right where they work. One leading consumer electronics retailer, for example, has been visionary in its thinking about how to use content management systems and leading-edge technologies to deliver supporting information to sales people in real time, right on the sales floor. As these applications mature, customers will get better service and the sales people will need less external classroom training. The company can put new hires on the sales floor and have them perform at acceptable levels more quickly than ever before. Are these learning solutions, knowledge management, or performance support? They are all of them.

A second trend pushing at learning and knowledge management from a slightly different angle results from changes in customer relationship management (CRM). For some years, companies have been seeking both an integrated view of the customer and the ability to deliver a unified customer experience. Customers have high expectations and can shift easily from one competitor to another, so companies are attempting to enhance their customer service capabilities and understand customer behaviors in order to sell to them more effectively.

Much depends on the quality of the content presented to customer service representatives. As tools mature to transform customer data into actionable insight, companies must also take advantage of the convergence of learning and knowledge management to make sure the right information gets to people in customer-facing roles. Consider an example from BT, the UK-based telecommunications provider. The BT Retail group set out to improve customer service as a core competence of the organization, and to create a capability that would deliver higher-quality service while reducing costs through more efficient and productive customer service representative interaction.

BT developed an innovative knowledge management portal, called 'OWL' (Optimizing Working Life). This portal has brought vital product, service and procedural information together into a single structured content architecture that enables easier access to vital information thanks to an intuitive portal interface. Using OWL, service reps for BT Retail can now readily access accurate information while handling and resolving customer inquiries on the first attempt.

One of the keys to success for BT was the design and implementation of a dedicated support organization that followed best practice workflow in content management to ensure the right people get the right information at the right time. BT has also integrated the portal into its overall internal communications programs.

Solutions like these also help support the rapid product development cycles companies need today. This is especially true in industries like telecommunications, where accelerating change may make content stale by the time a company develops training on new products and services. By centralizing content creation, a company can ensure that its content remains as fresh as possible.

IMPLICATIONS

This separation of content creation, management and delivery will have a major impact on organizations and their people, as well as on many vendors. Major CRM packages are reflecting this separation, and learning management systems are likely to follow suit. These systems will continue to perform important tasks: helping companies understand their learner base, register people for courses, track their attendance, and so on. These systems allow organizations to run the business process of learning. But they do not – and should not – demand that the content that serves every point in each transaction within the business process be tied up in that application.

The mix of a learning department's staff – and the resources it requires – will also inevitably shift in response to these trends, but the savings can be significant. Our experiences suggest that, today, a large company with a training organization of 1000 people might have a third of those employees devoted to documentation. Streamlining the content creation processes could deliver a savings of 30 to 40 percent and cut content development cycle times in half.

Different organizations will have different responses to the convergence of learning and knowledge management. Both functions bring important competencies to the table, and this convergence offers the opportunity for a huge business impact. Convergence means we are very close to realizing a vision many have had for years; delivering just-in-time support to workers, who can now share experiences and knowledge through collaborative applications, and find an expert immediately who can help solve a particular problem.

Conclusion

More than ever, senior management in both business and government is aware that enterprise learning can be a source of differentiation and make a significant contribution to achieving high performance. As the global economy gears up for growth, executives are turning expectantly to their learning organizations to help them become more innovative, to help them serve customers better and to help them deliver products to the market faster than their competitors. Investments in learning, and in learning technologies, are vital to enhancing revenue and increasing shareholder value.

Looking at the distinctive features of the best learning organizations, these leaders are ahead of the pack in a number of areas, including those dealt with here: aligning learning with the business – and also managing it as a business, developing learning programs that draw customers and channel partners more deeply into the value chain; and advanced learning and knowledge management technologies that are revolutionizing the way people work and the way they serve customers.

As businesses and governments begin to understand more deeply the enormous importance of learning to growth and success, learning executives are likely to be challenged even more by heightened expectations. But certainly it is an exciting time to be a learning professional – someone who is delivering measurable value, helping companies meet vital strategic needs today and preparing them for the demands of tomorrow.

Notes

1. H. Brakeley, P. Cheese and D. Clinton (2004) *The High Performance Workforce Study 2004*. New York, NY: Accenture (can be found on www.accenture.com/learning).
2. J. Meister and H. Brakeley (2004) *The Rise of the High Performance Learning Organization*. New York, NY: Accenture. (Executive summary can be found on www.accenture.com/learning.)
3. Portions of this section have previously appeared in *Chief Learning Officer* magazine: www.clomedia.com.
4. Portions of this section previously appeared in *KM Review*, November/December 2004, 'Customer management and the content revolution,' by Thomas A. Kraack and Kenneth L. Cundari.

Index